BLACK WOMEN IN
UNITED STATES HISTORY

Editor

DARLENE CLARK HINE

Associate Editors

ELSA BARKLEY BROWN

TIFFANY R.L. PATTERSON

LILLIAN S. WILLIAMS

Research Assistant

EARNESTINE JENKINS

A CARLSON PUBLISHING SERIES

See the end of this volume for a comprehensive
guide to this sixteen-volume series.

To Better Our World

BLACK WOMEN IN ORGANIZED REFORM, 1890-1920

Dorothy Salem

CARLSON
Publishing Inc

BROOKLYN, NEW YORK, 1990

See the end of this volume for a comprehensive guide to the sixteen-volume series of which this is Volume Fourteen.

Library of Congress Cataloging-in-Publication Data

Salem, Dorothy C.
    To better our world : Black women in organized reform, 1890-1920 / Dorothy Salem.
        p.   cm. — (Black women in United States history : v. 14)
    Includes bibliographical references.
    ISBN 0-926019-20-1
    1. Afro-American women—History—19th century. 2. Afro-American women—History—20th century. 3. United States—Social conditions—1865-1918. 4. Social reformers—United States––History—19th century. 5. Social reformers—United States––History—20th century. I. Title. II. Series.
E185.86.B543 vol. 14
973'.0496073 s—dc20
[973'.0496073]   90-1397

Typographic design: Julian Waters

Typeface: Bitstream ITC Galliard

The index to this book was created using NL Cindex, a scholarly indexing program from the Newberry Library.

Printed on acid-free, 250-year-life paper.

Manufactured in the United States of America.

Contents

I. FOUNDATIONS FOR REFORM

II. NEW PATHS FOR ORGANIZED REFORM

III. WAR AND ITS AFTERMATH

List of Illustrations

Acknowledgments

To bring a book to print requires intellectual, personal and financial support. Several libraries and archives provided the information from which the narrative and conclusions developed. The archivists representing the collections listed in the bibliography have my gratitude for aiding my search. Special thanks goes to a few who went far beyond the requirements to help me reconstruct the role that black women played. These include William Becker, archivist, Cleveland State University; Jacqueline Goggin, former archivist, Library of Congress; Olivia Martin, former archivist, Western Reserve Historical Society; and Elizabeth Norris, archivist/librarian, National Board of the YWCA. Those who shared personal insights into the personalities of the women and movements include Adelle Logan Alexander, Edward S. Hope, Amelia Fry and the late Alfreda Duster. Those who developed my intellectual interest in the topic include Curtis Wilson of Cleveland State University's Black Studies Department and August Meier, my advisor at Kent State University. All of you have contributed to the completion of this work.

I am thankful for the personal support and patience that I received from my husband and daughters, who learned to take care of each other during my travels to collections, my nights in classes, and my hours spent with the word processor. With the financial support from the American Association of University Women's American Fellowship, I was able to take time off from my full-time teaching to complete the writing during daylight hours.

When I started my research, a colleague questioned whether I would find enough material on the topic. When I finished, that same person apologized for having underestimated the breadth and depth of resources and the activities they represented. It is my hope that future researchers will pick up threads suggested in this tapestry and begin to weave new garments distinguishing individual women or quilts recognizing collective actions. As part of the first series on Black Women in American History, this book is only a beginning in the process to delineate their role. The best is yet to come.

Introduction

The reform role of black women during the thirty-year period at the turn of the century, 1890-1920, has received little attention from historians. Histories of the era mention blacks as the objects of a few programs developed by white reformers. Women's history tends to stress the work of the educated white elite in municipal reform, settlement houses, public health crusades, protective labor legislation, and woman's suffrage. Books and articles about racial advancement organizations relegate black women to footnotes or general statements about their importance. The lack of a recorded reform role, however, does not mean that black women were absent from organized attempts to improve conditions in American society. Their organizational records, personal correspondence, periodical articles, diaries, and autobiographies reveal a detailed record of their participation.

Placing black women in an historical period that called women into an active reform role, while simultaneously increasing the discrimination against and segregation of black Americans, reveals a curious paradox of an era that is popularly described as "reform." This thirty-year period encompassed rapid social change—increasing industrialization accompanied by expanding immigration and growing urbanization. These changes produced a wealth of social problems in health, housing, education, and working conditions. Many different cultures and peoples competed for an inadequate supply of jobs and housing. Fear, ignorance, and anxiety about the direction of such changes accompanied patterns of general intolerance. These seemingly contradictory strands raise many questions for the study of black women during the period.

The reform era attempted to deal with the immigration and adaptation problems of non-urban peoples. How did the patterns of migration and urbanization of foreigners compare to those of black rural migrants? How did the programs and theories of immigrant adaptation influence the programs for the black urban residents? Did black women establish services to help their race as did the immigrant groups who developed institutions to serve their aged, infirm, dependent children, and unskilled? Were such services established as a reaction to white discrimination, or did they emerge as the group developed greater organizational skills or resources? Were such services

1

a continuation of a cultural tradition? Did white-directed charities and reform groups display paternalistic attitudes toward immigrants and black newcomers to the city? How did black women deal with such attitudes and control?

The role of women in social reform expanded dramatically during these years. Did black women share similar sociocultural backgrounds and attitudes with the white women who were active in charity and social reform? What types of community and national reform activities did black women enter? During this time of increased racism, how did black women fit into such national organizations as the Women's Christian Temperance Union, the National American Woman Suffrage Association, the Young Women's Christian Association, the National Council of Women, General Federation of Women's Clubs, and the National Association of Settlements?

As racial violence and injustice escalated, a few progressive whites joined with black leaders to improve conditions through such interracial organizations as the Constitution League, the National League for the Protection of Colored Women, the NAACP, and the National Urban League. What was the role of black women in these groups dominated by white men or, in the case of the National League for the Protection of Colored Women, dominated by white women? Did the community ties of the black women help to build the black membership of these organizations and thus enable blacks to have more control? How did the dual status of being both black and female complicate intraorganizational politics?

This study answers these questions and, in the process, reveals a wealth of information about black women's dedication and caring involvement. They organized both locally and nationally, in segregated and integrated associations, to better the conditions in their communities. Three stages of their organizational development are chronicled. Part One discusses the foundations of organized reform on the local and national levels. Much of this early activity demonstrated a lack of organization, a lack of finances, and a defensive response to white America. Led by the black elite, most of whom had white lineage, occupied privileged positions, and were highly educated, the first stage of reform was an attempt to show white leaders that middle-class black women could care for the race's downtrodden, as white women had cared for their poor and ignorant. These first years, from approximately 1890 to 1910, laid foundations and built confidence and experience.

Around 1910, their experience, greater financial resources, and a more repressive racial environment led many black women into new areas of reform that required cooperation with whites. In this second stage, black women established reformatories, multipurpose community centers, and programs to improve the health and welfare of the community-at-large. They sought the cooperation of various white groups such as city councils, reform associations, and philanthropic foundations. White women began to attend the National Association of Colored Women's biennials, requesting the support of black women. Emerging interracial organizations such as the NAACP and the National Urban League relied on the community ties of black women to develop branches and affiliates.

The final stage evolved from black women's experiences during and after World War I. In the war effort, black women worked closely with many white female leaders unaccustomed to racial interaction. They not only proved their abilities, but also brought many needed services to their communities under the guise of patriotism and the rationale of contributing to the domestic war effort. When their wartime contributions produced few changes in postwar race relations, many black women became impatient and their rhetoric became more demanding. They organized to halt the postwar racial violence and pressed for greater representation in women's organizations. When frustrated in their attempts, black women left the white women's groups to devote their energies to racial justice through the NAACP and the National Association of Colored Women.

Black women attempted to cope with the impact of rapid social change. In so doing, they forged organizations and helped the grass roots development of institutions to protect and improve black communities. Many of these institutions survive and continue to shape the lives of black Americans. This is a study of their beginnings.

N.B.: Phillis Wheatley clubs often spelled the poet's first name "Phyllis"; the spelling used here is that of each individual club.

PART ONE

Foundations for Reform

Benevolence is the essence of most of the colored women's organizations. The humane side of their natures has been cultivated to recognize the duties they owe to the sick, the indigent and ill-fortuned. No church, no school, or charitable institution for the special use of colored people has been allowed to languish or fail when the associated efforts of the women could save it. . . .

> —Fannie Barrier Williams, "Religious Duty to the Negro," Address to the World's Parliament of Religions, Chicago, 1893, in Bert James Lowenberg and Ruth Bogin, eds., *Black Women in Nineteenth-Century American Life: Their Words, Their Thoughts, Their Feelings* (University Park: Pennsylvania State University Press, 1976), p. 274.

In the history of the Negro race no more heroic work has been done than that performed by the Negro woman.

> —Benjamin Brawley, *Women of Achievement* (n.p.: Woman's Home Mission Society, 1919), p. 7.

ONE

Foundations for Organized Reform

During the summer of 1896, the National Federation of Afro-American Women and the National League of Colored Women met in Washington, D.C., to consolidate the two groups into a common national organization to represent the interests of black women. The formation of the National Association of Colored Women represented the black female elite's attempt to combat the growing racism of the late nineteenth century, to build a national female reform network, and to meet the changing needs of the black community. Separated along denominational, community, and ideological lines, black women together faced the necessity of cooperating for their own self-interest and for the betterment of the race. They were both pushed and pulled into an organized reform role during the thirty-year period from 1890 to 1920.

The late nineteenth century challenged the black elite's faith in the American Dream. The Protestant ethic of hard work, frugality, and individual initiative had stimulated the drive for social standing, education, and material well-being among segments of black communities both in the North and the South. These promising gains were called into question as conditions worsened for the race in education, politics, popular image, public accommodations, and the legal system. In the South, where over 90 percent of blacks continued to reside, the disenfranchisement process was generally accomplished by the turn of the century. The federal government, to which blacks had turned for protection from state legislation, did little to relieve the situation. Republican presidents failed to speak out against the disenfranchisement and violence in their attempts to rebuild the party in the South, to effect sectional reconciliation, and to reflect popular opinion about the black race. The Supreme Court upheld state legislation that created segregation and disenfranchisement practices.

In this ideological and political climate, self-help became a means for racial survival. The voluntary creation of separate institutions became one way to deal with the increased discrimination. Excluded from white associations, black editors, teachers, farmers, and doctors organized their own groups to promote their interests. In 1890, black leaders held two major conferences to discuss the problems facing their race. In January, delegates met in Chicago to form the National Afro-American League. Led by T. Thomas Fortune, editor of the *New York Age*, the league sought to halt disenfranchisement, racial violence, Jim Crow segregation in public accommodation and transportation, inequitable expenditures in education, and injustices in the southern penal system. In February, an older, more politically involved group met in Washington, D.C. Led by J. C. Price, president of Livingstone College, Salisbury, North Carolina, the American Citizens Equal Rights Association emphasized the path to full citizenship rights through education, wealth, and good conduct, in contrast to the northern leadership's emphasis on active agitation. Unfortunately, both these groups suffered from the internal frictions and rivalries that made racial advancement efforts ineffective and led to inactivity within a few years.[1]

Black women, too, reacted to the worsening race relations. Negative racial stereotypes appeared in popular literature and scientific writings. According to one article in a popular magazine, the black woman had "the brain of a child and the passions of a woman, steeped in centuries of ignorance and savagery and wrapped about with immemorial vices."[2] The lowly condition of the entire race was blamed on the women as "the chief instruments of the degradation of the men of their own race. When a man's mother, wife, and daughter are all immoral women, there is no room in his fallen nature for the aspiration of honor and virtue."[3] This negative image demonstrated a widening gap between the Victorian lady, to which most black elite women aspired, and the treatment that black women received from the general public.

Black women with education and social standing rankled at the indiscriminate, legally enforced system of segregation in transportation. They argued that those who could afford to purchase first-class tickets and behaved as first-class citizens were entitled to first-class accommodations and treatment. Yet these women had to ride in the Jim Crow car with gamblers and prostitutes. Reacting with internal rage, legal suits, or physical resistance, black women sought to remove these legal and social barriers to their participation in American life.[4]

In their attempt to improve conditions, black women drew on their experiences in beneficial and literary societies, as well as church associations. Participation there did not lead directly to involvement in social reform, but it did develop organizational and fund-raising skills useful later. For example, in Philadelphia, which had the largest black population of any nineteenth-century Northern city, black women maintained a number of organizations to provide aid to ill and dependent women and children. Through the Dorcas Society, Sisterly Union, United Daughters of Wilberforce, Daughters of Absalom, and African Female Union, black women fought pauperism and crime. Within the churches, they provided support services in fund-raising and social welfare. The Philadelphia Home for the Aged and Infirm Colored Persons was managed by a standing committee of female board members led by Mary Campbell, wife of Jabez Campbell, bishop in the African Methodist Episcopal Church. These contributions continued to remain important throughout the nineteenth century.[5]

Black leaders noticed this female role in the 1890s. W. E. B. Du Bois stressed the role of women in *The Philadelphia Negro*, noting, "It is the women that do the larger part of the benevolent work in Negro churches."[6] Chicago clubwoman Fannie Barrier Williams said that in the church women "learned the meaning of unity of effort for the common good, [where] the development of social sympathies grew into women's consciousness."[7] By 1890, the women in five black Atlanta churches were already performing beneficial and benevolent work. Women of the First Congregational Church influenced its upper-class congregation to become the first black institution to enter social service through the establishment of a home for working girls and mission work in the city's poverty areas. In one sense, churches served as "the great preparatory schools"[8] for black women entering secular social reform.

Black women also began literary societies. Primarily a social improvement association, these societies created opportunities for racial self-expression and aspiration. Held in members' homes, the meetings brought like-minded women together to discuss current topics.

Most of these earlier efforts had been narrow in scope, limited to particular denominations, society members, or "deserving" individuals, and short-lived due to lack of administrative knowledge or finances. Nevertheless, these organizational experiences provided black women with a structure through which they became informed about current issues and skilled in fund-raising, accomplishing limited projects, and conducting meetings. The leadership of

9

some of these benevolent societies expanded the social goals and activities and by 1890, several groups moved in the direction of black female reform.

The conditions of the late nineteenth century directed many women's groups into an expanded social role. The problems faced by benevolent societies were becoming more complex as the character of the urban poor changed. Leaders from different social backgrounds expressed perspectives and techniques that varied from earlier elitist dominance. White women had faced similar limitations caused by social or religious divisions in their nineteenth-century associations, but by 1890, the major white women's organizations had consolidated or formed national associations. The Women's Christian Temperance Union (WCTU), the "goliath of women's organizations,"[9] had become national during the 1880s. Women privileged in the acquisition of higher education formed professional associations, such as the Association of Collegiate Alumnae (1882), the National Council of Women (1888), and Mother's Congresses. Some of these women founded settlement houses in which they could put their educations to use. Two experiments emerged in 1889 independent of each other: Vida Scudder's College Settlement in New York and Jane Addams's Hull House in Chicago attempted to meet community needs and satisfy the settlement workers' desires to apply their knowledge of the social sciences to real life.

Two major organizations became national in 1890. The National Woman Suffrage Association merged with the American Woman Suffrage Association to form the National American Woman Suffrage Association (NAWSA). Although each separate organization had originally differed in tactics, goals, and issues, the two wings realized the value of cooperation and consolidation of resources, membership, and goals to attain a national amendment to enfranchise women.

The consolidation of local women's clubs in 1890 created the General Federation of Women's Clubs (GFWC). Responding to the needs of middle-class women for self-improvement, the federation sought to develop women's minds, social graces, and involvement in the community. By the end of the year, national women's organizations had developed to guide temperance, suffrage and club activities.

As these organizations became national in structure, black women's participation became increasingly restricted. To become national, these organizations had to gain or retain southern support. To expand, they had to reflect, or at least not threaten, popular racial attitudes. The WCTU, which had started to organize in the South during the 1880s, found race a controversial issue to be ignored or handled tactfully in order to gain members and support. By the early 1890s, the three major women's organizations for suffrage, clubwork, and temperance had become national not only in scope, but also in attitudes. The late-nineteenth-century ideology advocating segregation and subordination penetrated policies and practices.[10]

Black women were in a paradoxical position. On the one hand, women, especially middle-class, educated women, were increasingly drawn into participation in organized reform. On the other hand, blacks were increasingly rejected as equal participants in these movements. For middle-class, educated black women the situation was filled with conflict or potential conflict. Depending on local conditions and leadership, most black women organized to meet immediate local needs, as did their white counterparts. Expanding beyond the denominational or social restrictions of the female church or literary organizations, black women formed clubs to improve themselves and their communities. As clubwork spread among the white women, a similar movement, though different in content, emerged among the black women of the major black communities.

The black women's clubs were neither imitations of white women's groups nor formed solely as reactions to discrimination. Fannie Barrier Williams attributed the rise of the black club movement to "the organized anxiety of women who have become intelligent enough to recognize their own low social condition and strong enough to initiate the forces of reform."[11] Mary Church Terrell, perhaps the best-known black woman of her time, felt clubs evolved to raise the standards of black women. Margaret Murray Washington, wife of Booker T. Washington and leader of several community projects in Alabama, felt that black women had responded to concerns stimulating all women. Rosetta Douglass Sprague, daughter of Frederick Douglass and social leader in Washington, explained the club movement as black women's organized attempts to ameliorate existing conditions for the race.[12] Several years later, Robert R. Moton, then principal of Tuskegee Institute, reassessed the origins of the black club movement as "an inspiration coming from within the race."[13]

White perceptions agreed with those expressed by the black leadership. Historian Eleanor Flexner noted the "organization among Negro women owed its particular character not so much to the fact that by and large they were excluded from white women's groups, as to the totally dissimilar circumstances of their lives."[14] A contemporary observer, Mary White Ovington, felt that the black women's clubs differed from those of white women in that the black clubs "from the first have engaged primarily, not in cultural, but in philanthropic work."[15]

Early club activities among black women dealt with moral reform issues or provision of services to the aged or children. The Harper Woman's Club, organized in 1890 in Jefferson City, Missouri, held mothers' meetings to instruct women in the latest techniques of child care, temperance meetings to counsel against the evils of alcohol, and classes to improve skills in sewing and millinery. The title of the club demonstrated black female pride in the achievements of Frances Ellen Watkins Harper, antislavery lecturer and leader in the Colored WCTU, and emphasized the club's commitment to reform. Similar clubs emerged as a response to the needs of middle-class women for self-improvement and community betterment.[16]

The national club movement among black women was the culmination of three factors. First, by 1890 the women had developed local leadership attempting to respond to specific community needs. Second, common interests and/or issues brought women together as a group above denominational or regional rivalries. Finally, several incidents demonstrated the need for a national organization to promote a positive image of black women, to preserve their relatively privileged status, and to provide moral and educational guidance to the less privileged in their communities.

An examination of activities in three centers of club life, Washington, D.C., New York, and Boston, documents how local leadership developed and how the organizations responded to the common interest of black women.

In Washington, a center of the black elite, the process of preparing women for organized reform was evident during the late nineteenth century. The wives and daughters of the black elite joined other educated black women at conventions and conferences of national organizations that led to stimulating lectures and discussions. Their participation in Washington's noted Bethel Literary and Historical Association provided opportunities to gain current information, develop skills in oratory, and establish a network of individuals interested in reform.

The Bethel Literary and Historical Association included women among its leaders, speakers, and participants from its founding in 1881. The first executive officers included two women as vice presidents, one as librarian, and two on the five-member executive committee. Women contributed frequently as lecturers and debaters during the first ten years of the society's existence. Mary Ann Shadd Cary, the first black female editor of *Provincial*

Freeman, a weekly Canadian newspaper for fugitive slaves during the 1850s, and practicing lawyer in the nation's capital, lectured about the "Heroes of the Anti-Slavery Struggles." Women lectured on the elements of "true womanhood," botany, separate schools for blacks, fashion, political roles for the race, black musicians, increasing social and educational opportunities for black women, and the role of the black female teacher in social reform. Sisters Mary Jane and Chanie A. Patterson debated Alexander Crummell and Robert Purvis on the advantages of professional versus trade education for the race.

By 1890, female participation in the Bethel Literary and Historical Association included several women who soon became leaders in the black club movement. Hallie Q. Brown, graduate of Wilberforce and Oberlin, lectured on "The Divine Art." Brown, member and lecturer for both the British and the American temperance movements, became the seventh president of the National Association of Colored Women and brought Wilberforce University worldwide recognition as a center of black education. Another Oberlin graduate and teacher in the Washington schools, Anna J. Cooper, spoke about American literature and the worth of the race. Cooper, known primarily for her contribution to black secondary education in Washington, became a leader in the National League of Colored Women. Mary Church Terrell, Oberlin graduate and daughter of Robert Church, the first black millionaire, served not only as a frequent speaker, but also as the first female president for the Bethel Literary and Historical Association in the 1892–1893 season. Terrell became the first president of the National Association of Colored Women. Fannie Barrier Williams, who became a leader in the Chicago and national club movements, told the Washington group about the opportunities for western women. Black women continued to hold leadership positions and participate in the Bethel Literary and Historical Association, an organization that influenced black intellectuals in the nation's capital and throughout America.[18]

Washington's black women not only participated in the literary societies, but also took part in benevolence and education. Many volunteered their services at the Home for Friendless Girls founded in 1886 by Caroline Taylor. Most of the black women taught in public schools and were therefore aware of the problems of the city's black children. Mary Jane Patterson, one of the first black women to receive a B.A. degree, had served as the principal of M Street (later Dunbar High) School from 1871 to 1872 and 1873 to 1874. Both Mary Church Terrell and Anna J. Cooper taught at the same school. Cooper went on to become the principal of M Street School (1901-1906), a position also held by Robert H. Terrell, husband of Mary Terrell. Leaders in education, benevolence, and literary societies, these women expanded their roles and became founders of reform organizations.

During the summer of 1892, many of these same women joined together to accomplish the goals they had earlier discussed on the speaker's platform. Organized in June 1892, the Colored Woman's League of Washington, D.C., proposed to improve the education and to promote the interests of black women. The league reflected the strong influence of female educators and wives of government bureaucrats in its original membership. Helen A. Cook, wife of the Honorable John T. Cook, served as the first president of the league. Charlotte Forten Grimke, former antislavery lecturer, teacher of the ex-slaves in Port Royal, South Carolina, and wife of Presbyterian clergyman Francis J. Grimke, served as the recording secretary. Coralie Franklin Cook, wife of George W. Cook, educator and administrator at Howard University, worked with Sara Iredell Fleetwood, wife of Christian A. Fleetwood, army officer and bureaucrat. Josephine B. Bruce, the first black teacher in the Cleveland public schools before her marriage to Senator Blanche K. Bruce, joined with Anna J. Cooper, Mary Jane Patterson, Mary Church Terrell, and fellow schoolteacher Anna E. Murray to form the core of the league's leadership. As the educated elite of Washington society, these women sought to establish themselves as leaders in the charity and social reform movements developing locally and nationally.[19]

Black women in New York City were also involved in a variety of activities by the early 1890s. They worked in white-founded charitable institutions such as the Colored Orphan Asylum, Colored Mission, and Lincoln Hospital and Home (for the Aged). Organized and controlled by well-meaning whites interested in providing charity for blacks, most of these institutions provided care only for the extremely needy or ill and did not allow black interns or doctors to serve on the staff, as in the case of Lincoln Hospital and Home. That did not stop the women from contributing goods and services to the blacks cared for by these institutions. Black women often pressured their churches to assume a more active role in social service. Their formation of the Dorcas Home Missionary Society of Concord Baptist Church in Brooklyn and the One Thousand Women of Bethel Church in New York City demonstrated the increased interest of black women in social services.

A few months after the Washington women formed the Colored Woman's League, black women from the New York–Brooklyn community organized a testimonial dinner in honor of antilynching crusader Ida B. Wells. Held at Lyric Hall on October 5, 1892, the banquet brought together the leading black women from Philadelphia, Boston, and New York. Victoria Earle Mathews (also spelled Matthews), widow of a coachman, William Mathews, had become an admirer of Wells. As a junior reporter for many of the New York dailies, Mathews understood the difficulties faced by a black female journalist. Joining with public school teacher Maritcha Lyons, Mathews spearheaded the celebration honoring Wells. The cooperation between Mathews and Lyons demonstrated a combination of journalism and social welfare experience with the skills of an educator. Lyons, who had worked with black abolitionist Charles Remond, was a teacher in the New York public schools for forty-eight years, twenty of which were spent as the assistant principal of Public School 83. Mathews, unable to complete her education due to family responsibilities, had devoted time to social welfare activities with the Sanitary Commission during the war years and to the writing of children's stories for juvenile magazines. As a widow whose only son had died at the age of sixteen, Mathews had a great deal of time and commitment to devote to social reform.[20]

Mathews and Lyons joined with other black women of the New York community to help black women and children. Sarah Smith Garnet, another public school teacher/principal of a Manhattan grammar school and wife of Henry Highland Garnet, and her sister, Dr. Susan Smith McKinney, a Brooklyn physician, united forces with leading women from other communities. Gertrude Bustill Mossell, editor of "Our Woman's Department" in the New York *Freeman* and wife of physician Dr. Nathan F. Mossell, attended with Boston reformer, Josephine St. Pierre Ruffin, wife of judge George L. Ruffin. This small group from the New York-Philadelphia-Boston communities headed a committee of 250 women who raised money for Wells to resume publication of her paper, *Free Speech and Headlight*, the offices of which had been recently destroyed by a Memphis mob angered by her editorials condemning the lynching of three black men.

Wells's activities epitomized the courage praised by the women in attendance. They recalled her refusal to move to a Jim Crow car when she had moved to Memphis from Holly Springs, Mississippi, and her successful legal suit against the railroad for damages. They recognized her journalistic criticism of immoral or unprepared black clergy and teachers. Their presentation of five hundred dollars and a gold pen-shaped brooch to Miss

Wells symbolized their support of her activities while simultaneously increasing their own sense of pride.[21]

The testimonial dinner has been called the beginning of the organized black women's movement.[22] Leading women came together to honor one of their own group and to discuss pertinent topics. The dinner also stimulated the formation of two of the most important women's clubs: the Woman's Loyal Union, organized by Mathews and Lyons later that same month, and the Woman's Era Club of Boston, organized by Josephine Ruffin in January of 1893.

As with the leadership of both Washington and New York, the Boston women had for years been active in charity and reform work. Josephine St. Pierre Ruffin had worked with the Sanitary Commission, Kansas Relief Association, Women's Industrial and Educational Union, and Moral Education Society. As a member of the racially mixed Georgia Educational League, a club supporting a kindergarten for black children, Ruffin regularly socialized with many of the leading white female reformers, including Ednah D. Cheyney and Julia Ward Howe. Ruffin was joined in the local reforms by her daughter, Florida Ridley, and by Maria Baldwin, black principal of Agassiz School, one of the most prestigious white schools in Cambridge, Massachusetts. Together, these women collected data, published and disseminated tracts and leaflets, and attempted to improve the image of black women through their own example.[23]

As black women were organizing clubs in Washington, New York, and Boston, three events emphasized the need for a national club movement. The Columbian Exposition, intending to open in Chicago in 1892 to celebrate the four hundred years since Columbus had discovered America, demonstrated the inability of black community women to cooperate with other women representing different communities. The World's Fair wanted to celebrate the achievements of women through a pavilion designed by female architects and displays of women's contributions. A Board of Lady Managers encouraged women from all countries to participate in the international demonstration of progress.

Black women sought to participate in the Columbian Exposition to show the progress both of blacks in general and of black women in particular. Fair rules required the submission of all displays to state committees. Since most blacks lived in the South, state committees impeded the efforts to display the race's progress. The Board of Lady Managers received petitions asking for inclusion in the planning process from black women's groups in Chicago and

Washington. When there was no response to the petitions, black women called for meetings. The "representative colored women" intended to meet in Washington "to resent the insult offered by the white women managers of the Columbian World's Fair."[24] Before the meeting could take place, conflicts erupted between the black women's groups over representation and tactics. The appointment of Chicagoan Fannie B. Williams to the fair's Bureau of Publicity was dropped due to the objections from other race leaders. The Washington *Bee* criticized the women's lack of cooperation in mid-October, 1891, saying, "We are too much divided among ourselves. We are more like informers. We like to talk too much of our business to our enemies."[25] Within a few weeks, the *Bee* criticized the Chicago women's retreat from the conflict with the white women's board. When the Washington meeting failed to materialize, the *Bee* summarized the situation, saying that the white women gave the black women "the usual bribe."[26] The newspaper was probably referring to the appointment of the wife of Provident Hospital surgeon Austin M. Curtis to the position of Secretary of Colored Interests at the Fair. Described by Gertrude B. Mossell as "refined and cultivated,"[27] Curtis had no real power and soon resigned.[28]

By mid-1892, with the formation of the Colored Women's League, a new avenue for recognition opened. Hallie Q. Brown, former dean of Allen University, appealed to the head of the board, Mrs. Potter Palmer. Palmer told Brown that representation went only to national women's organizations. Since none existed among black women, representation on planning committees could not be extended to them. Accordingly, Brown tried to assemble quickly the existing networks of black women into a national organization. She contacted fellow Oberlin graduates Mary Church Terrell, Mary J. Patterson, and Anna J. Cooper, all of whom were working or residing in Washington, participating in the Bethel Literary and Historical Association, and serving in various types of literary or charitable activities. Brown suggested that black women meeting in convention could declare the Colored Woman's League of Washington, D.C., a national body. But, unable to secure the cooperation of enough women from other communities, black women failed to achieve inclusion in the planning stages and in the women's pavilion displays.

Quickly, black women responded to their exclusion from the World's Fair, which opened early in 1893 following delays in building construction. Frederick Douglass, head of the Haiti exhibition, enlisted the help of journalist Ida B. Wells in exposing the discriminatory policies of the fair administration. Wells, in turn, enlisted the help of Chicago black women in raising money to finance the writing and publication of *The Reason Why the Colored American Is Not in the World's Columbian Exposition*. At least ten thousand copies received distribution during the last few months of the fair.[29]

The exposition emphasized the lack of cooperation among the centers of black club activity and the need for a national organization to represent black female interests. These difficulties and needs did not lead directly to the formation of a national organization. As the centers of club activity improved and expanded, the idea of national cooperation became a potential reality. The Washington Colored Women's League was the first to suggest the formation of a national organization. In an article by Mary Church Terrell in *Ringwood's Afro-American Journal of Fashion*, the league invited "women in all parts of the country to unite with it, so that we may have a national organization . . . a vast chain of organizations extending the length and breadth of the land devising ways and means to advance our cause."[30] Soon after the appearance of Terrell's article, the league established affiliates in Kansas City, Denver, Norfolk, Philadelphia, and South Carolina.[31]

In Chicago, women embarrassed about their inability to gain participation in the preparation of the fair and stimulated by the rapid growth of white women's clubs, needed an incident to galvanize the various groups into a solid local group. Black men, reacting to the racial exclusion of the fair, organized the all-male Tourgee Club, named after the liberal white columnist and civil rights lawyer who tested the constitutionality of the separate car law in *Plessy v. Ferguson*. Having opened each Thursday afternoon to women, the club decided to invite a speaker who could gather an audience to increase their meager female attendance. They choose Ida B. Wells. Many women came to hear her describe her activities as an antilynching lecturer throughout the Northeast and in England. She spoke about the organization of white women into suffrage and women's clubs. Stimulated by her discussion, the leading black women organized the Chicago Women's Club in September 1893.[32]

By the end of 1893, centers of black club activity had formed in Washington, New York, Boston, and Chicago. None of these centers, however, could speak for black women nationally. The club movement needed more internal commitment within the individual clubs and expansion of the club network into other communities. In January 1894, the Washington Colored Woman's League incorporated with affiliated leagues. The incorporation documents demonstrated Washington women as the national leadership, but the leadership of specific committees was shared with affiliate leadership from Baltimore; Cambridge; Newport; Philadelphia; Denver; Norfolk; St. Paul; Kansas City, Missouri; and Harpers Ferry, West Virginia.

Two months later the Boston Woman's Era Club began the first monthly magazine published by black women, *The Woman's Era*, which informed its subscribers about fashion, health, family life, and legislation. To enhance the national character of the magazine, women from different cities headed the departments: Victoria Earle Mathews (New York), Fannie Barrier Williams (Chicago), Josephine Silone-Yates (Kansas City), Mary Church Terrell (Washington), Elizabeth Ensley (Denver), and Alice Ruth Moore (New Orleans). Most of these cities had already affiliated with the Washington Colored Woman's League.

The representatives from Kansas City, Denver, and New Orleans had personal ties to the northeastern reform communities. Josephine Silone-Yates grew up in New Jersey and graduated from Rhode Island State Normal School in Providence, the city where Maritcha Lyons of the Woman's Loyal Union resided. In 1889, she married Professor W. W. Yates, head of Lincoln University in Missouri. Marriage also moved a second northeasterner to the West. Elizabeth P. Ensley had taught school and developed a circulating library in Boston before she married Nowell Ensley in 1882, which brought her to Colorado. Alice Ruth Moore had resided in New Orleans, but received her education at the University of Pennsylvania and Cornell University. These women brought the reform messages to their particular communities in the West, Midwest, and South. Their contacts demonstrated the geographical mobility of black elites seeking jobs, education, and expanding opportunities during the late nineteenth century.

The Woman's Era built on personal relationships among the black elites throughout the United States. The magazine appealed to the black female elite possessing education, skills, and experience in social organization. As members of the upper classes, many had the leisure time and the social expectations to pursue reform work. Since many had married later in life or had remained single, children seldom interfered with social activities. Their local clubs, the common racial issues, and *The Woman's Era* provided the membership and means of communication to create a viable national network of organized black women.[33]

As the black women of Washington and Boston spread their influence through affiliation and publication, the Chicago women again were exposed to their weaknesses as an organization in early 1894. Headed by Mary R. Jones, wife of John Jones, a wealthy tailor and community leader, the Chicago Women's Club suffered from conflicts stemming from loyalties to various churches, lodges, and social groups and from lack of commitment to club activities. The club primarily served as a vehicle through which the women could raise money for race issues and could attend inspiring lectures. Not until the women heard William T. Stead, a white reformer and proselytizer for the Social Gospel ideals, did they realize the direction of their commitment. Stead asked the women what they were doing to help themselves. Their responses indicated the internal division within the black community. Stead responded to their quibbling by saying, "You have not been lynched enough to drive you together."[34] This speech instigated the women to subordinate their differences for the common good, and the club renewed its commitment to the organized improvement of black life in 1894.[35]

Although the Colored Woman's League and the Boston Woman's Era Club aspired to form a national organization, neither held a national convention. An invitation by the National Council of Women to the Colored Women's League renewed the movement to form a national association. The National Council of Women included some of the most prestigious female organizations in the country. For a black woman's organization to gain membership in such an association would be a demonstration of racial progress. On October 9, 1894, the National Council invited the league to become a member and to send a representative to their spring 1895 convention. To be eligible for membership, the league called itself "national." Through columns in *The Woman's Era* the league requested members of other clubs to become delegates, but only a few accepted. The Woman's Era Club sent no delegates. To have done so would have been a public recognition of the national leadership of the league at a time when the Woman's Era sought that same leadership role. The league called itself national and behaved as a national within that convention, but as yet no national convention of black women had been held and no permanent national organization existed.

It was a slanderous letter about the character of black women that served as the catalyst to the calling of a national conference. James W. Jacks, president of the Missouri Press Association, wrote to Florence Balgarnie, white secretary of the Anti-Lynching Society of England. Reacting to criticisms of white church and reform leaders[37] by American anti-lynching lecturers in England, Jacks attacked the source of the criticisms—black women. He stated that the race was devoid of morality and that the women were prostitutes, natural liars, and thieves. The content of the letter was not unusual for the times, but the reaction to the letter demonstrated changes in the attacked group.

Instead of printing the letter in the English press as Jacks had wanted, Balgarnie, a supporter of racial reforms, sent the letter to Josephine Ruffin, editor of *The Women's Era*. Ruffin felt the letter "too indecent for publication,"[38] but included a copy of it in a communication to subscribers asking for their written opinions. Women from many centers of reform reacted. Margaret Murray Washington, wife of Booker T. Washington and lady principal of Tuskegee Institute, reported that black women were "suddenly awakened by the wholesale charges of the lack of virtue and character."[39] Fannie Barrier Williams felt the letter would have received "scarce notice" twenty years earlier, but by 1895, it was "instantly and vehemently resented. . . . [It] stirred the intelligent colored women of America as nothing ever had done."[40]

Although the charges of immorality were nothing new, the response of the black women—organizing into clubs, entering community reform, possessing newsletter and interorganizational communications networks, and seeking to promote the position of the black elites—was finally successful. The June 1895 issue of *The Woman's Era* called black women to Boston, saying, "Let Us Confer Together."[41] The First National Conference of Colored Women of America brought together "sisters all over the country, members of all clubs, societies, associations, or circles [to discuss] our position, our needs and our aims."[42] The conference attracted over one hundred delegates from ten states to discuss the charges in the letter and to develop "plans and work to redeem the unredeemed among them."[43]

The leadership represented an alliance of competing groups. Ruffin, of the Boston Woman's Era Club, became president. Helen Cook, of the Washington Colored Woman's League, and Margaret Murray Washington, of the newly formed (March 1895) Tuskegee Woman's Club, served as vice presidents. Elizabeth Carter, a leader in charity work in New Bedford, Massachusetts, was the secretary.

The delegates reflected the mixture of traditional and newly formed groups. Women's traditional emphasis on religious and moral reform was evident in representation from the Calvary Circle of Kings Daughters, Bethel's One Thousand Women, Concord Baptist Church of Brooklyn, and local chapters of the Colored WCTU. Delegates from the Boston Woman's Era Club, the Tuskegee Woman's Club, the New York Woman's Loyal Union, and the Washington Colored Woman's League took part in the discussions. Speeches by T. Thomas Fortune, editor of the New York *Age* and the central leader in the Afro-American League; William Lloyd Garrison, Jr., son of the abolitionist and supporter of women's rights; and Henry Blackwell, former abolitionist and husband of suffrage leader Lucy Stone, added to the interracial reform nature of the conference.[44]

Not wishing to draw the color line as was done by the southern white women of the Georgia Women's Press Club, Ruffin invited whites, saying, "We are not drawing the 'Color Line'; We are women, as intensely interested in all that pertains to us as such as all other American women."[45]

On the other hand, the leaders expressed an awareness of feeling superior to the lower classes and their discussion topics showed no attempt to increase their involvement with their social inferiors. They discussed women and higher education; organizational needs and methods; mental improvement in childrearing; training of nurses; women in law, business, and journalism; and the general "Negro Problem." The speeches delivered by female physicians, leading clubwomen, and teachers seemed out of touch with the conditions for the majority of the race. They nevertheless promised "to exercise a more helpful sympathy with the many of the race who are without guides and enlightenment in the ways of social righteousness."[46]

Before leaving the conference, the delegates voted to form a permanent organization, the National Federation of Afro-American Women (NFAAW), pledged to correct the image of black women. Membership was open to any club whose work reinforced the promise of the national body to uplift the masses and improve the skills of the middle-class homemaker.

The middle-class interests continued to prevail. Many of the same black women who headed the significant women's clubs and had participated in the formation of the NFAAW served as delegates to the Congress of Colored Women at the Atlanta Exposition in December 1895. Again, the women pledged themselves to social purity, improving the homes of the "lowly," child culture through children's clubs, and other forms of social uplift. Fannie Barrier Williams represented the Chicago Women's Club and Victoria Earle Mathews represented the Woman's Loyal Union. Coralie Franklin, superintendent of the Washington Home for Destitute Children and member of the Colored Woman's League, spoke. Josephine Silone-Yates from Kansas City joined Nettie Langston Napier, daughter of John Mercer Langston and wife of Nashville banker and lawyer, J. C. Napier. Ariel Hedges Bowen, wife of Rev. J. W. E. Bowen, president of Gammon Theological Seminary and staunch supporter of Booker T. Washington, attended, as did the suffrage and temperance leader Frances Watkins Harper. Harper, a popular novelist and poet, had worked with William Still on the Underground Railroad, lectured for the antislavery movement, organized black women for the WCTU, and took part in two conventions of the American Woman Suffrage Association before her appearance at this 1895 conference. Together, these women demonstrated an expanding concern with issues and interests beyond their immediate communities. Seeing themselves and their clubs as vehicles through which reforms could reach families, communities, and regions, black women sought to prove their abilities and to demonstrate their morality to America.[47]

The National Federation of Afro-American Women and the National League of Colored Women had to clarify their interrelationship as national organizations to be effective in their work for reform. The leadership had to resolve many of the problems inherent in early club activity. For example, many of the early clubs were small and exclusive (membership limited to fewer than twenty and extended only to women recommended by current members), leading to local jealousies and factionalism within and between elites. Josephine St. Pierre Ruffin warned black women to avoid conflicts caused by "trivialities and personalities."[48] Janie Porter Barrett, Hampton teacher and community leader, criticized black women's "silly bickerings and petty jealousies."[49] These conflicts were common.

In the white women's clubs, bickerings and jealousies were also evident. White women were similarly moved to organize after having been refused participation in a major social gathering. When the Press Club of New York denied women tickets for the Charles Dickens dinner in 1868, they recognized the need for an organized group to meet their needs and interests. Sorosis became the first club in 1868 to join women into a common association to discuss literature, science, education, art, philanthropy, house and home, drama, and current events. During the same year, the New England Woman's Club emerged as a philanthropic association. These two groups began competing with each other over which was first in organization and achievements. Both black and white women had to struggle to suppress these conflicts in order to build their separate club movements.[50]

Not only women's clubs suffered from conflicts during their early development. Racial organizations experienced similar problems. Ida B. Wells-

Barnett compared the factional conflicts of the black clubwomen to conflicts in racial organizations. Ironically, Wells-Barnett herself contributed to many of these conflicts. Nevertheless, most of the leading black women agreed that there was a need for cooperation; competition for members, financial resources, and attention of the white press could endanger the emerging club movement. Internal divisions and lack of money had weakened other racial organizations, such as the Afro-American League and the American Citizen's Equal Rights Association. As the national conventions approached, the leadership of both groups searched for ways to unite.[51]

Unity became a pervasive theme voiced by the leading clubwomen during the summer of 1896. Fannie Barrier Williams felt that "union is the watchword of woman's onward march."[52] The Preamble of the Constitution for the Colored Women's League emphasized that, "in union there is strength, . . . we, as a people have been and are the subject of prejudice, proscription, and injustice, the more successful, because of lack of unity."[53] The black women needed one national group to represent them at expositions, to present a suitable image to the white press, and to deal with issues of particular interest to their constituency.

The appearance of two national black women's groups holding their national conventions in the same city during the same month attended by some of the same women made the efforts seem ridiculous. The National League held its first convention at Francis Grimke's Fifteenth Street Presbyterian Church in Washington, D.C., from July 14 to 16, 1896. A few days later, the National Federation held its meeting at the Nineteenth Street Baptist Church, only a few blocks away.

The league and the federation showed a high degree of similarity between their leadership, ideologies, and programs. The league had representatives from urban areas: Kansas City, Washington, D.C., Norfolk, Harpers Ferry, Chicago, Baltimore, St. Paul, Denver, Newport, Philadelphia, and New York. The leadership reflected proximity to the nation's capital. Charlotte Forten Grimke, Helen Cook, Mary Church Terrell, and others had husbands employed in the ministry, law, or teaching fields there. Coralie Franklin was the superintendent of the Home for Destitute Children. Anna Cooper taught at the M Street High School.[54]

The federation's convention reflected similar backgrounds and interests. The participants represented "the best women in the land . . . to lift up and ennoble the womanhood of the race."[55] Compared to the league, the federation had more southern participation. Margaret Murray Washington of

Tuskegee; Rosa D. Bowser, teacher at Peabody Normal Institute in Richmond; Selina Butler of Atlanta; and Addie W. Hunton of Richmond, were joined by women from other urban areas: Ida B. Wells-Barnett of Chicago; Fannie Jackson Coppin of Philadelphia; Victoria Earle Mathews of New York; Josephine St. Pierre Ruffin of Boston; and temperance leader Libby C. Anthony of Jefferson City, Missouri.

The different geographical representations did not indicate a Washington-radical split. Those positions had little relevance for this early period of the black women's work in general. Both the league and the federation held similar goals, membership, and tactics. Most of the women were married to ministers, educators, lawyers, or civil servants and were educated in colleges or normal schools that prepared them for the most common occupation—teaching. Both organizations sought to improve the popular image of black women, educate them to become better homemakers and mothers, and assume their responsibility to uplift the "lowly and fallen" of the race. Their philosophies of education did not differ greatly. They supported manual or academic training depending on the needs of the student and the perspectives and politics of the community. Both the league and the federation tended to represent urban areas and/or centers of black education.[56]

The topics discussed during the league's convention displayed its privileged positions and middle-class interests. Ida R. Cummings, a kindergarten teacher and founder of the Woman's League of Baltimore, discussed child development. Sara Iredell Fleetwood, wife of former army officer, editor, and bureaucrat Christian Fleetwood and leader of the Washington Mignonette Club and Monday Night Literary Club, spoke about nursing programs for black women. Ida Platt, representing the Chicago League, provided information about the law profession, while Florence A. Lewis of Philadelphia talked on journalism as a career. Dr. Rebecca J. Cole, graduate of the Women's Medical College of Pennsylvania, spoke on the general race issue, and Josephine Silone-Yates of Kansas City discussed business careers. Their speeches and experiences stimulated resolutions calling for the development of kindergartens, industrial training programs, and rescue work in the cities.

As with the league's speeches, the topics discussed at federation meetings reflected elite interests. Josephine Beall Bruce called for black women to raise their social and moral inferiors to a higher plane. Frances Ellen Watkins Harper argued for improvement of the home. Several women focused on education as the means to uplift. Fannie Coppin urged the women to encourage education in trades, while they continued to seek formal education in order to lead their race in racial progress. Jennie Dean, founder of Manassas (Virginia) Industrial School, requested help from the federation in developing more industrial schools.[57]

The federation demonstrated its origins as an organized reaction to the defamatory letter of James W. Jacks. Rosetta Douglass Sprague, daughter of Frederick Douglass, and Mrs. L. B. Stephens called for improved socialization methods for young black women to rectify their image as immoral and inferior. The federation as a whole reacted to the "unjust and unholy charges."[58] The women declared, "Now with an army of organized women standing for purity and mental worth, we in ourselves deny the charges . . . not by noisy protestations of what we are not but by a dignified showing of what we are."[59] These upper-class ladies emphasized their commitment to prove that they were ladies.

The obvious duplication of membership, efforts, and goals stimulated the league's appointment of seven women to meet with seven women similarly appointed by the National Federation. These fourteen women[60] convened the first day of the federation's convention. Mary Church Terrell, the representative of the federation and one of the founders of the league, was elected chairman of this joint committee. The group recommended a merger of the two organizations. Their creation of the National Association of Colored Women reflected the attempt to overcome the factionalism and conflicts that had historically constrained the effectiveness of black women.

The interaction between various clubs and factions was not easy at first, but the women realized there were many bases for cooperation. Although the spread of legalized segregation was slower in some cities than in others, Jim Crow became a national phenomenon affecting even cities with liberal traditions, such as Boston and Cleveland. Increased segregation made the black elite more interdependent. Increased participation in reform requiring travel from city to city made the elite more dependent on local black leaders for shelter and information. As speechmaking increased through professional lecture companies and Chautauquas, mutual intercourse and cooperation became more frequent. As racial institutions proliferated, the elites sought the advice of successful fund-raisers. When a member of the elite faced discrimination in employment or housing, reliance on a network of supporters frequently became necessary. For self-protection, self-advancement, and social interaction, the elites gradually came together, lessening the city and/or class divisions that had historically prevented their unity.[61] The NACW became such a vehicle.

The women from both the league and the federation demonstrated the strength of conflicts and compromise during the formation of the NACW. Both groups wanted retention of association titles; in the end they compromised.[62] Choosing new leaders created further conflict. As the chairman of the joint committee, Mary Church Terrell described the election process as her "hardest day's work [which wore her] . . . to a frazzle."[63] Every name on the joint committee received nomination. Intermittent prayers released the tensions somewhat. Eventually, Terrell received a second nomination, which broke the deadlock and made her the first president of the NACW. This subordination of organizational and regional rivalries to attain one national organization for black women won the NACW favorable press coverage. Since the women sought a more positive image of black women, their cooperation achieved a part of that goal.

The 1896 meeting symbolized the fading of one generation of black female leadership and the rising of a new group. By the first meeting of the NACW, Sojourner Truth, Mary Patterson, and Mary Shadd Cary had died. The oldest delegate was the antislavery lecturer and "Moses" of her people, Harriet Tubman. This past conductor of the Underground Railroad introduced the youngest in attendance, the infant son of Ida B. Wells-Barnett. The aged, ex-slave Tubman epitomized experience in movements for temperance, abolition, and women's rights. Others with similar reform involvements in an earlier era included Frances Ellen Watkins Harper, Charlotte Forten Grimke, Fannie Jackson Coppin, Sarah Garnet, Rosetta Douglass Sprague, and Sara Iredell Fleetwood.

Few of the new leadership group had experience with slavery or mid-nineteenth-century reforms. Although many came from privileged backgrounds, many others had achieved their social positions through marriage, education, and/or such respectable occupations as teaching, charity work, and the legal and medical professions. As with their earlier counterparts, the members of the new leadership group possessed strength of personality and intelligence.

The delegates reflected the dominance of the original centers of club organization and the characteristics of the emerging leadership. Seventy-three delegates represented twenty-five states, one district, two territories, fifty cities, and eighty-two clubs. The strength of the NACW remained in the Northeast. Washington, D.C., and the Boston area predominated.

Black women valued self-help, protection of women, honesty, and justice. Thus, their clubs included the Lend-A-Hand Club, Woman's Protective Club, Golden Rule Club, Equal Rights Council, and Woman's Uplifting Club. They honored black leaders in names, as the Sojourner Truth Club, Phillis Wheatley Club, Lucy Thurman WCTU Club, Ada Sweet Club, and Ida B. Wells Club. The religious roots appeared in such names as the Calvary Circle, Temperance Social Assembly, and Christian League.[64]

Joining heroines of the past with younger, ambitious women filled with hopes for the future, merging old traditions with new scientific methods of social organization, the NACW became a major vehicle through which black women attempted reform during the late nineteenth century.

TWO

National Movements and Issues: Women, Race, and the National Association of Colored Women, 1890-1910

After the official founding of the National Association of Colored Women, black women responded to the general reform context as both a sexually and a racially subordinate group. As educated, elite women, they actively supported the major women's reform movements seeking moral purity, temperance, self-improvement, and suffrage. Their racial identity, however, complicated participation in the national organizations that included the National Congress of Mothers, the Women's Christian Temperance Union, the National Council of Women, the General Federation of Women's Clubs, the National American Woman Suffrage Association, and the Young Women's Christian Association. Black women had different perspectives on the women's issues; they possessed a triple consciousness of being an American, a black, and a woman. During the pre-1910 period, their activities in the NACW demonstrated the ambiguous goals and personal rivalries typical of most contemporary racial and women's organizations. As the women dealt with the issues and clarified their goals, the NACW evolved from a social and informational network to become more of a widespread, well-organized racial advancement organization.

Black women reassembled in Nashville from September 15 to 18, 1897, to formalize the organizational structure of the NACW and to demonstrate their worth and capabilities. Held during the Nashville Centennial, this first annual conference became a platform of racial self-defense. The organization's mission proposed "to furnish evidence of the moral, mental and material progress made by people of color through the efforts of our women."[1] The opening address by Mary Church Terrell described the reason for inclusion of the word "colored" in the organizational title: "our peculiar status in this country at the present time seems to demand that we stand by ourselves in the special work."[2] The women called for less criticism and more emphasis on the progress of the race. Self-help and racial solidarity echoed in every speech.

Unlike their rejection during the Chicago Exposition, the black women received recognition from the Nashville Centennial Woman's Department. In response to this recognition, the NACW modified its program to include topics and speakers that neither threatened the white power structure nor discouraged the attendance of new members. The speeches, therefore, reflected contemporary viewpoints about the nature of women and women's role in reform.[3]

The Victorian model of the lady influenced the behavior of the black elite women. Columns in the black press frequently quoted white women's magazines about appropriate dress, language, demeanor, and values. The photographs of black women and the advertisements indicated that the Gibson girl appearance was the acceptable style of the day. Leading black clubwomen advised avoiding ostentation in apparel. Mrs. C. C. Pettey remarked that "gorgeous dress and fine paraphernalia don't make a woman."[4] Fannie Barrier Williams recommended "refinement of conception, good taste, and the proprieties."[5] Good manners, social purity, cleanliness, and home care would eventually demonstrate the inaccuracy of the white conception of the black woman as immoral.

The members of the NACW believed in the woman's sphere, which emphasized women's moral superiority, nurturance of children and social inferiors, and imposition of middle-class standards on the lower classes. Richmond clubwoman Rosa D. Bowser felt the primary duty of women was the "systematic and wise ordering of the household."[6] Angelina W. Grimke, poet and daughter of Archibald Grimke, a lawyer and activist in the Boston and Washington communities, warned women to remain within their sphere effecting improvements in the home, noting, "As soon as she puts her foot outside the door and enters other spheres, she leaves behind her power and mingles with the palled [sic] throng"[7] who are fighting and struggling. At the Nashville meeting, Mary Church Terrell called for black women to begin in the home. To the clubwomen, the improvement of the home and family was primary.[8]

Through columns in the black press and articles in race periodicals,[9] women received advice to remain in the home and also to become more active outside the home. These messages did not contradict each other. The respectable lady did not participate in the labor force unless absolutely necessary. The management of the home, domestic workers, and the family utilized her energies. To accomplish these goals efficiently, however, women were encouraged to form literary or cultural groups in which they could develop more expertise about the latest methods of childrearing, housekeeping, and home management. The Nashville meeting of the NACW emphasized this process when it called for expanding the organization of Mothers' Congresses.

Once women had improved their own homes, they could extend their sphere into the larger family: the community. The educational and economic advantages of the elite black women placed them in a position to uplift their inferiors. They functioned as mothers to their communities. Lucy Laney, founder of Haines Institute in Augusta, Georgia, called women to action by appealing to their "God-given, blessed"[10] status as mothers. Fannie Barrier Williams told them to "become the civic mothers of the race by establishing a sort of special relationship between those who help and those who need help."[11] The destiny of the race was "in the hands of its mothers."[12] The women were expected to "reach down and assist"[13] by teaching lessons in purity, cleanliness, and economy to make "honest, industrious Christians of the future."[14]

The NACW reflected the elitism of its members. Rosa D. Bowser of Richmond called for the clubwoman to help her "weak sisters . . . [who know] she is NOT of them, but with them in their efforts to improve."[15] Mrs. M. E. C. Smith called for women "to have compassion for the lowly and extend a helping hand toward the elevation, comfort and restoration of their inferiors."[16] Fannie Barrier Williams said that the club movement reached into "the sub-social condition of the entire race."[17] Mary Church Terrell's opening address at Nashville reinforced these values when she called for more kindergartens where the "waifs and strays of the alleys come in contact with intelligence and virtue."[18] Her closing lines called for the clubwoman to protect and sympathize with her fallen sisters, not only by preaching, but also by practicing race unity and race pride.

The Nashville meeting showed the concerns of black women for racial issues. Sylvania Williams, president of the New Orleans Phillis Wheatley Club, delivered a "forceful paper"[19] on the separate car law. Sylvia M. Maples, from Knoxville, spoke out about the humiliation encountered while riding Jim Crow cars. Such segregated transportation offended the black elite who could afford first-class tickets. Their sense of justice was offended by the convict-lease system. Selma Butler presented a "harrowing picture"[20] of the system in her state of Georgia. The delegates responded to the speech so favorably that they had it printed for distribution.

The women not only called for improvements in segregated transportation and racial injustices, but also called for the building of race pride. Mary Church Terrell suggested that courses about "African Ancestors" could encourage race pride rather than "race suicide."[21] The delegates heard reports about the achievements of black women. Information about the "Steele Home" for orphans in Chattanooga, modeled after the Atlanta Carrie Steele orphanage, efforts to establish an orphanage and sanitarium in New Orleans, and the proliferation of temperance programs in black communities reinforced optimism that attempts to improve the social environment would lead to a better American society.

With the constitution and officers approved at the Nashville meeting, the NACW began its role as a national organization presenting a positive image of black women to white America. The clubwomen had to avoid open conflicts, demonstrate their organizational abilities, and garner positive notices from the white press and white reformers. Examination of the clubwomen's activities at and between the NACW's biennials demonstrated a gradual achievement of their goals.

Conflict threatened to halt the precarious unity of the national club movement before it had gained momentum. The ideological and personal conflicts present in the Chicago club community caused problems for the NACW leadership planning the first biennial convention to be held in Chicago in 1899. President Mary Church Terrell relied on the local clubwomen for assistance in planning the meeting. The Chicago women warned Terrell that she would lose their cooperation unless she excluded Ida B. Wells-Barnett. Dependent on the local leadership for the program, Terrell decided not to invite Wells-Barnett. Offended, Wells-Barnett charged that Terrell was afraid of losing her leadership position to her.

Although Terrell admired the accomplishments of Wells-Barnett, her decision to exclude the antilynching crusader was based on practical considerations. Since the convention took place in Chicago, Terrell could not offend the leading local clubwomen. Attempting to unite factions of black women and to provide a public image of reserved, ladylike leadership, Terrell knew she would have to omit this controversial confrontationist. Terrell also based her decision on the fact that Wells-Barnett, secretary of the Afro-American Council, would be busy with the council's activities during the same week as the NACW biennial. Terrell was an excellent judge of the politically expedient. Both Terrell and Chicago clubwoman Fannie Barrier Williams were supporters of Booker T. Washington. Their lawyer husbands, Robert H. Terrell and S. Laing Williams, gained Washington's support for political appointments. Ida B. Wells-Barnett and her lawyer husband, Ferdinand Barnett, were consistent critics of Washington.

Terrell understood the need to build an organization for black women that could attack racial injustices effectively. Wells-Barnett, as one of those "powerful personalities who had gone their own ways fitted for courageous work, but perhaps not fitted to accept the restraint of organization,"[22] posed a threat to the infant organization. As president of the NACW, Terrell based her decisions on what she saw as best for the organization, trying to leave aside personal issues.[23]

The conflict over Wells-Barnett was only the beginning of problems for the Chicago biennial. When the meeting opened on August 14, 1899, disagreements developed over the recognition of credentials, selection of officers, and parliamentary procedure. Some of the delegates arrived with no credentials. To avoid setting a negative precedent for the NACW, Terrell, as "able presiding officer and parliamentarian,"[24] ruled that those delegates lacking proper credentials could not take part in the proceedings. When Josephine St. Pierre Ruffin attempted to speak, Terrell ruled her out of order due to improper credentials. The past rivalry of the Boston and Washington clubs was reinforced by the credentials/parliamentary procedures difficulties.[25]

These regional rivalries reappeared in the selection process of new leadership. The NACW constitution prevented a president from serving more than two consecutive terms. Since Terrell had served as the head of the joint committee in 1896 and as the president when the NACW was formally organized in 1897, many thought her ineligible to run for office in 1899. Since the constitution had received approval only in 1897, other delegates wanted Terrell to seek reelection. Terrell's husband and father did not want her to run because of the time and travel required by the position. Terrell ultimately agreed to serve only if she received a two-thirds majority of the votes.

Several women were interested in the presidency and Terrell's running made the competition vocal. Terrell received 106 votes, which placed her eight votes beyond the two-thirds majority, and she accepted the post. The position of first vice president placed Ruffin; Libbey Anthony, St. Louis temperance worker; and Josephine B. Bruce in competition. Ruffin and Anthony withdrew, giving the office to Bruce. For recording secretary, Chicago's Connie A. Curl competed against New Bedford's Elizabeth C. Carter and Pittsburgh's Mary Sutton. Carter withdrew, charging the NACW with playing power politics and saying, "All you seem to want of us is our money and our influence to help the growth of the association."[26] Carter was probably referring to the recognition problems met by Ruffin earlier and the withdrawal of Ruffin from the vice-presidential conflict after having lost the presidency to Terrell. Carter's own defeat reinforced the perception of the New England clubwomen that the NACW had treated that region poorly. Carter announced the withdrawal of the Northeast Federation (formed from the New England Federation of Women in 1896) and its membership. The Woman's Era Club and the Northeast Federation took their complaints to the press, thereby threatening the positive public image of the NACW.

The NACW leadership met the charges directly. The organization published an official "Refutation of the False Charges . . ."[27] in the same publications that had printed the charges by the New England women. After much debate, the New England clubs remained, but the bitterness also remained. Still, the clubwomen understood the need for unity.[28]

White reaction to the NACW biennial was favorable. Jane Addams invited the NACW leadership to visit Hull House for a luncheon. Although the white press reported Addams's entertainment of the black women "in a social way,"[29] the invitation symbolized acceptance of the NACW as a legitimate national women's reform organization. The white press was favorably impressed by the proceedings. The *Times Herald* felt the black women "a continual revelation, not only as to personal appearance, but as to intelligence and culture."[30] The Chicago *Tribune* said the clubwomen's "efforts are calculated to command public respect and cannot fail to have in many ways, far-reaching influence."[31] Conflicts had not paralyzed the young organization, but continued to threaten its ultimate success.

The next major conflict resulted from the organization's success in gaining members and spreading influence in areas beyond the Northeast. The NACW represented only one regional federation and five thousand members in 1897, but thereafter the club movement expanded considerably. By the 1904 St. Louis biennial, membership had climbed to over fifteen thousand women from thirty-one states. Since the Buffalo meeting in 1901, state federations had grown from six to eighteen. The leadership of the NACW showed the growing influence of southern or border states with segregationist traditions. Until the 1901 Buffalo biennial, the NACW leadership had reflected the prominence of the northern urban areas and Washington, D.C. In 1897, of fourteen offices, only four were occupied by representatives from the South. By 1899, the South received only three of eleven offices. The number increased by two for the 1901 meeting and remained at five of the ten offices for the 1904 St. Louis meeting.[32]

The growth in membership and changes in leadership eventually contributed to the raising of the color issue during the 1906 Detroit convention. Of five candidates seeking the presidency, most were light-skinned representatives of the elite. The competition narrowed to former president Mary Church Terrell, Josephine Beall Bruce, and Lucy Thurman. Delegates complained that Bruce, wife of former Senator Blanche K. Bruce, was "too light in color and that she only went with people of her own color at home."[33] Terrell aroused antipathies among the women who were jealous of her intellectual and social abilities. Lucy Thurman, the dedicated leader of the Colored Division of the Women's Christian Temperance Union from 1895 to 1908, won the presidency because of her identity as a Michigan woman, her club and temperance work, and her darker hue. One of the delegates summarized the decision: "We prefer a woman who is altogether Negro, because while the lighter women have been the greatest leaders and are among the most brilliant of the association, their cleverness and ability is attributed to their white blood. We want to demonstrate that the African is as talented."[34] The delegate expressed a common perception of the white community. In the case of Mary Church Terrell, white reformers, reporters, and writers emphasized her white blood in their explanations for her achievements in speaking, writing, and organization. Terrell, herself, emphasized her mixed lineage, as did others of the black elite. Both in background and in appearance, proximity to white blood brought advantages and position.[35] The assertion of color consciousness was less of a rejection of the established elite than an assertion of racial pride by an expanding membership seeking racial recognition and their appropriate position in the

NACW leadership. The NACW averted a potential conflict by becoming more inclusive in its leadership.

The clubwomen continued to expand their interests as their organization grew. Their early emphasis on moral and educational concerns led to their support of the temperance issue. As with white women, black women pursued temperance through "the goliath of women's organizations,"[36] the WCTU. Stressing health concerns; prison reform; care and training of lower-class, needy, or delinquent children; dress reform; peace; social purity; mothers' meetings; and travelers' aid, the WCTU offered black women an organized vehicle through which they could improve family life, health, and morality.

The interest of black elites in temperance reform was not new. Black women had formed their own temperance societies during the mid-nineteenth century when they had been denied membership in the all-male organizations. After the Civil War, with increased political and social freedoms for blacks and women, black women continued to support temperance due to its stress on the family, morality, and self-control. When the WCTU expanded its activities among various groups and geographical regions during the late nineteenth century, black women became superintendents of "colored work." Jane M. Kenney held that position until 1883, when Frances Ellen Watkins Harper assumed leadership for seven years. Mrs. J. E. Ray took over from 1891 through 1895, followed by Michigan's club leader, Lucy Thurman, who occupied the superintendency until her election as NACW president in 1908.[37]

Although Rosetta Douglass Sprague regretted that little attention was paid to the WCTU by black women, most of the clubwomen supported the issue and organized to effect that reform at the national and local levels. Thurman, who served as one of the honor guards at the funeral of Frances E. Willard in 1898, was a potent factor in the establishment of a Temperance Department in the NACW. Frances Joseph, founder of the Colored Industrial Home and School in Louisiana, served as the American representative of the Frances Willard WCTU to the 1900 World's Women's Christian Temperance Union convention. Amanda Smith, founder of a Chicago children's home in 1899, had funded her institution with money raised as the "World's Evangelist of the WCTU."[38] These black women carried the temperance message beyond America's boundaries.[39]

On the state and local levels, black clubwomen combined temperance with other reform efforts. Frances E. L. Preston, a leader in the Michigan

Federation of Colored Women's Clubs, was a lecturer and organizer for the WCTU. Reverend Florence Randolph combined club, church, and temperance work in New Jersey. Ariel Hedges Bowen, president of the Georgia WCTU No. 2,[40] served as a club leader at the local and state levels. Laura A. Brown, organizer for the WCTU in Pennsylvania, found temperance reform "her happiest work."[41] Mary Cordelia Booze, daughter of Isaiah T. Montgomery, the founder of the black town of Mound Bayou, Mississippi, spread temperance through the black community. Supported by individuals as diverse as Mary Church Terrell, Libbey C. Anthony, Margaret Murray Washington, Elizabeth C. Carter, and Dr. Susan McKinney Steward, temperance was a reform favored by clubwomen from Michigan to Missouri, from New York City to Mound Bayou, from Atlanta University to Tuskegee Institute.[42]

Examination of the NACW departmental organization reveals a continual interest in temperance and an expansion of concerns as the membership grew. In 1901, the clubwomen institutionalized their support by including temperance among the seven departments of organizational work. (The other six departments expressed interest in moral and educational reform through kindergartens, mothers' meetings, domestic science, rescue work, music, and religion.) By the 1904 St. Louis biennial, their interests had expanded into twelve departments, adding concerns for art, literature, professional women, business women, and social science. These areas responded to the rising membership from literary and culture clubs. The participation of educated women in business, social work, medicine and law appeared in delegate representation and in the topics covered during the biennial. Lectures on how women could encourage the development of taste for the "best music,"[43] how to be a good example in one's home and community, and how to influence moral uplift, combined with discussions about sexual discrimination in the professions and advice on business management. The NACW resolved to work vigorously for suffrage, to develop closer ties with the WCTU, and to create a better environment for children.

Again, at the 1908 Brooklyn biennial, the expansion of departments reflected further growth and experience of the black club movement. Greater concern for young people had become specialized to include departments for juvenile court and day nurseries in addition to the standard departments for kindergarten, mothers' meetings, rescue work, art, literature, and music. The church-related concerns had been replaced with departments of parliamentary law, forestry, and humane interests. Business and the professions had been combined into one department. In an effort to gain representation from younger generations, the NACW organized a department for young women. The sixteen departments continued to include temperance among the priority reforms sought by the black clubwomen, who represented not only the Northeastern Federation, but also the North Central and the Northwest Federations.[44]

Temperance was not the only women's reform issue supported by the clubwomen. To black women, woman's suffrage "meant not only the future of the women of color in America, it also meant the correcting of many evils which if corrected would mean a new day for the American Negro."[45] Some of the older clubwomen included woman's suffrage as one of many reforms they supported. Several clubwomen had participated in the American Woman Suffrage Association, headed by Lucy Stone, and in the National Woman Suffrage Association, directed by Susan B. Anthony and Elizabeth Cady Stanton. The American Woman Suffrage Association, a conservative organization that sought to win suffrage rights through state amendments, differed from the National Woman Suffrage Association, which utilized protest tactics to win a federal suffrage amendment. Frances Ellen Watkins Harper, one of the few black members of the conservative American Woman Suffrage Association, included suffrage among her concerns for temperance, enfranchisement of blacks, and abolition. When faced with the conflict between enfranchising black men or women as a whole, Harper agreed with Frederick Douglass that the race needed the vote for self-protection more than women required that political tool. Most early supporters of woman suffrage belonged to the radical wing led by Elizabeth Cady Stanton and Susan B. Anthony. The National Woman Suffrage Association received the support of Boston clubwoman Josephine St. Pierre Ruffin and Washington club leader Mary Shadd Cary. Groups of clubwomen in South Carolina came together as the Woman's Rights Association under the American Woman Suffrage Association in the 1870s. The black women in Topeka, Kansas, formed their own group in 1887, the Colored Women's Suffrage Association.[46]

After the merging of the two wings of the woman suffrage movement in 1890, the National American Woman Suffrage Association (NAWSA) attracted the support of black women who were also organizing at the local and national levels. Oberlin graduates Anna Cooper, Mary Talbert, Mary Terrell, Hallie Q. Brown, and Ida Gibbs Hunt had become supporters of woman suffrage during their college days and carried that support into their club work in Washington, Buffalo, Boston, and Wilberforce. With the expansion of literary clubs and the Chautauqua movement, many more black women received information about the issue. Gertrude Mossell of Philadelphia, Fannie Barrier Williams and Ida Wells-Barnett of Chicago, Carrie Clifford of Cleveland, Coralie Cook of Washington, Mary E. McCoy of Detroit, Cora Horne and Sarah J. Garnet of Brooklyn, and many others worked for woman suffrage in the North. Their support was not typical of most black women during these early years.[47]

As with the white women[48] who opposed enfranchising women, many black women opposed any alteration in the "woman's sphere." Mary Terrell recalled, "In the early 1890s it required a great deal of courage for a woman publicly to acknowledge before an audience that she believed in suffrage for her sex when she knew the majority did not."[49] Susan McKinney Steward, sister of Sarah Garnet, said the great fear of that time was that a woman would "unsex herself"[50] by supporting woman suffrage. Angelina Grimke, whose father and uncle supported the issue, felt woman lost her true power within the home when she "mingled" with the outside world. Sarah Pettey thought the home environment offered higher power for the female sex. Men became the vehicles of female morality when they entered public affairs "to execute what woman has decreed."[51] Even Margaret Murray Washington belittled the importance of the female vote, saying, "Personally, woman suffrage has never kept me awake at night."[52] Before suffrage became a more popular public issue during the post-1910 period, most black clubwomen considered it a subordinate interest.[53]

Suffrage support was even more difficult for a southern black woman. Support for the suffrage amendment challenged the South's values of states' rights, paternalism, and racism. Yet when white suffrage leaders toured the South speaking to church and college groups, a few black women became interested. For Adella Hunt Logan, wife of the Tuskegee treasurer Warren Logan, supporting woman suffrage caused extremely difficulties. A graduate of Atlanta University, Logan became one of the early educators at Tuskegee Institute. She and her husband lived next to the Booker T. Washingtons. This proximity and conservative atmosphere caused Logan internal conflict over her support of an unpopular issue. She participated in the NAWSA as the only life member in Alabama in 1901. Attending conventions of the white suffrage association, Logan frequently relied on her ability to pass in order to take part in the proceedings. Her achievements received coverage in the *Woman's Journal* and she, in turn, gave the suffrage issue coverage in black periodicals. In the Tuskegee Women's Club, Logan pursued her suffrage interests and participated in departmental suffrage work in the NACW. Logan's intensity was somewhat unusual for southern black women. For most, lack of awareness, commitment, or interest was commonplace.[54]

For many black clubwomen, participation in the suffrage movement required passing for white or frustration with the growing anti-black attitudes and policies of the NAWSA. By the 1890s, the suffrage movement and black rights had moved so far apart that "only a few liberals . . . supported both causes."[55] Expediency required white suffrage leaders to accommodate prevalent attitudes. Carrie Chapman Catt expressed a racist argument in 1894 when she argued that female enfranchisement would counterbalance the power of the ignorant immigrant vote in the northern cities. By 1904, she argued that female enfranchisement would balance the black vote in the South. When the NAWSA officially bowed to states' rights at their 1903 convention, woman suffrage became the "medium through which to retain supremacy of the white race over the African."[56] Yet in this increasingly hostile atmosphere, black women continued to attend the conventions of the NAWSA.[57]

Several black members of the NAWSA made it a point to inform white women about issues affecting black Americans and to persuade the suffrage organization to support justice. At the 1899 NAWSA convention, Michigan clubwoman Lottie Wilson Jackson made a motion that the organization oppose publicly the treatment received by black women in Jim Crow railroad cars. Frances Watkins Harper used her suffrage participation to enlighten white women about her personal suffering as a black woman. Mary Church Terrell, a frequent speaker at NAWSA conventions in Washington, told the delegates of the 1904 convention, "I want you to stand up not only for children and animals but even for Negroes. You will never get suffrage till you . . . give fair play to the colored race."[58] Terrell used her speaking engagements at the 1898 and 1900 conventions to impress the white women with the abilities of her race. Reprints of her 1898 speech, "Progress and Problems of the Colored Woman," were sold to raise funds for kindergartens developed through the NACW.

Terrell's popularity with the white suffrage leadership led to an invitation to address the Sixtieth Anniversary Celebration of Women's Rights at Seneca Falls, New York, in 1908. Her two speeches, "Frederick Douglass" and "Woman Suffrage," delineated the main reasons for black women's support of suffrage. She emphasized the historical roots of this support when she told how Frederick Douglass had saved the suffrage issue from death by seconding Elizabeth Cady Stanton's motion at the first Seneca Falls convention. Terrell also showed how women as workers, taxpayers, property owners, and citizens deserved the same tool for self-protection and representation as males. American democracy could not be realized as long as women remained voteless. Blacks as a doubly powerless group could benefit from women voting for justice and moral reforms.[59]

Other clubwomen used different arguments for supporting woman suffrage. Ida Wells-Barnett emphasized the political power and protection available through the vote. During her Illinois residence, Wells-Barnett's membership in the women's suffrage organization had taught her the value of female enfranchisement. Organized voting could prevent restrictive legislation and elect candidates sensitive to racial issues. She tied the importance of the vote to her antilynching crusade. In those states where blacks had held the franchise, she argued, lynchings were infrequent or declining, compared to states where blacks had been disenfranchised. These statistics not only undermined Booker T. Washington's public subordination of the voting rights issue, but also served as an argument for blacks to support the woman suffrage issue.[60]

Even though many of the leading clubwomen expressed support for suffrage, the NACW as a whole paid little attention to the issue before 1910. The organization resolved to support the issue more vigorously in the 1904 St. Louis biennial and again in the speeches of the 1906 biennial. But woman suffrage did not receive full organizational endorsement until 1912, by which time the issue had gathered popular momentum and the official support of a non-suffragist national white women's organization, the General Federation of Women's Clubs (GFWC). Neither the NACW nor the GFWC led in the movement for woman suffrage.

The difficulties faced by the black clubwomen in the suffrage movement were repeated in their treatment by the General Federation of Women's Clubs. Formed in 1890, the GFWC failed to consider the problems resulting from participation of black women. Some black women participated indirectly through receptive state federations, as in the case of the Phyllis Wheatley Club of Racine, Wisconsin. Others belonged to white women's clubs that admitted a few of the black elite. Fannie Barrier Williams was the only black member of the Chicago Women's Club. Josephine Ruffin was the only black member of the New England Federation of Women's Clubs. By 1900, their indirect or direct participation became a major issue at the fifth biennial of the GFWC in Milwaukee.

Black participation became an issue because a black woman attended that national convention as a delegate. When Josephine Ruffin arrived at the biennial, she represented both a black woman's club, the Woman's Era, and a white women's group, the New England Federation of Women's Clubs. Finally, the white leadership of the GFWC had to face its lack of policy concerning black participation. Both the Woman's Era and the New England Federation had received legitimate affiliation with the GFWC. The chairman of the Massachusetts delegation had approved the application of the Woman's Era Club and had sent a copy of the club's constitution along with the proper application forms to the GFWC. Officials of the GFWC failed to notice the club's stated goals to help the Negro race.

The positive action by the Massachusetts delegation did not reflect the general attitudes held by most of the white clubwomen. In fact, the GFWC newsletter had recently published a story, "The Rushing in of Fools," which described how a prosperous black family moved into a white neighborhood and how the women of the black household and a white household became friends. The white neighbor helped the black woman gain admission to her women's club. Soon, the son of the black family became a physician and married the daughter of the white neighbor. Even though he was even fairer than his socially accepted mother, the son's first child was born "jet black." The young white mother died of shock after the birth. This story vividly illustrated the fears of social equality held by many of the white women in the GFWC. It was a cautionary tale warning white clubwomen what could happen if black women were admitted.[61]

The GFWC also faced fears of organizational disintegration if black women received official rights to participate. The Georgia delegates threatened to resign if the constitution did not go through the amendment process to restrict membership to white women. The amendment was made unnecessary by the tactics of the GFWC leadership. The white women voted to accept Ruffin's credentials as a representative from the white women's group, effectively eliminating recognition of the black women's club. The white leadership then advised the state federations to choose their delegates more carefully in the future to avoid other awkward situations.

Most state federations followed the suggestions of the GFWC leadership. The Illinois Federation, for example, created a "subtle evasion clause,"[62] which made black participation impossible. Yet even these restrictions could not prevent black participation at the local levels in city or county federations. When the Chicago Women's Club led the movement to organize all women's clubs in Cook County, the Ida B. Wells Club received an invitation to join the Cook County Federation of Women's Clubs. Wells-Barnett became one of nine women elected to the first board of directors for the new county federation. This type of schizophrenic policy reflected the GFWC's needs to maintain the loyalties of prejudiced northern women and southern women accustomed to segregation. Possessing their own national club movement, few black women fought for admission to further national conventions of the GFWC.[63]

Not all white women's groups attempted to exclude black women. The National Council of Women (NCW), founded in 1888, had invited the National League of Colored Women into membership in 1894. The National Association of Colored Women sought to legitimize their position as the national black women's organization by gaining membership in the NCW. Following the stormy Chicago biennial, black clubwomen renewed the movement for institutional membership in the National Council of Women. In the December 1899 issue of the NACW newsletter, *National Association Notes*, Adella Hunt Logan summarized the political and social arguments for membership. As American women, members of the NACW would join in the NCW's efforts "to promote the welfare of all women of the country."[64] Affiliation would mean greater public esteem for the NACW. Since separation of the races produced ignorance and increased prejudice against the race, affiliation would give both races "opportunities to work in sympathy."[65] Politically, membership in the NCW would give black women a voice in and influence over the policies and issues dealt with by the NCW. Membership provided attendance for the NACW at all triennial meetings, two votes on all issues before the national body, representation of a black women's organization, and invitations to speak before national and local women's councils. Through the NCW, the NACW would gain closer relationships with the WCTU, Sorosis (the founding club of the General Federation of Women's Clubs), Universal Peace Union, and NAWSA.

Logan's arguments demonstrated the main reasons black women sought membership in national white women's groups. Black women desired inclusion not for the goal of social equality, as was often stated by the white women's groups, but for an institutional voice and recognition of their role. Mary Terrell, president of the NACW and leader of the Colored Women's League in Washington, D.C., supported the move for membership in the

National Council of Women. In fact, she delivered greetings from the NACW to the 1900 Minneapolis convention of the NCW, at which time the National Council of Women formally approved the NACW membership.

During the spring of 1904, Mary Church Terrell brought prestige to both the NACW and the NCW: she represented American women at the International Congress of Women in Berlin. Terrell delivered her address to the delegates in German, English, and French. The speech and Terrell's "presence" impressed both the European and American press representatives. *The Independent* reported that "Southern ladies will have to drop the Empress of Germany from their calling lists on account of her reception of this negress."[66] Terrell used the situation as Logan had earlier posited. Terrell's comparisons of the position of Jews in Germany to blacks in America raised the consciousness of a few international representatives. The "hit of the congress"[67] displayed the inaccuracy of racial stereotypes held by most of her white female contemporaries. Subsequently, the NACW and its leadership continued to maintain a working relationship with the National Council of Women.[68]

The National Council of Women was not alone in trying to include black women. In New York City, a center of social reform, two women's organizations were formed in 1906 to lessen the problems of urbanization for women. Black women were coming north seeking employment as domestics. Often lured to the cities by unscrupulous employment agents, the young women faced economic problems and immoral conditions. The leadership of both the National Board of the YWCA and the National League for the Protection of Colored Women (NLPCW)[69] sought to include black women as recipients of and participants in their ameliorative efforts. Both movements, although founded by white female reformers, were directly influenced by New York's black-founded White Rose Home. Established in 1897 by a small group of black women led by Victoria Earle Mathews, one of the founders of the Woman's Loyal League, the White Rose Home attempted to protect, direct, train, and aid black female migrants entering New York City. Mathews's agents met women at the boat and train stations, provided an escort to their new jobs or the White Rose Home, and made available temporary lodging and meals until they could find work. Mathews aided their adjustment to the city by providing instruction in manners, dress, and domestic skills. She increased their inner strength through instruction in race history from books in the home's library and from lectures by visiting race leaders.[70]

The program of the White Rose Home influenced the development of the National League for the Protection of Colored Women, which sought to create on a national scale what the White Rose Home had accomplished locally. Frances A. Kellor, hired by the Woman's Municipal League of New York to investigate employment agencies and lodging houses, realized the need for an organization "primarily interested in the industrial problems of Negro women."[71] Her study, *Out of Work*, found black female migrants employed as maids and cooks in sporting houses, threatened by agents until they accepted jobs of questionable morality, and induced to come north with no knowledge about the specific destination, costs of travel, or city information. As the general director of the Inter-Municipal Committee on Household Research, Kellor tried to coordinate services in Philadelphia and New York.

Both cities had established methods to protect black female migrants by 1905. Philadelphia had a Home for the Homeless to provide temporary aid and the local Association for the Protection of Colored Women. Workers met boats, investigated employment agencies, disseminated information through black colleges and churches in both the North and the South, and provided a homelike atmosphere in the city. During one year, 1,351 girls received aid from the Philadelphia Association alone.[72] New York's Association for the Protection of Colored Women aided black women in that city.

As separate agencies, the Philadelphia and New York Associations for the Protection of Colored Women could not accomplish their goals without establishing a national organization. The dishonest agencies, agents, and lodging house operators from one city merely moved to cities without such protective agencies. The National League for the Protection of Colored Women emerged in 1906 to consolidate efforts throughout the major cities of the North and the port cities of the South. The interracial leadership of both the Philadelphia and New York associations[73] created the basic leadership under Kellor's direction.[74]

The National League sought to check the emigration from the South and to protect the migrants during their journey. Once the migrants were in the city, the league directed them to proper lodgings, assisted them in finding suitable employment, and provided them with wholesome recreation. To accomplish these ends, the league sent information about the northern cities and employment to churches, women's clubs, and schools in the South. For those who had already left the South, agents met the incoming boats and trains to provide advice and prevent dishonest manipulation of the ignorant. The league compiled lists of reliable employment agencies and lodging houses and organized social and recreational clubs. To provide shelter, the league cooperated with existing facilities or established their own homes for temporary lodgings. In Philadelphia, the existing home met the need. In New York, the White Rose Home, the Colored Mission, and the black YWCA in Brooklyn cooperated with the league.

The report of the league's results during the last year of its separate existence[75] demonstrated the cooperation between white and black associations. In 1910, travelers received aid from branches in Philadelphia, Memphis, Baltimore, Norfolk, and New York. The White Rose dockworker met the boats in Norfolk and New York. The Philadelphia Association provided lodging, served as a center for local social and educational programs, and aided destitute women in finding domestic employment. In New York, black women provided lectures on etiquette, sex hygiene, and health care through the Amusement Center. The fifty members held socials and dances to provide acceptable recreation. The New York probation secretary dealt with thirty-six cases. In the two major cities serving black women, the officers were still white or men, but the actual delivery of services—involving dockworkers; probation officers; volunteers for the development of lectures, socials, and dances; and employment agents—depended on the unnamed black women active in the city clubs or social services.[76]

The influence of the White Rose Home penetrated the leadership of a second white women's organization, the National Board of the YWCA. Grace Dodge continued the Dodge family tradition of leadership in the Young Men's Christian Association by serving as the mediator in the conciliation of two rival groups in the Young Women's Christian Association. The International Board, dominated by upper-class women of large eastern cities, competed with the evangelical American Committee, centered in Chicago. Grace Dodge united the two groups in 1906 to form the National Board of the YWCA and became the organization's first president. She had been active in establishing industrial education in the early 1880s and had been a supporter of Booker T. Washington's work with blacks. She had worked with Mathews' White Rose Home and had established in 1905 the first non-sectarian branch of the National Traveler's Aid Society in New York City. As president of the National Board, Dodge began to clarify the role of black women in the YWCA. She wanted to incorporate the already existing black women's Christian organizations under the auspices of the National Board.

Like contemporary black organizations, the YWCA encouraged self-help activities. As the working classes expanded in northern urban areas, YWCA workers attempted to "reach girls where they were."[77] Black women came into membership, at first, as individuals. But as the urban black populations increased, racially separate Christian organizations evolved. In 1893, the first black YWCA[78] began in Dayton, Ohio. On friendly terms with its white counterpart, the black YWCA was not an organic part of the Dayton YWCA. Similar black YWCAs existed in black communities in Philadelphia; Baltimore; Harlem; Brooklyn; and Washington, D.C. Most lacked any official interaction with the structure of the white YWCA.[79]

The YWCA's work in the South proceeded slowly prior to the turn of the century, due to the region's lack of rapid urbanization, progress in education, reception to new ideas, and liberal religion. Evangelical groups reflecting a strong missionary zeal developed among women of the black colleges prior to the formation of the National Board. Spelman had the first such group, organized in 1884—followed by Tougaloo University of Mississippi (1885); Wilberforce University of Ohio (1891); Normal and Industrial Institute of Ettricks, Virginia (1893); Talladega College of Alabama (1896); Normal Agricultural and Mechanical College of Normal, Alabama (1900); Langston College of Oklahoma (1902); Tuskegee Institute of Alabama (1902); and Southern Christian Institute of Edwards, Mississippi (1904). After the formation of the National Board, student associations began at Claflin (1906), Knoxville College (1906), Alcorn Agricultural and Mechanical College (1908), Paine College (1908), State Normal College (1908), Western University (1909), and Howard University (1909).[80] The black women in these organizations reflected the influence of the northern missionary spirit and movement for higher education for women. Segregated by race, the female students attended coeducational conferences of the black YMCA-YWCA.[81]

The de facto existence of black YWCAs in cities and at black schools caused the newly formed National Board to deal with the issue of affiliating with the black organizations. A YWCA conference, held June 11-17, 1907, in Asheville, North Carolina, met to develop programs and policies regarding "Negro work." The decisions reached at this conference had a major impact on the form of race relations and black female participation for years to come. The Y decided to continue allowing student groups to affiliate with the national association. To avoid thwarting the growth of YWCAs in the southern cities, the conference accepted the dominance of black locals by the local white YWCAs. Although each black branch received affiliation approval through the National Board, the white "central" YWCA remained the predominant local influence. Operating as the subordinates of the central white YWCAs in each city, black women continued to organize both city and student associations as group self-help efforts.

The YWCA rationalized its acceptance of racial segregation on several grounds. First, the separate black organizations started by black women under the name of the YWCA were allowed to continue in their parallel development. Second, the association believed in the natural groupings of people along occupational, nationality, and racial lines. Last, the association followed contemporary "American folkways"[82] for the separation of the races. The National Board realized that the process of organizational growth, especially in the South, would require accommodation to local racial practices. During the twenty-year period from 1890 to 1910, segregation grew as the accepted form of racial policy.[83]

In this context, black women worked for the National Board in the investigation of needs and programs for the black community. Their efforts resulted in the YWCA's moving "slowly but always surely in the direction of a truer realization of democracy."[84] In September 1907, Addie W. Hunton, wife of William A. Hunton, the first black secretary of the YMCA, became the first paid black worker of the YWCA. Appointed by the National Board, Hunton investigated possibilities for association work among black women. During the winter of 1907-1908, she found fourteen existing student associations. The strongest associations, those in Orangeburg, South Carolina, and in Petersburg, Virginia, conducted programs related to the national YWCA goals. Four city associations met the needs of black women in New York, Brooklyn, Baltimore, and Washington. At this time, only the New York City branch had officially affiliated with the National Board. To partially solve the organizational irregularities, the National Board established in 1908 a training school to develop skills for young women to become secretaries of the YWCA.[85]

In the spring of 1908, Elizabeth Ross, who became the wife of George Edmund Haynes, the first executive secretary of the National Urban League, joined the national staff as the student secretary for black women. In this role, Ross investigated the city and student organizations and found lack of regularity in association work. As a trained social worker, Ross described programs in Philadelphia, Baltimore, and Washington as "rescue work, Sunday School work, Epworth League work and kindergartens."[86] This variety of programs, lack of coordination with the National Board, and general distrust by black women of the YWCA led Ross to pursue active city work in 1909.

Fourteen cities declared intentions to begin association work. To avoid chaos, Ross called for the National Board to outline general plans and principles for the development of work among the black women. The first new branch association began in St. Paul, Minnesota, in October 1909. Within two years, Ross had attended student conferences at Talladega, Claflin, Tougaloo, and Fisk; charted the development of thirty-eight additional student organizations; and sought to build on the existing reforms and organizations. Her work in Kansas City emphasized the active social service role of black women in organizing art and reading clubs, lodges, hospitals, and orphanages.[87] The work of Ross and Hunton reflected the expansion of interest of the YWCA in black community work.

Both the YWCA and the National League for the Protection of Colored Women sought the support of the National Association of Colored Women. Delegates to the 1908 Brooklyn biennial heard presentations by Mrs. S. W. Layton, head of the Working Girls' Home in Philadelphia, and by the National Association (formerly called League) for the Protection of Colored Women.

In 1910, Elizabeth Ross came to the Louisville biennial to discuss the goals and principles of the YWCA, hoping to convince the four hundred clubwomen of the YWCA's efforts to overcome prejudice. She described the proliferation of organizations throughout the South that called themselves colored YWCAs. In Norfolk and Charleston, black women had organizations doing work similar to the YWCA, but without formal affiliation. Ross advised against using the name of the YWCA unless certain requirements had been met. The black organizations had to follow general guidelines and utilize trained leadership to become part of the national YWCA movement. Her discussion produced favorable responses. Soon other organizations sought to cooperate with the YWCA in helping black women. The National League for the Protection of Colored Women expressed a desire to combine efforts with the YWCA. The black clubwomen were courted by both of these national organizations, and although black women increased their involvement with both groups, their awareness of the white control and racial segregation/separation policies of the two bodies made the NACW reluctant to endorse the activities of either. They continued to listen to the speeches from white representatives, but they increasingly came to recognize the importance of working for racial issues through the NACW.[88]

The black clubwomen expanded their racial concerns as the national club movement matured and as the racial climate worsened, but during the early biennials their concerns reflected the interests of their elites. They protested the humiliation of educated, moral black ladies forced to ride in Jim Crow cars with gamblers and prostitutes. At the Nashville convention in 1897, New Orleans clubwoman Sylvania Williams condemned the separate car law and Knoxville leader Sylvia M. Maples described the humiliation of the Jim Crow experience. Similar presentations about the Jim Crow practices occurred at the biennials in Chicago (1899), Buffalo (1901), and St. Louis (1904).

A second injustice that captured the attention of the clubwomen during the early years was the convict-lease system. Blacks convicted of petty crimes were the chief victims of the system of leasing prisoners to landowners and industrialists for labor in mines, railroad construction, road building, and agriculture. Often, young homeless boys had to work in these same gangs because the county lacked facilities for youth. The clubwomen were offended by this practice and protested it at the Nashville convention and at the biennials in Buffalo and Detroit.

The clubwomen's methods reflected a naive optimism during this time. In 1897, they hoped that exposure of the injustices to the white leadership would gradually improve the conditions as prejudice declined. By the time they reconvened in Chicago in 1899, the women felt that prejudices were too ingrained for immediate change. They recommended proper education of both black and white children as the beginning of the process to correct racial misconceptions.

Education and reeducation were the most commonly advocated methods for the improvement of race relations during the early years of the NACW. Industrial and agricultural education, frequently associated with the programs advocated by Booker T. Washington, had held the attention of educators throughout the nineteenth century. The teaching of domestic science sought to develop values of thrift and morality as well as efficiency and cleanliness. As previously mentioned, Grace Dodge of New York City was a proponent of this type of education. She helped to found the Kitchen Garden Association in 1880 and the Industrial Education Association in 1884. By teaching household skills and values to young working-class girls, Dodge and others felt the working class could increase their chances for social mobility and ease adaptation to the city. This type of education also appealed to the educated elite because it placed them in the position of instructors over their social inferiors, thereby reinforcing their class identity.

Proper education of the lower classes of the race was a necessary prerequisite for improved white attitudes. Since the leadership of the NACW represented the racial elite, the women believed that most of the race could reach a higher plateau if exposed to the cleanliness, morality, and manners of the elite women. Aligned behind the slogan "Lifting as We Climb," the black clubwomen symbolically emphasized their belief that they could teach proper behavior and attitudes while simultaneously improving their own social status. The elites would "lift" the lower classes as they "climbed" the social ladder. Many leaders goaded the black female elite to become more active in this role. Mary Terrell criticized the clubwomen for the "inertia of some of our brainiest and most reliable women."[89] As "the more favored portion . . . [the black clubwomen had to] strive to illumine the minds and improve the morals of those who it is in their power to uplift."[90] Frequently criticized as being "too much aloof from the less fortunate of their people,"[91] the women officially dedicated the NACW to the uplifting of "those beneath them."[92] They wanted to create middle-class citizens out of "poor little barbarians,"[93] to improve the white perceptions of the race. The elitism predominated in the issues of these early biennials, but was joined by more inclusive issues as the organization expanded.

Lynching had always been "a readily acceptable issue around which to mobilize the black community, North and South."[94] Black clubwomen had played an active part in the grass-roots organization of the antilynching movement. Ida B. Wells-Barnett led the movement against lynching during the late nineteenth century. Her work received recognition and support from the black women of the Woman's Loyal Union. After her children were born, Wells-Barnett retired from the active crusade, but continued to be involved through club and church activities. Whenever a noteworthy lynching occurred, as that of a South Carolina postmaster in 1898, she emerged from semi-retirement. She went to Washington to protest, but lack of organization in the Chicago black community and an unresponsive white political structure produced no results. America's entrance in the Spanish American War was the main interest of both politicians and public during Wells-Barnett's trip. During the Chicago biennial (1899), the Afro-American Council created an antilynching bureau under the direction of Wells-Barnett. That same year, Pauline E. Hopkins, a Boston clubwoman, published an antilynching novel entitled *Contending Forces*. The Michigan Federation of Colored Women's Clubs petitioned President McKinley to appropriate $40,000 for the postmaster's widow. Again, inaction followed.[95]

By 1900, black women were displaying a growing concern. The Northeast Federation developed a separate department on lynching. The Michigan Federation protested all forms of mob law at its annual meeting in 1900. At the 1904 St. Louis biennial, NACW resolutions deplored and condemned the increasing numbers of lynchings and asked the federal government to take a firmer stand in its efforts to halt the practice. Although the number of lynchings had declined, the barbarity of the lynchings and the character of the victims had captured the attention of the well-organized clubwomen. The mob violence in Springfield, Ohio; Brownsville, Texas; and Atlanta, Georgia, further demonstrated the intensity of racial hatred in the North, West, and South. By the spring of 1908, the politically astute Mary Church Terrell was delivering throughout the South lectures that were characterized by the white press as "a most scathing rebuke to mob and lynch law violence."[96] The NACW kept the lynching issue constantly before the American public and its representatives in Washington.[97]

Critical protest and direct action were not the main activities of the black clubwomen during the pre-1910 period. They tended instead to reflect the tactics used by groups lacking power. From 1890 to 1910, most blacks and women lacked suffrage rights and socioeconomic power. Although the individual federations petitioned the president, protested inequities, or collected statistics, the NACW did little beyond issuing verbal protests. The 1906 biennial issued the most direct advice to its delegates. Dissatisfaction over increasing segregation in transportation and shock about heightened mob violence led the NACW to advise blacks to refrain from using conveyances where discrimination existed, avoid excursions into areas where discrimination prevailed, and fight southern discrimination with the boycott. This advice reflected the attempted boycotts of schools and streetcars in cities[98] from which many of the leaders originated. In the contemporary context, they continued to advocate conservative protest based on avoidance rather than direct confrontation. They continued to believe that the future of the race depended on "the people getting up and doing something . . . individuals . . . work[ing] and depend[ing] on themselves."[99] The women continued to emphasize the values of self-reliance and racial solidarity.

Black women viewed the successful growth of the NACW as an example for further organization of professionals and for black urban communities. In

1908, black women formed the National Association of Colored Graduate Nurses. The professional training programs that had emerged as a result of local efforts had produced a handful of graduates who felt mutual interest in developing a national association to pursue their goals and further develop their profession. In 1908, black college women banded together at Howard University to form the sorority Alpha Kappa Alpha, which appealed to the noble ideals of life through literary and cultural programs, social interaction, and discussions. Alpha Kappa Alpha and Delta Sigma Theta (begun in 1912) supported high educational, moral, and spiritual attainment; sought to purify the home; encouraged protest against the double standards in morality; and taught race pride and race service. When Mary Church Terrell sought to renew her membership (she had been a member from 1905 to 1910) in the Washington branch of the Association of Collegiate Alumnae (called the American Association of University Women after 1921), the white women of the branch officially seceded from the national organization to form the University Women's Club. Increasingly, black women responded to the worsening racial conditions by expanding and improving their own national organizations.[100]

Victoria Earle Mathews (also spelled Matthews), founder of the New York Woman's Loyal Union and the White Rose Home, spearheaded the celebration honoring Ida B. Wells for her antilynching activities.
[*The Schomburg Center, NYPL*]

Mary Church Terrell, one of the founders of the Colored Woman's League of Washington, D.C., and the first president of the National Association of Colored Women, represented American women at the International Congress of Women in Berlin in 1904.
[*The Library of Congress.*]

Evangelical groups reflecting a strong missionary zeal developed among women attending black colleges. The Prairie View (Texas) Student YWCA Conference, with Conference leaders Mr. Jones and Mr. Kingsley, took place around 1910.
[*YWCA of the USA National Board Archives.*]

Janie Porter Barrett, Virginia club leader and wife of Hampton University bookkeeper Harris Barrett, initiated the first southern settlement developed by black women: the Locust Street Settlement.
[Hampton University Archives.]

Janie Porter Barrett with a girl's club of the Locust Street Settlement.
[*Hampton University Archives.*]

Maria L. Baldwin, a teacher and later an administrator at the Agassiz
School attended by the children of Harvard professors, served as a
counselor and taught classes in English Literature at the Robert Gould
Shaw House in Boston.
[*The Schlesinger Library, Radcliffe College.*]

Lugenia Burns Hope, wife of John Hope, the president of Morehouse College, was one of the first women to do volunteer social work in Atlanta and the founder of the Atlanta Neighborhood Union in 1908.
[*Dr. Edward Hope.*]

Lucy Parsons, widow of white activist Albert Parsons, who was hanged for his part in the Haymarket Square riot, agitated for radical labor reform. Her leadership in the International Workers of the World (Wobblies) demonstrated her class, rather than race, emphasis.
[*University of Illinois at Chicago,*
The University Library, Department of Special Collections.]

The black clubwomen involved in the NACW or in black settlements would not have picketed Jane Addams's Hull House about hunger issues, as did Lucy Parsons in 1915.
[*University of Illinois at Chicago, The University Library, Department of Special Collections.*]

Settlement work developed in Mt. Meigs (Alabama) through black colleges. Hampton students Georgia Washington (left), J.G. Johnson (right) and A. Hall (standing) performed social service in Mt. Meigs with the support of the Tuskegee and Alabama State Federation of Colored Women's Clubs.
[*Courtesy Hampton University's Archival and Museum Collection, Hampton University.*]

THREE

Community Action: Black Women Respond to Local Needs, 1890-1910

The national growth in women's organizations was both a product of their increased association at the local levels and a stimulant to further reform in their communities. The National Association of Colored Women emerged from the local centers of club activity and responded to the need for a national vehicle for self-defense and reform. The biennial conferences of the NACW served as forums where women of different regions and ideological perspectives could present their programs and gain information about other reforms in other communities. The local club activities often preceded or moved beyond the resolutions and speeches of the NACW to address individual community needs. As whites organized programs to ameliorate the problems caused by rapid industrialization, immigration, and urbanization, blacks sought to improve their own communities, which became increasingly segregated and without services. Research on the late nineteenth century and the Progressive Era has often left out the activities on the local level, as well as the participation of both blacks and women in social reform. The local experiences of black women reflect the interaction of race, sex, and reform in community contexts.[1]

National approaches to social welfare activities shaped the programs and content of many of the black women's local reforms during the late nineteenth and early twentieth centuries. Organized charity work mobilized resources to meet the needs of the deserving poor and urban masses. Through systematic observation of the social problems and application of data gathered through the social sciences, the charity organization applied scientific philanthropy. The charity organizer sought to rebuild the sense of neighborhood and create orderly, efficient workers. The Charity Organization Society (COS), National Conference of Charities and Correction, and similar federations for charity and philanthropy used summer outings, penny savings societies, success clubs, friendly visitors, playgrounds for city slum children, day nurseries, and distribution programs of food, clothing, and medical care to teach middle-class values of thrift, cleanliness, order, efficiency, and self-denial to the lower classes. The charity worker did not question the origins of the social problems, but instead tried to alleviate the extremes by teaching the values necessary to achieve success and by providing the basic necessities until such uplift occurred. Charity workers did not seek to alter the economic, political, or social order. They merely met expanding needs within the contemporary context.

As a woman gained more leisure time, charity work provided a socially acceptable outlet for her energies. She donated time to friendly visitor programs. She would befriend a few poor families and establish a long-term relationship through provision of Christmas baskets; some clothing or shoes for the children; and exposure to the demeanor, dress, and values of the upper classes through her occasional visits to the slum residences. These visits did not threaten the woman's image as a Victorian lady. She did not have to move into the neighborhood or neglect her responsibilities to husband or children. She gave up none of her luxuries in order to serve the poor. Her work reinforced the contemporary image of the woman as nurturer, as natural educator of children and social inferiors, and as moral guide in social uplift.

While charity work expanded during the late nineteenth century, a second social welfare approach emerged. Social reform work, epitomized in the settlement, differed in goals and techniques from organized charity work. Unlike the charity worker who focused on the individual cases of poverty, the settlement worker focused on the social and economic conditions that caused poverty. Charity workers attempted to lessen pauperism, whereas settlement workers looked to equalize opportunity for the poor and working classes. Unlike the charity organizations that sought to utilize the leisure time of wives and daughters of men engaged in business and the professions, the early settlements organized groups of college women to live with and aid residents of poor urban neighborhoods. This type of "service" justified the privilege of these women in gaining college educations.

Most of the settlement workers, unlike the charity workers, were young, unmarried, college-educated descendants of old-stock American families with traditions in social reform. Such reform offered "a new kind of pioneering, an excursion into the unknown appealing to the generosity, the courage, the restlessness and the deep desire of youth to make the world over."[2] These differences in population and experience produced the different goals and programs of the two approaches to social welfare.

The educational background of most of the early workers led them to create the settlement house as an educational innovation. Lecture series, extension courses, classes in art and music, conferences, and manual training were part of most programs. Generally, the most useful projects focused on children, especially the kindergarten idea that settlement houses popularized.

The paternalism of most charity work was consciously avoided by settlement workers attempting to overcome feelings of superiority when dealing with the neighborhood residents. The settlement intended to "awaken the dormant side of society to a social consciousness . . . not inspired by a desire to reform or to uplift . . . [but] with a passion to understand."[3] Charity, though temporarily helpful, could not create the goal of settlement work—community self-help.

These two approaches shared several characteristics. Both developed as responses to the unstable economic and social environments created by panics, immigration, industrialization, and urbanization. Both tended to be located at first in the large to medium-size cities of the Northeast and Midwest. Either type of activity was acceptable for the leisure-class female; both roles were "a perfectly natural extension of the interests and duties of the woman in her own home and in normal neighborhood society."[4] Such social reform work placed the woman as "foster-mother to thousands of human beings that are worse than motherless."[5] The approaches of the charity worker and the social reformer appeared within the community programs of black women.[6]

Although the national trends influenced the form of the community programs, the local context determined the priorities and size of the reforms. The interests, education, and financial resources available to the community leadership shaped the choices of programs and their potential for success. Since women generally lacked the financial resources of men, reforms initiated by individual or small groups of black women frequently failed or ran into financial difficulties as the costs increased. The black women with solid support in the white community or in well-organized black institutions such as the church, fraternal groups, or schools produced more long-lived services. Likewise, the services initiated by the educated elite, women whose husbands and/or fathers held positions of status or power, had a greater chance to survive. Leisure time, knowledge about organized reform, and access to money enabled many programs to meet community needs during the Progressive Era and beyond. As more blacks came to the cities of the North and Midwest during the post-1910 period, greater reliance on the black community was possible. Most of the programs instituted by blacks during the years 1890-1910 remained small, dependent on white philanthropy and/or the volunteer time of black middle-class women, and responsive to the race's dependents: the aged, the infirm, children, and women.

Typically, care of the race's aged was the first type of organized reform initiated by small groups of local black women. During the late nineteenth century, lack of programs to care for aging ex-slaves became apparent. Existing beyond the traditional benevolence of black churches or fraternal societies, many black elderly lacked adequate or sensitive care. Through their clubs, church societies, or community coalitions, black women went beyond mutual aid to provide care for the aged and, within a few years, these programs were evaluated by the annual Atlanta Conference organized by W. E. B. Du Bois as "the first and best institutional work"[7] existing in the black communities.

Many of these ventures reflected the problems of early social welfare programs for blacks. Dependence on white support often ensured the survival of the organization, but it created white control or direction of projects. On the other hand, black autonomy frequently meant lack of experience as well as insufficient financial resources and, therefore, inadequate services or short-term viability of the organization.

Services to care for aged blacks were not new. In centers of reform traditions and/or large black populations, nineteenth-century white-founded institutions existed. New York, for example, had Lincoln Hospital and Home (for the Aged) to care for indigent aged and infirm and the Colored Mission and Colored Orphan Asylum to help the young. Philadelphia, with the largest nineteenth-century northern black population, maintained a Home for Aged and Infirm Colored Persons.

These white-founded institutions displayed the difficulties inherent in one race dominating the services to another race. Blacks were frequently excluded from participation in policy-making, management, or service roles. The paternalistic racial relationship often created a "cold and business-like"[8] atmosphere for black residents. White administrators determined which blacks were worthy of the services. As in the case of Lincoln Hospital and Home, black interns and doctors could not serve on the staff of the institution serving their race.[9]

These institutions suffered fewer financial difficulties than the black-founded and supported ones. If not supported by a well-established church or fraternal order, most nineteenth-century homes for the aged lacked adequate financial resources. Those founded by individual black women emerged from the founder's concern for the forgotten elderly. Harriet Tubman converted her home in Auburn, New York, into the Home for Indigent and Aged Negroes. Despite her widespread popularity and her constant fund-raising on the lecture circuit, maintaining the home was a continuing struggle.[10]

Once black women began to organize community projects, several of their earlier efforts were salvaged and reorganized. For example, the St. James Old Folks Home in Louisville, Kentucky, expanded and became financially solvent after a "younger set"[11] of women reorganized the Society of St. James in 1893. In Kansas City, black church women joined with the Codaya Circle literary club in 1896 to reorganize the Old Folks and Orphans Home. Their joint efforts enabled the home to survive and expand.[12]

The reorganization and expansion under black community women was especially evident in the case of the Alpha Home in Indianapolis. The Alpha Home emerged in 1883 from the concern of Elizabeth Goff, an illiterate maid, for neglected, aged ex-slave women. Depending on the advice and financial contributions of her wealthy white employer, Goff soon realized her limitations. Leadership of the Alpha Home Association soon passed to a more literate and financially privileged black woman, Huldah Bates Webb, wife of a bank president. Webb mobilized socially concerned black women in community fund-raising activities and in gaining county monies. Through annual fund-raising picnics, the women raised enough money during the 1890s to cover services and purchase new facilities, eventually expanding to an eight-room house accommodating both women and men.[13]

In 1896, a black woman active in the Cleveland community called a few women to her home to discuss the idea of founding a home for the aged. Eliza Bryant's idea circulated from this small group into the black churches. Black women received encouragement to begin organizing, charging membership fees, holding socials, and providing entertainments to raise money for a home. Incorporated in 1896, the Cleveland Home for Aged Colored People opened to both sexes in 1897. Following the motto "Let us not be weary in well-doing," the black women of Cleveland organized both the old and the new elites into supporting the home. The all-female managing board for the Association of the Home for Aged Colored People were the spouses of members of the old elite—Charles W. Chesnutt, nationally recognized author, and Harry E. Davis, lawyer and politician—and members of the new elite—S. Clayton Green, owner of a drug store and grocery; Welcome Blue, co-founder of the Cleveland *Journal*; and Thomas Fleming, the first black city councilman.

The Cleveland Home intended to board, lodge, and care for elderly blacks, but the early fund-raising in the black community did not provide adequate financing. In a few years, the original structure fell into serious disrepair. The women then created a men's auxiliary[16] with the main purpose to raise money, pay dues, and give advice to the trustees, of whom the majority were required to be women (to avoid loss of power to the men). This creative use of the men's auxiliary, together with aid from the Cleveland Federation of Charity and Philanthropy, allowed the Home to move to a newer building and pay off the mortgage just in time to accommodate the influx of blacks during the Great Migration.[17]

As with the Indianapolis and Cleveland examples, small groups of black women established homes for the aged in Chicago, Brooklyn, New Bedford, Newark, and Philadelphia. The Home for Aged and Infirm Colored People took root in Chicago (1898) after Gabrella Smith, the founder, had gathered homeless old people into her house. Smith interested other black women in her project. Anna E. Hudlun organized a club for the placement of needy old people into the home. In addition to the funds raised by the club, Bena Morrison donated a house, property, furnishings, and another piece of property to be used as an endowment for the home. Smith served as the superintendent without compensation, even though she had to work for a living. By 1904, a group of "Volunteer Workers" began to take over many of the responsibilities, including the crucial role of fund-raising in the black community. These women organized an annual bazaar that successfully raised most of the necessary funds for operation.[18]

In the mid-1890s, Brooklyn women established their Home for Aged Colored People. Unlike the Lincoln Hospital and Home, the Brooklyn Home was a product of black women's efforts. Through the Woman's Loyal Union and the leadership of black professional women, including Dr. Susan McKinney Steward, Sarah Garnet, and others of the Brooklyn–New York black community, the home expanded to meet the needs of the increasing numbers coming into the New York area.[19]

The Brooklyn home stimulated clubwoman Elizabeth Carter to found the New Bedford Home for the Aged. Accustomed to friendly visiting with the elderly, Carter planned the home in 1896. She brought together individuals who had been caring for the elderly, secured a house, found furnishings, and by 1897 moved the first residents into the home. Carter had started her venture as an individual paying for the home with $105 of her own money. The furnishings and other monetary donations came from black women's groups united behind the leadership of the Woman's Loyal Union. The home soon developed such a favorable reputation, disseminated through the national woman's club movement, that Addie W. Hunton called it the greatest enterprise established by the race.

Similar activities started by small groups of concerned black women looking for facilities sensitive to black needs appeared in other areas of the North. Stephanie Smith, Mary A. Campbell, and Margaret Boling helped to establish the Old Folks Home in Philadelphia. Black women in Wilmington, Delaware, established the Sarah Ann White Home in 1896. In Newark, New Jersey, the Colored Aged Home started on a small scale in 1895. Within ten years, the home moved to larger quarters in Irvington, New Jersey.[20]

Black women's clubs originated the plans and maintenance of other homes in the North. The Women's Twentieth Century Club of New Haven, Connecticut, started as a literary club to discuss race literature. Through discussions and lectures, and through the personal volunteer activities of the members who paid friendly visits to the community's elderly, the clubwomen became aware of the Hannah Gray Home. Named after a black woman who had bequeathed her house to a white board of trustees for the use of aged black women, the home was about to be sold for the payment of back taxes. The club representatives approached the trustees, promising to take control of the facility. Soon after this meeting, the club raised money for the home's repair and maintenance and for Gray's burial expenses, and persuaded the city to abate taxes each year. The club enlisted the help of the public schools, in which many of the black clubwomen taught. The schools contributed goods and food. White benefactors provided Christmas trees and gave money to the various fund-raising drives. Fairs in the black community provided enough money to move to larger quarters as the number of residents expanded. New Haven's Twentieth Century Club was joined by a Detroit club bearing the same name, which founded the Phillis Wheatley Home for Aged Colored Women under the leadership of Mary E. McCoy, wife of inventor Elijah McCoy and founder of the Detroit club.[21]

The North was not the only area to witness the proliferation of homes for the aged founded and operated by black women and their clubs. In black communities of the South, border states, and the District of Columbia, similar ventures took root during the pre-1910 period. In Washington, D.C., a white woman, Maria Stoddard, bequeathed land for a Baptist Home. Court battles between her heirs delayed development of the home until 1901. Opened to Baptist ministers and their widows or orphans, the home depended on the efforts of black women for its operation and its maintenance. The management fell to a body of women delegates representing each Baptist church in the District of Columbia. Responsible for raising the money for programs, care expenses, and house repair and maintenance, the women relied on their networks in the black churches and clubs for financial and moral support.

In Virginia and North Carolina, the black women's organization of Tent Sisters established homes for the aged. In Hampton, Virginia, the head of the society donated land for a home in 1897. The organization raised money to build the structure, furnish the rooms, and maintain the programs. Forbidden by society rules from soliciting donations from the general public, the women raised enough money from their own members to open that same year. The board of directors consisted of nine "sisters" of the order. The Tents supported a similar venture in Raleigh, North Carolina. For this home, 250 working women pledged one pound of food a month plus 25 cents cash each year to maintain the small facility. Individuals volunteered time after completing their daily employment. Almost two-fifths of the women were over sixty years of age, showing their self-interest in making the home successful for their own retirement years.[22]

The 1909 Atlanta University publication, *Efforts for Social Betterment Among Negro Americans*, although not definitive, surveyed many of the facilities for the aged established through the efforts of women's church and club associations. The Daughters of Mercy in Selma, Alabama, established the Priscilla Brown Mercy Home, named after a black "sister" who donated two lots for the home's construction. The aged needed the recommendation of their pastor before admission to this facility. Black churchwomen in Richmond, Virginia, founded the Negro Baptist Old Folks Home. Each home accepted the "morally qualified" aged, as determined by its religious group.[23]

A variety of denominations and societal affiliations provided services. The Wednesday Afternoon Sewing Club managed the St. Louis Old Folks Home in 1902. In Vicksburg, Mississippi, clubwomen established a home for their aged in 1905 by refurbishing an old mansion that overlooked the city.

Charleston, South Carolina, clubwomen persuaded the city government to support their home for the aged, which continued to operate under black administration in the early 1900s. Similar ventures emerged in Hot Springs, Arkansas; New Orleans, Louisiana; Pueblo, Colorado; Augusta, Georgia; St. Paul, Minnesota; Cincinnati, Ohio; Des Moines, Iowa; and many other communities.[24]

In many cases, the black population was neither large enough nor financially stable enough to support a separate home for their aged and for their infirm or orphans. Several communities, therefore, offered more than one service at the same facility. In Springfield, Illinois, in 1898, Eva Monroe led the Springfield Women's Club in establishing the Lincoln Old Folks and Orphans Home. In the early 1900s, Pittsburgh women started their Home for Aged and Infirm Colored Women; clubwomen in Anniston, Alabama, raised money for their home for old women and orphans; and Gainesville, Florida, women established an all-purpose center, the Home for the Friendless. Memphis had its Old Ladies and Orphans Home, Mobile had its Colored Old Folks and Orphans Home, and Pennsacola had its Home for Orphans and Aged. Clubwomen supported homes for the aged more "than any other one enterprise."[25] The pre-1910 period was truly an age for the aged.[26]

Through their clubs, black women contributed to ongoing efforts, reorganized failing ventures, and established new homes. These homes reflected the charitable approach to social welfare. Many accepted only the respectable aged and poor, those whose indigency could not be attributed to intemperance, laziness, or immorality. Some depended on the initial donation of land or money from white benefactors. Many of the founders gained knowledge about the aged's plight through their experiences as friendly visitors, as church workers, or in similar charity involvement. Some founders had personal experience with similar homes in other cities, but most began their organizations with only a strong motivation to help the needy in their own communities.

Most services began on a small scale, housing only a few residents. As the women gained experience and success, community support increased. Black women pushed their churches to increase financial and volunteer activities. Both blacks and whites bequeathed property and money. Persuaded by the black women's clubs, city governments contributed through tax abatement or regular funding. Frequently, success made expansion to larger facilities necessary. Through the black press and the community, the homes for the aged received wide support. Conflict over their segregated nature was not evident in press accounts, correspondence, or association records covering the pre-1910 period.[27] The wide community support, population served, and the fact that professional training was unnecessary made homes for the aged one of the first services attempted by black women.

Closely related to the care of the aged were the local programs to aid the infirm. As black populations increased, white hospitals became more discriminatory in their admission policies and in their allowance for black physicians, interns, and nurses. In response to the need for more black medical care and for institutional experience for black medical personnel, black hospitals emerged during the 1890s.

Most of the larger ventures were founded by men, usually physicians, who depended on the organized fund-raising, volunteer work, and management skills of black women. Even in the white-founded hospitals serving the black communities, black women provided vital support functions serving the black infirm while expanding the potential activity for black medical personnel. For example, at the Lincoln Hospital and Home in New York, black physicians and interns could not practice or admit patients to the institution. Yet, black women, through the White Rose Association or various women's clubs, contributed food and clothing and services in the form of lectures, music, and entertainment. The 1909 *Efforts for Social Betterment Among Negro Americans* mentioned the black woman's role in segregated hospitals. Black women's organizations emerged to aid the colored department or colored wards. Clubwomen in Frankfort, Kentucky, established the Charity Organization. Those in Galveston, Texas, provided clothing, holiday extras, and entertainment through the Colored Women's Hospital Aid Society. The Colored High School in that city had two hospital clubs to provide special items for the black patients. Black women formed the Charity Club to assist Christ Hospital in Jersey City, New Jersey. Although the exact dates of these services are difficult to determine, they did not appear in the surveys by Atlanta University in the 1898 *Some Efforts of American Negroes for their Own Social Betterment*. They did appear in the 1909 *Efforts for Social Betterment Among Negro Americans*. The expansion of the surveys completed by Atlanta University was probably a result of the improved communications networks and organized vehicles at the national level through which local experiences could be shared. The NACW biennials also neglect specific date citations. Since the purpose of such reports was to mention new or improved services, one could infer that the services existed around the general time of such biennial meetings.[28] These services were cited during the pre-1910 period.

Black male physicians founded hospitals in Philadelphia, Chicago, Savannah, and many other cities throughout the North, South, and Midwest, assisted by black women who shaped programs and services. In Chicago, Daniel Hale Williams, the first doctor to perform a successful heart suture, founded Provident Hospital and Training School for Nurses in 1891. Black clubwomen led by Fannie Barrier Williams helped to raise funds and manage the services of that facility. In Philadelphia, Dr. Nathan F. Mossell founded the Frederick Douglass Hospital in 1895. His wife, Gertrude Mossell, established the Douglass Ladies Auxiliary, which provided extra food and linens for the patients. During the first year of operation, the hospital depended on the fund-raising expertise of black women, who raised approximately 86 percent of the operating expenses from contributions of the black community. By the second year, these women helped to administer the drug department under a female pharmacist, a graduate of Howard University. As expenses increased, the Ladies Auxiliary provided more services to reduce the costs of operation.[29]

Similar women's auxiliaries aided black hospitals and sanitaria in southern towns. Dr. L. A. Scruggs, a black physician, founded a sanitarium in Southern Pines, North Carolina, for black consumptives in 1897. The black women of nearby Raleigh, North Carolina, formed the Ladies' Pickford Sanitarium Aid Society to furnish the building and to provide the basic necessities for the patients. St. Louis clubwomen performed a similar function for their People's Hospital. The Woman's Central League Hospital in Richmond, Virginia, depended on the black women in the churches and societies for its support. The Douglass Hospital of Kansas City, Missouri, depended on the women of the A.M.E. Church groups for funds and administrative skills.[30]

Black women's groups aided individual black women in creating hospitals and medical facilities for black communities in the North and South. Dr. Caroline Still Anderson, daughter of William Still, received the aid of the Berean Church women in her establishment of a dispensary with mission work in Philadelphia. Dr. Alice Woodby McKane, a Boston physician, founded a hospital with her husband in Savannah, Georgia. Supported by black physicians and women's clubs, McKane's Hospital provided medical care for the race's poor. Dr. Hallie Tanner Johnson, the first woman to practice medicine in Alabama, established a nurses' school and dispensary with the aid of the local women's club at Tuskegee. The first licensed female physician in South Carolina, Dr. Matilda A. Evans, founded a hospital and nurses' training school in Columbia, with the aid of the local women's clubs.[31]

Concerned black women, many of whom had received training as nurses, founded small hospitals. In Houston, a trained nurse founded the Feagan Hospital to care for the race's infirm for a small cost. Mary E. Burwell, organizer of the Virginia State Federation of Colored Women's Clubs, founded Richmond Hospital. As a member of the executive board and president of the Hospital Auxiliary, Burwell ensured the contributions and influence of black women to a medical care facility serving the race. In Montgomery, the contributions from women's clubs aided the operation of Hale Infirmary, founded and constructed by a black woman, Anna Hale.[32]

In addition to serving in auxiliary and fund-raising roles, organized groups of black women established their own facilities. The New Orleans Phyllis Wheatley Club founded a black hospital and sanitorium, which opened in 1897 and received city appropriations in 1898. By 1902, the club supported a program of black visiting nurses and planned fund-raising events for the establishment of a maternity ward. In Greenville, Mississippi, the King's Daughters cooperated with white groups to build and operate a small hospital serving the black community. In Cairo, Illinois, the Yates Women's Clubs supported a small black hospital. In 1905, Margaret Murray Washington described the changes in rural health care as a result of the new services and the dissemination of the "laws of health"[33] through the women's clubs and by thirty-five woman doctors. That same year, the Woman's Improvement Club of Indianapolis established the Oak Hill Tuberculosis Camp, the first of its kind in the country. This facility showed the gradual movement away from charity services, which sought to alleviate the manifest symptoms of the disease, toward social reform grounded in scientific investigation, planning, and alteration of the environment.[34]

Many of the ventures demonstrated group self-interest: black women seeking training as nurses and the correction of inaccurate information about black health. White philanthropy supported services to improve health care for blacks and to train black women in delivering those services. White reformers and philanthropists felt that black women were especially suited for the nursing profession, but few white institutions provided that training. Mary Beard, northern white reformer, said, "The negro woman is especially adapted through her past experience for the profession of nursing."[35] White women who studied the training programs for the Slater Fund concluded that "a nurse can be no more trained without a hospital, than a cook without a kitchen."[36] They praised the work of Dixie Hospital in Hampton, Virginia, and Spelman College in Atlanta, but recommended that the Slater Fund support more programs in the health field, especially those training black nurses. Most of these interested whites blamed high black mortality and morbidity on ignorance or disregard of basic laws of health and morality. The white founders of Spelman College established a nurses' training program to correct the improper sanitary conditions and general lack of knowledge about health precautions in the black population. By 1901, MacVicar Hospital opened to serve black women and provide practical experience for the Spelman nurses. The presence of black women in medical care offered different perspectives. When W. E. B. Du Bois reported that his research on *The Philadelphia Negro* had shown the high death rate from consumption due to black ignorance of hygiene, Dr. Rebecca J. Cole, a thirty-year veteran in the health field, disagreed with the young writer, citing the mutual responsibility of the slum landlords.[37]

With such white support, black women's groups became active in establishing new programs. The Charity Hospital of Savannah was chartered June 1, 1896, "by a few hard-working, energetic women anxious to take up and learn nurse training, that they might assist others of the less fortunate."[38] The women solicited donations, disseminated health information, overcame local superstitions, and developed professional nursing skills to help themselves and the local population. Black women pressured Lincoln Hospital and Home to establish a nurses' training program in 1897. Six black women from New York graduated in 1900 with most entering private duty. The graduating classes soon included students from as far away as Berkeley, California, with most returning home to work. Most soon found employment in public health, schools, and settlement houses. They served as supervisors in black hospitals and nursing schools, as operating room nurses, and as visiting nurses. When Provident Hospital and Training School opened in Chicago, only one training school received black women as nursing students. Within fifteen years, both black- and white-founded institutions provided nursing training. The formation of the National Association of Colored Graduate Nurses in 1908 demonstrated the development of the profession and their intention to actively pursue interests of their minority status.[39]

The activities of black women through hospital auxiliaries, women's clubs, and hospital/sanitorium administration helped to provide health care for their communities. Those efforts that were developed in the 1890s emerged from the charity approach to social welfare that stressed the alleviation of the manifest symptoms of disease, to take on more characteristics of the social reform approach. Gradually, the health care efforts supported scientific investigation, planning, and alteration of the environment to improve morbidity and mortality. By 1910, many of the programs attempted to prevent disease rather than merely to administer to the infirm. Changes in care of the infirm reflected the general trends in Progressive reform.

While black women continued to care for the aged and infirm, they did not neglect services for children. Programs to shelter, protect, and educate orphaned, abandoned, or unsupervised children responded to particular local needs and reflected the interests and capabilities of local leadership. Black women established kindergartens and day nurseries, founded orphanages, and improved education. The orphanages and day nurseries tended to display characteristics of charity, whereas the kindergartens and educational activities were motivated by a desire for social reform.

Black women felt that the most efficient way to re-form a society was properly to instruct and care for the young. Mary Terrell eloquently summarized this philosophy: "Through the children of to-day we believe we can build the foundation of the next generation upon such a rock of morality, intelligence and strength, that the floods of proscription, prejudice and persecution may descend upon it in torrents and yet it will not be moved."[40] Along with homes for the aged, kindergartens were among the first service provided for the local community. Brought to the United States through the immigration of German liberals, the kindergarten philosophy sought to release children from harsh discipline in order to encourage their natural development. Kindergartens were usually established by educated, privileged women with leisure time. Founders and residents of settlement houses, also educated women, established kindergartens as part of their efforts to serve the community. Most kindergartens, as educational programs, charged parents for the service. These programs fit into the mainstream of social reform during the Progressive Era.

Day nurseries, unlike kindergartens, originated in the charity tradition. The caretakers were wealthy women, and the care was custodial for children of the poor. For black women, the distinction between the welfare agency of day nurseries and the educational purposes of kindergarten did not apply.

They usually developed kindergartens first, followed by day nurseries as a supplemental program for younger children. Since most reforms were initiated by the educated elite who formed clubs and literary societies, and since education was considered the primary means to racial uplift, it was not unusual to find kindergartens among the first reforms supported by black women. Unlike the homes for the aged, orphaned, and infirm, kindergartens and day nurseries required little expenditure for facilities or staff. The services could be provided in a church basement, a clubwoman's home, or a rented house. Since many of the clubwomen were educated, they could provide well-qualified instruction and positive role models. Day nurseries needed only to rely on black women who had some type of child care experience as mothers or older siblings. Clubs provided the vehicle through which dedicated, educated, and motivated black women could care for the future generation.

Kindergartens spread among organized black communities. The women tried to provide training through free kindergartens, motivated by both charitable and educational considerations.[41] The women reasoned that such training was "doubly important for the child who starts in life handicapped with parents who are ignorant, with surroundings of poverty and its attendant evils, and with no chance to get a glimpse of anything beautiful . . ."[42]

Black women's clubs or church groups often combined services in their kindergarten programs. The female auxiliary of the Central Congregational Church in Topeka, developed kindergarten classes in 1893 and provided instruction for black mothers in child care, health, and hygiene. The Colored Woman's League in Washington inaugurated a model kindergarten in 1896. Two daily sessions accommodated forty children, most of whom had two working parents. Fifteen young women received training as kindergarten teachers. Washington's Colored Woman's League combined services with teachers instruction. From 1896 to 1898, the clubwomen funded the establishment of a Normal School to train teachers for the six free kindergartens managed by league member Anna E. Murray. The league cooperated with the Zion Baptist Church in opening a seventh school. Sara I. Fleetwood, a trained nurse and leader of the Washington social community, supervised the Mothers' Meetings, which presented information on the care and training of children during the evening to accommodate the needs of working mothers. The league women donated or raised funds for the purchase of shoes and clothing. Pupils in the Mending Bureau, supervised by the Industrial Committee, repaired the donated clothing while they learned to sew. These efforts were so successful that Congress made kindergartens part of the regular public school system and employed as teachers the first graduates of the Normal class in June 1898. That same year, the league began rescue work among black women and institutionalized four special fund-raisers during Thanksgiving, New Year, Valentine's Day, and Easter. The Colored Women's League reflected the leadership of college women and their approach to solving urban problems. Education for young children through kindergartens, for mothers through Mothers' Meetings, and for youth through domestic science classes became the mode of reform for this local Washington club.[43]

Black women also cooperated with white-founded services. The New York Free Kindergarten Association, formed in 1895 by three wealthy white women, depended on the black teachers of the West Forty-first Street Public School. During the first three years, a black teacher served as principal, aided by a white assistant. The need for expanded facilities led to relocation in a large vacant building in one of the worst black sections of the city. Financial contributions from Jacob Riis and other white benefactors enabled the new facility to open in April 1900. The original sixteen students had expanded to over eighty by the year's end. But, segregation remained. White students were taught in a separate afternoon session. After the school incorporated in 1904 and changed its name to the Walton Free Kindergarten, black women continued to teach and serve on the board of managers. This program combined charity services, as in the penny provident banks, home visitation, and free service to the poor. Social reform was also present in the class for older children, country outings for improved health and recreation, mothers' meetings, and educational programs. Both the black and the white women emphasized the inculcation of middle-class values of thrift, cleanliness, obedience, and order. Even though the white children could have been integrated when the demand increased, the decision to remain segregated reflected contemporary attitudes. The presence of the black women ensured the continual delivery of services to black children.[44]

Separate kindergarten programs were not always well received. In Chicago in 1897, Ida B. Wells-Barnett led a movement to establish a kindergarten at Bethel Church. Several members of the black elite wanted their children to attend the school, but they were afraid that attending a segregated black kindergarten might lessen their children's future educational opportunities. Wells-Barnett thought the kindergarten was sorely needed and persisted in her efforts, but support was difficult to obtain. Gradually, the black clubwomen saw the importance of the project and raised the necessary money for the segregated services. Soon new kindergartens developed to serve other neighborhoods. By the turn of the century, the Women's Christian, Social and Literary Club of Peoria, plus several others in the Illinois Federation of Colored Women's Clubs, supported kindergartens. Due to the integration of social services in Boston, the clubwomen there supported a kindergarten for black children in Atlanta through their Georgia Educational League. Clubs from New York to Chicago to Detroit developed organized kindergartens for their communities before massive immigration from the South overburdened urban social services.[45]

In the South, the kindergarten movement grew rapidly. Both the NACW in the 1897 and 1899 biennials and the Atlanta Conference in 1896, 1898, and 1905 called for more kindergartens, reforms that were immediately practical and dependent on local cooperation. Each of the Atlanta meetings revealed a definite and urgent need for day nurseries for mothers who "earn an honest living."[46] After the presentation of Gertrude Ware, a kindergarten training-school teacher at Atlanta University, conference director W. E. B. Du Bois requested that Ware meet with black women to begin an organization. In May 1905, black women of Atlanta[47] formed the Gate City Free Kindergarten Association. The first kindergarten started in "Johnson's Row," a notorious black district on Cain Street. The second opened in the fall of 1905 in a poor district near the Air Line shops. Both kindergartens served around thirty children daily. Black clubwomen, led by Alice Carey cooperating with black churchwomen of the First Congregational Church, established more kindergartens.[48]

Other southern clubwomen were similarly active. Meeting in Montgomery, during the Christmas season of 1899, black women discussed methods to raise funds for kindergartens. Presided over by Margaret Murray Washington, this conference developed the Colored Women's Kindergarten Association, which organized kindergartens in large black communities. In New Orleans, Frances A. Joseph, a black clubwoman and WCTU Superintendent of Prison Reform, established the first kindergarten for black children. In Augusta, Lucy Laney of Haines Institute developed the first kindergarten. Bringing a teacher from the North, Laney had her train other women for teaching. These programs were compassionate efforts to avoid future social problems. The women heard about children locked into or out of rooms all day, free to roam the streets unsupervised. As mothers, they sought to educate children in the higher planes of culture before they became "the wayward and criminal element of our city."[49] Children under six received daily baths, an hour's rest, nutritious meals, and exposure to well-educated Christian women. The older children went to public schools neatly dressed and returned to the center to study after school under a matron's supervision. Here, the children gained "their first notions of cleanliness, of truthfulness, of politeness, of honesty, of pure-mindedness."[50] These kindergartens in the black communities were "not merely charity, but . . . an investment in human life."[51]

When these expanded services were not handled by kindergartens, the black women developed day nurseries. Since five times as many black married women as white married women worked, child care presented an enormous problem. Day nurseries tried to prevent "the slaughter of innocents."[52] The early day nursery development followed the organization of women's clubs in established black communities. In Philadelphia, the Woman's Missionary Society established a day nursery to serve the seventh ward. By the turn of the century, day nurseries existed in West Philadelphia, four in Central Philadelphia, and in Germantown. The Civic League of Englewood, New Jersey, followed measures similar to those used by the Susan B. Anthony Club of Yonkers—renting a home, setting aside three rooms for a day nursery, and hiring a supervisor and trained nurse. A black graduate nurse, Mrs. E. E. Greene, founded Hope Day Nursery in New York City with the financial help of white philanthropist Mrs. Arthur M. Dodge. Black women, through church or club groups, supported nurseries in Pittsburgh, Brooklyn, Los Angeles, Lexington, Louisville, Austin, Athens, Atlanta, and Richmond. Black women worked in white-funded nurseries in Columbus, Washington, D.C. and other cities.[53]

In addition to providing care for the children of working parents, black women established orphanages. At first, these institutions reflected the charity response to local community needs by a single group or individual emotionally moved by the orphans' plight. These limited endeavors soon became community projects allowing the construction or purchase of larger buildings and the expansion of services. These efforts were often initiated by non-elite, ex-slave women expressing a need for family. The services that succeeded were eventually taken over by organized groups of club or church women to ensure the continuity of a valued service.

Early examples of this type of institutions can be seen in Georgia and in Illinois. The Carrie Steele Orphanage began in Atlanta in 1890 with five children in a two-room house. As a matron at Atlanta's railroad depots, Steele came into direct contact with abandoned and orphaned children. Herself orphaned as a young child, ex-slave Steele made a commitment to help. She wrote a book about her life to raise money for the venture. The proceeds from the book, combined with donations from black and white communities, enabled her to purchase four acres of land to begin.

Within a decade, the Carrie Steele Orphanage became a community project. Club and church groups not only raised money for the center, but also sent children to "Aunt Carrie." With this added support, by 1900 the orphanage expanded to a three-story building sheltering 225 children, a hospital, and a schoolhouse on land leased from the city. Steele continued to direct negotiations with the city and county, making sure black control would be maintained through the Board of Trustees, black men and women appointed by Steele. As with other examples of uplift education, the orphanage provided the rudiments of an English education, domestic training so that each youth could find employment, and moral guidance through Christian religion.[54]

Amanda Smith, daughter of Samuel Berry, followed a different path to establishing the Amanda Smith Industrial Home in 1899. Smith's work as an international evangelist and temperance lecturer served as the basis of her autobiography, which she sold to raise money for the Amanda Smith Orphan Home in Harvey, Illinois. With her original $10,000 investment, the aid of black women's clubs, and aid from the State of Illinois, the home expanded to care for over sixty children and thirty-one residents by 1908. Smith was over sixty when she began the orphanage and aid from women's clubs and from the state assured the continuation of the institution after her death. As with the Steele example, industrial education and Christian guidance permeated the instruction.[55]

These two individually initiated orphanages, which rapidly received group support of black women's social, club, or church associations, were not unique. In Raleigh, North Carolina, the founder of the Tent Sisters brought a few young girls into her home to live. With the help of her Tent Sisters, the orphanage soon emerged in that town. In the early 1900s a black teacher in Covington, Kentucky, received the first one thousand dollars to found an orphanage. The Reed Home and School, named after the benefactor, Mrs. H. C. Reed, housed over forty orphans in a ten-room structure providing shelter and instruction in agriculture.

Those orphanages founded by groups of women had a better chance of survival and usually began on a larger scale. Founded in 1890 to care for black girls in Atlanta, the Leonard Street Orphanage relied on community leaders for support. As with many of the southern examples, the official leadership went to whites and black male leaders such as Alonzo F. Herndon, John Hope, and Dr. L. B. Palmer. The records of local black women's groups such as the Neighborhood Union and Gate City Free Kindergarten displayed fund-raising and community cooperation of black women. Serving as matrons, volunteers, and fund-raisers, black women actively participated. The Orphan Aid Society of Charleston, South Carolina, depended on the church women organized under the leadership of the founder's wife, Mrs. E. C. Jenkins. The Weaver Orphan Home for Colored Children in Hampton, Virginia, was managed by the founder's wife, Mrs. W. B. Weaver, and received financial support from the black women of the community.

In addition to support roles, black women's groups founded homes. The Yates Women's Club supported the Children's Home and Day Nursery in Cairo, Illinois. Chicago clubwomen aided the Louise Children's Home and Home for Dependent Children. The Wednesday Afternoon Club sponsored the development in 1901 of the St. Louis Colored Orphans Home. The Pennsylvania State Federation of Colored Women's Clubs supported the Home for Destitute Negro Children. The New Bedford Women's Club supported a children's home founded in 1904. As far west as California, clubwomen supported the Oakland Children's Home founded in 1903. In Topeka, Kansas, the Young Ladies Charitable Union began homes for orphans. As with the homes for the aged, the segregated facilities did not provoke conflict because of their charitable nature and due to the belief that the race could better care for its own.[56]

Black women wanted not only to care for the needs of orphans, but also to improve the racial awareness of all black children. Improvement of education meant many things. For some, having black teachers who were knowledgeable about the heritage of the race and about racial problems was an improvement over white teachers. Other black women pushed for integration into white schools for better education. Several communities fought against the segregation of a previously integrated school system. Many believed the best education came through classical training; others felt industrial education most practical. Most of the women saw the value of both types of education.

Uplift through education mirrored the times and conditions of America. Since black women were 80 percent of the teachers instructing black youth,[57] they organized into groups as mothers, teachers, and community leaders to improve the curriculum, teachers, or educational access for black children. During the 1890s, black mothers refused to send their children to school in New York and Brooklyn. Insisting on the employment of black teachers, the mothers' boycott improved the educational possibilities for their children while increasing the employment of black teachers. In Topeka, black women also wanted black teachers to provide role models for their children. Fannie Barrier Williams, who had received her own education in an integrated New York school, advocated black teachers, noting, "Our race habit of looking up to somebody as superior to ourselves . . . is a great handicap to the cultivation of manhood, courage and pride of race."[58] The black women in Topeka agreed and pressured the Board of Education until, in 1894, black teachers received appointments to the schools. In Chicago, black women fought against segregation in education. Aided by Jane Addams and other influential whites, Wells-Barnett led other clubwomen to persuade the white community to maintain integrated schools to avoid social problems and to ensure an educated, efficient workforce. The persuasion and white aid halted the local movement for segregated education. In addition to the efforts of parent and club groups, black teachers themselves organized into the National Association of Teachers in Colored Schools in 1904. In this organization, black women cooperated with black men. Race increasingly became the most important identity for black women concerned with improving society.[59]

In addition to using pressure and protest as a means of improving their schools, black women bargained for a more active role in organizations concerned with policy and curriculum of black schools or for black students. In 1899, the female auxiliary of the Kansas Industrial and Educational Institute brought black women into positions where they could bargain for changes in curriculum and personnel in return for their fund-raising and administrative support. Women in the A.M.E. Church used their fund-raising skills to obtain $500,000 for education over a twenty-five-year period. Individual women's clubs supported black students financially through scholarship funds ranging from kindergarten through college. Most of these scholarships aided schools founded by black women.[60] The Cambridge Charity Club supported a student at Wellesley College. The Woman's Loyal Union maintained a student at Manassas School in Virginia. The College Aid

Society at Wilberforce, Ohio, aided many needy students. The Anna M. Duncan Club of Montgomery, Alabama, supported students in kindergartens, in normal schools, and at Talladega College. The Boston clubwomen supported children in Georgia educational institutions.[61]

Monetary contributions coexisted with efforts to include race history and literature in the educational process. Reflecting the current interest in African heritage, the black women's groups wanted both black and white children to learn about the "character in ebony as well as in ivory."[62] Several groups worked through school boards to get race history into the curriculum. The Akron branch of the Loyal Hearts of the Legion, the female auxiliary to the Loyal Legion of Labor, prepared race history examples for education boards to incorporate into existing history courses. The American Negro Historical Society of Philadelphia, which included both men and women as members and administrators, pushed for the inclusion of race history in education. Mary Church Terrell led black Washington clubwomen in the movement to celebrate February 14 as Frederick Douglass Day. The school system adopted the practice for the black schools, which continued for several years.[63]

In addition to institutional incorporation of race history, black women's groups developed libraries and reading rooms to give the black population access to information closed to them by segregated "public" libraries and considered unimportant by most library collections. The Sojourner Truth Club of Montgomery developed a reading room when the race was refused admission to the Carnegie Library. The club also sponsored a contest for the best paper written by a high school student about racial achievements. To raise money, the club brought in nationally known race leaders for their lecture series. In Guthrie, Oklahoma, the Excelsior Club maintained a library, as did clubs in Dallas, Jacksonville, and many other communities. In New York, the collection of race literature at Mathews's White Rose Home received widespread recognition through the national club movement. The Woman's Loyal Union tried not only to support that collection, but also to disseminate some of its information. The club sent leaflets arguing for such a dissemination process to white politicians and reform groups. As black women developed settlement houses, these reading rooms and libraries became a common expression of racial pride.[64]

Settlement houses served as significant centers of racial reform. Most of them emerged in the North and Midwest. Since 90 percent of the black population continued to reside in the South, few settlements expressed much concern for the needs of the black population. But, compared to purity crusaders and white clubwomen, the settlement workers appeared less paternalistic and prejudiced to racial minorities. Ideally, social work intended to build "a natural federation among all our different racial groups, which [would] in reasonable degree preserve all that is valuable in the heredity and traditions of each type."[65] The black population, however, presented a "particularly difficult problem of delayed assimilation."[66]

Although the settlement intended to provide "neutral territory traversing all the lines of racial and religious cleavage"[67] and avoid the motivation "to reform or to uplift,"[68] most provided little or no services for blacks. In a few cities with significant black populations, settlement houses established separate branches for blacks to meet the needs of the segregated residential communities or initiated new settlements. In New York, the Henry Street Settlement established the separate Stillman Branch. Chicago's Hull House helped to establish the Wendell Phillips Settlement. Residents from Boston's South End House initiated the Robert Gould Shaw House. Indianapolis had its Flanner House, and Washington had its Colored Social Settlement. All of the major cities that had significant black communities and well-developed women's clubs possessed some type of services through settlement houses.[69]

The experiences in settlements dealing with many different cultural groups influenced some white workers to become leaders in racial reform. Susan Wharton of the Philadelphia College Settlement initiated the study completed by W. E. B. Du Bois, *The Philadelphia Negro*, the first study of the urban black population. Mary White Ovington lived in the all-black Brooklyn's Greenpoint Settlement, where she became interested in conditions for blacks through her work at the settlement and through her activities in the New York Social Reform Club. John Daniels, author of *In Freedom's Birthplace: A Study of the Boston Negroes*, developed interest as a resident of South End House. William English Walling, one of the initiators of the NAACP, developed sensitivity to black problems as a resident of New York's University Settlement. Lillian Wald, public health nurse and founder of the Henry Street Settlement, sought to provide health care by employing black visiting nurses to help the black community in New York. The correlation between settlement work and black reform was evident in the signatories of the "Call" for the formation of a national committee to discuss the problems of the race. One-third of the signatories had been or were currently settlement house workers.[70]

Most of the early settlement activity initiated by whites for black populations had lacked the sensitivity of those established later by these noted white reformers. Those begun in the North reflected the sectarian traditions of nineteenth-century charity. In New York's San Juan Hill area, St. Cyprian's Chapel, founded by white Episcopalians, demonstrated the missionary style in settlement work of the 1890s. The center provided formal instruction in meal preparation, sewing, and exercise for children. Meals prepared by the cooking school provided luncheons for needy schoolchildren and the adult poor of the community. Yet even this type of center relied on the cooperation of the black community. Black priests and community service workers volunteered their time. Black and white doctors lectured about proper infant and child care through community lecture series and weekly mothers' meetings. This charity emphasis was also present in the white-founded settlements in Philadelphia: Starr Center, Spring Street Settlement, and the Eighth Ward Settlement. Moral uplift through missionary/charity services characterized all of these founded in the 1890s by white philanthropy.

In the South, similar attitudes pervaded both urban and rural programs during the 1890s. The Presbyterian Colored Missions established a sewing and cooking school, carpentry shop, and public playgrounds to serve the Louisville community. Started in 1897, the centers received most of their funds from southern whites. The Woman's Home Mission Society of the Methodist Episcopal Church started work in 1901 when Belle Bennett, head of the society, returned from a tour of British settlement houses. Transforming missions into "Wesley Houses," the white women sought to combine Christian and social welfare projects in meeting the needs of the urban poor.

Similar to the northern and urban southern examples, white initiative and philanthropy characterized southern rural settlement work. Two New England-born teachers from the Hampton Institute moved onto the Shelby plantation in Lowndes County, Alabama, in 1892 and began the Calhoun Colored School. These young women desired to work with "a community of cotton-raisers as neighbors."[72] Relying on the advice of Booker T. Washington, a Calhoun trustee, the women stressed industrial education and land ownership, training the hand, eye, and soul. Serving thirty thousand plantation blacks, the twenty-one black and white settlement residents directed a farmers' conference, thrift society, fathers' and mothers' meetings, and a night school. They combined industrial training with activities encouraging thrift, morality, and cleanliness. Forty to fifty families eventually pooled their resources to buy homes. Home ownership and employment served as the foundation for this rural white-founded settlement.[73]

This same emphasis on morality, social uplift, and industrial training appeared in the black-initiated settlements of the 1890s. Those in the South emphasized moral and educational uplift, while those in the North evolved from rescue and protective missions and working girls' homes. The first southern settlement initiated by black women emerged from the interests of Janie Porter Barrett, Virginia club leader and wife of Hampton's cashier and bookkeeper, Harris Barrett. Shortly after her marriage, Barrett began to invite neighborhood girls into her home to show them her "Palace of Delight."[74] She felt exposure to a refined, tastefully decorated home could raise the aspirations and habits of the young girls. These friendships led to the formation of clubs, a kindergarten for younger siblings, home visitation, and lecture series. By 1890, black clubwomen joined Barrett in formalizing these services into the Locust Street Settlement. With the cooperation of local white women, a community center was soon erected to house a reading room, clubhouse, kindergarten, and "practice house" to be cared for by the girls themselves. This center provided integrated entertainment through concerts, lectures, and athletic events. As community clean-up campaigns gained in popularity among clubwomen of both races, these groups cooperated. The Locust Street Settlement became a model for other centers among black clubwomen who learned about it from presentations at NACW biennials and through the columns of *The National Notes*.[75]

Woman's clubs frequently carried on settlement-like activities in the South. Nannie Burroughs, later founder of the National Training School for Colored Girls in Washington, organized a Woman's Industrial Club in Louisville, during the late 1890s. The group rented a house; taught millinery, home work (skills associated with the efficient management of the home, as sewing, cooking, laundry, sanitation, child care, dress, and hygiene), and health care; served inexpensive lunches for working people; and provided short-term lodging. To provide these services, each woman paid dues of ten cents a week, sold pies and cakes at fund-raisers, and garnered the support of white women of the city. As the club and services expanded, special teachers took charge of the various classes and the center became more professional.[76]

Rural settlements initiated by black women's groups differed little from those established by white women's groups. Margaret Murray Washington and the Tuskegee Women's Club established the Russell settlement in 1897, to improve the farmers' efficiency and to counsel land ownership. The Russell Plantation Settlement included fifty-five men and seventy-two women as residents serving 112 children and their parents. Three community women volunteered as non-residents. The women wanted to improve black family life through education, cleanliness, and morality. As with the Calhoun example, industrial training and the inculcation of middle-class values typified the activities of the rural settlements.[77]

In the North, homes or missions for the protection of women coming to the urban areas frequently developed into settlement programs. During the late nineteenth century, travelers' aid services developed. Most of these services could not or did not meet the expanding needs of black women migrating in search of better wages, working conditions, or opportunities. As the demand for general housekeepers increased among northern housewives, conditions worsened for the "unemployed who are strangers often without resources, and who must find other employment, or drift into immorality."[78] Black women established services to meet these needs.[79]

The White Rose Mission and Industrial Association, founded in 1897 by Victoria Earle Mathews and a small group of black women,[80] demonstrated the flexibility of working girls' homes in meeting the expanding needs of an urbanizing female population. Mathews, president of the Brooklyn Women's Club and the Woman's Loyal Union, had been concerned about young women since her stay at the Atlanta Exposition in 1895, when she witnessed the problems in the southern context. After her only son died, Mathews, already a widow, turned her energies to helping young women of her race. She gathered a group of black women together in 1896 at the house of Mary L. Lewis to discuss plans to develop a social service for young working girls. The White Rose Home proposed to "protect self-supporting colored girls who were coming to New York for the first time."[81] The name utilized the white rose as a symbol of purity, virtue, and goodness, characteristics often lost through ignorance. The center sought first to meet the arrivals, suggest appropriate accommodations or take them directly to the home, and then begin to help them adapt to the urban environment.

Black women served as founder, administrators, teachers, and volunteers in the White Rose Home. Alice Moore Dunbar taught in the kindergarten. Hallie Q. Brown served as assistant superintendent. The girls received training in the "art of doing things"[82] in classes of cooking, laundry, sewing, chair caning, and wood burnishing. They also received were trained for domestic service, the occupation of most black women at that time.

While the home was portrayed as the protector and preparer of domestic servants, it also strongly encouraged black pride. As in other settlements, nationally known lecturers such as Mary Terrell, Booker T. Washington, W. E. B. Du Bois, and Paul Laurence Dunbar spoke to the women. Mathews's collection of race literature served as the basis for an excellent reading room. Classes in race history also provided pride in heritage.

As with other settlements, the White Rose Home depended on white support. Winthrop Phelps, a philanthropist interested in racial concerns, donated a five-room apartment for the original center. Mrs. C. P. Huntington, Grace Dodge, Misses Stillman, and Mary L. Stone, all representatives of wealthy white families, contributed money and served as volunteers at the center. The conservative goal of protecting and training black domestics received the support of white benefactors and the black community. Black control allowed the center to expand its visions as the black community expanded.[83]

Many black women's clubs established similar rescue work during the late nineteenth and early twentieth centuries. A few expanded their facilities and programs to perform settlement work similar to that of the White Rose. Many overlapped in function and lacked coordination under a single administration. For example, Washington clubwomen established the Sojourner Truth Home for Working Girls in 1895. Under the direction of Amanda Bowen, leader in the Bethel Literary and Historical Association, the center received financial support from the Metropolitan A.M.E. Church for directing and protecting young female arrivals. In addition to this program, other services replicated the purposes. The Colored Women's League started rescue work in 1898. The Home for the Friendless and the National Association for the Relief of Destitute Women and Children also provided similar services. Lack of overall coordination prevented the Washington services from becoming settlements.[84]

Other cities created protective services to aid new migrants. Chicago's Beulah Home and Erring Girls' Refuge showed the problems of white control in their requirements for black girls to leave "after the first false step has been taken."[85] Hence, the Phyllis Wheatley Woman's Club organized the Phyllis Wheatley Home to protect young women from the "human vultures ever ready to destroy young womanhood."[86] The club raised money to purchase a home providing the typical accommodations, instruction, and employment counseling and placement services. In Indianapolis, lack of YWCA services for black girls led to the black clubwomen forming the

Young Colored Women's Protective Association to serve as a literary, social, musical, and industrial center. Similar to other centers, the Indianapolis example served as a training school in domestic science, an employment agency seeking better hours and benefits for working women, a protective association assisting females new to the city, and a liaison between the newcomer and social or educational agencies in the city. Both the Chicago and the Indianapolis centers began as reactions to white indifference.[87]

Similar associations arose to meet local needs. The Dorcas Home Society of Yonkers, New York, maintained a home and employment office for black women. Michigan's women's clubs contributed to fund-raising for the Detroit Phillis Wheatley Home. White benefactors aided black women in Grand Rapids. The Sojourner Truth Club in Los Angeles raised money for a Home for Working Women and Girls, while Oakland's Fannie Jackson Coppin Club provided aid to young women. By the end of 1908, black women had established the Negro Working Girls' Home in Springfield, Massachusetts; the Sheltering Arms Home of Los Angeles, and similar centers in Lynchburg, Virginia; Columbia, South Carolina; and Little Rock, Arkansas. Although many of these did not qualify as official settlement houses, several expanded services as the needs grew, as in the case of the White Rose Home. In other examples, as in the Washington case, the presence of several black-founded services was finally consolidated with white aid into the Colored Social Settlement. This interracial cooperation led to the development of several major settlement houses during the pre-1910 period.[88]

One of the first examples of cooperation between the races to establish a settlement for blacks was the Flanner Guild of Indianapolis. Developed in the late 1890s through a gift of property to the city's blacks from a white undertaker, Frank W. Flanner, the center's male management sought to improve the morality and industrial skills of black youth. Relying on black women as matrons in the employment agency, as supervisors of the reading room games and literature collections, and as instructors in the domestic science classes, the Flanner Guild offered the typical services of an urban settlement house. Young women learned food preparation and serving for jobs in clubs, for receptions and other social gatherings, or as domestics. The center helped the women find employment, and then, for ten cents a day, supervised their children while they worked. Black women held club meetings and social events at the center and raised money for the center's operation. The course trained cooks, carpenters, milliners, and bookkeepers. By 1905, the renamed Flanner Guild Industrial Neighborhood House had graduated over 150 milliners. To encourage neighborhood pride and provide food, the settlement dispensed seed and instruction to community people to cultivate vacant lots. They displayed their produce at the Land, Food and Industrial Exhibit in 1905.

The center "took on a new vitality"[89] under female direction when Gertrude Guthrie, a black community leader, became resident director in 1907. The center gained more land and a grant from the county. The erection of a new assembly hall provided space for lectures, athletic events, and entertainments. The center gained national attention through its voluntary probation officer program. Through its cooperation with the Charity Organization Society, the settlement aided charity cases, expanded services to help "fallen" women and unwed mothers, and helped travelers. With the financial help of the Christian Women's Board of Missions, the financial burdens eased. As blacks migrated to Indianapolis, the settlement became more involved with preventive health care programs. The direction and support of black women enabled the white-initiated settlement to serve the black community. Yet their support of a segregated facility presented a paradox. According to Ruth Crocker's study of settlement houses in Indiana, Flanner House became a source of black pride and definite improvements for the black community, but the maintenance of "segregation and inequality . . . ultimately made black progress limited."[90] In the context of the 1890s, most black communities lacked the financial resources and/or professional expertise necessary for the establishment of their own settlement houses and few examples of sensitive interracial efforts existed. Judging Flanner House in this context, the programs improved the conditions faced by blacks.[91]

Settlements founded after 1900 continued to show a lack of intergroup understanding. Just as the settlement leadership serving the immigrant populations looked down on the women as intellectually inferior, naturally suited for domesticity, and un-American,[92] the white initiators of black settlements held similar stereotyped notions about the client population and, frequently, about the black clubwomen with whom they cooperated. In 1905, the Newark Social Settlement began. Interested whites initiated the program, prepared the prospectus, and then called together black male and female leadership to help plan fund-raising and organization. The white leadership wrote to W. E. B. Du Bois for advice on the appointment of a head resident. They wanted a well-educated black woman to "bring the cultured and uncultured together in fellowship and uplift."[93] They wanted someone with industrial training, since the black population to be served had few skilled workers. Within a few months, Sarah Hunt, sister of Adella Hunt Logan, was selected as resident. Having graduated from both Atlanta University and Tuskegee Institute, Sarah Hunt possessed the ability to interact with both the "cultured" and the "unskilled."[94]

The settlement work of the Civic League of Englewood, New Jersey, demonstrated another type of racial insensitivity. When black women were called together to encourage black participation, the white settlement worker remarked that "there is nothing colored people enjoy quite so much as meetings."[95] This resident felt that blacks sometimes lacked ambition and were lazy, but on the positive side were "easily influenced and responsive to any advice or suggestion given by the [settlement] workers."[96] Although black women participated in these and other settlement[97] activities as fund-raisers, administrators, organizers, workers, or volunteers, their actions and words were restricted by the social and economic context of the times.

Occasionally, white-founded settlements gradually increased black control and direction. The Colored Social Settlement in Washington, D.C., began as a result of white initiative and developed as a result of black energies. Charles F. Weller came to the city as the executive officer of the Associated Charities. Interested in the conditions of the black poor, Weller rented a room in an alley community. From this position, he studied the conditions of life. Weller cooperated with the black men and women of the Colored Conference Class in the formation in 1902 of the "first colored social settlement in Washington, and perhaps the first distinctive settlement of its kind in the world."[98] The goal—encouragement of wholesome home life—reflected the influence of black women. As members of the executive committee, they directed the program and also worked in the settlement. Most were members of the Colored Women's League and had experience in rescue work, kindergarten teaching, friendly visiting, and industrial instruction. Together with black male leaders—Francis J. Grimke, Presbyterian clergyman; Kelly Miller, teacher and critic of Du Bois; and Sterling N. Brown, black writer and poet—the black women appealed to their clubs' missionary societies and circles for financial support. From the lists of "Givers of Goods" and "Contributors and Subscribers," individual women and women's organizations predominated. The list of "Volunteer Helpers" included only ten men out of seventy-two volunteers. Many of the women were simultaneously members of the Colored Women's League, the Prudence Crandall Club, and other charity and literary societies.

The Colored Settlement utilized the services of professionally trained black women. Sarah Collins Fernandis, graduate of Hampton and the New York School of Philanthropy and wife of John A. Fernandis of Baltimore, was one of the first black professional social workers in America. She helped to organize and served as the head resident of the settlement. For working women, the settlement provided a nursery for five cents a day. A free kindergarten helped supervise small children, and clubs provided activities for the older boys and girls. A stamp savings bank encouraged thrift and reputedly decreased the number of applications for charity and the intemperance of the neighborhood. Instruction in dressmaking, sewing, military drilling, and singing provided skills or enrichment for the varied age groups. A playground allowed recreation and fresh air, two reforms for children. These activities were typical of most settlement houses, but in the case of the Colored Social Settlement were "by and for colored people."[99]

In cooperation with the Colored Conference Class, the settlement behaved in typical progressive fashion. Investigations by the settlement professionals produced two specialized organizations. The Sanitary Housing Company constructed brick row apartments renting at reasonable rates in the crusade against the shanty living of the black residents. The Citizens' Neighborhood Improvement Association, negotiated with the city government and the Board of Education over greater industrial opportunity for the school children of the area, abatement of public nuisances, and establishment of public playgrounds. These changes demonstrated the ability of the privileged black female leadership to remain sensitive to the needs of poor or working-class black women and their children. Appraised as "one of the best social settlements,"[100] the association provided necessary services, studies, and changes in the Washington community.[101]

As the Washington women negotiated with school boards and city governments, the Chicago reform community developed "a glorious scheme,"[102] the Frederick Douglass Center on Wabash Avenue. Celia Parker Wooley, a white reformer seeking to decrease racial prejudice resulting from segregation, initiated the move to purchase a building to house interracial settlement work. Wooley brought together black clubwomen and with their help and regular contributions opened the center in 1904. As in the Washington example, settlement workers represented both races. The activities included a sewing class, lectures, kindergarten, and a woman's club. Reflecting the influence of the Chicago Musical College, training site for many national black female singers, the center offered children singing classes, orchestra, and quartette. After a few years, the center incorporated manual training, cooking, dressmaking, and child care with lectures from Booker T. Washington and, in 1906, from Max Barber, editor of the anti-Washington publication, *The Voice of the Negro*. As did other settlements, the center conducted investigations of housing conditions affecting the black community to ascertain needed changes.

Since the center's primary objective sought to "promote a just and amicable relationship between the white and colored people,"[103] black and white women united in the Douglass Woman's Club. As with the NACW, Ida Wells-Barnett found conflict with both white and black leadership. She resented that a club with two-thirds black membership had a white woman, Mrs. Plummer, as president, and a black woman, herself, as vice president. When Plummer retired, Wells-Barnett expected to become president. When a black physician, Dr. Fannie Emmanuel, received the position, Wells-Barnett accused Wooley of "double dealing"[104] Wells-Barnett took disagreements over lecture topics as personal affronts. Most of the other women, such as Fannie Barrier Williams and Mrs. Charles Bentley, interacted more effectively.[105]

Soon several social settlements arose to meet the needs of the black communities. In 1907, Robert A. Woods, a resident of Boston's South End House, established the Robert Gould Shaw House. Woods soon came to depend on a black resident worker and two black women, Maria L. Baldwin and Florida Ridley, as counselors. Baldwin, a teacher at white Agassiz School, taught English literature. The paid and volunteer teachers were black women. Dora Cole Lewis organized a neighborhood league as one of the women's clubs responsible for achieving cleaner streets, improving public parks, and cooperating with the Women's Municipal League, the Watch and Word, and other reform organizations. The Shaw settlement cooperated with other agencies concerned with black employment. Each year the center hosted one or more conferences concerned with industrial training. Young black women trained in the YWCA course in domestic science received placement in jobs through the settlement. Others received the aid of advisers and resident workers in securing clerical and stenographic jobs.[106]

During the same year, other communities formed similar centers. In Philadelphia, the Armstrong Association, supported by white philanthropy and directed by white managers, depended on black women and men for volunteer teaching and for service as executive officers. The center trained workers for the public schools and provided classes in industrial education. Through its employment bureau, the association helped skilled blacks find work and attempted to open new areas of employment for the race. The center employed a full-time trained social worker to work with black schoolchildren in two school centers. Thus black women brought settlement work into the black schools, which developed into a social center and night school. Since black social workers handled such services better than white workers, the association supported further expansion of professional social work programs for blacks.[107]

These settlements in the North shared many common characteristics. Most were initiated by interested whites who immediately sought the cooperation of the black reform community. The programs emphasized industrial education and employment-related services in addition to the standard kindergarten, clubs, and social activities. The black women who participated had experience with kindergartens and day nurseries, domestic training, and literary interests in their own women's clubs and societies. Their work as teachers in the school systems enabled many ventures to become institutionalized in the public school systems. As these centers proliferated during the pre-1910 period, black control increased and the reform interests in housing and health also expanded. Chicago added the Wendell Philips Center in 1907 to join the Frederick Douglass Center and settlements established by black male leaders Richard Wright, Jr., and Reverdy Ransom. As black populations increased in New York, Chicago, Boston, and Philadelphia, black women helped to increase services to meet changing needs.[108]

Yet the greatest number of blacks continued to live in the South. In Atlanta in 1908, a group of black women founded the most professional settlement organization for a black community to date. The segregationist traditions and special character of Atlanta racial leadership stimulated a black-initiated, black-directed, and black-funded settlement, the Atlanta Neighborhood Union. Lugenia Hope, wife of John Hope, the president of Morehouse College, came to Atlanta in 1898 after growing up in Chicago. She and her husband shared similar interests in social settlement work and urban reform. She became "his best emissary"[109] to the Atlanta community and became "among the first . . . to do volunteer social work in Atlanta and to organize the city for social work on a volunteer basis."[110] When a young mother died unnoticed by her neighbors, Hope called together a small group of black women to discuss the tragedy. They proposed united action to make the black community more responsible. Hope consulted Jane Addams for advice about settlement work. Within the month, the Atlanta Neighborhood Union began its efforts to improve the black community.

Adopting the motto "And Thy Neighbor As Thyself," the black women banded together to enlist the aid of others in general community reform. Hope's speeches acknowledged the great strides made by the race since emancipation, but expressed fears that current trends could lead to racial retrogression. Children roamed the streets, ill-clothed and unfed, while parents worked all day to provide for them. Hope criticized the black women who rationalized their lack of involvement by saying that they lacked time, had their own family concerns, or did not want their children mixing with those of the lower classes. Such reasons, said Hope, were "Hard-hearted, thoughtless, self-centered."[111]

Reflecting the progressive belief in the mutual interdependence of cultural groups and classes, Hope explained how the elite's self-interest was involved with the improvement of conditions for the lower strata. Bad housing and extreme poverty produced crime. Physical and moral uncleanliness, encouraged by lax law enforcement, produced health and vice problems for the entire city. Urban conditions could be ameliorated through human efforts. "People living in slums do not have to die in slums, nor do slums have to continue to be slums."[112] The slum child who survived this type of life was the true victim, not the slum child who died. Indicating all the currents of progressive thought, Hope encouraged individuals actively, scientifically, and humanely to enter the arena of community reform.

Hope led an expanding group of elite women in organized reform. They proposed to have a settlement house in each neighborhood for gatherings, clubs, classes, and community projects. Through lecture courses, fresh air work, clean-up campaigns, clubs, reading rooms, and instruction, the women hoped to develop good work habits, rid areas of immoral or criminal influences, provide beneficial sports or games, improve the health and sanitation of surrounding areas, and stimulate community responsibility. To accomplish these goals, efficient organization to investigate conditions and make recommendations was primary. Hope divided the city into sixteen zones, each of which was subdivided into neighborhoods and then into districts. Each district had a leader selected by the Neighborhood Union (NU) and endorsed by the district residents. Through this method, community problems became known to the local social workers while giving the community a feeling of self-direction.

The NU initiated work through four departments: moral and educational; literary; music; and the arts, which comprised industrial work in dressmaking, embroidery, millinery, cooking, and nursing. At first, these interests reflected the middle-class perspective of the leaders. As experience increased and the problems became more apparent, the departments expanded to include churches, health and sanitation, child welfare, finance, publicity, investigation, recreation, industry, relief, interracial, home economics, and literature and music. The black community received services from the NU while it raised the consciousness of the NU's middle-class leadership. This awareness, when coupled with their skills and experience, improved the efficiency and efficacy of black social work.

Black women served as the officers, board of directors, committee women, and foot soldiers of the NU. They understood the needs of the black community and the corresponding lack of money for the programs. Their first activities depended on their volunteer work as instructors in classes, as playground supervisors, and as investigators. Solicitation of donations was discouraged, leaving the women to think up creative fund-raisers: carnivals, box parties, fairs, bake sales, track meets, pageants, and house parties. For special projects, the women encouraged donations of money, services, and goods. Led by many efficient workers who received the professional advice and cooperation of Morehouse College and black churches, the programs lagged from time to time due to periodic lack of funds. The spirit and volunteer work continued to sustain the community services during the periods of financial difficulty. Within a few years, the NU had established the first playground at Morehouse College, which also allowed the neighborhood youths to use the athletic field and gymnasium. As coordinator of emergency relief to blacks, the NU cooperated with city charity agencies, turning cases over to Family Welfare to handle. Families received food, clothing, shoes, and coal directly through the NU with the support of the city and Welfare Department. Under the supervision of the Red Cross, the NU provided fire relief. As with Hull House in Chicago, the NU served as a social center, organizer of political action, and educational leader for Atlanta blacks.[113]

From 1890 to 1910, the Atlanta Neighborhood Union served as a beacon for other black communities seeking urban reform. The organization founded by black women demonstrated the highest form of social reform techniques and attitudes. This settlement organization and the others founded by interracial efforts continued developing to meet community needs. They did not revolutionize conditions for or attitudes about the race, but they did improve life for those they served. They demonstrate the progress of black female activity from the early charity work through the homes for the aged, infirm, and orphaned. During the two decades spanning the turn of the century, black women laid the foundation for major social services in their communities. As blacks migrated to the urban areas, these services expanded and changed to meet new conditions and new populations. As the services changed, so, too, did the women.

PART TWO

New Paths for Organized Reform

It is . . . no "woman question" alone. . . . It is a human problem—a problem of knowledge, intelligence, and morals—for individuals, families, communities, and states.

> —Mary Beard, *Woman as Force in History: A Study in Traditions and Reality* (New York: Macmillan, 1946), p. 332.

The Negro Question in America today is a white man's problem—Nay it is humanity's problem.

> —Anna J. Cooper, "The Ethics of the Negro Question." Speech delivered on September 5, 1902. Copy in the Anna J. Cooper Papers, Howard University.

FOUR

A Change in Direction: Women and Race, 1910 to World War I

A growing social awareness was obvious by 1910. That year revealed the variety of movements inherent in progressivism and all their contradictory facets. Varied ideas of justice appeared in actions and statements. Supporters for woman's suffrage were becoming more numerous and more likely to be heard as they sought a tool for political justice. In April, supporters of woman's suffrage presented petitions containing over five hundred thousand signatures to Congress. In August, Theodore Roosevelt echoed a different type of political justice in his speech at Osawatomie, Kansas. He called for "a square deal" for all Americans. To protect individualism, the government would prevent large corporations from limiting opportunity, preserve national resources for future generations, and protect workers from exploitation. The New Nationalism would support America's potential for greatness. Within a month, Woodrow Wilson, active in his New Jersey campaign, called for control of corporations and tax reform, allowing economic freedoms to open other paths to greater freedom for Americans. These interpretations of economic and political justice represented individual threads of the cloth of progressivism.

Racism, too, was part of that cloth. Stereotyped attitudes and discrimination marked America's treatment of ethnic minorities. Blaming various immigrant groups for the increased labor unrest, politicians succeeded in amending the immigration laws to restrict the admission of paupers, the diseased, and anarchists. In 1910, the tired and poor immigrants were finding themselves unwanted in an America that sought to perfect itself. Within a few years, state and then national policy would limit land ownership for the Japanese and exclude Asiatic laborers from entering our country. In the settlement houses that epitomized progressive reform, European immigrants received manual training so that they might assume their destined "place" in society as laborers and as domestics. Blacks migrating to urban areas and those in southern schools received similar training. The Jim Crow attitudes became national. Although the northern cities had no legal segregation restricting blacks to certain areas of the city, to the back of public transportation, or to particular schools, social and economic discrimination increasingly produced de facto segregation in city social services, housing, and recreation. Under progressive leadership, federal departments became increasingly segregated, blacks were downgraded in Civil Service, and racial violence was ignored by leading politicians. Suffrage leaders argued that the vote for women would serve to counterbalance the ignorant immigrant vote in the North and the potential black vote in the South. The plight of the ethnic minorities demonstrated the narrow definition of economic and political justice of many progressives.

For a minority of white leaders, male and female progressives, and humanitarians, the race question amplified the contradictions of progressive thought. Together with black male and female leadership, interested whites would not allow the race question or racial injustices to be ignored. Through agitation, protest, and use of legal test cases, the NAACP worked for legal and political rights to improve opportunities for blacks. On October 16, 1911, the consolidation of the Committee for Improving the Industrial Conditions of the Negro in New York (CIICN), the National League for the Protection of Colored Women (NLPCW), and the Committee on Urban Conditions Among Negroes (CUCN) formed the National League on Urban Conditions Among Negroes. The Urban League sought to improve the social and economic conditions for blacks using negotiation, persuasion, investigation, and education. The professionally trained social workers of the Urban League worked on such problems as housing, unemployment, health, crime, and the training of blacks in urban areas. Black women cooperated with black men and white leaders to effect change through these organizations.

In the first few years of the decade, the black woman's role was changing in reform organizations concerned with women's issues. The National American Woman Suffrage Association (NAWSA) increased its interaction with the National Association of Colored Women (NACW), sending representatives to NACW biennials, extending greetings to club conferences, and encouraging suffrage organization among black women. During the 1912 biennial, the NACW officially supported the suffrage amendment, two years prior to the white clubwomen of the General Federation of Women's Clubs taking a similar stand. The white clubwomen, like many women of the time, saw no need for women to have suffrage guaranteed by the national government. Women, they felt, could express their moral positions through the family rather than through the ballot box. Black women formed their own suffrage clubs, marched in suffrage parades, picketed the White House, and argued for woman's suffrage in the columns of black periodicals. Discrimination continued to occur in the white suffrage movement, but black women fought for the vote as a tool for racial advancement, as white women fought for the vote as a tool for social improvements.

Black women showed similar concern for women's problems in urban areas. Addie Hunton and Elizabeth Ross Haynes, recently married to George Edmund Haynes, the first executive secretary of the National Urban League, continued to expand the role of black women in the YWCA. The National Board of the YWCA soon created a new position, executive secretary of colored work. In January 1913, Eva D. Bowles, a professional social worker, took over this position, shaping the role of black women in the YWCA movement. Bowles, a native of Columbus, Ohio, where she graduated from Ohio University, finished her professional training at the New York School of Philanthropy before becoming the first black social worker employed by the Harlem YWCA. Participating in segregated Phillis Wheatley YWCAs, black women met urban needs, while redefining their position in the white, evangelical association.

In their own club movement, black women demonstrated a change in direction during the first few years of the decade. The successful growth in the national club movement enabled black women to finance national and state projects, such as reformatories, training schools, and the Frederick Douglass Memorial and Historical Association. Their success increased the importance of the NACW to national reform organizations. White representatives from the YWCA, suffrage organizations, and the General Federation of Women's Clubs increasingly appeared alongside representatives of the NAACP and Urban League at the NACW biennials. Interorganizational cooperation expanded during these years as black women worked for their own version of progressive justice and increased the racial awareness of the white women's organizations and the consciousness of women's concerns in the racial advancement groups.

Evidence of this change in direction appeared in the 1910 biennial of the NACW. President Elizabeth Carter's travels to state and local federations had produced gains in membership and dissemination of successful programs. Through its 45,000 members, the NACW had developed a matrix of influence permeating local communities, national organizations, and families throughout the nation. Carter, reelected to a second term, felt the Louisville biennial could be a time of healing old wounds. She extended an invitation to Ida Wells-Barnett to attend. The unpleasant experiences of the 1899 Chicago biennial, combined with conflicts in the Chicago clubs, led to Wells-Barnett's failure to attend any NACW biennials since 1899. The invitation brought Wells-Barnett back to club leadership as chairman on resolutions and returned conflict to the proceedings.[1]

Whether due to Wells-Barnett's presence, the more radical context from which the NAACP emerged in 1909-1910, or the expanded membership represented by 278 delegates, conflict ensued over control of the *National Notes*. The NACW newsletter was printed by students at Tuskegee Institute under the supervision of Margaret Murray Washington. Some delegates complained that articles or editorials unfavorable to Booker T. Washington never appeared. Other delegates suggested that the post of editor was becoming important enough to require election. As chairman on resolutions, Wells-Barnett motioned for the elective editorship of the *National Notes*. Her motion provoked conflict between Washington supporters and opponents. Some disagreed with the editorial actions, but remained grateful for the "free" publication. The leadership by Wells-Barnett produced hissing from the floor and criticism from past president Lucy Thurman. The motion failed to pass, but this did not signify the dominance of one ideology over another. The NACW biennial continued to function as a forum for varying philosophies and organizations. Eva Jenifer presented the goals of the newly formed NAACP and received the NACW's endorsement "provided it did not interfere with the treasury or divide the working force of the National Association of Colored Women."[2] The NACW leadership was not, as yet, convinced of the dedication of white reformers. Elizabeth Ross failed to persuade the clubwomen about the YWCA's change in direction. The women had experienced too many instances of the racial insensitivity of the white YWCA to offer official endorsement now. The presence of radical and conservative organizations depicted the range of opinions in the forum of the NACW biennial.

As more blacks moved to the cities and as black women's groups gained experience in social service organization, the reforms expanded. The Brooklyn Lincoln Settlement, under the leadership of black physician Dr. Verina

Morton Jones, expanded health lecture series and day nursery programs to meet the needs of working mothers. In Cleveland, an interracial social service center developed in 1915 through the Cleveland Playhouse Settlement. Existing settlements developed employment agencies to fill requests for maids and day workers and to protect the treatment of black workers. The Frederick Douglass Center advised employers about fair wages and working conditions and frequently arbitrated labor disputes. Ida Wells-Barnett founded the Negro Fellowship League, which provided temporary housing, literacy training, and employment services for black men beginning in 1910.[3]

There was also increased activity on behalf of workers' children. The Alpha Charity Club of Anacostia joined the Social Purity Club of Washington to provide money, food, clothing and volunteer services for children in the N Street Day Nursery. Baltimore's Empty Stocking Club joined the Fresh Air Circle to provide toys and gifts for black children during the holidays and on special occasions. Led by Ida Cummings, clubwoman and NAACP supporter, the joint effort introduced city children to the experience of "Farm Delight"[4] by taking them to the countryside in the summer. Josephine Allensworth donated land for the construction of a library in Allensworth, California, a black town founded by her husband. Libraries, day nurseries, and fresh air work received the support of clubwomen during the years before World War I.[5]

Health programs became increasingly emphasized. Indiana's Sisters of Charity began their drive in 1910 to raise funds for the establishment of a black hospital. The Frederick Douglass Hospital of Philadelphia developed a social service department, allowing the hospital more efficiently to serve the needs of an urban population. The hospital developed postgraduate courses to improve the skills of its physicians.

Tuberculosis, which affected a high proportion of urban blacks, became a concern of many black clubs. Lectures about disease prevention and care proliferated. Between 1910 and 1912, the Colored Teacher's Association of New Orleans donated money to tuberculosis prevention work and aided the city's sanitarium. Chicago clubwomen led a national fund-raising movement for the establishment of the Paul Laurence Dunbar Memorial Sanitorium for the prevention, care, and treatment of black tuberculosis patients. In 1913, black clubwomen in Birmingham organized tuberculosis clinics. Local clubs sponsored health campaigns and worked for improved sanitation conditions.[6]

The cooperative effort led by Atlanta women demonstrated the increased expertise in social organization of health campaigns. During the 1913-1914 year, the city's Child Welfare and Public Health Exhibit utilized the work performed in the classes of the Neighborhood Union. Attended by over four thousand people during the four-day exhibition and demonstration, the activities increased public awareness about health and the activities of the Neighborhood Union. To bring attention to the widespread presence of tuberculosis in the black community, the head of the Neighborhood Union, Lugenia Hope, approached the Anti-Tuberculosis Association (ATA) seeking some type of cooperation between the two agencies. Rosa Lowe—white reformer, former head resident of the settlement house in the Atlanta Fulton Bag and Cotton Mill community, and current secretary of the ATA—supported the idea saying, "It is absurd to undertake to fight disease in one section of the city and leave the other part untouched. . . . Tuberculosis knows no color line."[7] Lowe realized interracial cooperation would prove difficult because blacks had little faith in whites or their motivations. Lowe sought cooperation by allowing the black women control of the program in their community under the direction of the main organization, the ATA. Not confined to the cure of tuberculosis, the program stressed prevention through improved living conditions, sanitation, education, and recreation.

The black women launched the Atlanta Health Campaign on June 12, 1914. Organized along the same lines as the Neighborhood Union work, the women divided the black community into zones and neighborhoods to conduct intensive investigations of conditions. The Committee on School Surveys evaluated each building in terms of ventilation, lighting, overcrowding, and sanitary surroundings. The Committee on Housing observed home construction, ventilation, lighting, plumbing, air space between houses, application of present codes, family occupation of home, supervision of children, house maintenance, street lighting, and pavement conditions. In addition, the women investigated the conditions of such public buildings as grocery stores, lodges, churches, and recreation and amusement centers.

This organization and commitment produced results. The women effected the passage of ordinances eliminating privies, providing for city sanitation department removal of garbage from black neighborhoods, achieving the placement of physicians and nurses in the black schools, conducting periodic clean-up campaigns, and informing the public about health issues. The Neighborhood Union held free clinics throughout the city, conducted house visits, and lectured in schools and churches. The excellent organization and delivery of services impressed the whites in the ATA. Rosa Lowe became an admirer of the black female leadership and an ally for future interracial efforts in Atlanta and throughout the South.[8]

Similar health campaigns followed the Neighborhood Union's example after their presentation at the 1914 Wilberforce biennial. Richmond clubwomen, under the direction of Janie Porter Barrett, conducted health and clean-up campaigns cooperating with white women. The Indianapolis Woman's Improvement Club attempted to gain admittance for black tuberculars to Flower Mission Hospital and to establish a tuberculosis clinic at Flanner House. When they failed in these attempts, the women launched an educational campaign about the causes, treatment, and prevention of the disease. Joined by the black ministers, the women's clubs circulated health information within the community institutions. A second club in Indianapolis, the Woman's Council, worked for child health through the establishment of neighborhood clubs to instruct and advise black mothers in child care, nutrition, and clean environment. Atlanta women established a Free Children's Clinic at the Neighborhood House in 1915. The white Board of Education not only consented to a school lecture series, but also required all teachers to attend the presentations. The ATA employed a black visiting nurse to care for those unable to attend the free clinics, lectures, and neighborhood meetings. Suggested by the Negro Race Committee of the ATA, Rosa Lowe requested the city to establish more recreational facilities for black children and criticized the injustice of segregating the current facilities. Community health concerns were beginning to challenge segregation. By 1916, the emphasis was not focused on cleanliness as a moral quality or as a way to gain acceptance from whites, but as a practice to avoid health problems based on scientific evidence.[9]

The increase of white cooperation in health and clean-up campaigns, when combined with the growth of the black women's club movement, produced larger, more expensive, professional projects. The stress by progressives on investigation led black women to study black criminality and establish programs to alleviate the suffering of the incarcerated and prevent juveniles from becoming adult criminals. The rise of reformatories and juvenile work demonstrated the change in direction of club work during the post-1910 period. Most of the reformatory work had developed in the North and border states. By 1911, only eleven reformatories existed in the South, out of 105 such facilities nationally.[10] With the development of state federations, black women were able to raise the necessary funds for such expensive facilities, gain the cooperation of white organizations, and convince state legislatures to appropriate greater amounts of money for these services.

The club network spread information about state reformatories. As the Mt. Meigs reformatory in Alabama developed from the efforts of the Alabama State Federation of Colored Women's Clubs, the Arkansas Federation developed a reformatory using Mt. Meigs as the "model" The "model" was granted state funds in a bill presented to the Alabama legislature by the Alabama State Federation of Colored Women's Clubs, which then began fund-raising for the establishment of a girls' reformatory. The Texas Federation established a reformatory for black youths. The will of a black domestic worker provided a gift of 365 acres in Guilford County, North Carolina, to help black women establish a reformatory and manual training school for black youth. Black clubwomen in New York began fund-raising in 1913 for the establishment of a girls' reformatory. During the first few years of the decade, the presence of state federations stimulated a phenomenal growth in the number of reformatories in black areas that had previously been without them.[11]

The best-known reformatory developed from the interracial cooperation in Richmond, Virginia. When the NACW held its 1912 biennial at Hampton Institute, Janie Porter Barrett, president of the Virginia State Federation of Colored Women's Clubs, used the opportunity to gain attention and raise money for the establishment of a girls' reformatory. Barrett, founder of the Locust Street Settlement in Hampton, led tours for the clubwomen interested in her settlement work, while persuading delegates to support her reformatory. She lectured about her experience with the jailing of an eight-year-old girl, punished due to lack of facilities in the area. She told about her efforts to seek advice from the Russell Sage Foundation and financial help from black and white clubwomen. Her story and leadership produced results. By 1913, Barrett had raised $5,300, making the reformatory a practical venture.

Barrett ensured the viability of the institution by establishing interracial leadership and funding. Advice and financial help from the Russell Sage Foundation, combined with two prominent white women serving on the board of trustees, provided an acceptable project to receive funding from the Virginia State Legislature. Barrett and the two white female trustees testified and received state appropriations for the reformatory. A farm of 147 acres became the site for the Virginia Industrial School for Colored Girls in Peake. With funding from the state, local white benefactors, the Russell Sage

Foundation, and the Virginia Federation of Colored Women's Clubs, the success of the venture was virtually assured. The daily management fell to black women—Ethel G. Griffith, superintendent, and Janie Porter Barrett, secretary on the board of trustees.

The facility officially opened in January of 1915, but not without difficulties. Local residents protested its presence in their area. In response to political pressure from these residents, the state delayed its maintenance appropriation until the matter had been successfully resolved. During this time of conflict, Barrett's husband died, leaving her a sense of personal loss, but also freeing her from family responsibilities. The white residents agreed to cease their protests only if Barrett agreed to become the head resident superintendent. Barrett at first reacted negatively: "I, give up my pretty home to live in a dormitory and eat from thick plates with a tin fork?"[12] But, after much consideration, she did just that. Turning down an offer to become the dean of women at Tuskegee Institute, Barrett became the head resident at the reformatory. She imprinted her ideas about education and child rearing on the girls. Although her techniques could be labeled progressive, they arose from her personal preferences. She disliked corporal punishment, believing that Peake's Turnout should be a "moral hospital"[13] instead of a place for punishment. Through "loving discipline" and an honor system rewarding positive behavior, Barrett believed the girls could develop character, knowledge, and responsibility. The fences surrounding the reformatory were only as high as neighboring farm fences, but few girls tried to escape the home, guidance, and new start offered by the reformatory.[14]

Barrett's emphasis on interracial cooperation was founded on her personal philosophy and the practical reality of the South. The white members on the board of trustees provided the necessary influence, advice, connections, and money for the reformatory to function. The whites also brought the achievements of the reformatory to the attention of white philanthropy. The Russell Sage Foundation felt that Peake's Turnout was "one of the best five reformatories in the country."[15] Produced and nurtured by black clubwomen, the reformatory movement provided services for black youth and demonstrated black abilities.

In addition to reformatory development, black women increased their activity in juvenile work and as probation officers. In Chicago, Ida Wells-Barnett became the first female probation officer. The organized efforts of clubwomen won similar posts in Denver, Atlanta, and Pittsburgh. Several leading clubwomen entered juvenile work to aid black children, victims of poverty in urban environments. Existing schools or orphanages expanded their services to include reformatory or juvenile work. For example, both the Johnson's Orphanage in Macon and the Carrie Steele Orphanage in Atlanta added reformatory work to their services from 1910 to 1914. Assisted by juvenile probation officers, the Neighborhood Union placed children in reformatories, orphanages, and private homes. When community members received unjust treatment from the white justice system, the Neighborhood Union represented their cases. During 1913-1914, one individual received a release, while another won a shorter sentence due to the ombudsman role of the Neighborhood Union with white authorities. Such reformatory and juvenile probation work increased the experience of black women with the white political-legal structure as well as promoted contact with similarly interested white reformers. These experiences and white contacts aided future interracial efforts.[16]

Black women also increased contact with white school boards. Nannie Burroughs and the Woman's Convention Auxiliary of the National Baptist Convention worked with the District of Columbia School Board in the establishment and operation of the National Training School for Women and Girls.[17] A graduate of the M Street School in Washington, Burroughs furthered her education and gained the support of black churchwomen to launch fund-raising and organization for the first national trade school for black women in 1909. Only a few years later, buildings and programs were in place and the institution was providing an environment in which girls could live and learn marketable skills. Since 58 percent of black women worked as domestics, the school sought to develop a strong academic program with instruction in a "first-class trade." Although this school continued to emphasize industrial education, as was typical of the earlier years, its organization, fund-raising, and national character reflected the greater experience of black women and the increased interaction with white power structures of the pre-war years.[18]

Black women pressured school administrations to improve education for their children. Black mothers marched to a white school in Roslyn, Long Island, demanding admission for their children.[19] The Atlanta Neighborhood Union formed the Women's Civic and Social Improvement Committee in 1912 to investigate and improve the black schools. First, the committee inspected and investigated the conditions of every black school in Atlanta, finding unsanitary conditions, poor lighting and ventilation, congested rooms, and double sessions with the same overworked teacher instructing both groups. After gathering the data, the black women sought the cooperation of influential white women. Initially skeptical, the white women visited the schools. What they saw convinced them to give their support. Second, the black women visited each councilwoman, sought the support of white ministers, met with the mayor, and, finally, reached the public through mass meetings, public lectures, and community meetings. Black ministers urged their congregations to become more aware and involved in the schools. Atlanta black women had mobilized the black and white communities to improve black schools.

After gaining the support of community groups, the black women moved to improve conditions. A petition drive sought separation of the feeble-minded and defective children from the regular classes, improvement of sanitary conditions, addition of another school in south Atlanta, and elimination of double sessions. The Board of Education reviewed the conditions and issued recommendations. To lessen overcrowding, the board suggested reducing the literary course by two years and increasing the industrial education. Although the black women knew the value of skills training, they refused to accommodate to the loss of higher literary training. Instead of direct protest, the women used flattery and logic to persuade the white leaders. Less literary training would result in "less morally and economically efficient graduates."[20] Industrial education could lead to black advancement only if added to the normal curriculum. Overcrowding could be solved only by more facilities, not fewer. Finally, they argued that the "fair-minded citizens of Atlanta . . . [would never approve such a] fundamentally undemocratic and unjust" program.[21]

The investigations, political maneuvering, and arguments did result in improved black education. The Atlanta School Board added a school in south Atlanta and raised the salaries of the teachers. Black male leaders joined with the women in monitoring and improving the schools. The superintendent allowed school buildings to be used for community programs requiring only a three-day notice. During the summer, the buildings became centers of the Neighborhood Union's Daily Vacation Bible School. The physical conditions of the schools improved through increased expenditures and attention. After a bill calling for white teachers to be prohibited from instructing black children passed the Georgia Senate, black women testified before the Georgia House of Representatives. They noted that the bill was both unconstitutional and contrary to southern traditions, which encouraged northern and southern whites, motivated by intellectual or moral ideals, to spread knowledge to

113

southern black children. Their testimony prevented changes in instruction. The Atlanta women demonstrated how self-interest and racial cooperation on certain issues created the beginnings of intergroup understanding.[22]

The organized groups of black women not only improved local and regional social services, but also increased interorganizational cooperation with national women's or racial advancement associations. The 1910 Louisville biennial received presentations from both the NAACP and the YWCA. Encouraged by the president, Elizabeth Carter, the NACW sent representatives Mary Talbert of Buffalo and Joyce Jackson of Columbus to the Cleveland convention of the National Council of Women. The NACW took part in programs honoring Harriet Beecher Stowe during the centennial year of Stowe's birth in 1811. Those attending the June 1912 NACW biennial at Hampton heard reports about the successful development of the Phyllis Wheatley YWCA in St. Louis and the NACW/NAACP cooperation in the case of Virginia Christian, a seventeen-year-old girl found guilty of murdering her mistress. NACW representatives Mary Church Terrell and Hallie Q. Brown had met with the governor of Virginia to argue for clemency. The NACW made the NAACP aware of the case. The combined efforts helped to alter the sentence to life imprisonment and showed the expansion of NACW influence in the state executive offices. The 1912 convention of the National Municipal League heard black women discuss overcrowded housing conditions resulting from segregation. At the Child Welfare Conference in Richmond, a black woman told the white audience, "We do not prefer dilapidation and discomfort, nor being forced to live in districts where there is only depravity and low surroundings; but the better ones of us have too much self-respect to force ourselves on our white brothers, if they do not want us living alongside of them!"[23] These speeches stimulated women's associations to confront problems for blacks not only in the southern communities, but also in northern cities where increasing black population coupled with more restricted housing segregation caused severe congestion.[24]

Before the black women reconvened for the 1914 Wilberforce biennial, their cooperation with racial protest organizations expanded. The Northeastern Federation of Women's Clubs conducted public fund-raising meetings under the auspices of the NACW Department for the Suppression of Lynchings. At the meeting on February 27, 1913, at the Concord Baptist Church of Christ, Mary Terrell spoke about lynching. Maritcha R. Lyons and Elizabeth H. Mickens presented comments about lynching and the work of the NAACP. This type of rally, combined with the published articles about lynchings, served to raise the public consciousness about the injustice. The combined efforts of the NACW and the NAACP made lynching an American embarrassment.[25]

Intergroup cooperation was increasing in several centers of black reform. The Washington black elite increased community participation with the rising middle class. In Chicago, the City Federation of Colored Women's Clubs joined the United Charities during the fall of 1914. The 1914 Wilberforce biennial of the NACW demonstrated the intergroup cooperation in speeches and organizational representation. Five hundred delegates heard Eva Bowles, national secretary of colored work in the YWCA, describe her social work experience in Columbus, Ohio, compared to her work with the YWCA in Harlem and New York City. Her presence and the increased work of the YWCA with black girls led to the NACW's resolution to formally cooperate with the YWCA. Other white women's organizations sent representatives to the meeting. Zona Gale, of the General Federation of Women's Clubs, and Harriet Upton, president of the Ohio Suffrage League, urged the black women to cooperate in achieving common female reforms. The NACW protested to the governor of Illinois about his failure to appoint a black woman to the planning committee for a fair celebrating fifty years of black freedom and they endorsed Chicagoan Dr. Mary Waring for the post. Pressured also by local black women's clubs, the governor created a position and appointed Waring to it. These activities reinforced the pattern of increased interaction with political and reform representatives.[26]

The black clubwomen were proud of their influence and their successes. Coming to Baltimore during the week of August 6-10, 1916, they intended to celebrate their achievement as a race and as women. They heard a presentation by Madame C. J. Walker, who attributed her business success to hard work, efficiency, and skill. She epitomized the responsible black leader committed to the black community through her contributions to local and national organizations such as the NAACP, YMCA, and YWCA of St. Louis, Bethune-Cookman College, Tuskegee Institute, Haines Institute, and the City of Indianapolis. Walker was both a model to emulate and a co-worker in reform.[27]

Racial pride was evident throughout the meeting. The pageant "The Star of Ethiopia" portrayed the origin and progress of the race. Elizabeth Davis reported on the success of the Association. Since 1914, the NACW had gained over 5,600 new members representing 298 clubs. They had pledged

$1,000 to the Booker T. Washington Memorial Fund, contributed to the work of Baltimore's Fresh Air Circle, and entered into a campaign for the Frederick Douglass Home.[28]

The achievements of the past few years, coupled with the increased focus on racial pride as a prerequisite to racial advancement, led the NACW to take on the responsibility for the Frederick Douglass Home. Directed by the newly elected president, Mary B. Talbert, the NACW took over the financial obligation for the redemption and restoration of the residence of Frederick Douglass in Anacostia, D.C. Created by a special act of Congress after the death of Helen Douglass in 1905, the Frederick Douglass Memorial and Historical Association intended to preserve the home as a perpetual memorial to the great leader and a center for the collection, preservation, and exhibition of black history.

The Frederick Douglass Memorial and Historical Association had continually experienced difficulties raising money to pay the home's expenses. Booker T. Washington's efforts failed to raise the four thousand dollars to cancel the mortgage on Cedar Hill, the Douglass estate. The Cleveland *Gazette* lamented, "This is a sad commentary on this race of ours."[29] Another said, "it seems almost a tragedy that the colored people of the country should not be sufficiently interested."[30] The committee members charged with the original responsibility for the home included Francis J. and Archibald Grimke, brothers who were active in the Washington branch of the NAACP; Whitfield McKinley, Charleston-born friend of Booker T. Washington and a District of Columbia real estate dealer; and J. C. Napier, Nashville banker and lawyer before becoming the register of the Treasury in 1911. These men, with all their business and professional connections, could not raise the necessary funds. Their circular letters seeking donations seemed both visionary and indifferent. In 1915, the Indianapolis *Freeman* remarked that the committee had done more "harm . . . to the memory of Mr. Douglass by the weak show of trying to honor him than if the whole business was coldly dismissed."[31]

The NACW's sentimental relationship to Cedar Hill extended back to the Washington meetings of 1896. Just as the various clubs for black women merged into the NACW, Helen Douglass, widowed in 1895, invited the clubwomen to tour the home. The second Mrs. Douglass was a white woman and many people believed the interracial marriage led to popular opposition that created the difficulty in raising funds for the home. Others feared that relatives of Helen Douglass might claim part of the estate if and when the mortgage had been satisfied. Past alienation, future fears, and inefficient, unenthusiastic fund-raising attempts left the home as deep in debt as ever.

The current success of the national club movement provided a potential solution to the problems. The subject of the home had been discussed during the 1914 Wilberforce biennial, but the actual organization began when Talbert assumed the presidency in 1916. The Home Association requested to speak to the Baltimore delegates. After the committee explained the problem, Talbert prepared the way for the NACW assumption of responsibilities. Since most of the original committeemen had law degrees, they examined the charter granted by Congress and the will of Helen Douglass to ascertain the legality of transfer. No legal entanglements hindered the "the work of the preservation and maintenance of [Cedar Hill]."[32] A committee of five began the preparation for a national centennial celebration of Douglass's birth. This small group quickly enlarged with two committees headed by Hallie Q. Brown and Margaret M. Washington. These committees ascertained the cost of paying off the mortgage, restoring the home, and beautifying the grounds; the women decided on fifteen thousand dollars. To enhance the participation of black clubwomen in fund-raising, Talbert expanded the committee to fifty. Mrs. S. Joe Brown, president of the Iowa Federation of Colored Women, became the general chairman. For the NACW, Talbert said, "this is the psychological moment for us, as women, to show our true worth and prove that the Negro woman of to-day measures up to those strong and sainted women of our race."[33] To achieve the financial and psychological goals, Talbert led the mobilization of resources.

Newspapers, periodicals, schools, clubs, and churches became part of the NACW project. The black press provided publicity. *The Crisis* carried articles by Talbert and published a list of contributors. Since most of the clubwomen were teachers, Talbert sought their cooperation in making sure that the public schools observed the centennial of the Douglass birth, Friday, February 9, 1917. She recommended that a short program provide the basic history of Douglass and then each child should be asked to contribute one penny for the Douglass Home. By taking an active part in the redemption of the home, each child became a partner with the trustees in preserving for future generations the home of the "greatest man of our race of his time."[34] For children attending integrated schools with no formal programs, Sunday

Jane Edna Hunter, in response to difficulties she faced when she moved to Cleveland, founded the Phillis Wheatley Home to aid black women. She kept the organization independent of the direct control of the YWCA, while at the same time taking advantage of their training facilities, etc. [*The Western Reserve Historical Society.*]

The first home of the Phillis Wheatley Association (Cleveland),
1913-1918.
[*The Western Reserve Historical Society.*]

Lethia Fleming, wife of Cleveland's first black city councilman, Thomas Fleming, served on the boards of the Cleveland Home for Aged Colored People and the Phillis Wheatley Association.
[*Allen Cole Collection, The Western Reserve Historical Society.*]

The YWCA was more of a biracial than an interracial organization prior to World War I. The increased demands of the Great Migration led to an expansion of their programs. This photograph of the Brooklyn Colored Conference, taken in 1915, includes Eva Bowles (front), YWCA Executive for Colored Work.
[*YWCA of the USA, National Board Archives.*]

121

MAY B. BELCHER
War Worker
South Central Field

JOSEPHINE
PINYON
Special War Worker

EVA DEL VAKEA
BOWLES
Executive for
Colored Work

Mrs MARIA A
WILDER
War Worker
Southwestern Field

MARY E. JACKSON
Industrial Secretary

This photograph is identified in the Phillis Wheatley (Cleveland) archives as the officers of the National Association of Colored Women, 1937. Jane Edna Hunter is in the back row, second from right and Lethia Fleming is in the front row, fourth from right.
[*The Western Reserve Historical Society.*]

Facing page. This composite of five black YWCA staff members includes May B. Belcher, who helped organize the St. Louis Phyllis Wheatley YWCA, which developed the largest membership of either independent or affiliated black YWCAs by the end of 1912. Josephine Pinyon became a special worker among black students in 1912 and was involved in the Y's war effort. Eva D. Bowles, a professional social worker, shaped the role of black women in the Y as the Executive Secretary of Colored Work. Maria Wilder served as the war worker in the southwest. Mary E. Jackson, from Providence, Rhode Island, was also an organizer for the National Association of Colored Women and was the search committee's recommendation for NAACP National Secretary in 1916.
[*YWCA of the USA, National Board Archives.*]

The segregated Phillis (Phyllis) Wheatley YWCAs helped black women meet urban needs, while redefining their position within the white, evangelical association. The building pictured above is the Chicago Phyllis Wheatley Home.
[*University of Illinois at Chicago, The University Library, Department of Special Collections.*]

schools were asked to hold a memorial service on February 11, again requesting the contribution of a penny each.

To enhance the public awareness of donations, Talbert proposed to have the names of every individual or club donating over $25 inscribed on memorial tablets. Special recognition for the highest donation from an individual and a club would prove to coming generations the race loyalty of the present generation and disprove the "false accusation so long brought against us that we show no gratitude for benefactors if doing so costs dollars and cents."[35] Talbert's methods appealed to racial identity, to female pride, and to individual needs for recognition. Her methods of organization involved all levels, ages, and institutions in the black community. Through black women, Talbert reached all these groups and raised the money where the men had earlier failed. The symbolic burning of the mortgage at the 1918 biennial in Denver demonstrated what could be accomplished when black women worked together through their communities to achieve a common goal.[36]

This pride also appeared in black women's interaction with the white women's groups seeking suffrage and with the YWCA. As the movement for woman's suffrage gathered momentum during 1910-1914,[37] elite women increasingly joined the National American Woman Suffrage Association (NAWSA); the Progressive Party incorporated the issue into its program; urban political machines increased support; and black women saw the value in possessing a political tool to effect social change. From the early issues of *The Crisis*, the suffrage issue emerged as one area of social reform in which both races could benefit. The wife of the founder of the Constitution League, Mrs. John E. Milholland, opened the 1910 *The Crisis* series "Talks About Women" by inviting black women to join their "white sisters" in the suffrage crusade. Milholland charted the simultaneous growth in the black club movement and black support for woman's suffrage showing how racial and sexual progress were interconnected. W. E. B. Du Bois wrote a pamphlet on disenfranchisement for the NAWSA and addressed a Philadelphia suffrage convention. Martha Gruening, white reformer active in the newly formed NAACP, composed a resolution, presented by a black delegate, for the 1911 NAWSA Louisville convention. The resolution advised the white suffragists to express public sympathy with the common fight of blacks for justice and to recognize "it is as unjust and as undemocratic to disfranchise human beings on the ground of color as on the ground of sex."[38] Expediency concerns prevented the reading of the resolution in 1911, but the increased interest of a small group of white female reformers in racial issues and the expanded participation of black women in women's issues made the NAWSA the target for criticism about its racial policies.[39]

Before the white club movement gave its official endorsement to the suffrage amendment in 1914, black women had increased their public support of suffrage. Light-skinned black women participated in state campaigns for suffrage, as in the case of Adella Hunt Logan's work in the 1912 Ohio campaign. During the 1912 Hampton biennial, the NACW officially endorsed the suffrage issue. A few months after the biennial, *The Crisis* devoted a lengthy section of its September issue to a discussion of woman suffrage. Both Adella Logan and Mary Terrell appealed to American principles while tailoring arguments to black interests. They argued that denial of the franchise contradicted the ideals of "government by the people" and "all men are created equal." Such betrayal lessened the potential achievements of American society and damaged the American image. Female suffrage, however, could help black women achieve improvement in housing, sanitation, food purity, and justice through better political appointments for inspectors, judges, and prosecutors. The vote would also provide political negotiating power for women working with state legislatures for reformatories, larger school expenditures, and social services. No longer should the race be a victim of its environment. Politics could not be defined as outside the woman's sphere because "politics meddle constantly with her and hers."[40] Logan's arguments reflected the increased activity of clubwomen with city councils, mayors, governors, and state legislatures to improve city recreation, schools, health services, reformatories, and justice for black youth and adults.[41]

Participation in white suffrage associations increased awareness of political power. As a member of the predominantly white women's suffrage organization in Chicago, Ida Wells-Barnett saw the value of suffrage. Yet her fellow black clubwomen expressed little interest on the issue until she informed them about the "white women . . . working like beavers"[42] to restrict black suffrage in Illinois. Racial self-defense motivated the women to form the first black woman suffrage club, the Alpha Suffrage Club, on January 30, 1913. The group resolved to study, organize, and develop support for legislation and candidates helpful to the advancement of the race and the betterment of society. Led by Wells-Barnett, the club adopted a format similar to that used by literary societies, combining musical recitals, poetry readings, discussions, and lectures. The club's business produced resolutions expressing formal gratitude to white politicians for their "faithful discharge of duty in defending and protecting . . . rights . . . of the Afro-American."[43] The club offered formal support for black or white candidates and assumed public positions on political issues. It successfully worked against discriminatory legislation and helped Oscar de Priest win the position of alderman. Black women were finding local and national reasons for supporting woman suffrage.[44]

While the black women worked for women's suffrage as a tool of social justice, they brought the white suffragists into direct contact with the American dilemma of race. The suffrage parade, held during the inauguration of Woodrow Wilson in March 1913, illustrated the inconsistencies over black participation. Visitors to the capital witnessed the march of women clad in white. Leading the parade on a white horse was Inez Milholland, daughter of John E. Milholland, leading spirit of the interracial Constitution League. These "ladies" walked down Pennsylvania Avenue to demonstrate their lack of rights in a so-called democratic nation. To the hoots and insults of "hoodlums," five thousand women fought against the Washington police, cavalry troops from Fort Myer, and an uncontrollable crowd to protest their lack of voting rights and to turn public opinion toward the suffrage issue.

The "whiteness" of this parade went beyond the clothing and horse. Letters and comments from suffrage supporters throughout the country exposed white female opposition to participating with black women in the parade. Some threatened to drop out of the parade if black women marched. White female reformers as Alice Stone Blackwell, Mary Beard, Inez Milholland, Carrie Chapman Catt, and Alice Paul expressed support for black female participation. Each leader had worked with the black elite in social reform work or had a family tradition of supporting interracial concerns. Alice Stone Blackwell was the daughter of feminist-abolitionist Lucy Stone and Henry B. Blackwell, abolitionist and brother of America's pioneer female physicians, Elizabeth and Emily Blackwell. Both Mary Beard and Carrie Chapman Catt had worked with the black female elite in the New York reform community. Mary Church Terrell, although a resident of Washington, worked with both women in New York reform activities. Catt became a close friend of Terrell, who served as a frequent speaker for the National American Woman Suffrage Association, which was headed by Catt following the retirement of Susan B. Anthony in 1900. Inez Milholland, too, was active in the New York reform community with Harriet Stanton Blatch, daughter of Elizabeth Cady Stanton. Active in the Women's Trade Union League, the

127

NAACP, the National Child Labor Committee, and the Fabian Society of England, Inez Milholland supported radical causes related to women's rights and racial justice. Alice Paul, a young, highly educated Quaker woman, was also drawn to movement militance, but, unlike Milholland, Paul placed a woman's suffrage amendment above all other goals.[45]

The threat of white reaction to black participation caused a few of these liberal, though realistic, white suffrage leaders to take publicly ambivalent positions on race. The leadership of the NAWSA decided not to "encourage" black participation. Alice Paul reported to Alice Blackwell that only one black woman inquired about participation and did not sign up after all. To avoid negative reaction from southern states, the suffrage leadership decided the state organizations could determine the form of black participation. Each state handled the matter differently. Although this exclusion or segregation did not reflect official NAWSA policy, black leadership understandably remained suspicious about the attitudes of white leaders.

The actual parade included black women. Ida Wells-Barnett marched in the Illinois ranks with two white women on each side of her. Michigan and New York had black women carrying the state banners. The parade included twenty-five college students from Howard University, teachers, lecturers, physicians, actresses, writers, trained nurses, clubwomen, and an "old Mammy from Delaware."[46] These women, like their white counterparts, represented the "ladies" of the race. Carrie Clifford, founder of Cleveland's Minerva Reading Club, had been in charge of appeals to women for the Niagara Movement before becoming a leader in Washington's NAACP and Colored Woman's League. Mary E. McCoy, founder of the Detroit Twentieth Century Club and the Phillis Wheatley Home for Aged Women, marched with the author Alice Dunbar Nelson and black physicians Drs. Amanda Gray and Eva Ross. Black clubwoman Mary Church Terrell marched with black female leaders from the Washington area: Mrs. Daniel Murray, Harriet Shadd, May H. Jackson, and others.[47]

Black and white "ladies" received jeering, shoving, and insults from the masses of spectators on each side of the street. Although the crowds reflected the southern predominance of the inaugural celebrations, Carrie Clifford reported that the black women marchers received "no worse treatment from the bystanders than was accorded white women."[48] However, Bertha Campbell, another black marcher, felt that the black women received worse treatment than the white women. Perceptions in any mass demonstration are usually contradictory, based on personal experiences and perspectives. The white suffrage participants expressed appreciation for the quiet, respectful behavior of black men in the crowd.[49] The respectful behavior, however, was not a reflection of male perspectives on woman suffrage. All black men were not suffrage supporters.[50]

Although the husbands of the black female suffrage leaders were advocates of female suffrage, this does not prove greater black male support for woman suffrage than white male support.[51] Many elite, enlightened, reform-minded men of both races advocated female suffrage. Black women continued to educate black men about the need for woman suffrage. Anna Cooper complained that black men "drop[ped] back into sixteenth century logic"[52] on the woman question. Adella Hunt Logan felt female enfranchisement could "arouse the colored brother . . . [to his] duties of citizenship."[53] Kelly Miller detailed the anti-suffrage arguments in the 1915 article "The Risk of Woman Suffrage." Few black men openly agreed that a voting female was a threat to the stability of the home, family, and society,[54] but many continued to believe that married women belonged in the home, untouched by the demands and corruption of economic and political life.

The black women who worked actively for suffrage generally had supportive husbands and co-workers. W. E. B. Du Bois was an early defender of women's rights and worked for woman suffrage. Robert Terrell was "an ardent believer in woman suffrage."[55] Likewise, the husbands of Elizabeth Ross Haynes, Ida Wells-Barnett, Geraldine Trotter, Grace Nail Johnson, and Lugenia Hope were supporters of the suffrage issue. In addition to Du Bois, Robert Terrell, George E. Haynes, Ferdinand Barnett, William Monroe Trotter, James Weldon Johnson, and John Hope, black male support came from Alexander Crummell, minister and nineteenth-century intellectual leader; A. Philip Randolph, founder of the Brotherhood of Sleeping Car Porters and editor of The Messenger; T. Thomas Fortune, chief leader of the Afro-American League/Council; Benjamin Brawley, professor and proponent for black history; black politicians and appointees: John R. Lynch, L. M. Hershaw, W. H. Lewis, C. W. Anderson, Oscar de Priest, and John Hurst; NAACP organizers and leaders: William Pickens, Archibald and Francis Grimke; and author Charles Chesnutt. Black accommodationists, radicals, pragmatists, and protest leaders saw values to woman suffrage.[56]

With the cooperation of black male leadership and the support of some white female and male reformers, black women increased their support of the suffrage issue. Fannie Barrier Williams noted:

They appreciate what it means and are eagerly preparing themselves to do their whole duty. They believe that they now have an effective weapon with which to combat prejudice and discrimination of all kinds. . . . these new citizens will cultivate whatever is best in heart and mind that will enable them to meet the common tasks of life, as well as the higher responsibilities, with confidence and hope.[57]

In Washington and St. Louis, the right of black women to vote was "openly recognized"[58] by the woman suffrage movement. Harriet Ahee, president of the Pittsburgh Anna H. Shaw League, represented black women at the 1913 Philadelphia NAWSA convention. Suffrage debates even penetrated the walls of Tuskegee Institute during 1914. In a debate between Selma University and Tuskegee, the Selma debaters, defending woman suffrage, won.[59]

The growth of suffrage support penetrated other organizations with strong black female membership. The National Association of Teachers in Negro Schools officially endorsed woman suffrage. *The Crisis* devoted its August 1915 issue to "Votes for Women"; black men and women representing education, politics, literature, the arts, diplomacy, and club work contributed.[60] Unlike the September 1912 issue, which counterbalanced the viewpoints of Mary Terrell and Adella Logan with those of liberal white reformers Martha Gruening and Fannie Garrison Villard, the 1915 issue concentrated on black perspectives. Both old and new elites found reasons to advocate female enfranchisement for greater political and economic power, more justice, improved commitment to reform society, less discrimination, and greater intelligence in decision making. By January 1916, even the conservative Tuskegee Institute had emerged as a supporter of suffrage. A Tuskegee report on lynching connected lack of female enfranchisement with lynching. Those states with no female vote had "the largest record of mob rule."[61] Echoing the same arguments as the 1910 Wells-Barnett article "How Enfranchisement Stops Lynching," the Tuskegee report demonstrated how far the woman suffrage issue had penetrated black leadership by the end of 1916.[62]

The difficulties the black women encountered with white female leadership in the suffrage movement were repeated in the YWCA. As with white female settlement workers, the young, college-educated blacks in the YWCA frequently left social work after marriage. Elizabeth Ross resigned her position as the student secretary of the National Board after her marriage in 1910 to George Edmund Haynes. Cecelia Holloway, "a young college woman of exceptional ability and strong personality,"[63] replaced Ross in 1910, and when she became Mrs. Cabiniss in 1912, the position went to Josephine Pinyon.

The married women, Hunton and Haynes, returned to their YWCA work early in 1911 to provide services for young black women. In March 1911, they took over responsibility for investigating city associations and attempting to place trained secretaries in these local environments. The first graduate of the YWCA's two-year training program became part of a pool from which Haynes and Hunton made their recommendations. In addition, Hunton called on Du Bois for advice about "a college young woman—fitted physically, spiritually as well as intellectually to be College Secretary for the National Board of the YWCA."[64]

Hunton's reliance on the advice of Du Bois was paralleled by Haynes's reliance on her husband's council. George Edmund Haynes headed the department of social science at Fisk University, which began functioning during the academic year 1910-1911. Through his connections at Fisk and the New York School of Philanthropy he knew the names of all of the few black women who had received professional training. Hunton and Haynes escalated the process to meet the rapidly expanding needs of the YWCA. During the summer of 1911, three black graduates of Radcliffe, Hartshorn, and Fisk entered the National Training School in New York City to prepare for serving black women through the YWCA. Although these women's names do not appear in any lists of YWCA trainees for that year, they might be part of an undated list compiled some years later.

The city associations needed close supervision, money, and intelligent volunteers, but they continued to provide services. The New York Y provided rooms for migrating women and girls, helped to find employment, offered classwork to improve urban skills, all the while emphasizing practical Christianity. Similar programs existed at the Brooklyn Association, which found permanent employment for 110 women in 1910 and temporary work for 544. The Baltimore Association had already paid off over two-thirds of the mortgage on its building. The Norfolk Association cooperated with both Travelers' Aid and the Protective Association of Colored Women. The Norfolk programs were so effective that white social workers invited the president of the Norfolk Association, Laura E. Titus, to speak at their meeting. City associations as in St. Paul wanted trained secretaries. Most suffered from limited space and lack of personnel to meet the needs of increasing numbers of migrants. By the end of 1911, Haynes and Hunton felt the future held "very positive results in increased volunteer service . . . more enthusiastic response to the call of the secretaryship by our best-educated young women, and larger facilities in buildings and equipment."[66]

The next few years offered promise for black women in the YWCA. The NACW endorsed the work of the YWCA in 1912. That same summer, the YWCA sponsored the First Conference of Volunteer and Employed Workers. Turnover in trained personnel continued. Cecelia Holloway left at the end of the summer; Haynes and Hunton left a few months later. For these black women in leadership positions, representation in a white-dominated and white-directed Christian group was difficult. They were criticized by the black women's groups dissatisfied with the prejudices and discrimination in the local YWCAs. They tried to moderate between the black women's groups and the white leadership of the National Board of the YWCA. Gradually, sensitivity developed at the New York headquarters, but local prejudices continued to plague local efforts.

As evidence of the successful work by Hunton and Haynes and the developing sensitivity to the National Board, Eva D. Bowles became the first executive secretary of colored work in January 1913. Bowles represented everything that the YWCA sought in its workers. She was a native of Columbus, Ohio, where she graduated from Ohio State University and worked as a professional caseworker after graduating from the New York School of Philanthropy. This education and professional training, combined with her service at the Harlem YWCA, prepared her for the executive position at the national headquarters. In addition to her education, training, and experience working with Christian groups, Bowles possessed a personal ability of "gaining and holding the best wishes of the white people as easily as she does the colored."[67] This ability was crucial for black women in leadership positions during these early years.

Following the Bowles appointment, Hunton returned as a special worker. Her investigations of the local Ys led her to publish the first account of the work with black women and girls, *Beginnings Among Colored Women*, and to conclude that the "greatest need of the colored work at this time = leaders."[68] Without trained leaders, Hunton feared conflicts similar to those in Philadelphia, where "the zeal of local aspirants for the secretaryship and the clashing of members and friends"[69] prevented the organization from realizing positive goals for serving the city's black women.[70]

The need for leadership emerged during the period of expansion of local organizations attempting to meet the needs of migrating women entering cities. While some of these associations became black branches of the YWCA, others remained independent from both the National Board and local YWCAs. Local political traditions, conditions, and leadership produced contrasting patterns of social services for black women in St. Louis and Cleveland. The St. Louis Phyllis Wheatley YWCA emerged during the winter of 1911. The Cleveland Phillis Wheatley Association began around the same time, but resisted formal ties with the YWCA. (The correct spelling of Phillis Wheatley, the black female poet, was seldom used in the titles of the black YWCAs, thus most were Phyllis Wheatley YWCAs.)

St. Louis had traditions of both segregation and active participation of women in social services. The Women's Christian Association (white) began in 1868 to provide a boarding home for single working women and classes in Bible study, practical nursing, and domestic science. When the city hosted the 1904 Louisiana Purchase Centennial Exposition, girls came to the city seeking employment and pleasure. Their needs for shelter led to the founding of a home for Christian girls, which later affiliated with the National YWCA. During 1905-1906, the white YWCA actively campaigned to raise $500,000 in pledges to establish a new building and expand the services to include an Extension Department and Employment Department with boarding facilities, employment services, and home visitation. By early 1912, the new buildings, expanded services, and pressing needs made the St. Louis YWCA the largest in the world, with 7,420 members, of which 358 were black.

St. Louis black women had similar traditions in community service. Through their churches and clubs, they established aid for the poor, elderly, ill, and orphaned, as in the Old Folks Home (1902), Orphan's Home (1889), and Provident Hospital (1901-1902). Sociologist Lillian Brandt described the black female leadership in 1903 as exceptionally well-educated and responsible to the lower class. Through the Mississippi Federation of Colored Women's Clubs, the St. Louis Association of Colored Women's Clubs, and the NACW, black women stimulated social reform and provided services to the race. Through the federations or through their local clubs, the Harper's WCTU, Informal Dames, the Wednesday Afternoon Sewing Circle, and Booklovers Club, the women contributed to racial survival and advancement with their financial contributions and their personal involvement.

The St. Louis clubwomen received recognition for their programs by the NACW, which held its 1904 biennial in the city and became incorporated under Missouri law. St. Louis black clubwomen Maria L. Harrison, Mary

Ford Pitts, Susan P. Vashon, and others entertained the national clubwomen through visits to the Old Folks Home and a Grand Ball at the St. Louis Exposition. They observed that both black and white women had migrated to the city seeking opportunities. Outside of their churches and clubs, black women had few outlets for social recreation; they needed a YWCA. Although the St. Louis YWCA had over three hundred black members, they received no invitation to the dedication ceremonies or building tours held during the grand opening of the Central YWCA in May 1912. "Colored visitors" received no welcome in the YWCA. If black women wanted similar services, they would have to organize independently.[71]

Cleveland, in contrast, was a city of relatively liberal race relations and a small black community. Cleveland had a home for their aged, but lacked separate facilities for infirm and children. Small black population and integrationist traditions did not encourage the establishment of separate YWCA or YMCA facilities. As the black population increased and segregationist behaviors spread throughout the nation, racial segregation became a goal supported by white and black leaders.

The leadership and city traditions shaped different institutions for aiding black women and girls. In Cleveland, the impetus for the establishment of a working girls' home came from a "newcomer." Jane Edna Hunter had arrived from the South in May 1905. Born in South Carolina, educated at Hampton Institute and Dixie Hospital and Training School for Nurses in Virginia, Hunter came to Cleveland to work as a masseuse. Her own difficulties in finding safe lodging, suitable employment, and moral recreation made Hunter aware of the need for a home for black working women. When Hunter arrived, the favorable patterns of race relations were beginning to show signs of change. The Cleveland YWCA, actively engaged in fund-raising for a new building, was increasingly discriminatory in its admission policies and services open to black women. Until the influx of blacks after 1910, which changed the numbers and characteristics of the black community, the movement for a secular all-black institution to provide social and recreational opportunities failed until the development of the Phillis Wheatley Association in 1912.[72]

In St. Louis, black clubwomen accustomed to segregated institutions led the movement to establish an all-black association to meet the needs of black women and girls. Early in 1911, around 150 black women met in the Berea Presbyterian Church for the formation of a Colored Women's Christian Association. Most were teachers and members of the various black women's clubs throughout the city. Representing the black middle class, these women embraced the YWCA's emphasis on the family and morality.

Initially intent on forming an independent association, the black women had already established linkages with the Central YWCA. Lillian Trusdell, an associate secretary of the Central YWCA, addressed the women during this first meeting. Pearl Porter, editor of the local YWCA magazine, presented a lecture about the YWCA's work in foreign countries at a meeting of charter members in June 1911. The National Board of the YWCA received an appeal for advice from the St. Louis black women during the summer of 1911. With the approval of the Central YWCA in St. Louis, the National Board sent Elizabeth Ross Haynes to work with the women to stimulate interest and secure pledges for a black YWCA branch.

At first, the Central YWCA feared the establishment of the black branch. The white women thought the fund-raising might prove to be a double burden to many prospective donors. The board consulted an attorney to see if they could avoid the responsibility of a black branch. They feared a branch would drain potential resources from the Central Y, already overburdened by the costs of operating the newly opened buildings. Others feared attendance of both races at regional conferences and meetings. Haynes, however, advised the Central Y to make the work accomplished by the black women into a branch of the city association. The Central Board voted on December 1, 1911, to organize a black branch, "reserving to ourselves the right of supervision over them—both as to financial and general management—and that a legal contract be made to that effect."[73] A fear of separate programs lacking white control stimulated the branch approval.[74]

The Cleveland YWCA followed a different course. The fear of integration, where black girls attending YWCA functions would frighten off potential and existing white membership, motivated the Cleveland YWCA to encourage the formation of a separate black organization. The Phillis Wheatley Association emerged in 1912 from very different beginnings. Unlike the widespread support of clubwomen given to the St. Louis Phyllis Wheatley Branch, the Cleveland organization developed from a meeting of less than a dozen working women in the fall of 1911. Whereas teachers and clubwomen predominated in the St. Louis meeting at the Berea Presbyterian Church, domestic workers and nurses initiated the Cleveland meeting at the home of Hattie Harper, daughter of the presiding elder of the African Methodist Church. As with earlier reforms by black women, these working women felt the need to effect change. Jane Hunter noted, "The city government isn't going to do anything about it. The white folks have their own YWCAs and settlement houses to look after . . . how could they even know anything about the conditions which confront the Negro woman worker?"[75]

To expand the membership and support for the Working Girls' Home Association, the black working women assessed low dues of a nickel a week. The early fund-raising in the black community through concerts, meetings, donations-in-kind, and speeches raised little revenue for the proposed home. The St. Louis women also tried to raise money first in the black community. They sought to pledge one thousand members at five dollars apiece to begin their services. Although the St. Louis women appealed to a higher class of black women than did the Cleveland women, both fell short of their expectations and had to seek money from the white community. Moreover, before the Cleveland women could progress they had to persuade important segments of the black community to support the venture.

The integrationist traditions of Cleveland continued to influence the Old Guard black leaders. Accustomed to interaction with whites in politics, business, and society, the Old Guard disliked any action that would encourage segregation. The fight for a black YWCA, which began in 1906, failed during the pre–World War I period. Harry C. Smith, editor of the Cleveland *Gazette*, harangued against any activity or trend that might impede segregation. He criticized the policies of the public schools, discrimination in employment, and the establishment of separate facilities for the black community. Black clubwomen, too, opposed Hunter and her home. Seeing themselves as "the arbiters and guardians of colored society,"[76] the women emphasized the ideal view of racial relations, telling Hunter about their social interaction with the white community and about their dislike of a "newcomer" from the South trying to impose southern segregationist traditions on their city. This conflict between old and new elites was not unique to Cleveland. In Indianapolis, the attempt to convert the Young Women's Protective Association into a black branch led to opposition from the "older" group of black women and to support from the newcomers.[77]

In St. Louis, a border city with strong southern traditions, black women did not have to fight opposition in the black community. Arsania Williams, the leading voice in the St. Louis movement, had lived in the city since infancy. Her mother had been active in the community, taking girls needing assistance into her home. Like Hunter, Williams was "obsessed with what she wanted to do and what she thought should be done."[78] A product of the segregated St. Louis schools and a teacher in the black schools and a black church, Williams joined other black women operating in a separate community context.[78]

Just as Hunter had rallied co-workers, domestics and nurses, to form the Working Girls' Home, Arsania Williams rallied co-workers, teachers, church workers, and wives of prominent ministers, doctors, and educators. These prominent clubwomen used the support network of the NACW and the newly formed National Board of the YWCA to aid their efforts to establish services for black females in St. Louis. Building on these networks, Williams merged her venture into the established patterns of community and women's reforms. Hunter, the newcomer, had to create her own power base and accommodate to changing patterns of race relations. In so doing, she forged an organization that remained autonomous of the YWCA's direct control while remaining dependent on YWCA influence in money, personnel, direction, and training. Both groups of women recognized the value of self-help and separate racial institutions through which black women could develop leadership skills. Both of necessity sought the advice and counsel of white leadership in the YWCA. Through this relationship, the black women gained access to white funds and organizational expertise, while the white women felt increased control over the direction and personnel involved with the Phyllis/Phillis Wheatley organizations.

To balance the motivations of both black and white women required leadership adept at political manipulation. In this role, Hunter excelled by appealing to the self-interest of both groups. One student of Hunter's political techniques felt she "harmonized the purposes and desires of her people with the policies of her white benefactors."[80] To gain the support of the black community, Hunter held meetings with influential black ministers, who initially insisted on integrated facilities. Hunter's testimony about the immoral conditions facing young girls entering the city and about the discriminatory treatment of the white YWCA finally convinced the ministers to hold a meeting with the Board of Trustees of the YWCA, which confirmed its discouragement of black participation in YWCA activities. The ministers thereafter became active supporters of Hunter's association.

Hunter also sought the support of influential secular black leaders. She persuaded old guard leaders Walter C. Wright, secretary to the president of Nickel Plate Railroad, and Ohio Representative John P. Green to use their influence to gain community support and financial help for the Working Girls' Home. The new elite, newcomers to the city, generally supported Hunter's efforts. Products of their own racial uplift activities, they gained

137

social and economic power from the segregation permeating the major cities throughout the nation. Hunter received the support of the first black city councilman, Thomas Fleming, and his wife, Lethia Fleming. Black funeral home operators J. Walter Wills and Mrs. Elmer Boyd became Hunter's advocates. Cornelia Nickens, wife of a black physician practicing in the black community, saw the value of the association. As segregation increased in the city, even the Cleveland *Gazette* supported the activities of the Phillis Wheatley Association. Most factions of the black community recognized the changes in race relations after 1910 and supported the Phillis Wheatley as these changes became more pronounced.

To gain the support of white benefactors, nurse Hunter cultivated her contacts with wealthy white patients. Sarah C. Hills, wife of attorney Adin T. Hills, who constructed the constitution of the Phillis Wheatley Association, introduced Hunter to the influential Women's Missionary Board of the Second Presbyterian Church. From there, Hunter extended her contacts to the County Presbyterian Missionary Society. Hunter's speeches appealed for money and donations in kind to provide for the buildings and furnishings for the home. She played on the desire of these white women for efficient domestic workers. Hunter proposed to establish classes to train domestics, attributing the "root of the domestic problem to lack of interest, ambition, training, and association."[81] The home would provide black women with instruction in housekeeping, personal neatness, and domestic science while encouraging the development of personal loyalty to the employer, thereby providing white women with loyal, skilled, personable servants.

Having won the support of the old and new elites of the black community and the support of wealthy white women, Hunter moved to garner white male support. Henry A. Sherwin, president of Sherwin-Williams Paint Company, believed in racial separation and white control of social reform. His financial contribution to the Phillis Wheatley Association possessed strings that caused great embarrassment to Hunter. He agreed to contribute if a group of white women could be persuaded to advise and work with the black women in the venture. Hunter turned to the leaders of the YWCA for this help. They saw an advantage to a separate organization. Their advice and support could allow the Cleveland YWCA to overlook the National Board's guidelines established at the Asheville, North Carolina, conference in 1907, which advised white YWCAs to establish black branches whenever the black women of the community desired to organize services consistent with those of the YWCA. Through their support of the separate Phillis Wheatley

Association, the white YWCA leaders could maintain control over the local programs and leadership, while avoiding the conflicts of black participation in local, regional, and national YWCA conferences and conventions.

Hunter adjusted to the demands of her white benefactors. The original black Board of Trustees was abolished, and the white membership gained official recognition of the Phillis Wheatley Association. Hunter rationalized her accommodation, saying, "the inclusion of white members in the Board was necessary to acquire a larger range of influence and sufficient funds to carry on the work."[82] The new constitution, patterned after the constitution of the white YWCA, assured white control through its membership policies. Regular members paid dues of five dollars per year and five dollars on joining. For each five dollars of contributions, the regular member obtained one vote that could be cast in person or by proxy. Thus, wealthy whites could control the votes through their monetary contribution and would not have to interact socially to cast their ballots. Only from the regular members could trustees be selected. Associate memberships, which required annual dues of one dollar, applied more to the black community. Associate members gained the "privilege" of promoting the organization, raising money, and participating in the activities.[83]

Incorporated October 31, 1912, the Phillis Wheatley Association of Cleveland, so named because of a similar facility on Central Avenue bearing the title The Colored Working Girls Christian Home, began to provide services for black women similar to those provided white females by the Cleveland YWCA. The board of trustees included both past and present leaders of the YWCA: Mrs. Levi T. Schofield, Sarah Hills, Laura S. Goodhue, and Mrs. Henry A. Sherwin. Only John P. Green and Jane Hunter continued to represent black leadership on the board. Black support of the organization remained evident in the signatures to the constitution.[84] Mostly representatives of the new elite, the black signatories viewed the Phillis Wheatley as another facility providing service to the black community. The same leaders supported the local Urban League and the NAACP.

The white YWCA leadership retained a technical control over the Phillis Wheatley Association, but Hunter gained facilities and services through the YWCA connection. Hunter attended the National Board's Training School during the summers of 1914 and 1915. While she was away, the National Board tried to persuade the Cleveland YWCA to take on the Phillis Wheatley Association as a black branch. Eva Bowles came to Cleveland several times to aid the negotiations. Hunter, however, continually resisted assumption as a black branch. She said that only an independent association could meet the growing needs of black women. When faced with white support for branch affiliation, Hunter threatened to form another Phillis Wheatley Association, which would retain its independence. Hunter thwarted the branch movement, yet continued to attend meetings of the YWCA, gain training through the National Board Training School, and remain autonomous. The independence allowed Hunter to maintain her personal position of power in the Association and the Cleveland black community. As a branch of the YWCA, the association would have required a college-educated leader. Hunter lacked that type of education and would have faced subordination to the white central YWCA and National Board. The resistance to black branch status personally benefited Hunter.

Hunter's resistance to branch status, whether motivated by her personal desire for power or by ideological needs for black autonomy, resulted in the Cleveland Association becoming the largest Phillis Wheatley Association in less than a decade while providing lodging, parlors, cafeteria, beauty parlour, recreational center, employment department, instruction, and summer camps for black women and girls. Hunter pursued and gained a law degree from Baldwin-Wallace College to ensure her power if the association eventually became a black YWCA branch. She affiliated with the National Association of Colored Women and served as chairman of the Phillis Wheatley Department. Called the race's "most outstanding individual social worker"[85] by Mary McLeod Bethune, Hunter used the Association to provide services and a power base in the black community.[86]

A different pattern developed in St. Louis, where local volunteers and national YWCA workers broadened services to black women. During the fall of 1911, Elizabeth Ross Haynes aided the local women in raising money from the black community. These efforts gained the attention of a former St. Louis resident and YWCA board member, Louise Chapman of Detroit. To reward their self-help efforts, Chapman donated a house she owned in a black neighborhood. In honor of their benefactor, the group assumed the title Chapman Branch of the YWCA. It is unclear what discussions or activities transpired during the next few months, but by the time the national YWCA worker arrived in St. Louis in January 1912, the group had been renamed the Phyllis Wheatley Branch of the YWCA.

The national YWCA worker, May Belcher, arrived in St. Louis to "superintend the work and assist the women."[87] Educated at the University of Chicago and at Harvard University summer sessions, Belcher possessed professional skills. Although her appearance and demeanor allowed Belcher to pass for white, she remained strongly committed to her race. She sought to bring the finer aspects of life to poor, working-class black women. She taught them how to dress, manners, and responsibility to race. She related well to all groups, from wealthy whites to young YWCA workers to the women and girls served by the black branch. Not a sorority, club, or church woman, Belcher devoted herself to the YWCA. A young woman served by the Phyllis Wheatley Branch described Belcher as "a very highly cultured woman . . . [who] really knew . . . [her identity] and did wonderful work."[88] A co-worker described her as "truly a lady . . . modest . . . and a good manager who sought to develop the younger staff rather than retain total control."[89] Belcher's character and motivations contrasted sharply with those of Jane Edna Hunter.

Although Belcher had worked as a volunteer at the Brooklyn YWCA and with girls' clubs, the conditions in St. Louis surprised her. This large city had provided almost nothing for its black population. Belcher said in the March issue of *Christian Womanhood*, "there is no city that has so little for the colored girl or where her need is so great as St. Louis. . . . This field is a mountain of insufficiency . . . ripe for the YWCA."[90] Belcher felt the most urgent need was a boardinghouse to protect young women. Appealing to the readers of *Christian Womanhood*, Belcher requested donations of furniture, curtains, and anything needed to furnish the house. The Central YWCA was so concerned about its own needs, little attention went to the black branch. Belcher, aided by Arsania Williams and black church and clubwomen, shaped the programs and facilities of the branch.

The St. Louis example epitomized group self-help. The old Chapman house needed repairs and renovation; the women painted, plastered, and papered the house for the official opening on May 13, 1912. The Furnishings Committee of the Central YWCA gave the branch their castoffs. The house provided lodging for about a dozen girls. Black women volunteered to teach classes in sewing, jelly making, and canning. Experimental gardens developed in vacant lots. A small employment service placed girls in jobs. The branch provided story hours for children, held mothers' meetings, formed a choral group, and developed a library through the efforts of the Booklovers Club. The first Camp Fire Girls unit for black girls began at this branch. The Phyllis Wheatley YWCA provided black women "emotional support and validation of their middle class aspiration."[91] National YWCA workers such as Addie Hunton visited the branch and trained the volunteers. By the end of 1912, the branch had the largest membership of both the independent and affiliated black YWCAs.[92]

While the black women continued to develop services in local communities as in Cleveland and St. Louis, the National Board worked with black female leaders to clarify policies. The First Conference of Volunteer and Employed Workers in Colored Young Women's Christian Associations in Cities met in New York, June 6–9, 1912. Eight associations for black women discussed the problems and direction of "colored" YWCA work. Directed by the special "colored workers" of the National Board, the conference attempted to provide instruction, inspiration, and unification of the city associations. The workers listened to black women with experience in urban social reform. Frances R. Keyser, superintendent of the White Rose Home; Hallie Q. Brown, a former resident of the White Rose Home and current leader of the NACW; Josephine B. Bruce; and Channing H. Tobias, student secretary of the International Committee of the YMCA, delivered speeches about their experiences and presented their recommendations for Y work in urban areas.

The meeting for girls presented lectures and discussions on health, morality, hygiene, and special problems of working girls. Dr. Anna L. Brown, secretary for physical education and hygiene of the National Board; Helen Mars, physical director of the Brooklyn Association; and Dr. Verina Morton Jones, Brooklyn physician and head of the Lincoln Settlement, provided medical information. William A. Hunton, senior secretary of the Colored Men's Department of the YMCA, presented the program for black men. Representatives from centers of organized reform in Norfolk, Baltimore, Washington, Wilberforce, Philadelphia, St. Louis, Brooklyn, New York City, and Atlanta joined newcomers from Orange, New Jersey, and Gay Head, Mississippi. The women decided on "physical perfection," the development of health, hygiene, and morality, as their immediate goal. Although they lacked the funds and equipment to achieve the goal, the universal acceptance of the program enabled the YWCA to gain support of the conservative organizations in the black community.

Those conservative goals continued. The second and third conferences of black volunteer and employed workers held in Baltimore (February 6–9, 1913) and Atlanta (May 14–16, 1914) showed that the social prejudices of the YWCA continued to aggravate racial interaction. At the National Convention in Richmond, black Y workers sat in segregated seating in the balcony. The Atlanta conference echoed conservative accommodation. Booker T. Washington spoke about black progress, while doctors from Richmond,

Tuskegee, Hampton, and Nashville continued to stress health and hygiene. Speakers underlined the traditional role of women in teaching, social service, homemaking, and missionary work. Given the southern context of these meetings and the YWCA's attempt to spread organization into that geographical area, the tactics and topics upset few groups of either race.[93]

As the YWCA's black membership grew through black branches in northern and midwestern cities, the black Y workers developed new directions. At the Louisville Conference (October 14–15, 1915) "the best white and best colored women in the South"[94] met with the representatives of the black branches. Led by Eva Bowles, black women[95] made recommendations to improve the organization and operation of Y work, especially in the South. They formed the Cooperating Committee, one of the first instances in which Southern white women found themselves actively involved in a working relationship with black female leaders. The conference wanted more cooperation between city associations and branches, the development of black YWCA conferences for branch members, and a subcommittee on Colored Work in each geographical field as well as in national headquarters. To provide more trained leaders, the YWCA created a special national training course for black secretaries. Dr. Verina Morton Jones, experienced in working in the Lincoln Settlement, NAACP, and Urban League, tried to describe the ideal characteristics of black secretaries. The women should have administrative experience with the association, Christian spirit, intellectual abilities, and an appreciation of the group they are serving. The well-prepared secretary should "like a wise doctor study the needs and environment of a patient as well as the virtue of the medicine."[96] The Louisville Conference demonstrated a more confident, experienced black leadership seeking to develop more direction of Y work in black communities. But white domination continued to restrict the degree of black direction in the organization. The southern field remained under the direction of white women. Rigid by-laws existed for administering black branches. Progressive white branches had no means to bring blacks into their branches. Association publications continued to reflect white paternalism and insensitivity.[97]

A few benefits did accrue. Black women had one national colored secretary, sixteen local branches or centers, nine local paid workers, and 101 affiliated black schools by 1915. Separation offered the opportunity to function as officers, committee chairmen, and staff, positions that would have been lost in the general white-dominated membership of central Ys. Black participation and dependence on imaginative, improvised programs stimulated community involvement and concentration on realistic priorities. Yet separation continued to be a barrier to change and reinforced existing social patterns. Josephine Pinyon, one of the national black workers, felt that the distance between the races caused problems. For progress to occur, the "stubborn pride of educated colored women had to be overcome; barriers of prejudice on the part of white women had to be broken down."[98]

The YWCA was more of a biracial group than an interracial organization prior to World War I. The increased demands caused by the Great Migration led to expansion of independent and affiliated groups. In 1915, black girls slept on the porches of the St. Louis Phyllis Wheatley Branch due to overcrowding. By November they had to move to larger quarters; increased expenses and expanding needs required more involvement of the white Central YWCA. White awareness of needs, proprietary concern for the branch, more financial responsibility, and more interaction led to a closer approximation of interracial communication. By 1917, the Cleveland Phillis Wheatley had moved to larger quarters and it expanded again in 1919. In Philadelphia, Chicago, Brooklyn, and other urban areas, black branches enlarged programs and facilities to meet the needs of the ever-increasing numbers of black women entering their cities. Not until the war years did the YWCA receive recognition from and cooperative relationships with other social agencies and religious groups. As the practical expression of Christianity and service to women and girls, the YWCA gradually became an interracial organization through unintended, but not unexpected cooperation of black and white women.[99]

During the pre-war years, black women organized through clubs, suffrage associations, and the YWCA to meet the needs of their communities. When W. E. B. Du Bois spoke at Brooklyn's Lincoln Settlement in 1910, he summarized the results of black social reform: six social settlements separate from black schools, forty hospitals organized and operated by black people, over sixty orphanages and seventy-five old folks' homes, and thirty to forty YWCAs meeting the needs of black women and children.[100] More settlements, working girls' homes, reformatories, and YWCAs developed during the pre-war period. Greater professionalism, expanded services, larger facilities, and more black direction characterized these programs. These women's reforms existed simultaneously with their involvement in both the NAACP and the National Urban League. As women and as a race, black women filled many roles as they organized to improve American society.

FIVE

Black Women
and the NAACP:
Evolution of an Interracial
Protest Organization

During the decade 1910-1920, the National Association for the Advancement of Colored People emerged from a New York-based National Negro Committee representing the black elite and liberal or reform-minded white Americans into a well-organized, relatively broad-based protest organization receiving support, membership, and leadership from black communities throughout the United States. Black women played a prominent and often overlooked role in the development of the NAACP's branches, black membership, finances, and leadership.

By the end of the decade, the NAACP had developed an enlarged black membership and the origins of a national black leadership to display the organization's commitment to racial advancement. The appointment of James Weldon Johnson as national organizer in 1916 and as national secretary in 1920 established the black secretariat for the interracial organization. As the black man moved into such leadership positions, a few significant black women soon followed. Their leadership, however, depended on the grass roots organization in black communities performed by local and regional black female leaders.

The black women's role in the NAACP and earlier racial protection organizations has received little attention from historians. One could review the literature on the Afro-American League/Council, the Niagara Movement, the National Equal Rights League, the Constitution League, the National Association for the Advancement of Colored People, and the National Urban League without finding more than an occasional name of a black woman as a speaker or conference participant. This implies that black women played an insignificant role or that they did not take an active part in the development of organizations for racial progress and justice.

Neither implication is correct. Examination of autobiographies, organizational records, manuscript collections, newspaper and periodical accounts, and contemporary articles reveals that black women participated as speakers, conference participants, lobbyists, field organizers, fund-raisers, investigators, propagandists, branch or affiliate organizers, and administrators. They tapped the women's reform and community networks to anchor the organizations firmly in the black communities. In those organizations in which they played only an auxiliary role or were utilized primarily as speakers or convention representatives, black women were less successful in building such community support.

Black women entered the interracial NAACP with years of experience. The National Afro-American League had reflected the interests of the black female elite since its beginning in 1890. As with the National Association of Colored Women, the Afro-American League sought the elimination of Jim Crow transportation, reestablishment of voting rights, improvement of the justice and prison systems, and better education for blacks.

Black women began to participate more actively in the national meetings of the league after the formation of their own National Association of Colored Women in 1896. The 1898 meeting in Rochester reconstituted the league as the National Afro-American Council and elected Ida B. Wells-Barnett as secretary. The Chicago meeting in 1899 heard speeches from W. E. B. Du Bois and Mary Church Terrell and established an antilynching bureau with Wells-Barnett as its director. The black press noted the presence of both Terrell and Wells-Barnett at the Indianapolis meeting in 1900. Attendance remained small until the Louisville meeting in 1903. The Executive Committee included one black woman from each of the thirty-five states and two territories that sent delegates. This female representation led to the election of Fannie Barrier Williams as corresponding secretary; Mrs. R. Jerome Jeffrey, the national organizer for the NACW, as one of the vice presidents; and Martha V. Webster as assistant secretary. The Executive Committee included Lucy Moten, head of Miner Normal School in Washington, D.C.; Cornelia Bowen, founder of Mt. Meigs Institute; Sylvania F. Williams, president of the New Orleans Phyllis Wheatley Club; Josephine St. Pierre Ruffin; Mary E. McCoy, president of the Phyllis Wheatley Home for the Aged in Detroit; Lillian T. Fox, first black reporter for the

Indianapolis News; Nettie L. Napier; Josephine Silone-Yates; Alice Dunn Logan, club leader in Texas; and Ida Wells-Barnett. Fannie Barrier Williams, Mary Church Terrell, Nannie Burroughs, and other black women continued to deliver speeches to the national conventions through the last significant meeting in New York City in 1906.

The waning of the accommodationist approach, evident in these last meetings, stimulated the formation of a more militant organization, the Niagara Movement, started in 1905 by W. E. B. Du Bois and twenty-nine black men. Black women served in a female auxiliary of the Niagara Movement. Early in 1906, Du Bois wrote to Anna Jones, a club leader in Kansas City, Missouri, delineating the form and intent of a female auxiliary affiliated with the Niagara Movement. He suggested that Maria Baldwin, Mrs. John F. Cook, Mrs. Henry Bailey, and Mrs. Clement Morgan head a national committee. Carrie Clifford led the appeals to black women for support of the Niagara Movement, which she, at first, suggested might consider merging with the Afro-American Council. Mary White Ovington, probably the only white participant in the Niagara Movement, attributed the defeat of the Hepburn Railroad Rate Bill to the active work done by the black women of the Niagara Movement during 1906. In 1907, the Boston black women, Mrs. Morgan, Baldwin, and Mrs. George Forbes, raised money for the movement by presenting a play in Cambridge. By the latter part of 1907, the female members of the Equal Suffrage League in New York—which included Sarah Garnet, Lydia Smith, Verina Morton Jones, and others—and Addie Hunton, the national organizer for the NACW, pledged their support for the Niagara Movement and offered to help in any way they could. Black women worked diligently to aid the movement, but its organizational life was too short and too troubled.

By late 1908 and 1909, these groups were declining. Lack of money, organizational experience, and a secure organizational base, coupled with a general elitist nature in membership and issues, threatened the survival of black advancement organizations. Personal and ideological battles made stability and cooperation difficult. The black women aided the development of these early organizations through fund-raising and speech making, but even they could not make up for the basic weaknesses. In cases where the organization depended on a wide range of female talents, as with the NAACP, the black women helped to create an organization that increasingly represented the black communities.[1]

The NAACP began as a reaction to increasing racial injustice. Alarmed by the bloody race riot in Springfield, Illinois, on August 14, 1908, a small group of white reformers issued a call through Oswald Garrison Villard of the New York *Evening Post* for "all the believers in democracy to join in a national conference for the discussion of present evils, the voicing of protests, and the renewal of the struggle for civil and political liberty."[2] Sixty prominent men and women of both races signed the call.[3] Although one-third of the signers were women, only two, Ida B. Wells-Barnett and Mary Church Terrell, were black.

The female signatories had similar careers in reform and charity causes. The white women represented reform leadership in suffrage, settlement house, child labor, prison reform, pacifism, and women's labor reforms. Jane Addams, founder of the Hull House Settlement in Chicago, was the first female president of the National Conference of Charities and Corrections, a supporter of the labor movement, a peace crusader, and a leader in the National American Woman Suffrage Association. Through Hull House, Addams developed a female reform network, of full- and part-time residents, which included Florence Kelley, founder of the Consumer's League; Julia Lathrop, a lecturer at the Chicago School of Civics and Philanthropy and pioneer in occupational therapy for the insane; Sophinisba Breckinridge; Edith and Grace Abbott, Chicago women concerned with improving social services; Ellen Gates Starr, co-founder of Hull House; and pioneer public health crusader Alice Hamilton. Mary E. McDowell, a director of the University of Chicago Settlement and founder of the Women's Trade Union League (WTUL), shared a similar quest for social justice. The other leaders of the WTUL were Margaret Dreier, Leonora O'Reilly, Kate Claghorn, and Helen Marot. Jane E. Robbins, a physician concerned about public health, was the director of New York's College Settlement. Anna Garlin Spencer, a lecturer at the New York School of Philanthropy, worked for peace, temperance, woman suffrage, and labor reform. Harriet Stanton Blatch combined support of the National Consumer's League, the WTUL, and peace concerns, with her leadership of the National American Woman Suffrage Association. Another New Yorker, Fanny Garrison Villard, was a philanthropist for and participant in the National Consumer's League, New York State Suffrage Association, and later, the Woman's Peace Party. Lillian Wald, public health nurse and founder of the Henry Street Settlement in New York, came from a similar background in reform as Mary White Ovington, leader in the Consumer's League, Social Reform Club, resident of

Greenwich House, and founder of Greenpoint Settlement, a model tenement for blacks in Brooklyn. Leaders in women's education such as Mary E. Wooley, president of Mount Holyoke College, joined with wealthy white women who supported social investigation, such as Susan P. and Mrs. Rodman Wharton of Philadelphia and Helen Stokes of New York. Most of these white women signatories were educated reformers dedicated to social investigation and the organized improvement of urban conditions.[4]

Terrell and Wells-Barnett displayed similar activities. Both had participated in the Afro-American Council and the National Association of Colored Women as leaders, speakers, and local liaisons with both white and black associations. Mary Terrell, a frequent participant in the New York Social Reform Club, was one of the charter members of the Constitution League founded by John Milholland, white reformer and philanthropist, to protect the constitutional rights of black Americans. Terrell was an active speaker for woman suffrage through the National American Woman Suffrage Association. Ida Wells-Barnett, a member of the interracial Chicago women's suffrage organizations, gained recognition for her speaking, writing, and agitation in the antilynching movement both in America and abroad. Wells-Barnett worked with white female reformers from the Chicago area—including Celia Parker Wooley, founder of the Frederick Douglass Center and Jane Addams, Sophinisba Breckinridge, Florence Kelley, and others from Hull House. Both women lectured to white and black audiences about lynching and other injustices. Both also had personal contacts with white male and female reformers.[5]

Although both women supported similar goals, they represented different wings of the black movement and advocated different tactics for racial uplift. These differences were reflected in their past organizational experiences. After the National Afro-American League was reconstituted in 1898 as the National Afro-American Council (AAC), "the recognized National Negro protective organization in America,"[6] Ida Wells-Barnett became the secretary of the organization. In the Afro-American Council, Wells-Barnett reflected the anti-Booker T. Washington position long before the Boston Riot in 1903 that crystallized the opposition to the Tuskegean. At the 1898 meeting in Rochester, secretary Wells-Barnett criticized Washington's neglect of political and legal issues and his emphasis on economic progress. In 1899, following her conflicts at the NACW biennial, Wells-Barnett served as the toastmistress and a main speaker, along with Du Bois and Mary Terrell, at the Chicago convention of the Afro-American Council. As secretary, Wells-

Barnett pushed for and won the creation of an antilynching bureau, which she headed, and became part of the minority attack on Washington's philosophy.

She continued to attend meetings and participate in the AAC, but she and other "radicals" became offended by the steamroller tactics used to elect Washington supporters at the 1902 St. Paul convention. Even though the female representation increased to one-third of all delegates at the 1903 convention,[7] Wells-Barnett found little to support. Through the Chicago *Conservator*, the Barnetts criticized the Tuskegee leader. Wells-Barnett supported the views voiced by W. E. B. Du Bois in the 1903 publication, *The Souls of Black Folk*. Her own essay, "Booker T. Washington and His Critics," soon followed and proved to be her most concise appraisal and critique of Washington as a leader. She resented Washington's presenting a false public impression about the educated elite, the causes of lynching, disenfranchisement, and segregation, and the stereotyping of rural blacks as hog thieves. She blamed his leadership for the growing prejudice in the North, the limited opportunities in higher education, the restrictions in curriculum for blacks in the public schools, and the growing racial violence. Her resentment of and conflict with Booker T. Washington continued to define her rhetoric and actions in the NAACP.[8]

In contrast, Mary Church Terrell's experiences, although inconsistent depending on the issue and time, generally demonstrated public support for Booker T. Washington. Unlike Wells-Barnett, Terrell came from a privileged social and educational background as the daughter of one of the richest black families in America and a graduate of Oberlin College. She, as did other members of the black elite, supported Washington's leadership and opinions. She was referred to as "the female Booker T. Washington"[9] in the announcements of her lecture tours. Terrell had many reasons to support Washington. First, as the symbol of a black Horatio Alger, he represented the individual's struggling against the odds to attain property, position, prestige, and power. Second, Terrell received direct benefits from Washington's influence. Through him, she met Prince Henry of Prussia and her husband, Robert Terrell, received a federal appointment as a municipal judge. Washington's power through the black press, white philanthropists and reformers, and educators could aid or hinder black careers in lecturing, journalism, politics, and education.

Yet Washington's achievements and political power did not create a blind follower out of Mary Terrell. She admitted to feeling "indebted"[10] to him, but increasingly disagreed with some of his ideas and tactics. As a university graduate, she disliked his emphasis on industrial training to the exclusion of all else. She realized the necessity of industrial training, but advocated higher educational opportunities for qualified students. She resented how Washington made the highly educated appear ridiculous and felt his delineation of them "unwise and unfair."[11] As a visitor to Atlanta University and Tuskegee Institute, Terrell saw the value of both institutions and philosophies. She counted both Du Bois and Washington as her friends. Her correspondence with Du Bois demonstrated more affinity with him than with Washington, but her politically pragmatic view of race leadership allowed her to meander between protest and accommodation, depending on the audience, the context, and the goals.[12]

As race relations worsened and violence intensified, Terrell was one of those black leaders who became more open in their protest. In her lectures and articles, Terrell increased discussion of such controversial issues as suffrage, peonage, federal enforcement of antilynching laws, and racial violence. Warned by her friends not to present the graphic details of lynching, Terrell continued to deliver speeches that "incidently hinted" and "touched lightly on southern bonfires lit with living, human flesh."[13] Booker T. Washington criticized her speeches, but she continued to work for racial justice in the case of the Brownsville soldiers; criticize the white South's treatment of black domestics, farmers, and citizens; and shame black leaders who told dialect stories about the race. She felt that speaking out in a dignified, well-documented speech was necessary; silence would have been a betrayal of the race. In her diary, Terrell expressed bitter disappointment with Washington's failures to seize opportunities to improve conditions for the race. The worsening situation combined with the failure of the accommodationist approach led Terrell to shift her tactical emphasis to support more vigorous action as black opinion demonstrated a similar shift.[14]

When the Call went out to sympathetic whites and blacks throughout the country, Terrell and Wells-Barnett responded. They agreed with the Call's statement, "Silence under these conditions means tacit approval . . . Discrimination once permitted cannot be bridled."[15] By the time of the signing of the Call, both Wells-Barnett and Terrell recognized the need for a strong organization to protect the rights of black Americans. When a thousand invitations beckoned interested reformers, community leaders, and educators to the first conference of the National Negro Committee in New

York City, May 31 and June 1, 1909, the problems of black participation emerged.

Unlike the wealthy white initiators of the Call, the black male and female signatories earned their livings as teachers, journalists, lecturers, or ministers. Their ability to travel to New York City was limited. In Chicago, Jane Addams worked with Ida Wells-Barnett on a fund-raising committee to raise money to cover travel expenses for the trip. The time and expenses for travel limited participation of most black women, who possessed "no entrenched and comfortable security in even their achieved class status."[16] Aided by organizational funds and local fund-raising efforts, black participation of males and females reflected a predominance of New York-Brooklyn influence.[17]

Despite the costs, many black leaders attended the first conference with several hundred white representatives. A subcommittee of the National Negro Committee compiled a list of persons experienced in interracial cooperation to serve on the Committee of Forty on Permanent Organization.

Although the original list had not included Wells-Barnett,[18] the final list included her as well as two other black women: Mary Church Terrell and Maria Baldwin. Terrell, a fellow signatory of the Call with Wells-Barnett, was concerned about the National Negro Committee's resolution condemning Taft, but her doubts and fears did not deter her from "doing something to help remove the awful conditions which injure [the race] . . ."[19] She felt it would be a mistake to stay out of an organization simply because of the political and personal attitudes of a few members. Both Terrell and Baldwin, unlike Wells-Barnett, had experienced positive results from their reform work with white men and women. They hoped for similar results with the Committee of Forty.

All three women were well known in white reform circles and to W. E. B. Du Bois, the leading black influence in the National Negro Committee. Terrell was a well-known lecturer appearing through the Chautauqua circuit. A frequent visitor to New York City, she had established cordial relations with Oswald Garrison Villard, who encouraged her to write a book about the black woman's progress. John E. Milholland invited her to become a charter member of his Constitution League. Her appearances at Columbia, Wellesley, Oberlin, and other white institutions of higher education and at national conventions of the National Purity Congress, National Council of Women, National American Woman Suffrage Association, National Mothers' Congress, and the International Congress of Women brought Terrell into the limelight of progressive reforms. To many white reformers, Terrell was probably the most famous and respected black woman of her time.[20]

Ida Wells-Barnett had acquired an international reputation among white reformers by 1910. As the antilynching journalist and lecturer, she had traveled to England and throughout the North, describing the horrors and misconceptions about the racial violence in America. Her lectures to white audiences sought to develop public pressure for antilynching laws. But public criticisms of such white leaders as Frances Willard, head of the Women's Christian Temperance Union, and evangelist Reverend Dwight Moody, created animosity toward Wells-Barnett. Yet, she, too, had several white allies in reform circles. Jane Addams, Sophinisba Breckinridge, and Celia Parker Wooley supported and cooperated with Wells-Barnett in national and local reforms. These activities with white reformers, when tied to her national recognition as an anti-lynching crusader, made her well known to the white founders of the National Negro Committee.[21]

Maria Baldwin had less national recognition, but her prominence in Boston, an important center of radical agitation, provided influence with leading black and white reformers. As head of the Agassiz School, which catered to the children of the white elite, including children of Harvard professors, Baldwin held the "most distinguished position achieved by a person of Negro descent in the teaching world of America."[22] She was the first woman of any race to deliver the memorial address before the Brooklyn New York Institute on Washington's Birthday. Addresses to white reformers in New York and other cities and her associations with professors from Harvard and Radcliffe enhanced her reform contacts. The participation of Lincoln Steffens, Joseph Smith, Professor Charles Zueblin, William Lloyd Garrison, Jr., E. H. Clement, Moorfield Storey, and Albert Pillsbury—white Boston leaders in the National Negro Committee—suggested sufficient influence for Baldwin in active white circles.[23]

These three women also represented the active black communities working for racial advancement. Almost half the Committee of Forty came from the New York area; Boston, Chicago, and Washington, D.C., had the second largest representation with four representatives each. Although no black women represented the New York area, the three did represent Boston (Baldwin), Chicago (Wells-Barnett), and Washington (Terrell), cities that were also the original centers of the black club movement. Baldwin tied the Committee of Forty to the black leadership with a history of interracial cooperation and "elitist militancy."[24] Her friendships with Josephine Ruffin, founder of the NACW; Mary Wilson, active in charity work and wife of Butler Wilson, law graduate of Atlanta and Boston universities; Maude Trotter Steward and Geraldine Pindell Trotter, sister and wife of William Monroe Trotter, editor of the Boston *Guardian*; Agnes Adams, leader in the NACW; Mrs. Clement Morgan and Mrs. George Forbes, members of the women's auxiliary of the Niagara Movement, brought Baldwin into the inner circle of racial protest ideology demanding full equality and civil rights for blacks. Many of these women remained active in Boston social services. Geraldine Trotter devoted a great deal of her time to St. Monica's Home for elderly black women. Ruffin, Wilson, Morgan, and Forbes donated services to uplift the race in education, health care, and social interaction. For the Boston area, a contemporary observed that social services to aid the race were "composed of women."[25] The Boston women added the NAACP to their services to the race.[26]

Despite her quarrels with the female leadership in Chicago, Wells-Barnett represented Chicago on the Committee of Forty. Leaders in the female community included Fannie Barrier Williams; Mrs. L. A. Davis, founder of the Phyllis Wheatley Home; Anna E. Hudlun, organizer of a club to aid the home for the aged; Amanda Smith, founder of the orphans' home; Florence Lewis Bentley, writer of a literary column and wife of Dr. Charles Bentley; Mrs. John Jones; Martha B. Anderson; Lulu B. Shreves; Vera Green; Sadie L. Beasley; and many others. As teachers, writers, or wives of lawyers, doctors, or businessmen, these women extended their support to the new interracial organization.[27]

Terrell represented Washington, which by 1910 had become "to all intents and purposes a Southern city."[28] Prejudice had produced segregated seating in theaters; in churches, blacks occupied the back seats or gallery. Housing in good, respectable neighborhoods was increasingly difficult to find. Competent, intelligent black men and women lost employment when their racial identity became known. Despite these worsening conditions, the educated black leaders continued to work for social betterment. Black teachers—Emma Frances Merritt, founder of the Teacher's Benefit and Annuity Association, Nannie Burroughs, Anna Cooper, Lucy Moten, Amanda Bowen, and Anna Murray—joined with club leaders—Mary Cromwell, Coralie Cook, Helen Cook, Carrie Clifford, Josephine Bruce, and Mrs. S. H. Wormley—to strengthen the emerging NAACP.[29]

The Committee of Forty on Permanent Organization recommended that a National Committee of One Hundred elect an Executive Committee of thirty members from its select membership. New York clubwomen Frances R. Keyser and Maritcha R. Lyons served on the Committee of One Hundred. Together with O. M. Waller, Brooklyn physician and member of the Niagara Movement, Keyser and Lyons served on a subcommittee to select sixteen individuals to fill vacancies on the Committee of One Hundred. The influence of the black club movement was apparent in the selection of Josephine Silone-Yates, club leader from Kansas City, Missouri, and former president of the NACW (1901-1906); Carrie Clifford, club leader in Cleveland prior to the appointment of her husband, H. H. Clifford, in Washington, D.C., leader in the auxiliary of the Niagara Movement, and active in charity and social reform in the nation's capital; and Mary Talbert, clubwoman from Buffalo and president of the Empire State Federation of Colored Women. Keyser and Lyons utilized their contacts in the national club movement to expand the representation of black women in the leadership of the NAACP. Both were active in the administration of the White Rose Home in New York and so came into contact with Mary Talbert, fellow New York State Federation clubwoman active in vice and prison reform. Du Bois, who was often consulted about appointments, did not even know Mary Talbert in 1910. When asked about her in a letter, he recommended a white reformer for the post and indicated no knowledge of Talbert. Keyser, president of the New York State Federation of Colored Women's Clubs,[30] communicated regularly with Talbert, who also had held the presidency of that state federation. The hand of good luck guided the selection of Talbert, who became the president of the NACW and one of the most active national organizers during the early years of the NAACP.[31]

By the middle of 1910, black female leadership was evident in both the Executive Committee and the General Committee of the NAACP (formerly the Committee of One Hundred; though the plans called for an Executive Committee of thirty, the final list in December 1910 included twenty-one on the Executive Committee and sixty-six on the "General Committee"). Frances R. Keyser of New York, Mary Terrell of Washington, and Ida Wells-Barnett of Chicago served on Executive Committee along with five other female reformers, who had been members of the previous committees. The General Committee included not only Maria Baldwin, Mary Talbert, and Maritcha Lyons, but also a leading clubwoman from New Bedford, Massachusetts, Elizabeth Carter. The interracial organization continued to rely on the female reform network to expand black female involvement, which could then spread the philosophy, raise money, and increase membership for the NAACP. In

155

so doing, the black women assumed a significant role in creating a black-led NAACP.[32]

The black women immediately carried the NAACP into their communities. Buffalo leader Mary Talbert had the Phyllis Wheatley Club sponsor lectures by Mrs. Henry Villard and Du Bois. The Northeastern Federation of Colored Women's Clubs heard Maritcha Lyons describe the goals of the NAACP. The delegates to the Louisville biennial of the NACW heard speeches by Wells-Barnett and the executive secretary of the NAACP, Frances Blascoer. The New York State Federation of Colored Women's Clubs entertained Keyser and Blascoer, while Talbert described the NAACP's message to the National Convention of Odd Fellows in Baltimore.[33]

Lectures combined with fund-raising at the Berkeley Theatre on December 7, 1910. Mary Church Terrell discussed the social and economic progress of black women and Madame Azalia Hackley, a daughter of one of the original Fisk Jubilee Singers, entertained with her "thoroughly cultivated high soprano voice."[34] Du Bois related the details of the Pink Franklin case in which a black tenant farmer, charged with violating an agricultural contract, killed a constable who broke into Franklin's house at night. The NAACP, aided by the appeals to the governor by Mary Terrell and Frances Blascoer, was able to obtain a life sentence for Franklin, after the farmer had been sentenced to death for defending his home. Du Bois also told the audience about the NAACP's activities to form a positive public image of the race and the organization. The recital-lecture was both a financial and propaganda success.[35]

The black women participated in all the forms of proselytizing mentioned by Du Bois. They wrote articles, investigated discrimination, raised money, and developed contacts with community groups. As word of the association spread, white organizations requested speakers to present the goals of the NAACP. The second issue of The Crisis directed a call to greater participation: "The colored women have done their share in this march for progress and the betterment of their sex; but, as yet, their efforts seem to have been made principally within their own circle and among their own race. It is time now, however, that they come forward."[36] With this official encouragement, black women increasingly brought the goals of the NAACP before white organizations. Mary Terrell and Addie W. Hunton spoke to the Society of Friends and the Society of Ethical Culture. Mary Wilson presented NAACP goals in her speeches "Racial Discrimination and Segregation at the Capital" and "Race, Peace, and Brotherhood in Church." In 1911, Mary

Frances R. Keyser, New York clubwoman, served on the NAACP's National Committee of One Hundred and worked at the White Rose Home.

Terrell and Carrie Clifford represented the NAACP in presenting resolutions against lynching to President Taft. Since Terrell and Clifford were married to political appointees in Washington, they were able to use their connections to promote the NAACP resolutions reflecting principles of justice.[37]

Black women also used the columns of *The Crisis* to inform both black and white supporters about the activities of black women. Addie Hunton of the YWCA used "Women's Clubs," a regular column that began in May 1911, to chronicle social service activities of clubs and individuals. These columns not only informed the readers, but also stimulated black women to take on a greater role in the NAACP. Hunton's writings expanded articles by other such other black women as Adella Hunt Logan, Mary Terrell, Carrie Clifford, and Mary Talbert. As issues evolved, the women offered their opinions of woman's suffrage, discrimination by white reform groups, segregation in federal employment, and the female war role.[38]

Some of these same women came to the public platform to spread the message and early accomplishments of the NAACP. In 1912, Addie Hunton helped Carrie Clifford develop a committee of women to help the association in fund-raising and local speaking. They arranged for May Childs Nerney, the NAACP secretary from 1912 to 1916, to lecture to several groups in Brooklyn. Hunton served as an intermediary with the YWCA, arranging meetings for the NAACP and lectures to the YWCA leadership. At a mass meeting at Young's Casino on January 12, 1913, Hunton spoke to the audience about the NAACP and the need for active participation to fight the increasing segregation in Washington and other cities. In this and other speeches, Hunton discussed the progress of black women, a topic overlooked by the male speakers of both races and by white female reformers. Through the YWCA, reform clubs, and women's associations, Hunton cooperated with local black women to increase participation in the NAACP.[39]

Their role as speakers was important, but the most significant role played by black women during these early years was in the organization of branches. Their activities as field workers determined the ultimate survival and expansion of the NAACP in the black communities. Mary White Ovington said "Our Advancement Association would be a mere National Negro Committee but for the organized work of the women in the branches."[40]

Women's participation in branch development reflected sex roles typical of grass roots organization in other social movements.[41] Women pioneered actively during the early stages of associational development. They created mass support by spreading information and forming organizations. Once they had mobilized support in the black communities, black men received the first leadership positions opened to the race. Reflecting both the change in organizational needs following the development of a black community base and the societal discrimination against women, the black male leadership gained access to skills and networks restricted to women. As the organization began to form cooperative relationships with formal structures such as banks, courts, legislatures, and government agencies, male leadership again predominated. The women's role in the early stages, however, enabled the organization to grow and mature.

As volunteer field workers, who received commissions on the number of members enlisted and subscriptions to *The Crisis* sold, black women traveled throughout the major urban areas of the Northeast, Northwest, and Midwest. After the Amenia Conference in August 1916 and the subsequent appointment of James Weldon Johnson as national field organizer, black women penetrated fieldwork in the Southwest as Johnson penetrated the Southeast. As they built up the black membership of the NAACP, the women created the foundation from which blacks could launch their move for leadership during the postwar period. Not only did the women develop the NAACP from a National Negro Committee, but also they influenced the emergence of the NAACP as an organization *for* blacks *by* blacks.[42]

Black women participated as active, but often unofficial and unpaid, fieldworkers during the first five years, 1910 to 1915. Mary Talbert combined organizing activities for the NACW with those for the NAACP in 1913. The "first field worker,"[43] Kathryn Johnson, a public school teacher, began as an agent of *The Crisis* in Kansas City, Kansas. Her commissions on branch memberships and subscriptions barely covered her expenses, but her dedication spurred her on. During her travels in the South and the West during 1913, she reported unfavorable ground for branch development. The blacks in Texas feared organizing due to threats of violence. The high illiteracy of Louisiana blacks resulted in most never hearing about the NAACP. Johnson suggested the NAACP sponsor an educational campaign to raise the consciousness of southern blacks. Until they realized that they were "men" and "women," the NAACP would receive little support for its activities. With black pride instilled, Johnson predicted increased organizational efforts and less black reluctance to participate actively.[44]

Johnson's difficulties and successful branch development in the Northeast and the Midwest led to a concentration on those areas. Johnson's experience in the South and the Southwest was put to good use, however, in organizing and strengthening the branches in the Midwest. She relied on black women and black institutions. In 1914, she organized a branch at the Lincoln Colored Home in Springfield, Illinois. The officers were all women, reflecting the female participation in the founding and administration of homes for the aged. She had already organized a branch in St. Joseph, Missouri, and had plans for one in Des Moines when the NAACP made her role official. In February 1915, Johnson became a "reimbursed" field agent, receiving in addition to commissions on memberships and subscriptions, and one dollar per day for expenses.[45]

Johnson's career displayed many of the problems inherent in branch development. The interracial and intraracial conflicts of each community were compounded by similar conflicts in the NAACP structure itself. Johnson had organized eight branches before the summer of 1915. Most of them had white members. By the end of the summer, she had organized a branch in her hometown of Kansas City, Kansas, and had revived the "almost dead" Kansas City, Missouri, branch. In these cities of 12,000 and 31,000 blacks, she reported a great deal of antagonism to the NAACP. The editor of the black paper, Nelson Crews, held a grudge against Du Bois and the local loyalties were with the opposition. Kansas City, said Johnson, was a "BTW Center."[46] Johnson's work to increase membership in St. Louis was further frustrated by local efforts to raise funds to fight the implementation of segregation ordinances.[47]

Johnson tried to adjust her methods to the context. Her pragmatic approach, however, conflicted with NAACP directives. Her experiences had taught her that each branch had to assume its own form and direction. Some cities, such as Philadelphia, had black communities that did not want whites as their leaders. In other cases, only white leadership could produce a following. Although Johnson felt that whites should be members, a requirement of the national administration, she also felt that whites should not be "forced" into branches where blacks neither wanted them nor trusted them.[48]

Johnson utilized the black institutions to establish links with the black communities. She spoke to such organized groups as pullman porters, teachers, mail clerks, and neighborhood activists. Her speech at a black church in Alton, Illinois, brought her into conflict with a pastor of the largest black congregation, who found nothing wrong with the film *The Birth of a Nation*. Never one to evade direct confrontation, Johnson felt the minister "one of the worst degenerates in the country . . . a dope fiend . . . a white man's Negro."[49] Whereas St. Louis was used to being "Jim Crowed and disfranchised,"[50] Alton, Illinois, had no whites to stand up for the blacks in its community.

Her negative opinions did not stop Johnson from achieving success. In October 1915, the association commended her good work in the field and reported that another field agent, Nettie Asberry, newspaper editor in Tacoma, Washington, had not yet been successful in the Northwest. During the remainder of the year, Johnson worked with Mary Wilson to increase membership and branches. Johnson's success at organizing blacks, combined with her frank appraisals of people and situations, conflicted sharply with the diplomatic talents and interracial abilities of Wilson. Johnson had little faith in white direction of a black movement.[51]

Mary Wilson represented a different approach to branch organization. Coming from the interracial Boston community, Wilson was both accustomed to working with white leaders and reared in the ideology of full equality. Her marriage to attorney Butler Wilson and familiarity with the established white leadership of the NAACP made her comfortable in the social situations necessary for developing white membership. Throughout 1914, Mary Wilson traveled through Ohio, New York, and Pennsylvania to spread the word of the NAACP, delivering speeches at black churches and before clubs. She pledged members, organized branches, and informed audiences about the cases supported by the NAACP in Pittsburgh, Columbus, Springfield, Dayton, Cincinnati, Toledo, and Buffalo. Through the women's ties in the churches, she developed active support for the organization and its aims. Her Christmas 1914 message, "Race, Peace, and Brotherhood," combined the rhetoric and symbols of Christianity with the principles of the NAACP. Through the churches, Wilson sought to expand membership into the black communities and to avoid the narrow elitism of the earlier advancement groups. Her work was so effective that May Childs Nerney requested she speak to the Orange, New Jersey, branch in order to "vitalize" the branch, which had "fallen into the hands of those who care only to see their names on a letterhead or who are secretly supporting the Booker T. Washington propaganda."[52] Wilson's abilities with organizing blacks and whites continued to make her an asset to the local and national administration of the NAACP.[53]

In addition to their fieldwork during the first five years, black women helped to organize, manage, and raise funds for the local branches. Their specific roles in these branches is difficult to determine, except where their actions received attention by field-workers such as Hunton, Johnson, Talbert, or Wilson, or by the white secretaries of the NAACP, Frances Blascoer, May Childs Nerney, or Mary White Ovington. Often their contributions and activities received attention in *The Crisis* or in the reports of the annual conferences, especially when the conference was held in a city with active branches. The applications for branch admission, at first, varied in form. Some of the earliest list only names and addresses. The custom of women using their married titles further complicated identification. For example, is "Mrs. Hackley" the singer who helped raise funds for the NAACP during an event mentioned earlier in this chapter? It is known that she belonged to the Brooklyn branch, but certainty of the same identity is unclear. Also, is a "Mrs. W. T. Jones" the Brooklyn physician Verina Morton Jones, who served in the executive committee of the NAACP? It is much easier to identify a member who lists her entire name, as did Mrs. Lena Calhoun Horne, or who is married to a famous husband as in the case of Mrs. T. T. Fortune. These problems are magnified when attempting to identify women in less well-known communities.[54]

Sometimes there are indirect ways to ascertain their early role in branch organization. In southern branches, female participants are assumed to be black, since white women would not have joined. Photographs of the organizing committees of several NAACP branches include black women, but this method can only ascertain the identity of the visibly black women. Since many were able to pass as whites in reform circles, such visible identification is open to serious flaws. Cross-checks of application names with membership lists of the local and state federations of the National Association of Colored Womens' Clubs can reveal racial identity. Another method, again inadequate, compares the addresses to demographic maps detailing the black and white sections of the city. Since a few of the elite sought residence in mixed neighborhoods, this method too is unreliable. Detailed studies of local communities will have to be produced before their specific participation as founders can be accurately determined.[55]

The correspondence files, reports of the NAACP's secretary, and annual reports yield the greatest portrait of black female activity in the early branches. Most development followed "no formulated plan."[56] Some branches emerged from the local vigilance committees that existed to investigate cases of discrimination. For example, the Boston branch began as an integrated group of aristocratic sympathizers. In 1911, the NAACP held its annual

Dr. Verina Morton Jones, Brooklyn physician, served on the
NAACP's executive committee, directed the Lincoln Settlement,
and developed the YWCA hygiene programs for girls.

conference there. Maria Baldwin, Mary Wilson, Josephine St. Pierre Ruffin, and Florida Ridley reported cases of discrimination. They related the case of a Mrs. Grant, who became "dispossessed" because of her color. They told how black nurses could not find employment on the city's Floating Hospital. The employment of Dr. Thompson, a black female physician, led to white physicians threatening to resign from the New England Hospital. Baldwin discussed the "vicious" effects of housing discrimination on the character of individuals and communities. The group sought to monitor the policies and practices of social service associations. The Women's Trade Union League, Trade School for Girls, and Robert Gould Shaw House received the NAACP's scrutiny. Since the Boston women were the individuals most active in these social service organizations, one can assume that they monitored the racial policies of these three organizations. In 1912, the branch received official status when fifty-six members sought NAACP approval. Their six-person executive committee included one black woman, Maria Baldwin.[57]

The black women continued an active role in the Boston branch. While touring Ohio and Pennsylvania to organize branches and give lectures, Mary Wilson continued to help her husband, the branch president, expand activities in Boston. Her successful fund-raising, largely accomplished through parlor meetings, which threatened white participants less than mass meetings, consistently provided the NAACP with financial resources. Wilson channeled funds raised in 1914 through the Northeastern Federation of Women's Clubs. At the July 1915 meeting of the NAACP board, a resolution commended Mary Wilson for her efforts. At that same meeting, Agnes Adams of the Boston branch, reported on Boston's successful fight against *The Birth of a Nation*. A white Bostonian, Elizabeth C. Putnam, criticized William Monroe Trotter for bringing politics into the hearing against the film. She praised the testimony of Moorfield Storey, Butler Wilson, and Mary White Ovington. Wilson again received the board's praise in January 1916. She had held over 150 parlor meetings during 1915 raising money for the NAACP.[58]

Boston was not the only city association aided by black women. Late in 1912, Addie Hunton reported helping Carrie Clifford form a committee of women, from which emerged the core of female leadership in the Washington branch. The branch had to fight against proposed legislation that would worsen racial conditions and against political opportunism. With the start of 1913, the branch began an aggressive fight against the segregation that followed the election of Woodrow Wilson. When Dr. J.

Milton Waldron, pastor of the Shiloh Baptist Church and head of the Negro American Political League, attempted to use the prestige of the branch presidency for a political appointment, a faction led by black women thwarted his aims. Carrie Clifford; Julia Layton, leader in the Colored Women's League; and Charlotte Hunter mobilized a majority of the members against Waldron. They elected Clifford and the other women to administer the branch and keep it apart from partisan politics.

The election of Clifford and the others had not received official sanction from the New York headquarters. The independent action of the Clifford faction provoked internal conflict in the NAACP. Joel Spingarn, chairman of the board, disagreed with the action, while May Childs Nerney and Mary Ovington supported the move. Ovington warned Spingarn not to criticize the work of the majority, a criticism that would typify "rank paternalism"[59] of the white leadership. Nerney praised the branch for "backbone enough to act independently"[60] in the ouster of the "faker" Waldron. If the black women manipulated the Washington membership as effectively as Waldron accused, their organizational abilities displayed a great deal of political expertise and conformity to the original ideals of the NAACP.[61]

The Washington branch included the educated wives of ministers, political appointees, educators, and professionals as well as women who were accomplished in their own right: Coralie Franklin Cook, wife of George William Cook of Howard University and past superintendent of the Washington Home for Destitute Children; Helen Cook, founder of the Colored Women's League and wife of John T. Cook; Charlotte Hunter; Julia Layton; Mary Church Terrell; Nannie Burroughs, founder of the National Training School for Colored Girls; Carrie Clifford; Anna Cooper; and Dr. Sara W. Brown, one of the founders of the College Alumnae Club. The strong ties of these women to the social agencies and black institutions aided in branch development. With only 400 members in 1913, by 1915 the branch had become the largest, with 1,500 members. When Archibald Grimke headed the branch, black women helped it erase a $2,000 deficit. Mary White Ovington recalled that the women had done most of this work, having learned the necessary skills from their work in churches, where the ministers often turn to the women.[62]

The escalating discrimination in Washington occupied the energies of its NAACP branch. They utilized the legal resources of the NAACP to combat legislation to segregate streetcars, prohibit intermarriage, and limit the sale of homes in certain neighborhoods to blacks. Kelly Miller requested the branch to protest the lynching of an Anthony Crawford in South Carolina in 1916. Roscoe Conkling Bruce, assistant superintendent of the schools in Washington, requested that a committee be formed to obtain the reappointment of Susie Root Rhodes to the Washington School Board. The all-female committee chaired by Coralie Cook included the female leadership of the NAACP branch. An incident of discrimination at Goldenberg's Department Store led to plans for a consumers' league. Such a league would provide lower prices by cutting purchase costs, increase employment opportunities for blacks, and encourage further development of black business.[63]

In addition to fighting discrimination, raising money, and preventing the politicization of the branch, black women involved the NAACP in social and educational activities. Carrie Clifford's interest in children resulted in her heading the Juvenile Department. She believed that children had to learn "that all the races of mankind are one: to relate this group—which is constantly separated, segregated and divided from its fellowmen—to the human family."[64] She taught the Washington children about their humanity by providing living examples of racial excellence, by having children memorize and recite writings and speeches produced by the race, by taking the children to visit the Frederick Douglass Home at Cedar Hill, by performing race plays, and by raising money for such activities as the Anti-Lynching Fund. In an attempt to teach the children about racial accomplishments, Clifford created a game of cards with pictures, quotations, and information about leaders in journalism, public oratory, teaching, politics, literature, and science that was marketed through *The Crisis*. The women used the NAACP's resources and structure to improve the legal and political conditions for blacks in their city.[65]

Other cities in the East developed female leadership in the branches. In both Philadelphia and in New York, allegiance to the earlier-formed Constitution League produced problems. The 1913 annual conference of the NAACP was held in Philadelphia. Board members N. F. Mossell and William A. Sinclair, both physicians and administrators with Frederick Douglass Memorial Hospital, raised money to cover the expenses of the conference. Part of the money went to the Constitution League, although the NAACP had severed connection with the league earlier that year. Although the wives of the men were not involved in this effort, their fund-raising skills aided other racial institutions. *The Crisis* reported in 1916 that Gertrude Mossell of the Philadelphia branch had raised over $15,000 for the Frederick

Douglass Hospital by interesting such white philanthropists as Grace Dodge, Andrew Carnegie, Henry Phipps, Isaac Seligman, John Converse, and Mrs. Henry Villard to donate.[66]

In New York a similar problem occurred. John E. Milholland and Maritcha Lyons suggested the amalgamation of the league and the NAACP to avoid duplication and inefficiency. By December 1913, the board decided to reorganize the branch to correct the lack of purpose and stability. The national office took over the legal work and assigned the branch the task of money-raising for the New York area. In this function, black women excelled. The emergence of the Brooklyn branch was a reaction to the limited role of the New York branch. On March 31, 1914, Alice Wiley Seay, chairman of the committee to develop the Brooklyn branch, arranged for a mass meeting. The ties of Seay to the Empire State Federation of Women's Clubs and the Northeastern Federation of Women's Clubs enabled the Brooklyn branch to raise money through these groups and to disseminate the message of the NAACP through the state and the Northeast. The Brooklyn branch included many prominent black women tied to black institutions: Dr. Verina Morton Jones, head of the Lincoln Settlement; Addie Hunton, national organizer for the NACW and leader in the Brooklyn Suffrage League; Cora Horne, active in the Brooklyn Bureau of Charities, the Katy Ferguson Home, National Council of Women, NACW, and National Urban League; and Alice Seay, past president of the Northeastern Federation of Colored Women's Clubs. Little record exists of their accomplishments, but their fund-raising and speaking engagements are noted in the NAACP branch files.[67]

The women of the NAACP gradually won recognition from the male leadership. At the sixth annual conference, held in Baltimore, May 3-6, 1914, Joel Spingarn, chairman of the Board of Directors, opened the sessions praising female involvement: "in this cause as in so many other causes women have been preeminent."[68] Unlike the previous year's conference committee in Philadelphia, the Baltimore Conference Committee was headed by Baltimore black women: Lucy Diggs Slowe, graduate of Howard University, teacher in the Baltimore Colored High School, and secretary of the Baltimore branch; Jennie H. Ross; Ethel Lewis; and Margaret A. Flagg. The women described the local fight against the city segregation codes and included several female speakers for the conference sessions. In addition to Butler Wilson's delineation of "creeping racism" in New England and white reformer Dr. Katherine B. Davis's description of "The Delinquent Colored

Woman," several black women headed sessions focusing on children and the problems of black working women. Coralie F. Cook of Washington described the recent International Child's Welfare Conference, which had no black speakers, no representation from racial organizations, and mentioned the black child only twice during the entire proceedings. She urged black parents to interpret actions of discrimination to their children, rather than to try to ignore them. She urged black teachers to develop race pride, "tracing through the ages the thread woven by black hands."[69] Cook also called for efforts to achieve the loftiest standard in politics—equality of rights.[70]

The final session of the conference heard Alice Dunbar, wife of Paul Laurence Dunbar, describe "The Colored Working Woman." She refuted the idea that privileged black women belonged to a type of racial aristocracy: "We have no frivolous class."[71] The teacher, trained nurse, clerk, and stenographer served as the aristocracy. After describing the problems of black working women, Dunbar concluded, "the problem of the colored working woman is the problem of the colored child. . . . [We need] to give our children the care at home they need."[72] As in their club activities, black women brought the concerns of children, women, and the family into their activities of the NAACP.

The work in the branches in the East was more successful than developments in the Midwest, the Northwest, and the South. Much of the early work in Chicago was managed by Ida Wells-Barnett and her Negro Fellowship League. In 1910, when Frances Blascoer and William E. Walling were in Chicago trying to increase membership for the NAACP, Wells-Barnett organized the fight to aid Steve Greene, an illiterate laborer who killed a former employer in self-defense and was being extradited to Arkansas and possible lynching. Freed because of errors in the extradition papers, Green was helped to escape into Canada before the defects could be corrected. Wells-Barnett, a member of the Executive Committee of the NAACP, was not a typical representative of the Chicago branch.[73]

The Chicago branch was dominated by Booker T. Washington supporters. Jenkin Lloyd Jones, a Unitarian minister, and Julius Rosenwald, a philanthropist and major contributor to Tuskegee Institute, were quite influential during the early years. Former Niagara members Dr. Charles Bentley and Ferdinand Barnett joined liberal whites Jane Addams, Celia Parker Wooley, and Sophinisba P. Breckinridge to overcome the accommodationist financial and political influences, but by 1915 the problems still existed. The national headquarters felt the need to take direct action in the Chicago branch in order to make the local goals more in tune with national directives. The Chicago branch continued on the conservative path, gaining support from Fannie Barrier Williams and Dr. Mary F. Waring, leaders in local social welfare activities to improve health and hygiene education, homes for the aged, and settlement work. Wells-Barnett's earlier conflicts with these women and disagreement with the lack of movement in the Chicago branch led to her withdrawal from an active role in the branch. The Negro Fellowship League provided the vehicle for her protest and action.[74]

Local conditions and traditions shaped the female role in other Midwest branches. Jealousy and rivalry frustrated the development of a branch in Columbus, Ohio. The domination of black ministers in Springfield, Ohio, placed women in a subordinate role. Detroit's branch did not limit women at first. Within a few years, a Mrs. L. E. Johnson is listed as the Detroit branch's executive secretary under the presidency of Reverend R. W. Bagnall, who later took over as the director of branches at the national office.

These cities did not lack potential female leadership. St. Louis had a strong group of black female leaders, but did not develop a strong NAACP branch. May Childs Nerney attributed the difficulties to competition with the Urban League and the segregationist traditions. Both the strength of the league and the segregation went hand in hand. Black women devoted their limited resources and energies to causes that had a chance for success. In a city with a segregationist tradition, separated social welfare work through affiliates of the Urban League or the YWCA were not likely to succeed. Therefore, during the early years of the NAACP branch development in St. Louis, black women allocated their energies primarily to the Phyllis Wheatley YWCA and race institutions to help the aged, indigent, and orphaned.[75]

In contrast to the role of the St. Louis black women, the Indianapolis branch reflected almost total dominance of "a very fine lot"[76] of black women, most of whom were teachers. Rejecting the female dominance of the Indianapolis branch, men led by a Washington supporter, W. R. Valentine, sought to capture the branch and use it politically. Fearing this action, the NAACP directed the branch under the leadership of Mary E. Cable to admit men. Within a few months, however, only a few men had joined.

The female teachers lacked experience in the legal redress tactics of the NAACP. Nerney reported that they allowed several "good cases" to slip by unpursued. As teachers, however, they did excellent research work. For example, they investigated the treatment of black women in the women's prison to improve conditions for their incarcerated sisters.[77]

The leadership and experiences of the Indianapolis branch stimulated the later involvement of black women in Evansville, Indiana. There, Sallie Wyatt Stewart became a charter member and the first secretary. Stewart's reform work went beyond the NAACP, into church, business, and lodge organizations. She helped to found and/or manage day nurseries, tuberculosis programs and homes, the Phyllis Wheatley Home, and the Evansville Federation of Colored Women.[78]

In the Midwest involvement in more than one activity was common. Typical was Myrtle Cook, organizer of the Kansas City branch. Previous to her NAACP role, Cook had organized the Dorcas Club, joined the Woman's League and the Book Lovers Study Club, helped to organize the Kansas City Federation of Colored Charities, served as secretary of the Colored Children's Association, and worked as editor-manager of the NACW's *National Notes*. A teacher, YWCA worker, and active Republican Party volunteer, Cook brought years of experience in organizing and implementing reform to her NAACP work.[79]

Similar experiences were reflected in the female leadership in Iowa and Ohio. Sue M. Brown served in various leadership positions in the Des Moines branch. As founder of the Intellectual Improvement Club, Iowa Colored Women's Club, Mary B. Talbert Club, and National League of Republican Colored Women, Brown's social and political connections helped the Des Moines branch to grow and become more active in fighting discrimination.

Ohio showed a wide variation of backgrounds in the branch leadership. The branch in Wilberforce counted on the activities of Hallie Q. Brown, leader in movements for suffrage, temperance, educational reform, and clubwork. The Cleveland branch included Lethia Fleming, chairwoman of the Home for Aged Colored People, leader in the Phillis Wheatley Association, and member of the National Negro Historical Society, Urban League, and NACW; Eleanor Alexander, and Genevieve Davis. In Youngstown, most of the officers were women employed as YWCA workers, court stenographers, or homemakers. In Wellsville, the male leadership had difficulty gaining female members.[80]

In the West and the Northwest, black women helped to develop some of the branches. Nettie Asberry organized and led the branch in Tacoma. Beatrice Sumner Thompson helped to organize the branch in Denver. In

California, Mary Sanderson Grasses and Hettie S. Tilghman helped to build the Oakland and Linden branches. In Los Angeles, the NAACP received the support of Mrs. John A. Scott and Eva Buckner.[81]

The southern branch development came later and reflected patterns of patriarchy in the leadership. Yet even in the South, black women assumed an active role in the founding groups and in fund-raising. For example, in Charleston, South Carolina, the only female branch officer was Susie Dart Butler, yet the membership list of the branch application listed 81 women of the 228 members. The organizational meeting preparing the application for charter listed 11 women of 29 signatures. The branch indicated involvement in issues that aided or reflected female interests. It pushed for the employment of black women in the clothing factory at the Navy Yard and worked for the employment of black teachers in the black schools. In Columbia, South Carolina, Mrs. L. J. Rhodes and Mrs. R. T. Brooks served on the executive committee. The latter suggested female speakers for the NAACP to James Weldon Johnson. Her suggestions included Mrs. Louis F. Holmes of Florence, South Carolina, active in the modern health crusade for children; a high school teacher, Mrs. C. D. Saxon of Columbia; and Mary C. Jackson McCrorey, a former teacher at Haines Institute and currently associated with Biddle University of Charlotte, South Carolina. In addition to the branches in South Carolina, women represented over one-third of the founding members in Dallas.[82]

The female efforts as field-workers and branch participants did not lead to much participation in national administration; only a few prominent black women gained access to leadership positions. Mary Church Terrell became a member of the Board of Directors in 1912 with a term expiring in 1914. When the white journalist Mary D. Maclean died in July 1912, physician Dr. Verina Morton Jones served the remainder of her term on the board and received reappointment with a term expiring in 1918.[83]

Although black representation was small in the national headquarters, the successful growth of black branch membership was stimulating a move for greater visibility in leadership. May Childs Nerney reported the progress and problems of branch organization to the NAACP Annual Meeting in January 1916. Nerney showed how the branch membership and proportion of black members had increased and expressed hopes that soon the "whole burden" might be carried by the "victims" themselves. With such a growth in branch work, Nerney recommended the NAACP appoint a full-time field organizer to take some of the burdens away from the secretary. Before her resignation,

171

Nerney recommended Jessie Fauset and others for that position. With increased black membership and an increasing percentage of the NAACP funds coming from the black community, the organization seemed to support Nerney's recommendation for more black direction. The timing seemed conducive for a black woman to move into that position from a successful career in field organization.[84]

Several black women had achieved success in branch organization and field-work. At the annual meeting in 1916, the NAACP commended Kathryn Johnson for her successful work developing the black membership of the branches. Other black women organizers appeared before white groups for NAACP support. Mary Wilson represented the NAACP to Mary Beard's Fifth Avenue Suffrage Shop on "the Color Question."[85] Wilson accompanied Susan Elizabeth Frazier of the Brooklyn branch to try to gain the endorsements of the Empire State Federation of Women and the Northeastern Federation of Women's Clubs. Nannie Burroughs accompanied Mary Wilson to the National Conference of Charities and Corrections as representatives of the NAACP. In Chicago, the agent of *The Crisis*, Sarah Brown, addressed the Baptist Women's District Convention. The efforts of these black women not only reflected the traditional needs for white support, but also the NAACP's selection of black female leaders to fulfill the proselytizing and organizing functions.[86]

The position of national field secretary or organizer required an ability to court white favor, to present a favorable image to both black and white audiences, and to behave diplomatically in conservative or radical situations. Kathryn Johnson was unwilling or unable to court white favor and too direct in expressing her feelings about corruption and incompetence. Commended for her successful work in January 1916, Johnson no longer had a job with the NAACP by July. Both Mary White Ovington and Mary Wilson suggested to the new national secretary, Royal Freeman Nash, that Johnson lacked the "personality and intellect to interest either the more cultured members of the colored race or the white friends"[87] in the NAACP. Ovington felt the organization needed a fieldworker "whose personality is big enough to get our propaganda across before just the audiences which [denied Johnson] . . . a hearing."[88] Nash reported having heard Johnson speak to a Cleveland conference, where her favorable reception was based on "the almost exclusive blackness of those audiences and the fact that we have not over two or three strong white members in . . . Cleveland."[89] Johnson's inability to reach white liberals, her conflicts with "the most distinguished colored men and women,"[90] and her lack of tact resulted in the final insult. Nash described an interracial meeting attended by Johnson in New York City. Her appeals for funds and support made her seem to be going "after the dollars of men of large means and big affairs exactly as you would go after the dollar of a levee hand in New Orleans."[91]

Johnson's skills in organizing black branches were insufficient for a national leader. Unlike Mary Wilson, Addie Hunton, Carrie Clifford, Mary Terrell, and Mary Talbert, Kathryn Johnson was unable to either put on the "mask" or to cooperate with whites for black advancement. Unlike the other black women, Johnson came from areas with segregationist traditions; the NAACP needed someone more cosmopolitan.

As Johnson battled to save her job, the NAACP was considering candidates for the position as national organizer. Nash acknowledged the existence of five candidates prior to the Amenia Conference, August 24-26, 1916. She mentioned a white suffrage supporter who investigated the Waco lynching during the summer of 1916, Elizabeth Freeman. From other correspondence, the consideration of William Pickens, graduate of Yale University, dean of Morgan College, and former president of the Talladega College branch of the NAACP and John Hope, president of the Atlanta Baptist College (Morehouse), is evident. The other two candidates are unclear, but could have included the Nomination Committee's selection, Mary E. Jackson, and the successful candidate, James Weldon Johnson.[92]

The Amenia Conference influenced the final decision on a national organizer. The NAACP's national gathering of black leaders at the Spingarn estate in Amenia, New York sought to provide a forum for the discussion of racial problems and solutions. It was attended by moderates, radicals, and accommodationists. Mary Terrell felt the meeting represented an "effort to induce colored people of all shades and varieties of opinion to thrash out their differences and unite on some definite programs of work."[93]

Black women attended and received recognition for their role in racial advancement. Du Bois noted, "We had the women there to complete the real conference."[94] Mary Terrell, Mary Talbert, Addie Hunton, Lucy Laney, Dr. Morton Jones, Mary Wilson, and Nannie Burroughs participated. Visibly absent were the female field workers or branch leaders: Kathryn Johnson, Nettie Asberry, Mary E. Jackson, Agnes Adams, and Carrie Clifford.[95]

At the conference, James Weldon Johnson impressed Joel Spingarn with his ability to establish harmony. Johnson's performance on the panel "A Working Programme for the Future" led to Spingarn's consideration of

Johnson as national organizer. Both Spingarn and Nash realized the personal and professional attributes of Johnson and their value to the NAACP. The organization wanted to increase the black membership and develop more branches in the South, where the majority of the black population continued to reside. The organization also needed a person comfortable in situations requiring constant contact with government, legal, artistic, or church representatives. Instead of rewarding an experienced fieldworker already active in the NAACP, Spingarn chose Johnson, a man for all situations.

For Johnson to become the national organizer, however, a black woman had to be denied the position, creating an awkward, but resolvable situation. At the December 11, 1916, meeting of the board of directors, Mary White Ovington issued the "Report of the Committee on National Organizer." As chairman of the committee, Ovington recommended Mary E. Jackson for the position, beginning January 1, 1917, serving a probationary period of one year, and receiving a salary of $2,000 a year plus expenses. Board members Paul Kennady and William Sinclair moved for the approval of the committee report. After discussion, their motion lost. Sinclair then moved that the matter be laid on the table until the next meeting. His motion lost, too. Charles H. Studin then moved that James Weldon Johnson be appointed as field secretary and organizer. The recommendation was seconded and voted on, with one dissenting vote. Chairman Spingarn appointed Roy Nash to serve on a committee to contact Johnson. At the next meeting, January 8, 1917, James Weldon Johnson was present. He was voted field secretary and organizer. The wishes of the white male leadership predominated over the official committee.[96]

What advantages did James Weldon Johnson possess over the qualified black female candidates/fieldworkers? Johnson's ties with the Washington camp through his friendship with Charles W. Anderson could help unite black leadership after Washington's death. His ties with the Republican Party, acquaintance with Elihu Root, and his presidency of the New York Republican Club could help in lobbying efforts for antilynching legislation. He was a scholar, but mixed well among people of various racial, geographical, ideological, or class backgrounds. His diplomatic training coupled with his being raised in the South and his working in the northern urban areas gave Johnson adaptability and support. While Du Bois felt him an asset, Ovington found him a reactionary on the labor question, but nevertheless felt he was a good choice. Although Ovington had recommended a black woman for the position, she was not adamant in

At the 1916 Amenia Conference on the Spingarn estate, black female participants included Mary Church Terrell, Mary Talbert, Addie Hunton, Lucy Laney, Dr. Verina Morton Jones, Mary Wilson, and Nannie Burroughs. Seated in the center of this photograph are (left to right) Mary Church Terrell, Mary Talbert, William Hunton, Addie W. Hunton, and (perhaps) Lucy Laney.
[*The Library of Congress.*]

opposing Johnson's appointment. With support from Chairman Spingarn, Secretary Nash, and Du Bois, and with a lack of organized opposition, Johnson became the first black field secretary of the NAACP.[97]

Few of the capable black women could outshine Johnson's attributes. Mary E. Jackson, the recommendation of the nominating committee, had experience with labor problems through her employment with the Labor Department of Rhode Island. A close friend of Mary Wilson, Jackson had well-established contacts in the national club movement, the YWCA, and white reform circles. But as a female in the early twentieth century, Jackson lacked Johnson's access to the governmental, legal, and professional bureaucracies needed by the NAACP.

Most of the women had family or career responsibilities that could complicate their involvement in national fieldwork. Mary Terrell had to consider the tenuous position of her husband's career as the only black judge of the municipal court in Washington, D.C. As blacks lost offices under the Wilson administration, Judge Terrell required organized support for reappointment. Mary Terrell fought for her husband's political survival during the Wilson years, in which race relations deteriorated and southern white control expanded in the political structure.[98]

Priorities of husbands, homes, and other reform interests had their effects on the activities of the other potential candidates for the position. Mary Wilson aided her husband in the Boston branch while combining her social reform and fieldwork responsibilities. Nettie Asberry had home responsibilities in addition to being editor of a Tacoma paper and a field organizer. Her location in the Northwest also geographically isolated her from the center of the NAACP in New York. Even the extremely active Addie Hunton and Mary Talbert admitted to home conflicts with their limited fieldwork. Both were also active in other reforms through the YWCA, NACW, and local charities, which lessened their available time. Addie Hunton had to turn down offers to work in many community activities due to too many organizational commitments. She was able to expand her NAACP role only after resigning her YWCA role and her husband's death. Talbert took on a more active role after fulfilling her presidency of the NACW. By 1920, both Hunton and Talbert ascended to higher positions in field work in the NAACP.[99]

The appointment of James Weldon Johnson did not limit the role of black women. While Johnson focused on branch development in the Dixie district, Mary Talbert developed branches in the Southwest. As both Johnson and

Talbert penetrated the South, sudden growth resulted from the combination of organizing efforts and worsening conditions. Johnson reported that there were sixty-eight branches in the North and the West in 1916, but only three in the South: Key West, Shreveport and New Orleans. In January, 1917, Johnson began to organize in Richmond, Virginia, and additional cities in Florida. Although Johnson seldom recognized the role of women, he did mention their absence. He noted that the organizational conference in Atlanta "was unique; it was the only one in which no woman was invited to take part."[100] He also acknowledged the "supplementary work" completed by Mary Talbert in the South and Southwest. By the end of 1918, NAACP membership had increased to 43,994, of which 18,701 lived in the South and thirty-eight states held 165 branches. By the end of 1919, the NAACP had 310 branches, of which 131 were southern locals.[101]

The activities of Mary Talbert during these years illustrated many of the problems and conquests of black women in fieldwork. Travel to the South required courage and adaptability. On her return from branch work in Texas and Louisiana, Talbert wrote to John R. Shillady, newly appointed secretary of the NAACP, about her relief to be back in "God's country" after three months of rare "jim crow" privileges in the South.[102] Talbert's eighty-seven day trip carried her 7,162 miles, resulting in the formation of nine new branches in Texas and Louisiana, six campaigns to increase branch membership, and lectures to fifty-seven local groups, nineteen universities and schools, and three state conventions. Talbert estimated that she spoke to thirty-five to forty thousand people.[103]

Throughout her travels and communications, Mary Talbert used the existing female support network to advertise the NAACP. She worked in the NACW, Women's War Councils, and YWCA to get membership. The effectiveness of the personal character of female fieldwork was clearly evident in Talbert's letter of February 12, 1919. She had been invited to dinner by a wealthy, retired white couple. Since she always carried a copy of *The Crisis* with her, she showed the couple the magazine and proceeded to tell them about the antilynching fund and the NAACP. Later this couple sent her a generous check and a personal note about their interaction. Talbert advised the NAACP to do more of this type of personal work with white people. Field-workers would need more educational propaganda prepared for them to present the information effectively to potential white supporters.[104]

Field-workers like Talbert brought the NAACP into community social services. Even though the NAACP had earlier defined social service and employment areas as Urban League activities, the black women moved the NAACP closer to the communities by cooperating with such ventures. Mary Talbert helped to raise over $5,000 for a home for black working girls affiliated with Reverend Durham's church. As previously mentioned, the Charleston branch was active in employment and educational concerns. Black women frequently erased the rigid lines separating social from political-legal rights.[105]

Despite their devotion, some black women faced conflicts over their active roles in the NAACP. Talbert faced conflict in her own Buffalo branch. Described by Mary Ovington as "immensely busy and capable,"[106] Talbert was frequently unable to gain the cooperation from other branches because they felt Talbert was "getting glory out of it."[107] Talbert, herself, admitted a dislike for working where she was "not appreciated and misinterpreted."[108] At one time, she called on the diplomatic skills of James Weldon Johnson to settle the factional fights of the Salt Lake City branch so as to avoid chaos similar to her experience in Omaha. Addie Hunton complained about similar problems. Her Brooklyn branch included three female officers, Mrs. Temple Burge, Mrs. M. C. Lawton, and Miss Lillian Dodson, and suffered from "one lady with more ambition than principle . . . turning things topsy-turvy to get on the executive committee."[109] Intragroup conflict continued to plague the activities of racial and women's groups.

The successful development of black membership and finances, an achievement gained partially through the efforts of black women, led to greater black representation in NAACP leadership. James Weldon Johnson had assumed the position of acting secretary of the NAACP by 1920. Du Bois had advised the association to select a black man for that position because "no young, ambitious white man can find a career in this work."[110] As Johnson moved into that leadership role, a black woman, Addie Hunton, moved into his former position as national field organizer, a position that would frequently go to a black woman in the future. When Reverend R. W. Bagnall, formerly of the Detroit branch, took over as director of branches in 1920, the position of assistant director of branches went to a black woman with YWCA experience, Catherine D. Lealtad.

Both the black and the white leadership understood that the NAACP had reached a stage in its organizational development requiring visible black leader to display the advances made by the race within the organization and the organizational commitment to racial advancement. Black leadership could more closely reflect the interests of a black membership. By 1920, the

NAACP had moved a few black men into such positions. Following closely behind were black women. By 1920, the NAACP had become a very different organization from that started a decade earlier. From branch to national level, black women continued to contribute to the growth and maturation of the NAACP.[111]

SIX

Response to
Urbanization:
Black Women and the
National Urban League

The ten-year period from 1910 to 1920 moved thousands of black Americans into cities of the South and North. Although the process had been continuing during the entire period from 1890 to 1920, the rapid change during the final decade expanded the increasingly segregated cities of the North, creating the need for well-organized social services and professional social workers. The Urban League emerged as the principal agency handling the employment, housing, health, recreational, and adaptational problems of blacks in these cities. To become national in its program, the Urban League had to assess the social programs already in place and affiliate these voluntary associations under the league's supervision. Many of these local social welfare programs had been developed by and remained under the control of black women. The early development of the Urban League depended on the cooperation of these women and their social service organizations.

The urbanization of black Americans, when coupled with segregation and discrimination, created a need for a national response to the problems of the race. From 1890 to 1910, black movement out of the South and into the cities progressed at a steady rate. In 1890, 90.3 percent of blacks lived in the South, with 84.7 percent residing in rural areas. Within twenty years, 89 percent still remained in the South, but the rural residence had declined to 73 percent. Of those blacks living outside the South, over 60 percent lived in urban areas. In 1890, only Philadelphia ranked in the top ten urban black populations. Within ten years, New York joined Philadelphia, but the other eight remained southern cities. Clearly, the typical urban black resided in a southern or border city prior to 1910.[1]

The location of a statistical majority was not as important as proximity to reform and philanthropic centers. New York had a high black population combined with a myriad of philanthropic and protective organizations developed to meet the needs of the ever-expanding waves of immigrants arriving from Europe. Social services adapted to meet the needs of migrating blacks seeking the promise of northern life. The New York Colored Mission, originally founded by Quakers, expanded to meet the social and economic needs of the black community. St. Cyprian's on San Juan Hill became more responsive to the employment and recreational needs. Settlement houses set up branches to serve the black communities. White reformers and settlement house workers became more concerned about racial discrimination.[2]

As the radical black leadership joined together in the Niagara Movement, racial reformers established two New York-centered organizations dedicated to the study and correction of urban conditions affecting black Americans. In 1905, the Inter-Municipal Committee on Household Research established information bureaus in New York, Boston, and Philadelphia. Under the direction of white social investigator Frances A. Kellor, the Inter-Municipal Committee expanded from its origins as a source of information about employment bureaus, job opportunities, recreational centers, and boarding facilities, to an association to protect black women coming to the cities. In 1906, the association became the National League for the Protection of Colored Women (NLPCW), which sought to spread the programs available in New York, Philadelphia, and a few other cities to a national level. These two organizations anticipated the work of the Urban League.[3]

The employment problems facing blacks in New York City stimulated a group of white reformers, businessmen, and philanthropists to join black leaders in education, journalism, and business to form the Committee for Improving the Industrial Condition of Negroes in New York (CIICN) in May 1906. As with the NLPCW, the CIICN attempted to discourage migration to the North and to make those already in the city aware of available vocational opportunities and industrial education. Although both organizations cooperated with Philadelphia's Armstrong Association, New York's White Rose Home, and other local social service agencies, the lack of a permanent, paid, professional staff, absence of consistent fund-raising, and narrowness of organizational goals limited their achievements. Their presence, personnel, and programs aided the development of the Committee on Urban Conditions Among Negroes in 1910, which laid the foundation for the National Urban League in 1911.[4] The NLPCW, CIICN, and Committee on Urban Conditions Among Negroes consolidated their services in 1911 under the title, the National League on Urban Conditions Among Negroes.[5]

Black women continued to deliver services under the auspices of the Committee for the Protection of Women. They spread the information about northern life and requirements for migration through their institutions in the South. Volunteers investigated and sought improvement of the conditions for women on steamers. Agents continued to meet boats and "provide direction, relief, recovery of baggage, and protection from unscrupulous men."[6] Miss E. G. Burleigh in New York and Mrs. H. A. V. Proctor and Ida Bagnall in Norfolk served as agents in 1913. In Richmond, Ora B. Stokes served as a founder and supporter of both the NLPCW and, later, the National Urban League. Eventually, the dock work was turned over to the Travelers' Aid Society to avoid duplication of services.[7]

In the National League on Urban Conditions (Urban League), black women sponsored social clubs, recreational activities, and training programs. In New York, the women developed a child nursing program for black girls over the age of sixteen. Coming to the Lincoln Hospital and Home, the girls received instruction in child care and a certificate for their completion of the course. Black women started cobbling classes at the White Rose Home to improve employment opportunities in shoe repair. Through the league's cooperation with the Big Sister Program, black women implemented guidance counseling for girls growing up in the urban environment. Juveniles coming into the Children's Court received support from black female probation officers or from private black homeowners who cared for and supervised children placed there by the court due to overcrowding in the reformatories. Black community women helped the Urban League raise money for such racial services as the Sojourner Truth House, the Howard Orphan Asylum, the Harlem Neighborhood Club, and the Amusement Club of New York City. They organized mothers' clubs, campaigned for improved working conditions for black domestics, and worked on issues that benefited their neighborhoods. Although most of these women remain anonymous through official records and reports of the Urban League, their services enabled the league to make direct contact with urban populations.[8]

The black women developed these services and implemented such programs at the very time when black migration stressed available programs in the urban areas. The demographic changes between 1910 and 1920 demonstrate the impact of black migration. In 1910, Washington continued to attract large numbers. It continued to have the largest black urban population. New York increased its black population, making it second highest, followed by New Orleans, Baltimore, and Philadelphia. Although Chicago ranked eighth in 1910, the rapid influx of black migrants brought the city to fourth position by 1920. Only New York, Philadelphia, and Washington had higher black populations.

A similar though not as massive urbanization occurred in such southern cities as Memphis, Louisville, Atlanta, Charleston, and Savannah. Smaller cities in the Midwest and North underwent high percentage changes from 1910 to 1920. Detroit's black population expanded by 623 percent, Cleveland's by 308 percent, and Gary, Indiana's, by 1,284 percent. Similar growth occurred in Boston, St. Louis, and Cincinnati. By 1920, almost 85 percent of non-southern blacks were city dwellers, while southern urbanization accounted for over 25 percent of the black population.[9]

These "roving men and homeless women"[10] encountered hostility from existing black populations as well as increased racism and segregation on the part of white society. In New York, the newcomers were referred to as riff-raff, lazy, boastful, and creators of problems. They lived in tenements and alleys, created race fights, and encouraged vice.[11] In Boston and Cleveland, cities with relatively amicable race relations, the influx created a muted racism, unlike the blatant forms of discrimination and segregation that occurred in Indianapolis and Chicago.[12] While the Chicago newcomers were characterized as confused, unprepared people from the South who were continually taken advantage of by taxi drivers and lodging housekeepers, those in Boston were stereotyped as the "illiterate, shiftless, semi-vicious sort."[13] Whatever the city, the newcomers were always received unfavorably.

Black migration created social problems that concerned the Urban League. Jobs, family disintegration, wages, crime, housing, health, corruption, education, and recreation were all tied to rapid urbanization. The Urban League directed its efforts to improving the conditions facing the urban areas of the North and South. Dependent on the local social context for support, the programs varied in approach and goals. Affiliates grew as did the urban areas that each local league represented. In industrial centers like Chicago, Pittsburgh, Columbus, Detroit, Cleveland, Newark, and Milwaukee, labor concerns became a priority. The resulting difficulty in housing, sanitation, education, employment, recreation, and travelers' aid utilized the Urban

League's professional staff to survey conditions and ascertain the availability of programs capable of dealing with the problems. In the urban South, labor concerns were deliberately underplayed, giving health, recreational, and educational concerns priority. In both regions, however, the Urban League depended heavily on the existing social services and reform networks developed by black women.[14]

A close examination of the Urban League's entrance into the social service arena in Chicago and in Atlanta can provide a comparison between programs, leadership, and developments in northern and southern communities. Eugene Kinckle Jones, the first full-time secretary for the Committee on Urban Conditions, came to cities to survey conditions and ascertain the availability of necessary programs. To avoid duplication of services and competition with local organizations, the league tried to make use of established programs and institutions, many of which had been initiated and maintained by black women. Since many of these services depended on the meager resources of the black community, not all individuals or groups welcomed the entrance of the Urban League. The reception by black women ranged from total support to jealousy, resentment, or suspicion. Both Chicago and Atlanta illustrate the variety of responses.

In Chicago, the Urban League began at the height of the black migration. The conservative leadership of the Chicago black community supported the league's establishment. The white supporters, too, favored the practical reforms of the league over the "idealistic" goals of the radical protest leaders. Dr. George Cleveland Hall, the personal physician and a supporter of Booker T. Washington and head of Provident Hospital, used his connections as chairman of the YMCA board and president of the Frederick Douglass Center to anchor the Urban League in Chicago. The league started at the Wabash Avenue YMCA, but soon Hall was able to obtain the entire first floor of the three-story Douglass Center as headquarters.[15]

Hall's direction and support were not enough. The support of black women as community liaisons and fund-raisers helped the Chicago Urban League to survive and expand its services. According to one historian, the women's groups "made the most enthusiastic response"[16] to the league's appeals for financial and moral support. Irene McCoy Gaines turned in the first memberships from the black community. The Chicago Federation of Colored Women's Clubs became one of the first groups to endorse the league. The largest single contribution from a black group came from the two thousand members of the Baptist Women's Congress. Women from the

Wendell Phillips Settlement, local NAACP, State Federation of Colored Women's Clubs, Frederick Douglass Center, the Social Service Round Table, and black churches actively promoted the programs and cooperated with the league. A group of thirty women became the "Urban League Volunteers" under the supervision of a league worker. The league, in turn, helped to develop the professional social work in the black institutions. The services at the Wendell Phillips Settlement received supervision and development by the Urban League; the Douglass Center shared personnel and equipment.[17]

Not only did black women support the Urban League in their organizations, they also helped as individuals. Mrs. William Carey, president of the Baptist Women's Congress, became the director of the Chicago Urban League. Women's club leaders Joanna Snowden-Porter, Elizabeth L. Davis, Jesse Johnson, and Bertha Mosely served as representatives on the board of directors or as organizers. Jennie E. Lawrence, superintendent of the Phyllis Wheatley Home, cooperated with the league in an effort to extend services. Since the league's programs built on the social service areas traditionally developed by black women through churches or clubs, black women's groups supported the league's efforts to develop cleaner streets and homes, improve personal hygiene and deportment, and adapt to the norms of urban life. By improving the urban environment, the black women felt that the Urban League gave blacks "a chance to make [their] social, economic, and political status what the status of an American citizen ought to be."[18] Since both the league and black women's organizations worked in the same social service areas, most black women's groups supported the league.[19]

The league's emphasis on negotiation and persuasion to improve urban conditions for blacks received favorable responses from Chicago's social reform, business, and philanthropic groups. White female reformers Sophinisba P. Breckinridge, Edith Abbott, Amelia Sears, Celia Parker Wooley, and Jane Addams used their connections with the University of Chicago, Chicago School of Civics and Philanthropy, Juvenile Protective Association, and settlement houses to integrate the Urban League into the reform community.

White financial contributions allowed the Urban League to become established and professionalize its services. The contributions of Julius Rosenwald enabled the Chicago Urban League to meet the expenses for the first few years, while donations from other white business and professional groups aided expansion of programs. These white contributions accounted for 90 percent of the league's budget, while blacks accounted for 75 percent of the members. This reliance on white contributions allowed the league to professionalize urban social services. The large black membership, on the other hand, led to direct black influence in the delivery of services to the black community.[20]

Not all members of the black community embraced the Urban League. To Ida Wells-Barnett, the Urban League had studied her own methods of social work and then sought to displace her Negro Fellowship League in the direct delivery of social services to the black male migrants. As the originator of the Negro Fellowship League Reading Room and Social Center, Wells-Barnett jealously protected her domain from infringement by the Urban League and its pro-Washington supporters.

The Negro Fellowship League had emerged from Wells-Barnett's Bible study classes at Grace Presbyterian Church. The discussions moved to Wells-Barnett's home on Sunday afternoons around 1908. Gradually, the group of young men went beyond discussion to investigation of social problems and visitation of prisons and other institutions for firsthand information. The investigative journalism of Wells-Barnett had rubbed off on her prodigies.

As more blacks moved to Chicago, existing facilities became more discriminatory in their programs and policies. Wells-Barnett sought to provide the same type of service offered through settlements, YMCAs, and YWCAs to black migrants who could not afford or were unwelcome at the white-dominated facilities. She persuaded Victor F. Lawson, publisher of the Chicago *Daily News*, and his wife to withdraw their contributions from the YMCA until that organization provided services to the black population. They agreed to give Wells-Barnett money for the development of the Negro Fellowship League Reading Room and Social Center if she would keep their contribution anonymous.

Opened in May 1910, the center provided many of the services traditionally available in the local YMCAs. The first secretary had experience in YMCA work in Georgia. He visited the local poolrooms and saloons attempting to persuade the "lower types" to visit the center. As more migrants came to the city, Wells-Barnett expanded the services. She had a worker meet migrants at the Illinois Central Station. She provided temporary shelter for those seeking employment in a men's lodging house above the center. Downstairs, the center helped the men learn to read, provided space for playing checkers, and guided men through the job hunting process. By the end of the first year, the center had taught forty to fifty men how to read and placed 115 men in jobs.

The breadth and regularity of services of the Negro Fellowship League Center depended on the contributions of a few white donors and on the personal direction of Wells-Barnett. When the black YMCA reached completion, the Lawson donation reverted to that institution. Wells-Barnett moved to smaller facilities, contributed more of her own time and finances, and decreased some of the services. She sought funding from Julius Rosenwald, but her personal direction of the center became a liability. Wells-Barnett met with the head of the Rosenwald investigating committee, Paul J. Sachs, cousin of Julius Rosenwald and member of the Urban League's executive board. Sachs had been responsible for interesting Rosenwald in black issues after meeting Booker T. Washington in 1911. During the interview with Sachs, Wells-Barnett responded to his comments about Washington's jokes about chicken-stealing southern blacks. Wells-Barnett asked Sachs how he would feel if Rabbi Hirsh made similar jokes about Jews who burned down their buildings for insurance. Such direct responses did not raise funds for the center.[21]

Wells-Barnett viewed the Urban League's entrance into the Chicago community with suspicion. She was not one of its early supporters and on more than one occasion came into conflict with its leadership, due to competition and differences with its pro-Washington leadership. Dr. George Cleveland Hall, a leader of the league, received the Lawson contribution for the new black YMCA, for which he served as the chairman of the board. Wells-Barnett's Negro Fellowship League had lost Lawson's largess to her pro-Washington competitors. The conservative Chicago leadership opposed most of Wells-Barnett's efforts to raise money or support for protest action. She became more directly resentful of the Urban League's intrusion when police halted the representative of the Fellowship League from meeting the migrants at the train depots. The Travelers' Aid Society objected to the Fellowship League's duplication of its services and received the blessing to maintain control over the activity from T. Arnold Hill, the National Urban League's organizer for the western field and executive secretary of the Chicago Urban League. Later, Wells-Barnett disagreed with the Urban League over the placement of children left homeless by a fire at the Amanda Smith Home. Wells-Barnett wanted the children housed at the Frederick Douglass Center. Instead the league placed them in private homes. Wells-Barnett saw the Urban League as a conservative social welfare agency seeking to take over services provided by her center. Its reliance on persuasion and negotiation and dependence on conservative white philanthropy were very different from Wells-Barnett's confrontation and protest tactics and cooperation with white reformers. Both Wells-Barnett and the pro-Washington leadership had to gain funds and support from overlapping circles. The two groups would have to cooperate, or one side would fail. Since Wells-Barnett found cooperation impossible, she pursued her own goals outside of established organizations and channels. Eventually this lonely path would cause her organizations to fail.[22]

Women in other cities of the North aided the Urban League in delivering services to local black communities. The Utopia Neighborhood Club stimulated interest in the Sojourner Truth Home in New York. The club organized day excursions, health week campaigns, playgrounds, and Big Sister work for girls appearing before the Children's Court. In Philadelphia, the women cooperated with the churches in mission and friendly visitor work. Black women created a "Baby Saving Show" to improve the care of newborns. Delinquent girls and women received aid through the Court Aid Committee. The black women in White Plains, New York, raised funds and helped administer the Valley Rest Convalescent Home for Women. Detroit women in the Dress Well Club taught urban migrants about dress and decorum, while the New Comers Community Dance established socially acceptable contacts. Chicago clubwomen conducted house-to-house visitations to inspect the accommodations and added a day nursery to the Wendell Phillips Settlement to aid working mothers. Stressing instruction and investigation, the northern black women aided black adaptation to the urban environments.[23]

Southern racial attitudes affected the leadership and programs of the Urban League affiliates in that region. Many of the pre-World War I affiliates had totally black membership. The conservative southern philosophy supported programs patterned after settlement house work rather than emphasis on employment and labor conditions, as in the northern branches. The Urban League sought expansion in cities with high black populations: Savannah, Atlanta, Augusta, Birmingham, Nashville, Memphis, Chattanooga, and border areas such as St. Louis and Baltimore. In cities with conservative leadership, the league frequently gained a foothold through supporters of Booker T. Washington. In St. Louis, for example, Roger Baldwin's leadership of influential whites interested in Washington's types of reform produced an active affiliate.[24]

In the South, black women continued to influence the success of affiliates and programs. In 1911-1912, St. Louis women helped to develop facilities for feeble-minded and epileptics and worked for state assistance for tubercular patients. The next year they helped to defeat a city ordinance segregating residential areas. In Norfolk the Urban League women cooperated with the local YWCA to inform and aid travelers as they had done earlier through the National League for the Protection of Colored Women. The Richmond Neighborhood Association became an affiliate in June 1913, to continue caring for neglected black children. As an Urban League affiliate, the Richmond group organized Camp Fire Girls for black girls; participated in clean-up campaigns, travelers' aid, and vice regulation; and purchased and disseminated literature on health and morality.

Similar efforts expanded in other southern cities. In 1916, the league women worked at a Poor Farm in Savannah. The women in the Nashville League aided the Bethlehem Settlement House's domestic science classes, kindergarten, sewing school, public lectures, and Camp Fire Girls. Women in Augusta cooperated with the league's clean-up campaigns and temperance work. When the Nashville Public Welfare League assumed the Juvenile Court work previously done by the black women, the women continued their interest in children through the newly organized Big Sister program and in adults through the employment bureau at the Bethlehem House. Their Urban League activities resembled the social service work of the black women's clubs—helping dependent children, teaching domestic skills, and generally improving the health and hygiene of the black community.[25]

Of all the programs in the South, one of the most successful belonged to Atlanta. As in Chicago, the Urban League tried to affiliate successful local social service agencies under its direction. When the league sought the affiliation of the Atlanta Neighborhood Union, the suggestion received mixed reactions. Lugenia Hope, the founding spirit of the Neighborhood Union, felt that the league was trying to gather up existing institutions. She had developed a well-organized institution to meet the changing needs of the Atlanta black community. She feared the league's direction of the programs of the Neighborhood Union and the possibility that the league would accept the credit for accomplishments gained by a small group of dedicated black women. At first, the Neighborhood Union resisted affiliation. But as Hope saw the local autonomy allowed the affiliates, her reservations subsided. The Neighborhood Union became one of the strongest and most influential of the southern affiliates.[26]

The Neighborhood Union fit well into the settlement-like pattern of southern Urban League affiliates. Familiar with Hull House and Jane Addams in Chicago, Lugenia Hope used her Chicago experiences and commitment to urban reform when she moved to Atlanta with her husband, John Hope. As with the Urban League, Hope and the Neighborhood Union expressed concern for the children roaming the streets, ill-clothed and unfed while parents worked all day to provide for them. The poor housing and extreme poverty produced crime, vice, and health problems. Appealing to the elite's self-interest in reducing crime and disease, Hope gained white cooperation in clean-up campaigns, educational improvements, health lectures, and recreational activities.

The Neighborhood Union sought to professionalize social work. Hope's efficient manner of organizing community investigations depended heavily on the sociology department of Morehouse College. Groups of sociologists trained the volunteer women of the Neighborhood Union in survey and investigative techniques. Hope divided the city into zones and districts, with leaders selected by the union and endorsed by district residents. She accomplished democracy and efficiency simultaneously; the local community problems became known to the neighborhood social workers while giving the community a feeling "that it is their very own."[27] These methods not only enhanced the programs in Atlanta, but, through the Urban League, were disseminated to affiliates throughout the country. Similar organizations emerged in Jacksonville and Tallahassee[28]

Unlike Wells-Barnett in Chicago, Hope's experience with intra- and intergroup cooperation enabled her to find advantages in affiliation with the Urban League. Hope built neighborhood programs with whatever means were available. She identified strongly with the Atlanta Neighborhood Union, but she chose organizational survival over personal control. In making this choice, Hope continued to retain direction of the Neighborhood Union while spreading the influence through the black women's clubs, the YWCA, and the Urban League. Hope displayed "patient militance,"[29] while Wells-Barnett evidenced the opposite. During the Progressive Era, patience mixed with commitment and tenacity gradually produced results.[30]

Through the Urban League, the influence of the Neighborhood Union spread. Louisville's Committee on Neighborhood Improvement, headed by Georgia Nugent, utilized methods and programs similar to Hope's. By 1916, the Urban League told of a unit plan of social work to be used in the cities. Recommending the zone-neighborhood-district organization developed by the Neighborhood Union, the Urban League facilitated the spread of black social work based on the Hope model. By 1917, Eugene Kinckle Jones provided

191

The Atlanta Neighborhood Union purchased this house (Holman Home)
in 1915 to serve as the center for its diverse social services.
[*Atlanta University Archives.*]

The alliance with Atlanta University's sociology department helped the Atlanta Neighborhood Union develop scientific methods to ascertain community needs. Here Lugenia Burns Hope and John Hope pose with graduates of the Atlanta School of Social Work.
[*Atlanta University Archives.*]

the names and addresses of other Urban League affiliates so that Hope could offer advice more directly. In this way, Hope and her Neighborhood Union went on to influence social services in Philadelphia, Newark, Norfolk, Louisville, Tallahassee, Jacksonville, and many other cities that turned to the Urban League for advice or cooperation.[31]

The Neighborhood Union's inspection of the public schools, petitioning for improvements in schools and city neighborhoods, and organization of neighborhood gatherings, vacation Bible schools, anti-tuberculosis work, clubs, and neighborhood beautification campaigns received much attention in the Annual Reports of the Urban League. Finally, in 1920, the interracial cooperation of the Neighborhood Union and its leadership received the commendation of the Urban League. Advocating similar "Atlanta Plans" for other affiliates, the league sought to encourage efforts to "bring together forward looking white and colored for frequent conferences on mutual problems."[32] The Neighborhood Union's skills in developing publicity, completing surveys, and cooperating with other organizations, colleges, and industries, led to Atlanta becoming a major success story among Urban League affiliates.[33]

Most of the affiliates were not as successful as the Atlanta Neighborhood Union, but several reflected the grass roots leadership of black women. Lucy Laney of Haines Institute served as the executive secretary of the Urban League affiliate, the Colored Civic Improvement League in Augusta. Mrs. S. W. Layton headed the Philadelphia Association for the Protection of Colored Women. Almost half the members of the executive board of the Urban League of Greater Boston were women. Mrs. Clement Morgan and Maria Baldwin combined their activities through both the Urban League and the NAACP. Black women helped the Boston Urban League through their work with the Abraham Lincoln Settlement, YWCA, Baby Hygiene Association, Church Home Society, Boston Society for the Care of Girls, Children's Aid Society, Harriet Tubman Home, Home for Aged Women, Robert Gould Shaw House, Episcopal Mission Work Among Colored People, and Girls' Trade School. The New York League's female leadership included Cecelia Cabiniss-Saunders, an early worker for the YWCA; Adah B. Thoms, head of the Colored Graduate Nurses Association; and Mrs. E. P. Roberts, active in the New York War Relief Association. Catherine Lealtad, former YWCA secretary, served as the associate secretary of the New York branch of the Urban League. In these and other affiliates, black women served in local leadership roles.[34]

Few black women worked their way up in the Urban League to national administration. Most of those who achieved positions on the National Executive Board or served on organizational committees did so because their membership served to benefit the organizations. In 1915, both Lugenia Hope and Maggie Lena Walker served as advisers to local affiliates through the national Membership Committee. As director of the Neighborhood Union and wife of the president of Morehouse College, Hope could help increase support and membership in both black and white circles of southern educational and club groups. Walker's leadership of the St. Luke Penny Savings Bank, presidency of the Virginia Federation of Colored Women's Clubs, church and fraternal order associations, and membership on the biracial Board of Trustees of the Virginia Industrial School for Colored Girls provided significant connections for the Urban League in Richmond and other urban areas. Her financial and community work made Walker a valuable advisor for a northern-based social service organization.[35]

The influence of Booker T. Washington remained on the National Executive Board. Margaret Murray Washington completed the remainder of her husband's term after his death late in 1915. Her position represented a continuation of Washington's influence, as did the appointment of Robert Moton, Washington's successor at Tuskegee. After Mrs. Washington finished her term, she served on the Membership Committee where her club, suffrage, and educational ties were invaluable. By 1919 and 1920, two more black women joined the Executive Board. Nannie Burroughs, director of the National Training School for Colored Girls, and Mary McLeod Bethune, head of Bethune-Cookman College, brought their influence, outlook, and administrative abilities to bear on the direction of the National Urban League.[36]

The Urban League used the talents of black women at the local and national levels and sought to develop more professional talent in the group. Unlike the NAACP, the Urban League wanted professional social workers in charge of their affiliates. Through their fellowship programs, nine men and eight women were able to become professional social workers during the decade. Ellie A. Walls, one of the first two fellows, finished her education at the New York School of Philanthropy while living at the Lincoln Settlement in Brooklyn. During her fellowship, Walls completed research on the services for delinquent black females in both Brooklyn and Manhattan while serving as a caseworker for the United Charities Organization. Joined in "preventive work" by Hallie Craigwell, Vivian Johnson, and Nellie M.

Quander, who had worked with the future editor of the socialist *Messenger*, Chandler Owen, in friendly visiting and Travelers' Aid, Walls found many activities requiring a skilled social worker in New York City. But when she had to return to Texas to care for her mother, Walls had to seek employment as a schoolteacher. Social work remained a charitable, volunteer activity in most communities during the first decade of the Urban League's existence. Nevertheless, the foundation for further professional social work had developed during these early years.[37]

Black women helped to develop these early programs. During the fall of 1914, the Bethlehem Training Center opened under the auspices of the Urban League, Fisk University, and the Woman's Missionary Council of the Methodist Episcopal Church. The kindergarten and sewing school, operated by the Woman's Missionary Council, expanded to become the settlement called the Bethlehem House during the fall. Due to the cooperative efforts of the Nashville black women, the training center produced a new generation of black social service workers for churches, missions, kindergartens, children's courts, and other social agencies.[38]

This reliance on profession training and dependence on white philanthropy created an organizational development very different from that of the NAACP. The services and the professional staff required more money to support Urban League affiliates. Unlike the NAACP, the Urban League grew gradually. The NAACP had 310 branches with 88,292 members by the end of 1919. The Urban League had only twenty-seven affiliates by 1918 and only thirty-four by 1930. The NAACP's reliance on branch organizers and volunteers rather than the professionally trained workers of the Urban League brought a broader base of membership to the NAACP. This larger membership lessened the financial dependence of the NAACP on a small group of wealthy whites. The Urban League gained over 40 percent of its budget from three white patrons. In 1919, when the Urban League received 795 gifts, the NAACP received 62,300. The views of the white donors became more closely tied to the programs of the Urban League, while the leadership positions went to trained black workers. The NAACP membership was dominated by white reformers, but gradually the dependence on black funding produced more black leadership.[39]

By the time the organization officially adopted the title National Urban League in 1920, black women had served as the foundation of many affiliates built on the preexisting local services. The league relied on the women to raise money for league activities and to bolster support for the organization within the community. The Urban League provided contacts with sympathetic white business, educational, and reform interests. Its emphasis on professional training of social workers stimulated black women to improve the efficiency and organization of their community reform organizations and encourage young black men and women under their direction to seek further education in the field of social work. The local reformers formed a symbiotic relationship with the Urban League. Both groups gained from their contacts with each other and this interdependence continued.[40]

The ultimate significance of the community services was small. Only a few blacks received services and only in the few cities having affiliates or branches. But numbers do not tell the whole story. The services did influence lives. The aid did help some. Described by historian Nancy J. Weiss as "Useful services, but unspectacular results,"[41] the social programs developed and delivered by the black women helped the Urban League to realize some of its original goals. Ruth Standish Baldwin, a prime mover behind the National League for the Protection of Colored Women and the Committee on Urban Conditions Among Negroes, stated the ideals of the Urban League:

When we, colored and white people, banded together in our League, seek to better conditions among the *Negroes* of Harlem or San Juan Hill or Brooklyn, we seek also to make a better New York City for *everybody* to live in, and to help in some measure towards a truer realization of the ideals of sound community living in our Great Republic.[42]

From Atlanta to Boston to Youngstown, some of the same black women who were leaders in the club movement, founders of local branches of the NAACP, and community leaders became affiliated with the Urban League. Racial betterment in all forms gained their attention and support.

PART THREE

War and Its Aftermath

Our intolerance is cumulative. . . . We shall exert our righteous efforts until not only every eligible black man but every black woman shall be wielding the ballot proudly in defense of our liberties and our homes. . . . We are loyal and will remain so, but we are not blind. . . . What think you will be the effect on the morale of black men in the trenches when they reflect that they are fighting on foreign fields in behalf of their nation for the very rights and privileges which they themselves are denied at home?

> —Atlanta Neighborhood Union, "To the President, the Cabinet, the Congress of the United States, the Governors and the Legislatures of the Several States of the United States of America," March 1, 1918. Copy in the Neighborhood Union Papers, Atlanta University Center.

The highest development of civilization of the future depends of making a beautiful, healthful, community life that shall afford adequate stimulation to all this struggling, hungry desire of the individual. . . . The healthful growth of our democratic civilization is dependent upon the development of this more completely healthful social environment—the organized community.

> —Lugenia Hope, Memoranda, 1919-1924. Copy in the Neighborhood Union Papers, Atlanta University Center.

SEVEN

Wartime Reform

The First World War exacerbated conditions that black women had been attempting to improve. Pushed by worsening situations and declining opportunities in the South, young blacks came to the cities of the North seeking employment in industries engaged in war production, in occupations previously employing European immigrants, and in jobs left open by whites who went into better-paying factory work or joined the armed services.

As their numbers increased in the industrial towns of the North and Midwest, the problems of urban life expanded proportionately. Vice, ignorance, housing, health and sanitation, family disintegration, social isolation, crime, and social control required immediate attention. Since black women had been involved in these problems since the nineteenth century, they became an active element of the wartime reform work.

The outbreak of war in 1914 did not immediately concern black Americans. The election of Woodrow Wilson brought southern democracy to Washington, D.C. Bills flooded Congress seeking to segregate the races on public carriers, to exclude blacks from commissions in the Army and Navy, and to eliminate all immigrants of Negro descent. Municipal codes requiring residential segregation appeared in city after city.[1] President Wilson segregated federal restrooms and eating areas. U.S. Marines occupied Haiti. The brutality of lynchings increased, as in the public burning of Jesse Washington in Waco, Texas, where thousands of men, women, and children watched and cheered the "executioners." *The Birth of a Nation*, a film based on the ultraracist book *The Clansmen*, perpetuated the basis of lynching through its portrayal of black men as beasts lusting after virtuous white women. Conditions for blacks deteriorated in cities and rural areas of the North and the South.[2]

Black Americans did not accept this situation complacently. Petitions, lobbying with sympathetic congressmen, protests in both the black and the white press, public meetings with influential whites, and utilization of the court system halted passage of some of the detrimental legislation and challenged the constitutionality of the approved laws, such as residential segregation.[3] William Monroe Trotter served as a spokesman when black leaders from thirty-eight states protested the segregation policies of the Wilson administration. Ida Wells-Barnett participated in the interchange that resulted in Wilson's promise to look into the problems. After a year of increased segregation, the group returned. Trotter's persistence resulted in the segregation issue achieving national publicity when Wilson ordered the group to leave.[4] Black communities boycotted and protested the showing of *The Birth of a Nation*; several communities successfully pressured mayors and city councils to withdraw permits for the public showing of the film. Delilah Beasley's articles in the Oakland *Tribune* condemned the film and stimulated a local movement against it.[5]

The European conflict presented pressures and opportunities for black Americans. The country had been receiving 900,000 immigrants annually from Europe. With the start of the war, the number fell to 100,000, while the need for workers in manufacturing increased. The decrease in immigration created openings in jobs that had previously been closed to blacks; which enticed southern blacks to the urban, industrial areas of the North.[6]

Cities already experiencing problems in health, housing, and interethnic conflict faced intensification of these difficulties as the black population swelled. Cleveland's black population increased by 308 percent, Cincinnati's by 51 percent, Detroit's by 623 percent, Chicago's by 148 percent, New York's by 66 percent, and Gary, Indiana's, by 1,284 percent.[7] Even cities with relatively liberal traditions in race relations, such as Boston and Cleveland, experienced increased prejudice as numbers expanded.[8]

The population pressures on cities, already unable or unwilling to handle the housing, health, educational, and recreational needs of the black population, stimulated black women to expand existing facilities, programs, and services. In 1915, the Chicago Phyllis Wheatley moved to larger quarters and established an employment department to find jobs for the many black women entering the city looking for work. Most of these women entered the job market as domestics when white women took over the better-paying jobs in factories. The migration created a need for a black branch in Louisville, new quarters in Charlotte, North Carolina, and Brooklyn, and new services in Detroit.[9]

The war required citizens to cooperate with the government. Human and material resources had to be utilized as efficiently as possible. Intergroup and intragroup frictions often had to be subordinated to the overall aims of the nation. The elaborate systems of segregation often had to be changed or ignored to achieve intergroup cooperation. Once America officially entered the war in the spring of 1917, both separately and together with white women, black women effectively aided the American effort.

The role of black women began, as with white women, in patriotic service. They aided black soldiers and their families; raised money through the various Liberty Loans, War Savings Stamps, and United War Work campaigns; helped to produce and conserve foodstuffs, clothing, and industrial goods; and spread American propaganda through the press, lectures and schools.

As their initial efforts became successful, the black women keenly observed the possibilities in the wartime situation. The war forced whites to incorporate the work of black women into their agendas. As white women worked for the improvement of public health, black women grasped the chance to improve the nutrition, medical care, and recreational facilities for black children and families. The Red Cross classes in home nursing and dietetics improved the conditions in black communities. As white women worked for better safeguards for women in industry, black women tried to open opportunities for black women, using patriotic reasons for their endeavors. They argued that training of black women as nurses would allow white nurses to volunteer for the European field. Black women working as elevator operators would free men to volunteer for direct military roles. The improvement of city lighting and street conditions in black neighborhoods and the expansion of reformatories would lessen the potential immoral temptations for men stationed at nearby military camps. Ably manipulating the wartime rhetoric and goals, the black women aided the race by wearing the cloak of American patriotism.[10]

The First World War had a direct influence on the progress of blacks, women, and reform. To the social justice reformers, the war meant an end to laissez-faire. The government encouraged such reforms as industrial education, social insurance, national health campaigns, utilization of schools as community centers, and improved housing and urban development.[11] The war also served as a catalyst to the feminist movement. Government regulation, emphasis on the issues of prohibition, woman's suffrage, and war mobilization, the need for reform in education and physical training, and a surge in organizational activity created a growth in confidence and self-image. Women felt needed. Through the war, they proved their abilities, performed nontraditional jobs, and increased their expectations for postwar progress in pay and occupational status.[12]

The war affected black women as a race and a sex. The YWCA's War Work Council developed "the foundation of the community work for Negro women."[13] The YWCA emerged from the war more of an interracial organization. John Hope Franklin noted, "Not until the outbreak of World War I did a strong movement develop for the work among Negro women."[14] The black women worked in parallel or integrated organizations. When they found the local YWCA, State Councils of National Defense, War Camp Community Service, or American Red Cross unable or unwilling to accept their cooperation, they created their own vehicles to meet local or national needs. Alice Dunbar Nelson, a chronicler of the black female role in the war, described their contribution:

> They offered their services and gave them freely, in whatsoever form was most pleasing to the local organizations of white women. They accepted without a murmur the place assigned them in the ranks. They placed the national need before the local prejudice; they put great-heartedness and pure patriotism above the ancient creed of racial antagonism . . . the conduct of the Negro women . . . [is] a lesson to the entire world to what womanhood of the best type really means.[15]

Their services were not selfless sacrifices for the American war effort. They took advantage of opportunities to demonstrate ability and responsibility, showing themselves worthy of equal treatment.

When the United States officially entered the war in April 1917, women's groups throughout the nation offered their help. By April 21, the government had organized the Woman's Committee under the Council of National Defense. The major national woman's organizations, including the National Association of Colored Women, were represented on the Woman's Committee. The committee attempted to incorporate all groups of women into the domestic war effort to accomplish food conservation, production of knit goods, development of maternal and child protection activities (these included the establishment of milk stations, baby weighing and measuring programs, and recreational facilities), and creation of federal working standards for women in industry. According to Alice Dunbar Nelson, field representative of the Woman's Committee, the committee "made the best organized attempt at mobilizing the colored women of all the war organizations."[16]

The racial policies of the Woman's Committee varied due to its reliance on State Councils of Defense. In most of the northern states, separation of the races was "superfluous." Black women in California joined the State Defense Council. Yet, in some cases, black women formed distinct units to accomplish specific aims. Illinois organized a Committee on Colored Women that worked with the Urban League. Black women participated on the State Committee in Delaware. A separate division directed by the president of the Indiana Federation of Colored Women's Clubs, Gertrude B. Hill, organized the state's female war effort. In New Jersey, the Colored Woman's Volunteer League developed the black women's efforts through the Woman's Committee of the Council of National Defense.[17]

In the South, black women participated through many segregated organizations. Florida, Mississippi, and Maryland developed parallel black women's councils with black state, county, and local chairpersons. This allowed black teachers and clubwomen to organize and develop leadership in general state guidelines and direction. In Maryland, Ida Cummings served on the State Council of Defense. Sally Green, a Hampton graduate, teacher, and county agent, became the state chairman in Mississippi. In Florida, Eartha M. White headed the black women's department. In Kentucky, a state black men's organization incorporated black women into its organization. Missouri saw no need to organize black women. West Virginia had the state federation of the black women's clubs send a representative to the National Defense Council.[18]

Most of the southern states, however, appointed a "local black to cooperate, when needed, with the local county council."[19] Called the "Sumter County Plan," after the county in Virginia where the technique originated, this method led to various degrees of organization or disorganization in North and South Carolina, Virginia, and Georgia. For example, in Georgia, Alice Dugged Cary, president of the State Federation of Colored Women's Clubs, was appointed chairman of the black subcommittee of the state women's committee. Cary built on her strong organizational base in Atlanta, yet her influence did not reach Lucy Laney and Augusta, which approached war work independently. Similar cases of separate organization within the same state existed in Louisiana, Alabama, and Tennessee. In those states, work in New Orleans, Birmingham, Knoxville, Nashville, and Memphis developed into well-organized local efforts but did not penetrate beyond their boundaries.[20]

In addition to the Woman's Committee, the federal government requested cooperation of seven national organizations.[21] The American Red Cross was one of the first organizations approached by black women. In many northern cities, black women combined their Red Cross activities with white women. For example, black women of Freehold, New Jersey, formed an auxiliary to the Big County Branch; they worked in the same central headquarters under the same supervisor as did the white women. Laura A. Brown and Daisy Lampkin of Pennsylvania (Lampkin, a national organizer for the NACW and vice president of the *Pittsburgh Courier*, went on to serve as regional and national field secretary for the NAACP in the 1930s and 1940s); Lillian J. Craw of California; Susan P. Vashon of Missouri; Dr. Susan M. Steward, Susan E. Frazier, Cora Horne, and Mary Talbert of New York; and Grace Booth Valentine of New Jersey worked in Red Cross activities. Addie W. Hunton became one of the first blacks in Red Cross social work.[22]

In the South, the form varied. Nettie Napier was invited by the white women of Nashville to cooperate with the Red Cross. Blanche Beatty of Tampa formed the separate Booker T. Washington Chapter. Mary Cordelia Booze, daughter of Isaiah Montgomery, became the Red Cross committee chairman for the black town of Mound Bayou, Mississippi. Separation of the races remained the rule in the South.[23]

When nurses were called for overseas duty early in 1918, black women were eager to serve. The Red Cross served as an auxiliary to the Army Nurse Corps, recruiting, enrolling, and classifying nurses for both military and civilian duty. Since the surgeon general never expressed a specific call for black nurses and since most lacked the "necessary credentials," black women were excluded.

The participation of black women in Red Cross organizations or auxiliaries coupled with protests from Robert Moton, Emmett Scott, the NAACP, the NACW, and the National Association of Colored Graduate Nurses led to the secretary of war calling black women into national service for their own race in June 1918. Registered by the American Red Cross, the black women served in the six black base hospitals—Camp Funston (Kansas), Camp Grant (Rockford, Illinois), Camp Dodge (Des Moines, Iowa), Camp Taylor (Louisville, Kentucky), Camp Sherman (Chillicothe, Ohio), and Camp Dix (Wrightstown, New Jersey)—serving 38,000 black troops. Due to bureaucratic procedures, however, few black nurses had received the call to service before the armistice.[24]

In the Red Cross, black women's services fluctuated according to locality. Alice Dunbar Nelson reported over 300 nurses serving overseas by passing for white. In the United States, "local conditions, racial antipathies, ancient prejudices militated sadly against her usefulness in this work."[25] In Indiana, nurses enlisted as a contingent for service and received commissions in nitrate plants or where needed. During the influenza epidemic of 1918, the Red Cross called on black volunteers. Yet in the South, the Red Cross denied black women the "privilege" of doing canteen service, while allowing them to prepare comfort kits, knit garments, and maintain restaurants.[26] Black women "did all that could be done, all that they were allowed to do."[27]

Black women also formed their own organizations to aid the black soldier and his family. The old Fifteenth New York Regiment became the first New York State Guard during World War I. Composed solely of black men, the Fifteenth Regiment gained a Woman's Auxiliary of over one hundred members in May 1917. Organized by Susan Elizabeth Frazier,[28] a New York public school teacher and clubwoman, the Woman's Auxiliary investigated cases of men whose dependents claimed exemptions for them. Through their investigations, the women perfected the recruiting process and helped win commendations for the officers and staff.[29]

To provide services similar to those of the Red Cross, the Circle for Negro War Relief began during the fall of 1917. Originating in New York City, the circle expanded to sixty units by early 1918. Each circle promoted the welfare of the black soldiers as dependents by meeting specific individual and local emergency needs. For example, the Motor Corps of Haywood Unit of New York City visited hospitals, escorted the wounded to canteens, on sightseeing tours, and on shopping trips, and wrote letters for the soldiers and their families. The Ambulance Unit of New York City, composed of a small group of black women nurses, donated a two-thousand-dollar ambulance to the 367th Regiment at Camp Upton. The leadership of the circle included a few white reformers and philanthropists such as Ray Stannard Baker, Mrs. Amos Pinchot, George Foster Peabody, and Emilie B. Hapgood, but the direction remained in the hands of black men (W. E. B Du Bois, Colonel Charles Young, Dr. Robert R. Moton, Charles W. Anderson, and J. Rosamond Johnson) and black women (Lelia Walker, Dora Cole Norman, Saddie Dorsette Tandy, Ruth Logan Roberts, and Adah B. Thoms).[30]

Through these units, black women provided the soldiers with comfort kits, chewing gum, victrolas and records, southern dinners for homesick boys, lectures on social hygiene and race pride, niceties such as air cushions, and visits to hospitals and camps. They raised money to provide Christmas trees for Harlem residents, published and circulated pamphlets about the black soldier, and cooperated with the Red Cross. The Crispus Attucks Circle in

Philadelphia attempted to establish a base hospital for black soldiers with a staff of black physicians and nurses. Mary McLeod Bethune developed an Emergency Circle of Negro War Relief in Daytona. In Boston, the War Service Center developed a Soldiers' Comfort Unit. A dozen black women in Newport News responded to the urgent need for knitted goods. Within months, this group had affiliated with the Circle for Negro War Relief and expanded to include 177 women. Functioning as a black counterpart to the Red Cross, the circle eased adaptation to wartime civilian conditions.[31]

Black women responded not only to the race's needs, but also to humanity's. Most of their efforts emphasized equal treatment for all groups. The Josephine Gray Colored Lady Knitters of Detroit produced knit goods for "all American soldiers regardless of race, color or nationality."[32] In Boston, war work signs or mottoes noted a public policy of non-discrimination. Occasionally, the race organizations helped Europeans; the Colored American Society for Relief of French War Orphans had a National Woman's Committee. The call to service, especially in aiding children, fit in easily with the traditional role of black women. The war years merely redirected those energies.[33]

The war role of black women in the YWCA demonstrates the conflicts and potential opportunities for racial reform in a white woman's organization. The YWCA was one of seven national organizations summoned to wartime cooperation by President Wilson. In June 1917, the National Board of the YWCA established the War Work Council to protect the health and morals of American womanhood, especially in communities surrounding army and navy training camps.

To meet the needs of black women, the YWCA allocated $400,000 of its 1918 budget to "colored work."[34] Under the leadership of Eva D. Bowles, national secretary of colored work, black female leaders and volunteers came together to accomplish the general goals formulated by the War Work Council. Although the council aimed "to do everything for colored girls that is being done for the white girls,"[35] the conditions caused an immediate expansion beyond the original goals of protection of young women and aid to female relatives of servicemen.

A third goal became the most significant for black women. By openly encouraging them to demonstrate their skills and abilities both in war work and in industry, the War Work Council simultaneously provided the opportunity to prove equality and the context to raise expectations for equal treatment in the YWCA.

The YWCA served as a microcosm of race, class, sectional, and factional conflicts played out in a wartime environment permeated by patriotic rhetoric and personal sacrifice. The war provided the impetus for greater service to the black communities and expansion of the black female role.[36] Black women began their war work in 1917 with one national secretary, sixteen local centers or branches, and nine paid workers. Within two years, twelve national workers, three field supervisors, and sixty-three paid workers managed the work in forty-two centers, many of which later became branches of the YWCA. Under Bowles's direction, the black women worked in white-controlled organizational and community structures. As a Christian-based women's organization, the YWCA emphasized conservative values and techniques. The Colored Women's War Work Councils reflected adjustment to that conservatism.[37]

The black women tried to meet three basic needs of the black female community. First, through the establishment of hostess houses in training camps, they provided an information bureau for female relatives and friends of black soldiers, a "homey atmosphere" for soldiers and visitors, and a supervised environment in which rest, refreshments, and entertainment eased adjustment to military life and maintenance of morality. Second, through an Industrial Department, the YWCA met the needs of black women drawn to urban areas by traditional jobs in domestic service and employment in industry. Finally, the YWCA provided black girls with appropriate recreation, emergency housing, and self-improvement in health, social morality, and skills.

The YWCA utilized well-educated and experienced black women with demonstrated leadership abilities and organizational understanding of the Ys purpose and methods. The first war worker, Josephine Pinyon, fulfilled both criteria, having received her education at Cornell, Columbia, and Chicago universities and having served as the special worker among colored students since 1912. Assuming her position as special war worker in August 1917, Pinyon's first order of business was the development of interracial cooperation in communities adjacent to training camps.

Bridging the social gap between the races proved her most difficult task. White male officials were certain that they understood the race better than any black woman could. The prejudices of white women hampered effective cooperation, as did the "severe denominational conflicts" and "stubborn pride" of the black women.[38] In the South, such interracial cooperation exacted a "great psychological price to the black women involved."[39] Yet cooperation was necessary. To whites Pinyon argued that war created an interdependence of the races requiring cooperation rather than conflict. To garner black support, she appealed to the social consciousness of women through their women's clubs.

During her first month as special war worker, Pinyon faced the problems that would continue to plague interracial efforts of the YWCA. Conservative white women of Petersburg, Virginia, expressed concern about the mingling of girls with the soldiers at Camp Lee. Pinyon worked with the local black and white communities to establish a recreational center and hostess house. Failure of the black and white women to cooperate delayed the opening of that facility, but the hostess house concept rapidly progressed in areas outside the South.[40]

The hostess house program became the most significant achievement of the YWCA's Colored Women's War Council. (Most communities set up canteens for white soldiers. The hostess houses were organized to meet similar needs for black soldiers.) Bowles called the program the most spectacular wartime achievement.[41] White journals praised the houses and the effective work done by the black women volunteers.[42] The first hostess houses opened in the Northeast, where interracial cooperation and black Y work was firmly established. In November 1917, Camp Upton Hostess House was opened on Long Island through the efforts of Boston black women Mary Wilson, Hannah Smith, and her assistant, a Mrs. Norcomb.[43]

By early 1918, the direction of the Camp Upton House went to Lugenia Hope, founder of the Atlanta Neighborhood Union. The Upton house became the model for the succeeding fifteen facilities: Camp Custer (Michigan), Grant (Illinois), Funston (Kansas), Dodge (Iowa), Dix (New Jersey), Sherman (Ohio), Meade (Maryland), Taylor (Kentucky), Green (North Carolina), Gordon (Georgia), Alexander and Lee (Virginia), Jackson and Wadsworth (South Carolina), and Travis (Texas). It also served as the training center for black women supervisors assigned to other hostess houses. By the summer, training had been received by Mabel Whiting for Camp Funston, Amanda Gray for Dodge, Callie Edwards and Mary Cromwell for Dix, and Ruth Hucles for Gordon.[44]

The hostess houses served "all races and creeds,"[45] yet tended to concentrate on minorities shut out of other social services. At the Camp Upton house, black women registered and entertained the wives, mothers, and friends of black and Jewish soldiers. (Anti-semitism and racism brought the groups together.) When a soldier was injured or killed, the hostesses

At first directed by Boston black women Mary Wilson and Hannah Smith, the Camp Upton Hostess House became a model for hostess house development nationally. Lugenia Burns Hope assumed leadership in early 1918 and this photograph includes her (center) and her staff and volunteers.
[*YWCA of the USA, National Board Archives.*]

211

consoled and advised the women. For the illiterate men from the South, the house provided a center for literacy training. During the influenza epidemic in the fall of 1918, the hostess house became an emergency hotel where white and black women could stay while nursing the ill. For men drafted unjustly, the hostesses served as liaisons between the military bureaucracy and the soldier. For men called away from their homes, the center provided a homelike atmosphere in contrast to the dreary barracks. Old rose lampshades and curtains, books, games, records, musical instruments, homey furniture, and the presence of refined, educated matrons made camp life more comfortable.[46]

Although the YWCA provided funds, information, and direction in securing the buildings and training the black hostesses, the atmosphere, furnishings, and volunteer activities originated with black women who came from the surrounding communities and other centers of reform.[47] They instilled both patriotism and racial pride. Black soldiers received encouragement to fight to make the world safe for democracy and return to improve the future of their race at home.[48]

Although the impact of the hostess houses was limited, their success evolved from the combined efforts of black women who served as supervisors and volunteers, raised funds and goods to furnish and operate the various facilities, and adapted the often paternalistic program of the YWCA to the needs of the race. The YWCA booklets "Mothers All," "Heroines of Health," and "Suggestions to Lecturers on Social Morality" found their way into the hands of black volunteers and supervisors, where the information became transformed into useful guidance.

Not only the YWCA, but also the War Camp Community Service provided home ties for enlisted men. Organized in communities surrounding the training camps, black women provided clubhouses, canteens, cafeterias, and pool rooms. Similar to service clubs, the centers developed in Des Moines, Battle Creek, Washington, Louisville, Chillicothe, Charlotte, Petersburg, Newport News, Baltimore, Atlanta, Montgomery, and Columbia. (Other sources list also Richmond, Macon, Chattanooga, Hattiesburg, Philadelphia, and Greenville.) Some of these locations were already served by YWCA hostess houses. Depending on local acceptance and funding, these centers provided wholesome entertainment through chaperoned dances, picture shows, community sings, minstrel shows, and home hospitality. Thirty black workers shaped activities among forty-nine communities. Dr. Mary Waring served as the organizer for the War Camp Community Service

The office activities of the Camp Upton Hostess House with staff (Lugenia Burns Hope, center) and visitors. Jewish soldiers were also served by the hostess house, which brought both groups together during the war years. [*YWCA of the USA, National Board Archives.*]

in Illinois. Mary Burwell headed the canteen at the center in Newark. The Phyllis Wheatley Club in Columbia, South Carolina, opened a community center for use by the YWCA, Red Cross, and War Camp Community Service. Mary Church Terrell served as an organizer in the South, interviewing qualified black women to head centers there. The biographical data on black women indicate service as canteen workers, organizers, entertainers, fund-raisers, and supervisors[50]

Black women transferred their talents as fund-raisers to war work. They participated in the five Liberty Loan Drives, six Red Cross campaigns, the United War Work Campaign, and the thrift savings stamp program. Black teachers encouraged student contributions as evidence of patriotism. Black schools participated in war savings stamp programs. Selma women raised money through sale of thrift stamps. Laura Brown of Pittsburgh headed the campaign for black women as the appointee of the National War Savings Committee under the secretary of the treasury.

The National Association of Colored Women's Clubs organized successful drives in the Liberty Loan and Red Cross campaigns. Leading clubwoman Elizabeth L. Davis received an honorable discharge for her valuable service raising money for Liberty Bonds. In the Third Liberty Loan campaign, clubwomen raised over five million dollars and three hundred thousand dollars for the Red Cross. In that campaign, clubwomen of Savannah accounted for one-quarter of a million dollars, with South Carolina clubs giving $8,000. In Atlanta, the United War Work Campaign reported that blacks had greatly exceeded their allotment.[51] These successful efforts received praise. Mrs. Philip North, president of the National Council of Women, noted that, "No women worked harder than the women of the National Association of Colored Women."[52] Emmett J. Scott, special assistant in the War Department, felt the National Association of Colored Women had achieved the "most practical achievements of the womanhood of our race at this time."[53]

The war's effects on the American economy offered opportunities and problems for black females. New jobs opened as corporate firms and retail outlets developed and technology mechanized work previously done by hand. More jobs opened to women in industry as men entered the military service and as factories converted to wartime production. No longer could labor shortages be met by increasing the numbers of European immigrants. The war years cut the number of immigrant males in labor and factory work and immigrant females employed as domestics.

The Committee on Colored Work of the YWCA recognized the potential problems that these new opportunities presented. By December 1917, Mary E. Jackson brought her experience in the Labor Department of Rhode Island and in the NACW to her task as industrial secretary of the YWCA's Committee on Colored Work. Jackson built on the existing employment bureaus of Phillis Wheatley branches and developed industrial recreational centers. Her industrial work used a multifaceted approach. She wanted to develop training programs to improve skills and work habits, to save women from exploitation, to organize women into groups for increased bargaining power, and to use the opportunity of wartime to build long-range goals.

As a trained organizational worker, Jackson encouraged investigation as the first step in understanding the problems. Studies described the areas of employment, working conditions, wages, and problems caused by prejudice and rapid in-migration of black female workers. In June 1918, the New York City YWCA, under its president, Emma S. Ransom, cooperated with representatives of the Women's Trade Union League, the New York Urban League, the Russell Sage Foundation, and the Committee on Colored Workers of the Manhattan Trade School to investigate conditions for black women throughout the New York metropolitan area. Gertrude MacDougald interviewed other black women, while a white woman obtained information from business establishments. They found black women segregated from white workers, denied piecework competition, and paid lower wages. Employer and white worker prejudice, joined with the ignorance of black women workers and the absence of collective bargaining explained most of the inequitable wages and working conditions.[54]

The findings in New York City generally applied to black female employment in other industrial areas. The war years opened employment in Cleveland knitting factories, railroad yards, electrical supply houses, box factories, and packing houses; in Pennsylvania clothing industries; and glassworks, cotton-chopping plants, and lumberyards in Texas, Virginia, and Tennessee. Yet Jackson's surveys found wages unstandardized, unions evasive about organizing black women, poor working conditions, and racial separation and classification. For example, Ohio employed black women in railroad yards, but only as laborers. Employment as telephone operators remained closed to black women in Ohio.[55] To Jackson, the black woman worker was "denied the right to serve her country in many war activities."[56]

Jackson found some of these opportunities to be mixed blessings. In Pittsburgh, black women received the same wages and working conditions, but remained separated from the white working women, which implied inferiority. In St. Louis, a day manager of a drug company lauded the performance of black women but used racial stereotyping when he described their "naturally imitative" qualities. Factory girls in Philadelphia joined a successful strike that raised their pay, even though the black women received only one-third of that earned by the white women workers.

In their separate black branches or as agents of the industrial secretary, black women created employment services and training bureaus. Ransom's New York City branch offered vocational classes. The independent branch in Washington developed both an employment bureau and housing service to meet the needs accentuated by the exodus from the South. Under the leadership of Mrs. B. G. Francis, Frances Boyce, Marion P. Shadd, Alice Quivers, and Annie E. Cromwell, the Washington organization raised money for expansion of facilities and programs through Mardi Gras entertainments, Tag Day drive, and various membership campaigns. By the end of 1918, the War Work Council of the YWCA pledged to help the Washington group erect a new building.

The East was not alone in the growth of employment services. During the summer of 1918, Irene Goins cooperated with the WTUL to obtain employment for black women in the Chicago stockyards. By that fall, the Central (white) YWCA turned over a thirty-six-room building to black women, who developed the Industrial Women's Service Center. The St. Louis Phyllis Wheatley established an employment bureau, training courses, a housing registration service, and mediation for black women workers and their employers. Miss Z. O. Stratton organized industrial work in Indianapolis in a large room located over two stores. Mary Jackson established club activities for black working women in a four-room cottage in Nitro, West Virginia. Cooperation in East St. Louis among the YMCA, the Urban League, and the organized labor movement enabled Esther Fulks to develop an industrial center by March 1919. By May, black women had organized a community Phyllis Wheatley Club.[57]

The war years demonstrated the dual edge of discrimination. Black women finally entered jobs previously closed to them during peacetime. Yet their previous lack of access to industrial employment and employer failure to train black women for supervisory positions created laborers ignorant of industrial routine with no black foremen to instill pride and teach techniques. To correct this situation, Mary Jackson used wartime rhetoric to gain white support of programs to aid the black woman worker. White workers, labor unionists, and employers needed to encourage black working women in the name of general American patriotism. For black women to make their best contribution to the war effort, Jackson argued, they had to have a chance for advancement, equal wages for equal work, identical working conditions, and a patient attitude for their lack of experience. She emphasized, "It is now to the national advantage to give the Negro a square deal."[58] To the white women of the YWCA, Jackson used a different approach. She argued that the United States could not become "an ideal for world-wide democracy"[59] until black women received the right to compete in all areas.

Most black women, however, continued to be employed in domestic work. While Jackson's Industrial Department concentrated on opening opportunities in industry, the local women's Christian associations, clubs, and black branches of the YWCA serviced black women seeking to establish more efficient households or devote more time to patriotic activities. The pool of potential domestic immigrants had been steadily declining. Earlier generations who had viewed household work as a vehicle for upward mobility now sought jobs in industry, bureaucratic firms, and retail outlets. In addition, new reforms in child labor, compulsory education, and increased prosperity prevented many young white girls from filling the increased demands for domestic workers.[60]

World War I created a demand for black domestic workers. The South utilized "Work or Fight" laws requiring compulsory employment, which pushed many black women into positions as servants.[61] The low wages earned by black men compelled many women to work as washerwomen, maids, cooks, and scrubwomen. Although southern women frequently complained about the domestic's ignorance of duties, shortness of service time, and dishonesty, the high demand for domestic labor led to southern women's competition for available services.[62]

The conditions in the South and hope for a better life brought many black females to northern urban areas seeking employment. Since most lacked skills, they entered domestic service. The black women's clubs and YWCA organizations expanded programs in domestic science. Such classes had been a regular part of the work of the women's clubs, but increasing demands led to combining instruction with employment bureaus. Often the Phillis Wheatley branches mediated disagreements between the black girls and their employers. Black women through clubs, independents, or branches of the YWCA provided such services in Cleveland, St. Louis, Washington, New York, and Chicago.[63]

The employment and emergency housing services enabled local branches and independents to gain contact with the black migrants, who needed social, educational, and recreational services. In areas lacking YWCA branches or independents, the YWCA provided recreational or industrial workers to establish community services, many of which developed into branches following the war. A center in Houston provided a meeting place for the Patriotic Service League, the Rainbow Club, and the Tennis Club as well as classes in food demonstration, wartime cookery, French, and stenography. In Columbia, South Carolina, a recreation center held parties, outdoor games, and meetings for nine clubs. Patriotic Service Leagues expanded into social-recreational centers in Little Rock. A similar center emerged from girls working in war gardens to increase the food supply in Petersburg, Virginia. A trained YWCA worker organized the branch at Germantown, Pennsylvania. She developed a pageant of black folk songs to involve the community, a camping expedition for the girls, and a local auxiliary of the Red Cross for the adult women.[64]

Cooperation with other wartime agencies enabled black women to expand services. The independent organization in Washington and local center in Montclair, New Jersey, worked with the Red Cross and the War Camp Community Service. Louisville, "one of the strongest branches in the country,"[65] had eighty-one Patriotic Leagues, developed housing and protection for the two thousand girls employed in the city's factories, and established the first YWCA summer camp for black girls.[66] The college and training-school girls in Harlem and Brooklyn branches volunteered their services in the recreation centers. The New York branch heard lectures by W.E.B. Du Bois and viewed sculptures by May Howard Johnson. Throughout these branches and centers, black women provided wholesome lectures, recreation, social interaction, and patriotic activities.[67]

The programs and philosophy of the YWCA War Work Council did not differ considerably from those of women's clubs or state defense councils. The guiding philanthropy of the YWCA noted, "Wholesome fun, provided by the YWCA, makes the colored girl a better woman, a better worker, a better citizen of her country."[68]

The leadership in the black war work of the YWCA differed from that in the club movement. Married, middle-aged women predominated in the leadership of the clubs and woman's committees of the state councils of defense. The YWCA national staff and war workers tended to be younger, single women, as were their white counterparts in the settlement house movement. Most of these women graduated from the YWCA training school open to graduates of college or normal schools. The four-week sessions prepared them to establish YWCA programs at the local level, to become better administrators of local branches, and to assume leadership positions in their communities.[70]

Whatever the level of training or the form of organization, black women did not wait for white direction to begin helping the race. Typically started by teachers, college women, and/or clubwomen, most of the activities attempted to ease the burdens of military service of black soldiers and their families. In Chicago, the city federation under Ida B. Wells-Barnett's direction organized a committee to raise money to send Christmas boxes to the 1,200 black soldiers stationed at Camp Grant. Advertising in the Chicago *Tribune*, the women raised the money to make the Christmas of 1917 pleasant for the black soldiers. In Oakland, black women prepared boxes for their "Liberty Boys of the Race."[71] When Alice Dunbar Nelson became field representative of the Woman's Committee under the National Defense Council, she found black women already organized in the South. Atlanta women attempted to gain facilities, services, and just treatment for black soldiers.[72] The Atlanta Colored Women's Club raised over $1,800 to help furnish the colored YMCA so that black soldiers would have a "wholesome place to go."[73] In Mobile, an independent War Service Club carried on work similar to that accomplished by the white Woman's Committee. Black women in Bessemer, Alabama, worked through an active Council of Defense, supplying comfort kits and Bibles for soldiers and infant layettes for their spouses. Similar stress on comfort kits and care of families appeared in the activities of the Cobb County, Georgia, women. Florida women concentrated on the Mutual Protection League for Working Girls to find employment in such new fields as elevator operators, bellhops, and chauffeurs. Illinois women formed a Committee on Colored Women in cooperation with the Urban League to train black women for employment.[74]

Their role did not stop there. Black women aided the soldiers' convalescent care at Fort McPherson. Mary Church Terrell investigated and served as a liaison for black soldiers disabled or ill. Addie Hunton, Helen Curtis, and Kathryn Johnson led a contingent of volunteers to investigate the treatment of and provide counsel and aid to the black soldiers in Europe.[75]

As part of the domestic war effort, black women took an active part in food production and conservation, nutrition, and fund-raising through food sales to benefit the black communities in both rural and urban environments.

Building on the home economic demonstrations of county agents or state agricultural colleges, black women learned and then taught new canning techniques, formed canning clubs, and held county rallies providing prizes and nutritional information to local residents. One author described these food programs as "an important aspect of the drive for social reform."[76] Under the guise of patriotism, black women significantly improved the knowledge and health of black communities.[77]

Black women also used patriotism to improve neglected public health and safety concerns. The Children's Bureau of the Labor Department supported programs to cope with high infant mortality. The Woman's Committee sought to improve the life chances for infants and children by establishing baby weighing and measuring programs, improving the purity of milk, incorporating public nurses into the schools, and establishing more accurate methods of birth registration. Black women participated in these efforts through their separate black state councils, women's clubs, or settlement houses.[78]

Black nurses increasingly found employment in municipal health departments, clinic milk stations, public schools, settlement houses, and in hospitals, sanitaria, or medical wards with high proportions of black patients. Many became part of the expanding visiting nurses' programs in the major cities. The increased need for black nurses led to the development of more training programs and the Washington Woman's Committee published a list where they were available. Black women's clubs and white state councils gave their support to such programs in the form of scholarships and information to the communities. Black women entered training programs in Florida, Louisiana, and Mississippi as a result of these changes.[79]

Reformatories for black girls received more public support as wartime required more social control facilities. The Peake's Turnout reformatory received state funds to expand its buildings and services. With the help of the state commissioner of charities and correction, South Carolina clubwomen started their own reformatory using Peake's Turnout as a model.[80] Peake's Turnout used the wartime context to enlarge the facilities to work with black girls from the areas surrounding Virginia military camps. With the $40,000 from state and local agencies, Peake's Turnout added two new buildings and expanded services and won black clubwomen recognition from the state legislature for their "services and sacrifices . . . in . . . reform and conservation."[81]

The push for playgrounds that black women had long sought received impetus from the war context. The need for strong children to serve the country in the future and to avoid domestic unrest provided the rationale. The Georgia State Federation and Georgia Woman's Committee responded to the requests of black women and established two playgrounds for black children. In Jacksonville, black women raised $600 for equipment to provide a playground for that city. Atlanta women petitioned the mayor and park commission to improve the police protection and to eliminate the immoral practices in Washington Park. The Atlanta Playground Association donated playground equipment to the Carrie Steele and Leonard Street Orphanages. Black teachers in Atlanta supervised candy sales to purchase "a slide and a giant stride."[82] Using the wartime conditions as their rationale, black women attempted to gain reforms that they had sought for years.[83]

The activities of Atlanta black women demonstrated the breadth of reform possible under wartime conditions using wartime rationales. Cooperating with the Anti-Tuberculosis Association, black women organized an annual "Spring Campaign of Cleaning" from 1917 through 1919. Through the schools, mass meetings, and black motion picture houses, women informed the black community about the locations of Public Health Service lectures, venereal disease clinics, and portable clinics. Building on their institutional, occupational, and familial ties, they galvanized the community. Fifteen locations in churches, halls, kindergartens, and orphanages throughout Atlanta served as distribution centers for lime and as portable clinics. Black physicians and nurses volunteered to do physical exams and referrals for hundreds of black Atlantans. Schoolchildren enrolled as health "crusaders," to keep the schools clean and renovate their neighborhoods. Each school vied for the prize banner for the cleanest grounds. Talks on health and sanitation reached all grades of black schoolchildren. The organized efforts were so successful that they city won the prize for the National Campaign in 1917.

In 1918 and 1919, a Mid-Way Carnival offered health information and community entertainment. Promoted as "Fun! Jolly! Educational! Patriotic!,"[84] the carnival provided moving pictures, pantomime, gypsy fortune tellers, and a house of mystery for entertainment, while educating blacks about dental care, child welfare, tuberculosis, and infant care. By 1919, the professional organization of city health campaigns had produced a Social Service Institute to train zone chairmen at Morehouse College. Exhibits and lectures instructed neighborhood leaders in child dental care, home nursing, preparation of food for invalids and infants, and community organizing.

The health campaigns conducted under the banner of patriotic service provided an informational and social service base from which black women could argue for improved conditions. The Atlanta women advised the local War Department Commission on Training Camp Activities to improve the sanitation of black neighborhoods through regular collection of garbage and rigid enforcement of sanitary laws pertaining to surface closets and open wells. They recommended that prohibition and prostitution laws be applied equally to both races and rigidly enforced to improve the health and morality of black neighborhoods in which these practices were allowed to continue by police authorities. Atlanta women had argued for more street lighting for several years. The war allowed them to modify their arguments: "we recognize that the present inadequate facilities for lighting are in peace times, a menace to the welfare of the city, and will become especially menacing with the advent of this large body of soldiers in our midst."[85] To protect those who had to return home after dark, the black women requested the citywide cooperation of employers to release women earlier. Such actions, with the addition of street lighting, would serve the common good as "eminently patriotic and conducive to general public safety."[86] The black women's efforts from 1917-1919 gained lighting, employer cooperation, playgrounds, and health care.[87]

While continuing to aid the war effort and improve social conditions in the black communities, black women helped improve racial conditions in the overall American society. Utilizing the press, national women's conferences, and racial advancement organizations, the women tried to alter the present discrimination in accommodations, housing, public statements, justice, and racial violence. Their war work made them feel entitled to respect as Americans.

When they failed to gain that respect, they called public attention to the insensitivity or injustice. When the Reverend Billy Sunday proselytized in Providence, he proposed that the work of black men and women for the war entitled them "to work along side of any white girl in the munition factories."[88] Yet within the month, he advised holding a "Jim Crow" night at the Tabernacle. Nannie Burroughs criticized his insensitivity in a sarcastic reply utilizing patriotic rhetoric. She said that she spoke for "every sensible Negro in Washington" who felt insulted by his idea and suggested that he "shut up the Tabernacle on 'Jim Crow Gospel' thought and accept the saving in fuel as your contribution to the Government in its effort to conserve fuel."[89]

In addition, black women called attention to the labels used to designate race. Atlanta women criticized the public press of the city and the state for "heralding in glaring headlines to the world, every little weakness or recreancy . . . [while] suppressing the good and commendable qualities of the race."[90] They wanted a "keener sense of fairness"[91] in the printed word and a label of their own choosing on training camp signs. Instead of "Negro," the Atlanta women asked for "Colored" on signposts and camp printed matter.[92]

The Atlanta women correctly responded to the harsh treatment in the public press. The reports about black behavior had been partially responsible for the Atlanta riot in 1906. Racial violence continued to be feared by black Americans. During times of social chaos, as in wartime, the chances of such violence increased. For example, a black physician in Vicksburg, Mississippi, received a tar-and-feather treatment for his refusal to purchase $1,000 worth of war savings stamps. Black housewives were jailed for vagrancy when they refused to accept jobs picking cotton or working as domestics. In addition to these indignities, the war years were noted for frequent race riots and brutal lynchings.[93]

The war-produced competition for available housing, access to recreational facilities, use of transportation, and jobs led to racial confrontation in Chester, Pennsylvania; Philadelphia; East St. Louis, Illinois; and other areas.[94] Racial harassment of black soldiers led to retaliatory violence in Houston. The white-led violence of East St. Louis, which resulted in the deaths of at least thirty-nine blacks, resulted in the punishment of only a few whites. Yet the death of seventeen whites in Houston led to the execution of thirteen blacks in the winter of 1917. Sixteen more received death sentences, with several dozen sentenced to life imprisonment.[95] The inequities in punishments for racial violence increased black militance. The November 1918 issue of *The Crisis* reported the existence of a "New Negro" whose "sullen attitude" combined with the realization of injustice displayed a "growing determination on the part of the Negro to claim his rights at any cost."[96]

The brutality of lynching captured public attention. A mentally retarded black youth was tortured and burned before a crowd of thousands in Waco. A similar situation occurred in Estill Springs, Tennessee, on Lincoln's birthday. Such public torture and burnings became more frequent during the war years. Mass lynchings in Gainesville, Florida, and Brooks and Lowndes counties in Georgia stimulated public outcries. In the latter case, the pregnant wife of one of the victims protested her husband's innocence and was burned alive for her actions. In 1918, sixty-four blacks had been lynched. During the first four months of 1919, nine blacks were lynched in five southern states. Black soldiers appearing in uniform became victims of lynch mobs in Georgia and Mississippi.[97]

Descriptions of sadistic torture coupled with statistics about the number of lynchings and reputed reasons for them revealed an American public either participating in such brutalities or lending "tacit approval and active tolerance"[98] to such actions. The women of Atlanta protested in an open letter to the president, cabinet, Congress, governors, and state legislatures. They condemned the "massacre" of blacks in East St. Louis, and the punishment of black soldiers in Houston. They argued that the disenfranchisement of blacks in the South was an effort to "re-enslave" the race. In direct language, the women condemned the discrimination and admonished the politicians for their inaction. They warned:

> our intolerance is cumulative. . . . We shall exert our righteous efforts until not only every eligible black man but every black woman shall be wielding the ballot proudly in defense of our liberties and our homes. . . . We are loyal and will remain so, but we are not blind. . . . What think you will be the effect on the morale of black men in the trenches when they reflect that they are fighting on foreign fields in behalf of their nation for those very rights and privileges which they themselves are denied at home?[99]

They appealed to the political leaders to take action in the name of democracy, American citizenship, and God, but added, "*We will be heard!*"[100]

The Atlanta protest letter demonstrated an overt response to wartime injustice. Through the women's clubs, black women again voiced dissatisfaction with American racial policies. At the annual meeting of the National Council of Women, Mary Church Terrell's speech and presence as a delegate led to the passage of a resolution favoring equal opportunity for black women.[101] The biennial meeting of the NACW in Denver during the summer of 1918 produced similar resolutions. The black clubwomen reaffirmed their commitment to the war effort, pledging to continue supporting the Red Cross, relief work, food conservation, and fund-raising. Mary Talbert, the president of the NACW, praised the women for their success in raising millions of dollars for the Liberty Loan Drive and the Red

Cross. The NACW allocated money to send representatives to the war work councils. Talbert likewise encouraged the affiliation of white female reformers Jane Addams, Sophinisba Breckinridge, Zona Gale, Crystal Eastman, and Mrs. Robert LaFollette so that the women of both races could work together for passage of the Eighteenth and Nineteenth Amendments.

But their commitment to American and reformist goals did not cloud their concern for racial issues. The exclusion of black women from serving as Red Cross nurses brought condemnation and a national petition to the Red Cross. The women urged the passage of a federal antilynching amendment for which they promised active participation. They also refused to support segregationists running for office.

These black clubwomen demonstrated racial pride through many public activities. The 1918 biennial witnessed the public burning of the mortgage on the Frederick Douglass Home. This national monument to black achievement remained in the hands of black women. The memorial tablet with the names of black women who donated money to save the home served as a historical record for future generations. Talbert requested that black women compile biographical information and store memorabilia of their achievements at the home "so that our boys and girls may receive inspiration from your work and your life."[102] The home symbolized not only the success of one black man, but also the organized achievements of black women.[103]

The black clubwomen also resisted discrimination by covertly uncovering information for organized action. The NACW leaders toured the South during the fall of 1918 to increase sales of Liberty Bonds. Before their departure, they obtained travel expenses from the branches of the NAACP. During their tour the women gathered evidence for the NACW about railroad accommodations and conditions of travel for blacks throughout the South. Their confidential report to the NAACP demonstrated a continual pursuit of racial reform during the war years.[104]

As organizer for the War Camp Community Service, Mary Church Terrell was supposed to select qualified black women to head recreational centers in Illinois, Alabama, Tennessee, and Georgia.[105] These centers sought to provide "practical work" for returning soldiers. In addition to helping the returning men, Terrell also traveled through Florida, Mississippi, Alabama, Georgia, and Tennessee to ascertain the need and potential reception of local communities to work with black women. She spoke to white leaders who served on the local executive committees of the War Camp Community Service and boards of the YWCA.

Her experiences varied but generally reflected the deep prejudices of southern whites against improved conditions for blacks. In Pensacola, white leaders would allow no programs until "they could be persuaded that a Colored worker here would teach Colored girls to be better servants."[106] Although many black soldiers had already returned, the whites would not support a War Camp recreational center. One man compared the black soldier's service to a mule's contribution: "He will do the work if you will furnish the brain."[107] Despite such recalcitrance, the black women in Pensacola implored Terrell to do as much as possible, since neither the YWCA nor any other agency had attempted to meet the needs.

White opposition followed Mary Terrell. In public meetings Terrell became "she" so that white southerners did not have to address a black woman by the title of "Mrs." Since much of her work resembled that of the YWCA, cooperation with that organization was occasionally necessary. A white YWCA worker in Gulfport, Mississippi, advised Terrell "to go about it [colored work] quietly."[108] The Macon YWCA did not object to the sending of a black woman to work with the black girls, but emphasized it "would not assume any responsibility if it did not succeed."[109] In Atlanta, the city's two YWCA workers had accomplished little for over five thousand girls of that city. Terrell received some help from the Anti-Tuberculosis Association, but recommended sending at least one more black woman to help in Atlanta. Only in Memphis, the city of Terrell's family origins, did she receive cooperation. The Memphis Industrial Welfare Committee, an interracial group seeking to improve housing and employment for blacks, agreed to cooperate with the War Camp Community Service in establishing a community center as the headquarters for all work concerning black people."[110]

Little gains came from the War Camp Community Service in most areas of the South. Often goals could be achieved through protest, propaganda, and public pressure of the NAACP. Before Terrell left the War Camp Community Service in April 1919,[111] she sent copies of her reports and interviews to the NAACP. She requested that John Shillady pay particular attention to the attitudes expressed in certain interviews.[112] Apparently her reports stimulated action in the NAACP. A conference at the offices of the National Board of the YWCA attended by Eugene K. Jones of the National Urban League, Jesse Moreland of the YMCA, Eva Bowles of the YWCA, Mary Talbert of the NACW, and Mary White Ovington of the NAACP produced a letter from the five national organizations to the War Camp

Community Service requesting a conference to discuss the southern conservatism reflected in the agency's policies and practices.[113]

The War Camp Community Service work of Mary Terrell and the fund-raising tours of the NACW/NAACP women indicated that the armistice declared on November 11, 1918, had ended the fighting but not the war. Black women continued to work in fund-raising, government services, and reform organizations until all war-related activity stopped. Demobilization and peace became major concerns as the European situation seemed to be moving toward peace negotiations. Blacks wanted to ensure the safe return of their troops, to make certain that racial issues were acknowledged in the peace process, and to create a process of demobilization that protected the safety and welfare of all black Americans. From many directions, black women attempted to facilitate these goals.

Several black men and women applied for passports to go to Europe following the armistice. The United States government, wishing to avoid embarrassing public statements about American racial injustices, refused to approve passports of all but a few black men and women. To travel to Paris, black leaders had either to resort to deception or be engaged in activities considered acceptable by the government. The outspoken criticism of the National Equal Rights League caused the State Department to deny passports to the delegates. Ida B. Wells-Barnett and Madame C. J. Walker, the female delegates, could not reach Paris.[114] William Monroe Trotter, posing as a seaman, made it by May 1919. Du Bois used his position as editor of *The Crisis* to gain a position on the press ship that left the United States in December 1918. Unlike a fellow traveler, Robert Moton, who attempted to pacify the black troops remaining in France, Du Bois sought to collect data about the treatment and role of black soldiers and to organize a Pan-African Congress.[115]

Black women seemed less of a direct threat to the American self-image. Several black women were able to leave the United States through their connections with the YMCA, the YWCA, and the international women's organizations. They appeared in France in late 1918 and early 1919. Most were allowed to go because of their participation in "acceptable" activities. Immediately following the armistice, the Paris headquarters of the YWCA requested the services of "six fine colored women at once."[116] Under the guidance of the War Work Council of the YMCA, only three black women arrived in France to minister to the needs of over 200,000 black troops. These women represented a variety of organizational backgrounds. Kathryn

Johnson, former organizer for the NAACP; Addie Hunton, organizer for the YWCA, the NAACP, and the NACW; and Helen Curtis, clubwoman from Washington and wife of James L. Curtis, the minister to Liberia, talked with the soldiers, recorded their aspirations, and, in cases of discrimination, made recommendations for improving conditions or assignments. Hunton and Johnson recorded the discrimination against black soldiers and their exclusion from the Paris victory parade. They reported black soldiers confined to camps to prevent contact with white French women and slander by white officers. They told about American-originated propaganda spread among the French about the anatomy of black men. During the spring of 1919, sixteen more black women arrived as canteen workers to set up reading and reception rooms. Their work received the praise of white officials and commendation from General Pershing.[119]

The reports of the black women contradicted the official versions issued by Ralph W. Tyler, black appointee to the Committee on Public Information, who denied mistreatment of black soldiers. Robert R. Moton counseled the soldiers to return home displaying modest behavior. The black women served as surrogate mothers for the soldiers preparing to return to the United States. They listened to the personal stories of the soldiers and recorded their experiences for the NACW and the NAACP. They were in France to meet the needs of their soldiers as well as to ensure peace for future generations.[120]

A few black women reflected an international perspective in their European activities. Addie Hunton and Mary Talbert used their earlier work with the YMCA/YWCA to attend the Pan-African Congress in Paris, February 19-21, 1919. Ida Gibbs Hunt used her participation in the International Congress of Women, to be held in Zurich in May, to gain travel approval in order to participate in the Pan-African Congress. These women participated in the meetings seeking gradual self-government for Africans, the use of the League of Nations to supervise the rights of natives, and the promotion of mass education for Africans. Addie Hunton spoke about the role of women in this world reconstruction. The Executive Committee, which emerged from the Pan-African Congress, included Ida Gibbs Hunt as secretary. The Pan-African ideals became a prominent interest of the organized black women and their club movement.[121]

The international ideals included women. Ida Gibbs Hunt and Mary Talbert joined Mary Church Terrell in Zurich for the International Congress of Women, May 13-17, 1919. Accompanied by Jeanette Rankin, Jane

Addams, and nine other American female delegates, Terrell was the only non-white member of the delegation to the conference. Due to the important influence of the African countries during World War I, Terrell saw her presence at this conference as crucial to non-white countries. Terrell delivered the opening address in German and described the continual racial difficulties in the United States. The conference passed a resolution supporting educational opportunities, equal opportunities to earn a living, and elimination of discrimination and humiliation of "human beings on account of race, color, or creed."[122] Terrell's speech had been heard.

The experiences of the several prominent black women confirmed black disenchantment with both the American war efforts and the peace process. Each woman had gained her passport through the performance of "acceptable women's work," such as aiding soldiers or attending women's meetings. Mary Talbert admitted to other reasons for her going to France as a canteen worker. She intended to use the public platform of the international meetings to "tell of our treatment over here. France and England must tell America how the 'poor crackers' should treat us."[123] While in Europe, the women's contact with American racial prejudices through the Christian organizations, military, or women's groups made them very aware that postwar hopes were unrealistic.[124]

The black women returned to the United States during the spring and early summer of 1919. Demobilization produced thousands of returning soldiers, a reversion to peacetime economy, and readjustment to civilian life. Demobilization hastened the economic and social tensions that exploded in the Red Summer of 1919. The soldiers' return combined with the revitalization of the Ku Klux Klan, the persistent denial of suffrage, residential segregation, unemployment, strikes, and postwar hysteria against immigrants and radicals. Conditions were fertile for racial violence. By the end of 1919, seventy-seven blacks were lynched, including eleven soldiers. Twenty-six cities suffered race riots killing hundreds of blacks in Chicago, Omaha, Charleston, Longview (Texas), and Phillips County (Arkansas). Whites in Austin, Texas, severely beat the NAACP secretary, John Shillady.[125]

The warning of the Atlanta women from March 1918 came to bear on the nation's capital. When blacks were chased down streets and taken off streetcars and beaten or killed, the black mob retaliated against the white attackers. The Washington blacks had reached the "certain point"[126] mentioned by the Atlanta women. They had sacrificed "the best blood of our sons upon our Nation's altar to help destroy Prussianism beyond the seas."[127] They expected better treatment in the postwar world. Instead, they met increased intolerance and violence. Many felt that they could not and would not tolerate the treatment any longer. An anonymous black woman from the South responded to the Washington riot:

> The Washington riot gave me the thrill that comes once in a life time . . . our men had stood like men, struck back, were no longer dumb, driven cattle. . . . The pent-up humiliation, grief and horror of a life time—half a century—was being stripped from me . . . thank God for Washington colored men![128]

The war had changed black Americans. Many had emigrated to urban areas seeking jobs and a better life for their families. Their sudden numbers and social needs had led to the development and expansion of social services for the black community. Many of the ambitious among them had ascended to political and economic prominence from a community base. Organized, proud of their achievements under adverse conditions, and possessing a power base in the urban areas, communities of blacks had come to express the spirit of the New Negro in postwar America. As part of this metamorphosis, black female leadership emerged from their war roles with a resolve to bring democracy to their people.

EIGHT

Peace, Pride, and Protest: Black Women in the Postwar Period

The postwar period provided the context in which rising expectations collided with political reality. No longer needed to win the war, blacks found themselves unemployed, attacked by mobs, and subordinated in the organizations that had promised a better life. Yet black women approached their postwar reform role confidently and optimistically.[1] They worked for less charity and more justice. Armed with better training, interorganizational connections, and confidence, they sought a greater voice in organizations delivering services to their communities.

The war years escalated several changes that stimulated the development of the postwar New Negro.[2] Demographically, black Americans became increasingly urban. The population pressures stimulated the expansion of existing social services, the creation of new agencies, and the development of political organization. Restricted housing patterns meant that blacks could develop greater political power in areas where they retained the franchise. White politicians became more responsive in cities with organized black political groups. Black concentration in southern cities created social problems requiring municipal solutions. White reformers and politicians needed the cooperation of the black middle class to curb the spread of tuberculosis, to lessen crime, and to avoid social chaos. Their centralized numbers in both the North and South established an organized, educated leadership possessing greater power to protest discrimination and greater ability to improve social conditions.[3]

Many black men and women expressed a conscious awareness of how war work had changed their attitudes. Addie Hunton and Kathryn Johnson said the war developed a "racial consciousness and racial strength that could not have been gained in a half century of normal living in America."[4] Eva Bowles

231

of the YWCA felt the war provided the opportunity "to prove [the black woman's] ability for leadership and . . . she made good."[5] St. Louis black women gained confidence from their achievements.[6] Du Bois noted that in "the great rank and file of our five million women we have . . . new revolutionary ideals which must in time have vast influence on the thought and action of this land."[7] Another felt that their "quiet struggle over organization"[8] in the war work agencies helped to erode the southern caste system and to increase the responsibility and self-respect of black women.

War work enabled black women to extend their organizational networks. They carried out programs, raised money, conducted investigations, and offered suggestions to aid the civilian efforts. They received praise from white female reformers and from male heads of government agencies or social reform organizations.[9] They developed confidence in their abilities and expected to be treated justly in the postwar era. The wartime rhetoric stressing the principles of democracy raised the expectations of black women and made some whites more conscious of the racial injustices in America. In short, the war experience stimulated a growth in consciousness.

Demobilization and postwar racial violence required immediate action. The armistice enabled black women to work for reconstruction. Many continued their war work in Liberty Loan campaigns, hostess houses, and demobilization. The Circle for Negro War Relief dropped the word "war" from its name and revised a peacetime reform program covering health and child care in a national public welfare plan.[10]

The armistice also allowed leading black women to refocus their attentions on the chronic American problem of lynching. In May 1919, the NAACP sponsored a National Conference on Lynching that drew over 2,500 men and women to Carnegie Hall to hear speeches by black and white leaders. The meeting resolved to develop support for federal antilynching legislation, to organize state committees to create favorable public opinion, and to carry on systematic fund-raising and advertising campaigns. Before disbanding, the conference prepared "An Address to the Nation on Lynching" signed by leading citizens including an ex-president of the United States, an attorney general, seven state governors, university presidents, and leading reformers.[11]

Mary Talbert became the guiding force behind the postwar mobilization of black women against lynching. As president of the National Association of Colored Women (NACW), Talbert had worked with Congressman L. C. Dyer, sponsor of a federal antilynching bill, before the NAACP had begun such interaction. She relied on the extensive club structure to extract personnel, imagination, money, and volunteer activity to spread the information and create a political cadre. She succeeded in raising $12,000 for a defense fund and pledged black women to crusade against lynching.[12]

And crusade they did. Charlotte Hawkins Brown, founder of Palmer Memorial Institute in Sedalia, North Carolina, addressed the North Carolina Federation of Women's Clubs about the black antilynching campaign. The white clubwomen passed resolutions condemning lynching and mob violence. Esther Jones Lee served as the regional officer for the California crusaders. Ida B. Wells-Barnett served as the publicity director of the National Equal Rights League's antilynching activities.[13]

Black women used their organizations to mobilize support. The Georgia Federation of Colored Women's Clubs petitioned the governor of that state to use his office for action against lynching.[14] The War Work Council of the YWCA requested its members to provide "constructive help" and suggestions for the improvement of racial enmity: "As a world-wide organization for women, we stand ready and eager to do our part . . . to bring about a more friendly relationship, greater sympathy and understanding between the races, justice, and protection under the law."[15] The greatest work resulted from the cooperation of the NACW and the NAACP.

Through the NAACP, black women raised money to fund investigations, publicity, and public meetings to increase public support for the Dyer federal antilynching bill. Within a few years, Talbert mobilized black women into an ad hoc group for fund-raising and publicity (this group became the Anti-Lynching Crusaders on July 15, 1922). Broader based than the NAACP, this group directed religious fervor into their crusade to "unite one million women to suppress lynching . . . and make the Dyer Anti-Lynching Bill a law."[16]

The staff received no pay; every cent went for antilynching activities. For leadership of this volunteer group, Talbert built on networks developed during wartime. She had been a participant in the Zurich International Council of Women conference. Helen Curtis and Mary Wilson, the two vice-directors of the antilynching group, had been active in the YWCA canteen work and hostess house management. The publicity committee of the antilynching group was headed by Alice Dunbar Nelson, who had served as the field representative for the Woman's Committee on the Council of National Defense, and Grace Nail Johnson, who had been a leader in the New York City Circle for Negro War Relief. The role as national organizer went to Mary E. Jackson, who had served as the Industrial Secretary for the YWCA's Committee on Colored Work.[17]

Such leaders used their organizing experiences in the NACW, the YWCA, the war agencies, and the NAACP. Talbert, Wilson, Curtis, and Jackson had actively organized NAACP branches throughout the Northeast, Midwest, and Southwest. Grace Nail Johnson, the wife of James Weldon Johnson, the national field secretary of the NAACP, was also familiar with the organizational techniques necessary for such a national campaign. Together, these women relied on female networks to mobilize the black communities against the postwar violence. Talbert sent letters to clubwomen heading state and city federations, asking them to hold meetings, persuade ministers to deliver antilynching sermons, and mobilize their communities to sell and wear buttons publicizing the campaign. "Sacrifice weeks" sought to raise at least one dollar from every black woman throughout the nation. Pamphlets filled with descriptions of lynchings, statistics, and methods to organize campaigns went to clubwomen who sent in lists of volunteers and donations. As with her earlier success in saving the Frederick Douglass Home, Talbert relied on her "United Sisterhood."[18] With the help of supportive white female reformers,[19] the black women created the foundation for a movement against lynching and racial violence which finally came to fruition in the 1930s with the founding of the Association of Southern Women for the Prevention of Lynching.[20]

The black women not only tried to lessen the racial violence in America, they also joined the Women's International League for Peace and Freedom (WILPF). Mary Church Terrell, one of the few black women active in the American peace movement prior to World War I,[21] had refocused her peace efforts toward domestic reform during the war. Following the war, Terrell accompanied white peace advocates Jane Addams and Jeanette Rankin to the International Council of Women conference in Zurich. Terrell and the other black women who attended this conference tried to link the women's peace movement to other reforms.[22]

Terrell wrote a pamphlet for the WILPF's Americanization Committee. She argued that the Americanization process should teach an appreciation of the contributions made by the many races and cultures in America instead of imposing white, English cultural values on every immigrant and race. During the postwar period when conformity and nativist-racist hysteria escalated, Terrell was able to influence the constitution of the WILPF: membership was open to any woman who promoted methods of peace in American

Black female educators served as the core of leadership in the South. Pictured here at a 1907 teachers' convention at Hampton are (left to right) Lugenia Burns Hope, Jennie B. Moton (perhaps), Margaret Murray Washington, Mary McLeod Bethune, and two unidentified teachers. John Hope, president of Morehouse College, is at the left.
[*Atlanta University Archives.*]

society. After adopting the official title of the Woman's Peace Party, the Americanization Committee became the Committee on Citizenship.[23]

Black women's peace interests and international concerns continued to expand during the 1920s. Delilah L. Beasley, clubwoman and journalist in Oakland, participated in the League of Nations Association for Northern California and, later, in the World's Forum. Black women circulated petitions advocating the United States's participation in the World Court and supporting the Geneva Disarmament Conference, both actions showing a concern for international issues during the so-called isolationist 1920s.[24]

The international theme again appeared in a new woman's organization—the International Council of Women of the Darker Races of the World. Organized in Richmond, during the summer of 1921, the purposes of the organization were to study the history and present conditions of darker-skinned peoples, to develop race pride, and to acquaint other races about the problems throughout the world. The leadership reflected a variety of ideologies and regions. Margaret Murray Washington of Tuskegee was elected president. Addie Hunton of Brooklyn and Mary Church Terrell of Washington became vice presidents. Other officers included Elizabeth C. Carter (New Bedford, Massachusetts), Mary Jackson McCrorey (Charlotte, North Carolina), and Mame Stewart Josenberger (Fort Smith, Arkansas), all of whom were leading clubwomen. The Executive Committee was headed by Nannie Burroughs and included Mary McLeod Bethune, Nettie Langston Napier, and Maggie Lena Walker. Addie Dickerson of Philadelphia, Lugenia Hope of Atlanta, and Emily Williams of Hampton headed special committees. Others actively involved were Charlotte Hawkins Brown, Mary Talbert, and Casely Hayford, a black woman educated in New Jersey who was teaching in Sierra Leone. Led by these prominent black women, a subgroup of 135 women prepared study courses for clubs, schools, and leaders. They encouraged elementary and secondary schools as well as colleges to incorporate their information into the curricula. They believed that factual information about the darker-skinned peoples in America and throughout the world would create racial pride, erase racial ignorance, and promote understanding.[25]

Black women continued an interest in the Pan-African movement. At the Richmond biennial of the NACW, Jessie Fauset, literary editor of *The Crisis*, reported on the recent 1921 Pan-African Congress. The NACW delegates also heard speeches about West Africa and African womanhood. Through the congresses, the International Council of Women of the Darker Races of the

World, the Woman's Peace Party, and the NACW biennials, black women became more aware of their ties to people of the Third World. Study clubs formed throughout the century to investigate the readings available for education. The movement for black history received a valuable ally among the black women's clubs, teacher's associations, and interracial organizations in which many of the women remained active.[26]

The postwar period demonstrated a reaffirmation of interest in women's concerns. Most of the wartime reform activities required subordination of or incorporation into established war goals. The popular association of women and peace provided a stimulus to the passage of the woman suffrage amendment. Expediency continued to dominate the policies of the National American Woman Suffrage Association (NAWSA). When the Northeastern Federation of Women's Clubs, which represented over 6,000 black members, applied for a cooperative membership with the NAWSA, the white women deemed the black women's federation eligible, but advised postponement of their application until after the amendment had passed. Since the suffrage amendment was so close to passing, the white leadership wanted to avoid any last-minute conflicts. Ida Husted Harper asked Mary Church Terrell to use her influence to have the Northeastern Federation withdraw its application to avoid jeopardizing the final vote in the Senate. Again black women waited for equitable treatment.[27]

Conflict also occurred with the National Woman's Party and statements attributed to the organization's director, Alice Paul. When Paul had stated in a *New York Times* article that the suffrage amendment would have little effect on the voting rights of South Carolina black women, she explained that she had been referring to the effective methods of disenfranchisement used by the southern states. Nevertheless, many black women and a few interested white reformers took Paul and the Woman's Party to task and Paul was asked to repudiate the statements. The NAACP promised to turn its 187 branches against the amendment if it intended to limit the voting rights of any groups. Black women helped the NAACP pressure the National Woman's Party to deal with the race issues, but for Paul, gender equality continued to be the primary goal.[28]

During the whole long struggle for the suffrage amendment, the leadership of the NAWSA had never placed the organization on public record supporting the black woman's right to vote and no major leader had publicly repudiated the suffrage argument which implied reduction of black political power. When woman's suffrage became national law, black women began to prepare themselves as voters. The branch secretary of the Cleveland NAACP reported "Cleveland is alive as it never has been before due to the intense interest taken in politics by women. Meetings and classes are held all over the city where white and black women go to be taught how to vote."[29] By the fall of 1920, women's citizenship classes had been organized in Alabama, Georgia, Illinois, Kansas, Virginia, Oklahoma, West Virginia, Ohio, Missouri, and Kentucky. The NACW biennial at Tuskegee emphasized preparation for the vote. The evidence demonstrated a conscious effort to use the vote as a tool for racial and sexual reform.[30]

Black women continued to stress the use of the educated, informed vote to effect reform. Alfreda Barnett, daughter of Ida B. Wells-Barnett, urged black women to vote against non-supporters of the Dyer Anti-Lynching Bill. Lugenia Hope organized registration and education programs for women to "take on the duty of citizenship."[31] The NACW supported the movement for black women to "actively engage in politics wherever, whenever, and however they can without breaking the law."[32] They felt the need to become more politically active in order to break the double burden of racial and sexual powerlessness. In 1924, the National League of Women Voters established a Committee on Negro Problems; every state having at least a 15 percent black population received membership.[33]

The postwar period raised white womens' awareness of racial issues, but such consciousness did not come easily or automatically. Black women actively pursued more equitable treatment in white-led reform organizations that altered programs, perspectives, and policies. The emergence of both the New Negro and the New Woman during this period created changes in the NAACP, the National Urban League, and the YWCA.

The interaction and participation in the interracial NAACP and the National Urban League became more important. Since black women had played important roles as regional organizers and branch developers, the NAACP rewarded their work through appointments to offices. During the postwar era, both Nannie Burroughs and Mary Talbert served on the NAACP Board of Directors. Talbert became one of the six vice presidents of the NAACP and winner of the Spingarn medal. Addie Hunton became a field secretary after James Weldon Johnson advanced to national secretary. Mary White Ovington's advice to include more black women in leadership positions fell on receptive ears. The field organizer position passed from Hunton to Daisy Lampkin and on to contemporary leaders, such as Ella

Baker. In the NAACP, black women maintained a tradition as prime movers.[34]

The National Urban League, though more conservative in approach, relied on black women for its initial expansion and reinforced the woman's role in social work. Some of the same women who aided the growth of the NAACP also helped to develop the National Urban League. The Urban League rewarded a few national black women leaders; Margaret Murray Washington, Nannie Burroughs, and Mary McLeod Bethune gained national positions. But, most black female influence still remained at the local affiliate level.[35]

Black women became more involved in social work through the Urban League. The fellowship program trained nineteen men and nineteen women in the 1920s. Just as the Bethlehem House and Training Center in Nashville had emerged in 1914 from the cooperative efforts of the Urban League, Woman's Missionary Council, and Fisk University, the Atlanta School of Social Service began in 1920 to meet the need for professional social workers in the Southeast. The courses, held on the Morehouse campus, provided social and economic theory, social case work, statistics and record keeping, discussion of medical-social problems, and fieldwork. A course in community organization was jointly taught by Jesse O. Thomas, field secretary of the Urban League for Southern Field, and Lugenia Hope, president of the Atlanta Neighborhood Union. The tradition of cooperation among universities, the Urban League, and local social welfare organizations created another path to professional social work.

Together, these southern schools, when added to the older schools of social work in New York, Pittsburgh, and Chicago, provided trained black workers to serve as district agents, welfare workers in industry, executives in Colored Departments of Associated Charities, probation officers in juvenile courts, recreation directors, and secretaries for Urban Leagues, YMCAs, and YWCAs. This preparation of social workers led to expansion of Urban League affiliates and branches, which required direction under a professionally trained worker. Affiliates emerged in Baltimore, Omaha, Los Angeles, Kansas City, Tampa, and Minneapolis-St. Paul. Community houses provided services for the black urban populations, as did settlement houses for the immigrants. The black women who organized and staffed these centers made urban life more bearable. Picnics, camps, clean-up campaigns, essay contests, day nurseries, and clinics touched the lives of residents in many communities.

Municipal governments began to assume more responsibility for these essential social services. The Urban League's dental clinic in St. Louis became part of the local health department. In Atlanta, the health department took over the infant welfare station. The Detroit Municipal Court hired the probation officer for black juveniles. The Social Services Bureau in Newark hired four caseworkers to provide similar services for that city's black youth. The services started by black women had become institutionalized in many municipal programs by the 1920s.[36] Governments and white social welfare associations had come to "recognize the need for special colored work."[37]

During 1919 and 1920, black women also fought for racial recognition and inclusion in policy making. The YWCA's work with black women and girls had expanded during World War I. Demobilization challenged the earlier altruism and idealism. A new generation of black women had become vocal in the YWCA. Better-educated products of urban prosperity, critical of conservatism in black churches and other institutions, and proud of their wartime achievements, these women pressured the YWCA to fulfill its wartime promises.[38]

The return to peacetime reform led to the Ys closing all hostess houses by October 1919 and the absorption of the industrial and recreational programs into the general association work. Meetings and conferences held during that year reflected postwar changes and black criticism mounted about racial discrimination in the YWCA. At the national conference in Washington in February 1919, black women suggested that the Y work become interracial rather than biracial. Eva Bowles reported in September that the Student Conference at Talladega "felt different from other conferences,"[39] in the militance among the younger women. In Boston, the Urban League branch criticized the "exceedingly small . . . number of colored girls touched and helped by the YWCA."[40]

When the International Student Volunteer Convention met in Des Moines on December 31, 1919, the conflicts between YWCA practices and young, educated, proud black women became apparent. The black secretaries had been assured that no discrimination would occur. After they "demanded" accommodation in the same hotel as the white staff, only the YMCA black male secretaries were admitted. The YWCA senior secretary provided counsel only to "her colored women secretaries."[41] Catherine Lealtad, national secretary of the Department of Methods and one of four black secretaries, described the situation:

> Miss Conde told me that in demanding that I be accommodated in the hotel with the rest of my staff, I was acting contrary to customary policy of the Y.W.C.A. She further stated . . . that they could not afford to do so much,

Catherine Lealtad, increasingly disenchanted with the racial policies of the YWCA, resigned from her leadership position there to become the Associate Secretary of the New York Urban League. She later served as Associate Director of Branches of the NAACP.
[*Macalester College Archives.*]

because they might alienate the white constituency of the Association in that state.[42]

The women finally stayed in the local white YWCA to avoid direct conflict with hotel management. After the convention was over, however, the Y refused to accommodate the black secretaries for two more nights. They wanted to avoid setting a precedent.

In response to the attitudes and actions in Des Moines, the black field-workers attended a meeting in New York, which created the Bureau of Colored Work. The first meeting, on February 27, 1920, attempted to create "an understanding with the colored secretaries, so that there would not be another situation such as there was in Des Moines."[43] The general secretary of the YWCA told the black women about the approaching Triennial Convention in Cleveland. The YWCA did not want the black delegates to stay in hotels with whites because their presence might offend southern white delegates. Adelle Ruffin, the black secretary of the southeastern field, reminded the other black women that the black delegates at the Louisville Convention prior to World War I had promised to "go no faster in their work than the attitude of the southern white women would warrant."[44] This was not the last time that Ruffin supported white policy or practice.[45]

Many black women became increasingly disenchanted with the racial policies in the YWCA. Shortly after the New York meeting, Lealtad resigned to become the associate secretary of the New York Urban League and later the associate director of branches for the NAACP. She felt the YWCA had failed the "acid test" for public display of the Christian spirit.[46] Addie Hunton, one of the first black women involved in the YWCA work with the National Board, sought more activity in the NAACP in 1920 to replace her efforts in the YWCA.

In Atlanta, the turnover of YWCA workers reflected the interracial conflicts. Beatrice D. Walker became a social worker for women and girls at St. John's Institutional Activities, an affiliate of the National Urban League in Springfield, Massachusetts, after conflicts over white direction and problems with Adelle Ruffin. Walker told Lugenia Hope that Ruffin's "overbearing ways" made the younger workers "uneasy, afraid, uncertain."[47] Ruffin always looked for ulterior motives, undercut her workers in front of white women, and felt threatened by younger women. Due to these difficulties, Walker left Atlanta to take "less popular and smaller paying work just for the freedom to serve in peace."[48] Walker's replacement, Florence Kennedy, did not find the situation any easier. She performed well, but

Ruffin fired her. The Atlanta black women wrote to the National Board, demanding her reinstatement.

The problems in Atlanta epitomized the assertiveness of black women no longer satisfied with accommodation or compromise. The YWCA sought to remove Catherine Lealtad as national secretary of the Department of Methods and place her where she would be less apt to protest segregationist policies. Lealtad opposed reassignment and refused to work with the YWCA under the direction of a white supervisor. She sought the support of the black staff members of the National Board, who, in 1920, included: May Belcher, Crystal Bird, Caroline Bond, Eva Bowles, Mabel S. Brady, Juliette Derricotte, Frances O. Grant, Almira Holmes, Mary Jackson, Catherine Lealtad, Adelle Ruffin, Juanita Saddler, Mrs. D. W. Stokes, Jeanette Triplett, Clayda Williams, and Cordella A. Winn. Lealtad reported only Bowles ready to speak out. Bowles told the white supervisor that "a white woman could not do for the colored girls what one of their own could do."[49] When the supervisor suggested that a southern white woman might have better luck with race relations in the South, Bowles replied, "instead of having one woman who had the right attitude toward colored work, all of the secretaries of the National Board should have [an] understanding attitude toward the colored work."[50] These efforts produced no results. Lealtad resigned, disgusted with the "milk and water"[51] policies of the YWCA and the lack of support from the black staff.[52]

During the latter part of 1919 and early 1920, letters poured in to Lugenia Hope, who had been preparing a direct attack on the YWCA policies and practices. Helen A. Davis, the executive of the Field Work Department of the National Board, tried to lessen Hope's opposition by claiming faulty communications. Davis felt the English language inadequate to communicate policies and, thus, misinterpretations and inaccurate conclusions created misunderstandings.[53] The movement continued. Many black women of the South were dissatisfied and demanded change.

Hope called a meeting at Morehouse College of representative black women to discuss the attitude of southern white women toward the participation of black women in the affairs of the YWCA. These black women represented a variety of organizational experiences. Frances Keyser, former New York club leader and director of the White Rose Home, now represented the Florida club network, as did her co-worker, Mary McLeod Bethune. Mary Jackson McCrorey of Charlotte, North Carolina, had been the assistant to Lucy Laney at Haines Institute before her marriage and leadership in the club movement. McCrorey joined her fellow educator and North Carolina club leader, Charlotte Hawkins Brown. Lucy Laney of Augusta and Lugenia Hope of Atlanta represented Georgia. Marion Wilkerson of Orangeburg, South Carolina, and a Mrs. W. Hale, a substitute for Nettie Napier of Nashville, completed the group. They represented over 300,000 black women of the South. They criticized the misrepresentation of black women at the prewar Louisville Conference, denying that black women had agreed to advance no faster than southern whites would allow. They condemned YWCA statements that the "alley girl" was not acceptable to the YWCA. They voted to draw up an appeal to the National Board. Constructed by McCrorey, Brown, Hope, Wilkerson, and Keyser, the appeal received the endorsement of the delegates for presentation at the Triennial Convention to be held in mid-April 1920 in Cleveland.[54]

The militant petition, presented to the National Board by McCrorey, Laney, and Hope, requested an investigation of the South Atlantic Field, where black women remained dissatisfied. YWCA workers frequently left employment, and local conditions were ignored. The women recommended that colored work receive supervision, that student work gain direction from National Headquarters, that black women receive representation on the National Board, and that black women be permitted to form independent organizations wherever the branch relationship was not desirable or where no central association existed.[55]

The board responded favorably to some of the requests. The Cleveland conference agreed that black women had been misrepresented at the Louisville conference; nothing had been said about going only so fast as white women allowed. The white women's interpretation created a protest from the black women, "We would rather have no Y.W.C.A. and go back to our church organizations than have a special policy for Colored women under the direction of Southern white women who know absolutely nothing about us."[56] The demands for supervision and leadership led to the YWCA's creation of a new post for Eva Bowles as general secretary of colored work.

The white YWCA would compromise no farther. The board did not favor the black suggestions for independent organizations. They said the black representation on the National Board could not be settled until the election process allowed black women to receive such representation. Hope advised the black women to exert their influence to keep this issue alive. The convention decided that national secretaries could go wherever invited by interested groups. Thus, black women of the South Atlantic Field could invite individuals from the National Headquarters to visit their area for observation, but the representatives had no power to alter conditions.[57]

The National Board resolved some of the difficulties, yet continued to appease the prejudices of the southern white contingents. The National Committee told black delegates attending the Cleveland convention that the Statler Hotel waiters would go on strike if blacks attended the banquet. The Y's acceptance of Jim Crow practices received criticism from the black press. The Cleveland *Advocate* said the YWCA "is becoming more ridiculous every day, as some new evidence of their scorn of Colored people is given. . . . How long will these institutions continue to prostitute the word 'Christian' in their appellation . . ."[58] Another scathing editorial followed and posed the condition, if the YWCA remained segregated, then colored direction and control must follow. Current boards of managers are allowed to "function only up to the point the whites permit them to function."[59] The relationship with these "white overseers" had to stop.

Many of these problems had to be deferred to a later meeting in Richmond. The black women were not satisfied with the results in Cleveland. Nettie Napier said blacks wanted all that America had to offer. Having died for it in World War I, they would be satisfied with nothing less.[60] McCrorey felt the YWCA made their demands seem nothing like a protest. The Y had kept black women "strictly subordinated"[61] in Cleveland. Laney, too, felt uneasy about the results. She advised more agitation and diligence in holding to their stand.[62]

The women reassembled in Richmond on July 3, 1920. Again, the consideration of Colored Work disrupted the genteel proceedings. Held in the offices of the South Atlantic Field Headquarters, the meeting showed the organizational manipulation of white YWCA leaders. As with the perception of the Cleveland meeting, the official record of the YWCA made the black women's "questions" appear to be misunderstandings or misinterpretations of policy.

When faced with the charges that white women refused black women the chance for branch status, the National Committe's staff denied that such had ever occurred. The white women explained, "any hesitancy that a central Association might feel was due not to lack of interest or desire but to the financial burden that Association is already bearing."[64] Frequent turnover in personnel was blamed on the "fickleness" of young women dissatisfied with "climatic, physical, home, salary, distaste for the job, distaste for those with whom they work . . . [and] unwillingness to stand by a difficult job."[65]

245

Lugenia Hope's statement survived, noting that southern white women "do not know the colored women in their churches or in their homes or their educational institutions or in any but a very limited way."[66] The staff response to Hope's statement was regret at "so general a statement."[67]

The South Atlantic Field issued an official report to the National Board. The Richmond meeting of white and colored representatives had discussed the possibility of some branches becoming independents, but there had not been a fight because both groups desired good results and because the black women realized that they could not exist as financial independents. This official version of the Richmond meeting masked the results to the National Board. Black women did not forget the issues they had raised at Morehouse, Cleveland, and Richmond.[68]

The leaders of the YWCA black women's committee brought their grievances to the 1920 Tuskegee NACW biennial. Similar complaints about the YWCA came from clubwomen of the North, the Southwest, and the District of Columbia. Mary Talbert, the current president of the NACW who had just returned from Norway as the representative to the International Council of Women, described the discrimination of southern white women who had accompanied her to Norway, and the Jim Crow policies of the Paris YWCA, which was managed by American white women. Probably as a response to the failures of the Richmond meeting, Charlotte Hawkins Brown proposed that the NACW develop a Southeastern Field to serve as a parallel regional organization to the YWCA's white-dominated South Atlantic Field.

The action taken at the NACW biennial indicated widespread support of Hope, Talbert, and Brown. The NACW refused to endorse the work of the YWCA and resolved that all organizations affecting black women should have black representation. NACW delegates prepared petitions for the YWCA, requesting the right to black representation. Brown's suggestion for a Southeastern Federation also received support. Almost immediately, the cities in the South that had experienced problems with the YWCA began organizing their own federations to support the new Southeastern Federation, which soon became the "greatest organization in the whole country."[69] The black women had taken on the "Christian" YWCA.[70]

At the same time, racial advancement organizations gained the support of black women. The 1,000 delegates of the NACW biennial officially endorsed the work of the NAACP and the National Urban League. They reflected the current emphasis on political action for social reform. The women endorsed

By the 1920s, Jane Hunter's Phillis Wheatley Association (pictured here is their new building, completed in 1926) had become the largest in the nation. Hunter served as the chairman of the National Association of Colored Women's Phillis Wheatley Department and was praised by Mary McLeod Bethune as the "most outstanding individual social worker."
[*Phillis Wheatley Association, Cleveland, Ohio.*]

247

the Volstead Act, urged women to prepare to use the vote intelligently, and refused to endorse either the Republican Party's platform or its candidates due to their failure to take a strong stand against lynching. The clubwomen became advocates for a black man scheduled for execution for murdering a white streetcar conductor and the NACW sent a telegram to the governor of Alabama asking for a stay of execution. These women used political persuasion as a tool to aid the race.[71]

The black women were not alone at the Tuskegee biennial. Nine southern white women, interested in the newly organized Commission of Interracial Cooperation, came to this meeting by invitation from Lugenia Hope. Black and white women met at the house of Margaret Murray Washington following the day's proceedings. The white women faced suspicion and anxiety. Charlotte Hawkins Brown questioned their motives. She had always felt that white women of the South defined "uplift" as better preparation of domestic servants. She told the white women, "I am glad you have not any Negro servants and I am not going to help you get any."[72] Lugenia Hope emphasized the sacrifice of black women during the war years and underlined the need for progressive black and white women to cooperate. The black women requested that the newly formed Commission of Interracial Cooperation sponsor a conference on race relations for women's organizations of the South. When the commission agreed, the women prepared a seven-point agenda for the conference.[73]

Ninety-one white women attended the Woman's Inter-Racial Conference in Memphis, held October 6-7, 1920. As representatives of eleven southern states, the white women listened to speeches by four predominantly conservative southern black women: Jennie Moton, wife of Robert R. Moton; Charlotte Hawkins Brown; Margaret Murray Washington; and Elizabeth Ross Haynes. The first day's events included descriptions by the white women of their experiences at the NACW Tuskegee biennial and an accommodationist address by Margaret Murray Washington. On the second day, Elizabeth Ross Haynes described the humiliation of black women forced to endure Jim Crow practices in public accommodations. Charlotte Hawkins Brown related similar experiences and challenged white women to confront the lynching mythology of the immoral black man. She suggested that white women begin controlling the actions of their men by rejecting racial violence and lynching. White women could begin to treat black women better by calling them by their proper titles of Miss or Mrs. These speeches made the white women see "the aspirations and the determination and the longing of the Negro woman's heart as they had not seen it before."[74]

The conference became a model for interracial meetings of the next decade.[75] Sympathetic white women worked with articulate black women to improve the conditions for the "educated and developed Negro,"[76] while leaving the general system of segregation unchallenged. The women together reached the "revolutionary position that lynching did not promote their security."[77] They voiced a strong statement about the double standard serving as the basis of lynching and looked at the causes of lynching that black women had publicized since the early 1890s.[78]

The Memphis conference showed many of the difficulties present in interracial communication in the postwar South. Black women issued a seven-point statement calling for the protection of black girls working in white homes, the development of programs for black children, the end to humiliation and abuse of black passengers in railroad transportation, the need for improved education and facilities, the lessening of inflammatory headlines and articles in the white press, the need for free exercise of the ballot, and the end to the injustice of lynching and unfair trials.

This statement was not presented as written. Without consulting the black women, Carrie Parks Johnson, leader of the Woman's Missionary Council and chief organizer of the conference, altered the statement and read this version to the white women.[79] The suffrage point received no mention. To the lynching-injustice point, the white women added a statement deploring actions by black men that incited mob violence. The "Preamble" voicing the pride and militance of the Tuskegee biennial never appeared in the white presentation. The audience never heard that the black woman wanted "all the privileges and rights granted to American womanhood, for which she is ready because of her training in all activities of American life."[80] The white women again acted as the interpreters of southern black women.[81]

The black women reacted. Although Margaret Murray Washington advised moderation, Hope called together the original Tuskegee participants to reaffirm their commitment to the original agenda. They wrote to the white leadership, accusing them of being "too cautious, with too little faith."[82] Hope criticized the white behavior, saying, "Ignorance is ignorance wherever found, yet the most ignorant white woman may enjoy every privilege that America offers. Now . . . the ignorant Negro woman should also enjoy them."[83] Since the white women would not support the principles, black women tried another path. The newly formed Southeastern Federation of

Colored Women's Clubs adopted the seven-point statement as the platform for their organization.[84]

The interracialism of the postwar period emphasized conferences, meetings, and publications with little actual change in policy or power. The Committee on Woman's Work, jointly funded by the Commission of Interracial Cooperation and the Woman's Missionary Council, operated in a hostile southern environment that restricted changes sought by the black women. The YWCA, however, was primarily a northern, urban-based organization. Yet the racial changes in that organization remained limited. The racial awareness and commitment of the YWCA *appeared* to change, however. During the latter months of 1920, the YWCA hosted a Conference of Outstanding Colored Women at the National Headquarters in New York City. Twenty black female leaders received invitations to attend the conference for discussion of organizational difficulties and racial aspirations.[85] The black women issued a statement at the conference expressing a desire to carry responsibility, to develop initiative and leadership through representation on the National Board and Field Committee, and to monitor the practices of the local branches ensuring the proper interpretation of YWCA policies. Eva Bowles called for serious consideration of the recommendations so that the YWCA could gain a future endorsement from the NACW.[86]

During this period, the YWCA issued several publications addressing the conditions and work of black women. In 1919, *A New Day for the Colored Woman Worker* and *The Work of Colored Women* described the industrial and overall organizational contributions of black women to the YWCA and the American war effort. In 1920, *The History of Colored Work, 1907-1920* appeared. In most of these publications, problems in interracial communication were attributed to misinterpretation of YWCA policies by local white and black women. The official stories often left out the black perspective. Progress became the official theme.[87]

The national secretary for colored work then advised stronger action by the YWCA. The time had come for black women to gain representation on the National Board. No longer could the YWCA neglect black counsel and advice. Aware of the sterilization techniques used by the white leadership, Bowles warned that changes must "actually be put into operation and not so much talked about—if not, only antagonism and unrest will result."[88] Bowles's report to the Department of Research and Methods again called for a change in interracial policies, saying that the black woman would "work *with* but resents anything that savors of being worked *for*."[89] She advised northern cities beginning an organization for colored women to develop a movement *among* the black women and girls rather than *for* them.[90]

Her recommendations did not penetrate the white direction of the YWCA. Elizabeth Ross Haynes became the first black woman elected to the National Board in 1924, yet she acknowledged the discrimination in the "New Negro end of our YWCA."[91] Bowles lamented in 1922, "This year has proven the futility of an understanding if white people interpret colored people to white people . . . we can only be retarded by an unwillingness to be an association which in the true sense is interracial."[92] Anna Arnold Hedgeman, who later became a leader in the YWCA and executive director of the Fair Employment Practices Committee, expected greater racial understanding in the North, where she worked as a YWCA volunteer in the 1920s. Instead she found a "sugar-coated segregation pattern of social work and housing."[93] As a professional worker, Hedgeman could not use the gymnasium, swimming pool, or cafeteria in the Central Y. To her, "separate [was] inferior, despised and unequal."[94] Both black women and a few white reformers continued to criticize the discrimination of the supposedly Christian, interracial organization for women and girls.[95]

The postwar period had created not only a New Negro, but also a New Woman. The evidence of the blending of both changes appeared in the black female leadership in national conventions, correspondence, and organizational behavior. For the black clubwomen, the reforms that individuals or clubs had begun during the pre-war period now became institutionalized. The departments of the NACW described reform successes: Neighborhood Work, Phillis Wheatley, Peace, Inter-Racial, Frederick Douglass Historical Association, National Association of Colored Girls, Negro Women in Industry, and History.[96] The leadership still reflected a middle-class perspective, but conditions and an expanded membership brought a broader consciousness of the working woman to the NACW. At the 1920 Tuskegee biennial, the clubwomen called for working women to affiliate with the clubwomen. Within a few years, Nannie Burroughs, Mary McLeod Bethune, Maggie Lena Walker, and others joined together to form the National Association of Wage Earners to educate women about the importance of organization to achieve better wages, working conditions, and handling of worker grievances.[97]

Black women had come to realize that race was the paramount issue around which to organize their activities, yet they also understood that success depended on white support. They continued to press for inclusion in white female reform organizations seeking suffrage, Christian programs, and social work. Participation in these organizations served as a means for black women to improve conditions for the race. Woman suffrage, for example, received support primarily as a tool of social reform. Black women increased their participation in Republican politics after 1920 and demonstrated a continued faith in the efficacy of the political process.[98]

The war years and postwar disillusion had created a more practical, realistic, yet well-organized female leadership. They no longer tried to prove their "whiteness" in manners, goals, and social interaction. Many of the light-skinned women used their appearance to gain access to sources of white power or money.[99] But most of them were very sure of their identity. They were "careful publicly to eschew any desire for social equality, [while] most of them hammered away on equal rights in courts, an end to segregation . . . and the Negro's need for the ballot."[100] As individuals, many women had learned how to wear the "mask" to manipulate the necessary white leaders.[101] Others presented well-argued challenges to the white female organizations.[102] Both approaches proved functional in individual circumstances.

The women helped to create a viable NAACP. The increased role of black women and greater power of blacks in the association was especially evident in the Annual Conference in Cleveland, June 21-29, 1919. Black women presented reports about their individual branches. Men emphasized the importance of the female role. A. D. Williams of the Atlanta branch described the work of the women, noting, "the great success of the membership and registration and the campaigning was largely due to the activity of the women."[103] Chicago leader A. C. McNeal advised delegates that, "Ladies must be secured to your aid."[104] for ultimate success in the branches. Delegates elected Mary Talbert to the board of directors for her contribution to the race and to the NAACP. Power had shifted from the white-dominated board to the black secretariat headed by James Weldon Johnson. The NAACP had become an institution in black communities. The Cleveland conference reflected a different character from previous meetings in that "white delegates worked *with* the people we were trying to help."[105] Black women were partially responsible for the increased racial respect that served as the basis for the shift in attitude.[106]

The black woman's role in organized reform reflected the maturation of philosophy, structure, and personalities. Their reforms became part of the recognized changes necessary to build viable black communities. Although many of the reforms, such as the day care programs, old age homes, or community houses, provided necessary but unspectacular services, their reforms nevertheless touched the present and future generations. Their stress on building race pride might not have resulted in scholarly articles, books, and famous debates, as did the writings and actions of some black male leaders. The black women, however, incorporated many of the same principles in their services to children and mothers, thereby socializing future generations to accept and support the ideologies purported by the black male leadership. Their direct human services improved the health, knowledge, and self-concept of many black residents. As true spiritual progressives, the women wanted to improve the social environment in which the black children could grow and learn.

Mary McLeod Bethune described the black woman's role:

> By the very force of circumstances, the part she played in the progress of the race has been of necessity, to a certain extent, subtle and indirect. She has not always been permitted a place in front ranks where she could show her face and make her voice heard with effect. . . . But she has been quick to seize every opportunity which presented itself to come more and more into the open and strive directly for the uplift of the race and nation.[107]

Her role has continued to provide leadership for the present society.[108]

Supplementary Tables
and
Organizational List

TABLE I
Urban Black Population

1890[1]		1900[2]	1910[3]	
Percentage Blacks in Selected Cities		*Cities with Highest Black Population (Ranked)*	*Black Population in Selected Cities*	
Baltimore	15.49	Washington	Washington	94,446
St. Louis	5.49	Baltimore	New Orleans	89,262
Philadelphia	3.74	New Orleans	Philadelphia	84,459
Cincinnati	3.72	Philadelphia	Richmond	46,733
Boston	1.76	New York	Charleston	31,056
New York	1.55	Memphis	Nashville	36,523
Chicago	1.29	Louisville	Memphis	52,441
Brooklyn	1.27	Atlanta	St. Louis	43,960
Cleveland	1.14	Charleston	Atlanta	51,902
San Francisco	.61	Savannah	Savannah	33,246
		Montgomery	Birmingham	52,305
		Jacksonville	Louisville	40,522
			New York	91,709
			Jacksonville	29,293
			Pittsburgh	25,623
			Kansas City	23,929
			Boston	13,564

1890[4]

Cities with Large Black Populations

Washington	75,697
New Orleans	64,663
Philadelphia	40,374
Richmond	32,354
Charleston	31,036
Nashville	29,395
Memphis	28,729
St. Louis	28,672
Atlanta	28,117
Savannah	22,978

1. W. E. B. Du Bois, *The Philadephia Negro: A Social Study* (New York: Schocken, 1967), p. 50.
2. John Hope Franklin, *From Slavery to Freedom* (New York: Random House, 1969), p. 436.
3. Franklin L. Mather, ed., *Who's Who of the Colored Race* (Chicago: Memento Edition, 1915, reprint ed., Detroit: Gale Publishing, 1976), p. xviii.
4. Du Bois, *Philadelphia Negro*, p. 53.

257

TABLE II

Net Migration of Negroes by Region, 1890-1920

	Northeast	South	Northcentral	West
1890-1900	136	-185	49	—
1900-1910	109	-194	63	22
1910-1920	242	-555	281	32

Source: Reynolds Farley, "The Urbanization of Negroes in the United States," *Journal of Social History* 1 (1967-1968): 251.

TABLE III

Percentage Growth Rate, 1910-1920
Black Population in Select Cities

New York*	66	Gary, Indiana	1,283.6
Chicago	148.5	Cleveland, Ohio**	307.8
Detroit	623.4	Cincinnati, Ohio	50.9

Source: Philip Hauser, "Demographic Factors in the Integration of the Negro," in John Bracey, Jr., August Meier, and Elliott Rudwick, eds., *The Rise of the Ghetto* (Belmont, California: Wadsworth, 1971), p. 45.

* Gilbert Osofsky, *Harlem: The Making of a Ghetto* (New York: Harper and Row, 1966), p. 128.

** Kenneth Kusmer, *The Making of a Ghetto: Black Cleveland, 1870-1930* (Urbana: University of Illinois, 1978), p. 10.

TABLE IV

Percentage of Urban Negro Population, 1890-1920

	Total U.S.	South	North/West
1890	19.8	15.3	61.5
1900	22.7	17.2	70.4
1910	27.4	21.2	77.5
1920	34.0	25.3	84.5

Source: Reynolds Farley, "The Urbanization of Negroes in the United States," *Journal of Social History* 1 (1967-1968): 255.

MEMBERS OF THE
FREDERICK DOUGLASS COMMITTEE

Executive Committee: Nannie H. Burroughs, Chairman; Nettie L. Napier, Treasurer; Rev. Florence Randolph; Hallie Q. Brown, Chairman of Executive Board; Maggie L. Walker; Elizabeth C. Carter; Victoria Clay-Haley, Secretary.

General Committee: Margaret M. Washington, Jennie Moten, Lucy Thurman, Mary Church Terrell, Josephine Bruce, Rosetta Lawson, Mrs. Kelly Miller, Clara B. Hardy, Grace B. Valentine, Isabella W. Claphan, Mary E. Jackson, Judity Horton, Mrs. M. E. Goins, Mrs. S. Joe Brown, Mary H. Baker, Mary E. Josenberger, Meta Pelham, Mrs. F. W. West, Mrs. E. J. Freeman, Maritcha R. Lyons, Addie W. Hunton, Emma Keeble, Mrs. George Contee, Mrs. C. R. McDowell, Dr. Mary Waring, Charlotte Dette, Mrs. W.T.B. Williams, Lizzie B. Fouse, Eartha M. White, Mrs. Charles Banks, Lugenia Hope, Charlotte Hawkins-Brown, Mrs. G. L. Jackson.

Source: Mary Talbert, "The Frederick Douglass Home," *The Crisis* 15 (February 1917): 176.

Notes

CHAPTER ONE

1. The worsening racial conditions and self-help responses are in C. Vann Woodward, *The Strange Career of Jim Crow* (New York: Oxford University Press, 1966); Rayford Logan, *The Betrayal of the Negro* (New York: Collier Books, 1954; reprint ed., New York: Macmillan, 1970); George M. Fredrickson, *The Black Image in the White Mind: The Debate on Afro-American Character and Destiny, 1817-1914* (New York: Harper and Row, 1971), chapters 9 and 10; and Mary Frances Berry and John W. Blassingame, *Long Memory: The Black Experience in America* (New York: Oxford University Press, 1982). For information about the racial organizations see August Meier, *Negro Thought in America, 1880-1915* (Ann Arbor: University of Michigan Press, 1963) and Emma Lou Thornbrough, "The National Afro-American League, 1887-1908," *Journal of Southern History* 27 (November 1961): 494-512.
2. Eleanor Tayleur, "The Negro Woman: Social and Moral Decadence," *Outlook* 76 (January 1904): 270.
3. "The Negro Problem By a Colored Woman and Two White Women," *The Independent*, 64 (March 17, 1904): 589.
4. Examples of individual reactions to segregation in transportation include Alfreda Duster, ed., *Crusade for Justice: The Autobiography of Ida B. Wells* (Chicago: University of Chicago Press, 1970), pp. 18-19; Anna Cooper, *A Voice from the South: By a Black Woman of the South* (Xenia, Ohio: Adline Publishing, 1892; reprint ed., New York: Negro Universities Press, 1969), p. 96; Mary Church Terrell, *A Colored Woman in a White World* (Washington: Ransdell Press, 1940), p. 297; and Fannie Jackson Coppin, *Reminiscences of School Life, and Hints on Teaching* (Philadelphia: AME Book Concern, 1913), pp. 12-14. Treatment accorded lower classes especially concerned the black female leadership.
5. Anne H. Boylan, "Women in Groups: An Analysis of Women's Benevolent Organizations in New York and Boston, 1797-1840," *Journal of American History* 71 (December 1984): 497-523, noted that involvement in benevolent societies did not lead to reform activities. She recognized the development of organizational and fund-raising skills in the benevolent organizations and the justification of a public role for women. Social activism was due more to the social backgrounds of women rather than their participation in the benevolent

societies. Black female societies tended to reflect the common social and religious backgrounds of the participants. Many of the early societies were quite exclusive, dividing along denominational and social lines. As race relations worsened, however, the white failure to differentiate between the classes of the race created black membership and goals that were broader than those of the original elites. For information about black women's early activities in literary, church, and beneficial societies, see Dorothy Porter, "The Organized Educational Activities of Negro Literary Societies, 1828-1846," *The Journal of Negro Education*, 5 (October 1936): 556-76; Jacqueline Grant, "Black Women and the Church," in Gloria T. Hull, Patricia Bell Scott, and Barbara Smith, eds., *But Some of Us Are Brave* (Old Westbury, New York: The Feminist Press, 1982), p. 141; Leslie J. Pollard, "Black Beneficial Societies and the Home for the Aged and Infirm Colored Persons: A Research Note," *Phylon* 41 (Summer 1980): 232-32; and Linda Perkins, "Black Women and Racial 'Uplift' Prior to Emancipation," in Filomena C. Steady, ed., *The Black Woman Cross-Culturally* (Cambridge: Schenkman Publishing, 1981), pp. 317-27.

6. W.E.B. Du Bois, ed., *Efforts for Social Betterment Among Negro Americans* 14 (Atlanta: Atlanta University Publications, 1909): 22.

7. Fannie Barrier Williams, "The Club Movement Among Colored Women in America," in J.E. MacBrady, ed., *A New Negro for a New Century* (Chicago: American Publishing, 1900), p. 383.

8. *Ibid.*

9. Ruth Bordin, *Women and Temperance: The Quest for Power and Liberty, 1873-1900* (Philadelphia: Temple University Press, 1981), p. 94.

10. Resources dealing with white women's organizations during the late nineteenth century include Eleanor Flexner, *Century of Struggle: The Woman's Rights Movement in the United States* (Cambridge: Harvard University Press, 1959, reprint ed., New York: Atheneum, 1974), chapter 13; Lois W. Banner, *Women in Modern America: A Brief History* (New York: Harcourt, Brace, Jovanovich, 1974), chapter 1; Carl Degler, *At Odds: Women and the Family in America from the Revolution to the Present* (New York: Oxford University Press, 1980), chapter 13; Bordin, *Women and Temperance*; and David J. Pivar, *Purity Crusade, Sexual Morality and Social Control, 1868-1900* (Westport, Connecticut: Greenwood Press, 1973).

11. Williams, "The Club Movement . . . America," p. 384.

12. Terrell, *Colored Woman*, p. 148; Margaret Murray Washington, "Club Work Among Negro Women," in John Williams Gibson, ed., *Progress of a Race: or the Remarkable Advancement of the American Negro* (Naperville, Illinois: J.L. Nichols and Company, 1920), p. 178; Rosetta Douglass Sprague, "What Role Is the Educated Negro Woman to Play in the Uplifting of Her Race?" in D.W. Culp, ed., *Twentieth Century Negro Literature* (Toronto: J.L. Nichols and Company, 1902), p. 169.

13. Robert R. Moton, "Organized Negro Effort for Racial Progress," *The Annals of the American Academy of Political and Social Sciences* 140 (November 1928): 260.

14. Flexner, *Century of Struggle*, p. 186.
15. Mary White Ovington, *Portraits in Color* (New York: Viking Press, 1927), p. 185.
16. Gerda Lerner, ed., *Black Women in White America* (New York: Random House, 1973), pp. 450-58.
17. The women included Annie E. Geary and Amanda R. Bowen as vice-presidents, Chanie A. Patterson as librarian, and Belle Nickens and Julia R. Bush on the executive committees in John M. Cromwell, *History of the Bethel Literary and Historical Association and Programme for the Year 1895-1896* (Washington: R.L. Pendleton, 1896), pp. 1-22, in Bethel Literary and Historical Society Papers, Howard University, Washington, D.C. (hereafter referred to as Howard).
18. *Ibid.*, pp. 21-27. Other literary societies functioned in much the same way. The Forum and Lyceum in Cambridge, Massachusetts, offered "opportunity for racial self-expression and aspiration"; no pagination in manuscript of Robert Wood's *Zone of Emergence*, copy in the Social Welfare History Archives, University of Minnesota, Minneapolis, Minnesota (hereafter referred to as SWHA).
19. Other women included Ida Bailey, Miss A.V. Thompkins, Belle M. Howard, Emily Lee, Alice S. Davis, Hattie A. Cook, Elizabeth Shippen, Mrs. J.A. Taylor, Mrs. J.W. Cromwell, Dr. Julia Hall, Mrs. L.M. Hershaw, Mrs. A. Mays, Mrs. E.F. Merritt, Mrs. M.A. Wormley, Julia Mason Layton, Mrs. H. Saunders, Lucy Moten, and Amelia Douglass. Information about these women can be found in the file for the National League of Colored Women, Mary Church Terrell Papers, Library of Congress; Helen A. Cook, "The Work of the Woman's League of Washington, D.C." in W.E.B. Du Bois, ed., *Some Efforts of American Negroes for Their Own Social Betterment* 1 (Atlanta: Atlanta University Publications, 1898): 57-59; Mary Church Terrell, "History of the High School for Negroes in Washington," *Journal of Negro History* 2 (July 1917): 252-66. Although Mary Jane Patterson is often listed as the first black woman to receive the B.A. degree (Oberlin College, 1862), the first position belongs to Grace A. Mapps, a cousin of Sarah M. Douglass, who graduated in the 1850s from New York Central College. See Dorothy Sterling, ed., *We Are Your Sisters: Black Women in the Nineteenth Century* (New York: W.W. Norton, 1984), p. 202n. For further biographical and reform information concerning the Washington women consult Constance M. Green, *The Secret City: A History of Race Relations in the Nation's Capital* (Princeton: Princeton University Press, 1967), p. 144; Wilhelmina S. Robinson, ed., *Historical Negro Biographies* (New York: Publishers Company, Inc., 1967), p. 80; and Hallie Brown, *Homespun Heroines* (Xenia, Ohio: Aldine Press, 1926).
20. Information about the New York-Brooklyn black community can be found in "Wealthy Negro Citizens," *New York Times*, July 14, 1895; Sylvia Dannett, ed., *Profiles of Negro Womanhood* (Chicago: Educational Heritage, Inc., 1964), pp. 257, 313, and 289; Brown, *Homespun Heroines*, pp. 108 and 160-64; and the Annual Reports of Lincoln Hospital and Home in the Schomburg

Collection, New York Public Library, New York (hereafter referred to as Schomburg).

21. F.B. Williams, "The Club Movement . . . America," p. 392; Duster, *Crusade for Justice*, pp. 76-80; David M. Tucker, "Miss Ida B. Wells and Memphis Lynching," *Phylon* 32 (Summer 1971): 112-16; and Thomas C. Holt, "The Lonely Warrior: Ida B. Wells-Barnett and the Struggle for Black Leadership" in John Hope Franklin and August Meier, eds., *Black Leaders in the Twentieth Century* (Urbana: University of Illinois Press, 1982), pp. 39-62.

22. Paula Giddings, "Heritage of Black Women," *The Crisis* 87 (December 1980): 540.

23. For information about the Boston black community see Stephen R. Fox, *The Guardian of Boston* (New York: Atheneum, 1971); John Daniels, *In Freedom's Birthplace: A Study of Boston Negroes* (Boston: Houghton Mifflin, 1914); and Dannett, *Profiles*, pp. 291 and 309. Descriptions of the club organization are in Mary Church Terrell, *A Colored Woman*, p. 150; Duster, *Crusade for Justice*, pp. 80-81; and Margaret Murray Washington, "Club Work Among Negro Women," p. 178.

24. Washington *Bee*, October 11, 1890.

25. *Ibid.*, October 10, 1891.

26. *Ibid.*, October 31, 1891.

27. Mrs. N.F. Mossell, *The Work of the Afro-American Woman* (Nashville: Fisk University, 1894; reprint ed., New York: Books for Libraries Press, 1971), p. 21.

28. Several sources of information exist delineating the activities of the 1893 Chicago Exposition. See Reid Badger, *The Great American Fair: The World's Columbian Exposition and American Culture* (Chicago: Nelson-Hall, 1979); Ida B. Wells, *The Reason Why the Colored American Is Not in the World's Columbian Exposition* (Chicago: n.p., 1893), copy in the Frederick Douglass Papers, Library of Congress; Georgia Douglass Johnson, "Frederick Douglass and Paul Laurence Dunbar at the World's Fair: An Episode," *National Notes* 49 (January-February 1947): 10 and 29, copy in Mary Church Terrell Papers, Library of Congress; and Elliott Rudwick and August Meier, "Black Man in the 'White City': Negroes and the Columbian Exposition, 1893," *Phylon* 26 (Winter 1965): 354-61; Tulia Kay Hamilton, "The National Association of Colored Women, 1896-1920," (Ph.D dissertation, Emory University, 1978), pp. 19-20; Duster, *Crusade for Justice*, pp. 114-18; Mossell, *The Work of the Afro-American Woman*, p. 21; St. Clair Drake, *Churches and Voluntary Associations in the Chicago Negro Community* (Chicago: Report under the auspices of the WPA, 1940), pp. 87-88.

29. Although unable to participate as a national group during the preparation stages, black women participated during Negro Day and as individuals. Gertrude Mossell noted that Annie Jones, Lucy Moulton (probably Moten of Washington, D.C.), and Anna Cooper lectured on education. Imogene Howard of New York, Florence A. Lewis of Philadelphia, and Mrs. S.A. Williams of New Orleans took part in the "great celebration." See her account in Mossell, *The Work of the Afro-American Women*, p. 10. The other accounts

mentioned in note 28 cited attendance or speeches by Genie Burns (later Lugenia Burns Hope), Fannie Barrier Williams, Ida B. Wells, Frederick Douglass, and Paul Laurence Dunbar.

30. Mary Church Terrell, "The History of the Club Women's Movement," *Aframerican Woman's Journal* 1 (Summer/Fall 1940): 35.

31. Williams, "Club Movement . . . in America," pp. 387 and 395-96; Terrell, *Colored woman in White World*, pp. 149-50; Elizabeth Davis, *Lifting As They Climb* (n.p.: The National Association of Colored Women, 1933), pp. 171-72.

32. Duster, *Crusade for Justice*, pp. 114-18.

33. For biographical information about Silone-Yates, Ensley, and Moore see *The Crisis* 5 (November 1912): 16 and 20 (May 1920): 38; Dannett, *Profiles of Negro Womanhood*, pp. 299 and 333; Brown, *Homespun Heroines*, pp. 151-53, 178-81; Gloria Hull, "Researching Alice Dunbar-Nelson: A Personal and Literary Perspective," in Gloria T. Hull, Patricia B. Scott, and Barbara Smith, eds., *But Some of Us Are Brave* (Old Westbury, New York: The Feminist Press, 1982), pp. 189-95; Daniels, *In Freedom's Birthplace*, pp. 209-10; and Terrell, "The History of the Club Movement," pp. 34-36.

34. William T. Stead quoted in Duster, *Crusade for Justice*, p. 123.

35. *Ibid.*, pp. 122-25.

36. Terrell, "The History of the Club Movement," pp. 34-36. Copies of the *Woman's Era* in the Mary Terrell Papers (Library of Congress and Howard University) display a basic network of communications between the black female leaders of the major cities of the North and Midwest.

37. Often criticized for their silence on lynching and support of segregation were evangelist, the Rev. Dwight Moody, and the W.C.T.U. head, Frances Willard, both attacked by Ida B. Wells during her tour of England. Duster, *Crusade for Justice*, p. 82, views the Wells criticisms as the motivating force in the Jacks letter. Holt, "Lonely Warrior," p. 56, feels Wells was not necessarily the object of Jacks's slanderous letter, but contemporary accounts usually mention Wells as the object.

38. Josephine St. Pierre Ruffin quoted in Davis, *Lifting*, p. 15.

39. Margaret Murray Washington, "Club Work Among Negro Women," p. 179.

40. Williams, "Club Movement . . . in America," p. 397.

41. *The Woman's Era* 2 (June 1895): n.p., copy in Mary Church Terrell Papers, Howard University.

42. "Extracts from Reprints," in Davis, *Lifting*, p. 14.

43. Williams, "Club Movement . . . in America," p. 400.

44. "The First National Conference of Colored Women, July 29-31, 1895," *The Women's Era* 2 (September 1895): 14; Davis, *Lifting*, p. 21; biographical information about Margaret Murray and Elizabeth Carter (Brooks) can be found in Louis R. Harlan, *Booker T. Washington: The Making of a Black Leader* (New York: Oxford University Press, 1972), pp. 176-90; Gerda Lerner, ed., *Black Women in White America*, pp. 450-58; Davis, *Lifting*, pp. 168-69; and Dannett, *Profiles*, p. 231. The Georgia Press Club stated that

Southern white women were not bigoted, but "simply cannot recognize the colored women socially," cited in Logan, *Betrayal of the Negro*, p. 258.
45. Josephine St. Pierre Ruffin, "Address," July 29, 1895, quoted in Davis, *Lifting*, p. 19.
46. Williams, "Club Movement . . . in America," p. 400.
47. Hamilton, "The National Association of Colored Women," p. 16; Terrell, "The History of the Club Women's Movement," pp. 34-36; Mary Church Terrell, "History of the National Association of Colored Women," *The Sooner Woman* 1 (September 1950): 3, copy in Mary Terrell Papers, Library of Congress; Davis, *Lifting*, pp. 8, 14, 21-27; typescript from the files of the National Association of Colored Women's Clubs (n.d.; n.p.) and *Annual Proceedings of the National Association of Colored Women* (n.d.), pp. 114-15 in files of the National Association of Colored Women's Clubs, National Headquarters, Washington, D.C.
48. Josephine St. Pierre Ruffin quoted in "Extracts from the Reprints," in Davis, *Lifting*, p. 19.
49. Janie Porter Barrett to Mrs. Booker T. Washington, October 9, 1922, copy in Mary Terrell Papers, Howard University.
50. Jennie J. Croly, *The History of the Woman's Club Movement in America* (New York: Henry G. Allen and Co., 1898), pp. 1-62; Karen Blair, *Clubwoman as Feminist, 1868-1914* (New York: Holmes and Meier, 1980), pp. 93-94, describes the conflicts of the white women's clubs prior to merging into the General Federation of Women's Clubs. For examples of black club exclusivity: Informal Dames Prudence Crandall Club folders in the St. Louis Association of Colored Women's Clubs Collection, Western Historical Joint Collection, University of Missouri-St. Louis; Chautauqua Circle Collection, Atlanta University Center, Atlanta; and Minerva Literary Club folder in Myrtle Bell Papers, Western Reserve Historical Society, Cleveland, Ohio.
51. Duster, *Crusade for Justice*, p. 328.
52. Fannie Barrier Williams, "Religious Duty to the Negro," Address to the World's Parliament of Religions, Chicago, 1893 (Chicago: The World's Congress of Religions, 1894) in Bert Loewenberg and Ruth Bogin, eds., *Black Women in Nineteenth Century American Life* (University Park: Pennsylvania State University, 1976), p. 273.
53. "Preamble to the Constitution of the Colored Woman's League," in Mary Terrell Papers, Howard University.
54. For biographical and community information of these Washington women see Sterling, ed., *We Are Your Sisters*, pp. 418-36. For more insight into the relationship between ideology and class in the black middle class see August Meier, "Some Observations on the Negro Middle Class," *The Crisis* 54 (October 1957): 460-69. Black interdependence is also shown in the Archibald Grimke Papers, Howard University, showing the interdependence of black charity and social welfare organizations for aid in fund-raising and securing appointments.
55. "Welcome by Reverend Walter Brooks," *Washington Post*, July 21, 1896, p. 4.

56. See note 54 above.
57. *Washington Post*, July 23, 1896; and Davis, *Lifting*, pp. 14-19.
58. "Extracts from the Reprint," in Davis, *ibid.*, p. 18.
59. Davis, *Lifting*, p. 19.
60. The representatives on the Joint Committee included from the League: A.V. Thompkins (Washington), Florence A. Barber (Norfolk), Anna Jones (Kansas), Julia F. Jones (Philadelphia), Coralie Franklin (West Virginia), Fannie Jackson (Kansas), and E.F.G. Merritt (Washington). From the Federation, delegates included: Victoria Earle Matthews (New York), Rosa D. Bowser (Richmond), Selina Butler (Atlanta), Josephine Ruffin (Boston), Mary Terrell (Washington), Libby Anthony (Jefferson City, Missouri), and Addie Hunton (Richmond). Davis, *Lifting*, p. 37. Black women disagreed as to which group was first in national organization and/or intentions. For the varied viewpoints see Terrell, *Colored Women*, p. 150; Duster, *Crusade for Justice*, pp. 80-81; and Margaret Washington, "Club Work Among Negro Women," p. 178. Disagreement existed over which group proposed unifying both national groups into one organization. For those viewpoints see Duster, *Crusade for Justice*, p. 242 and Davis, *Lifting*, p. 21.
61. For information about black interdependence see note 54 above.
62. Due to the existence of two national groups plus the merging into a third national group, much confusion occurs in contemporary accounts according to names associated with the organizations. The National Association of Colored Women also received labels such as the National Federation of Colored Women, the Federation of Club Women, and the National Federation of Colored Women's Clubs. Similar variety occurs in accounts of the individual clubs. For an illustration: the Washington League, The Colored Women's League, and the Washington League of Colored Women refer to the Colored Woman's League of Washington, D.C.
63. Mary Terrell, "The History of the Club Women's Movement," p. 38.
64. The First Directory of Delegates, National Association of Colored Women, 1896, in Davis, *Lifting*, pp. 11-13; *National Association Notes* 1 (June 15, 1897): 4, in Mary Terrell Papers, Howard University.

CHAPTER TWO

1. Elizabeth Davis, *Lifting as They Climb* (Washington: National Association of Colored Women, 1933), p. 41.
2. Mary Church Terrell, "Address to the National Association of Colored Women, September 15, 1897," in Mary Church Terrell Papers, Library of Congress (hereafter MCT Papers, LC).
3. *Ibid.*
4. Sarah Dudley Pettey, "What Role Is the Educated Negro Woman to Play in the Uplifting of Her Race?" in D.W. Culp, ed., *Twentieth Century Negro Literature: Or, a Cyclopedia of Thought on the Vital Topics Relating to the American Negro* (Toronto: J.L. Nichols, 1902), p. 183.

5. Fannie Barrier Williams, "Religious Duty to the Negro," Address to the World's Congress of Religions, Chicago, 1893 (Chicago: The World's Congress of Religions, 1894) in Bert Loewenberg and Ruth Bogin, eds., *Women in Nineteenth-Century American Life* (University Park: Pennsylvania State University, 1976), p. 272.

6. Rosa D. Bowser, "What Role Is the Educated Negro Woman to Play in the Uplifting of her Race?" in Culp, *Twentieth Century Negro Literature*, p. 177.

7. Angelina W. Grimke, "Woman in the Home," Address, n.d. in Angelina W. Grimke Papers, Moorland-Spingarn Research Center, Howard University, Washington, D.C. (hereafter referred to as the Angelina Grimke Papers, Howard).

8. Davis, *Lifting*, pp. 41-44; Emma Fields, "The Woman's Club Movement in the United States," (M.A. thesis, Howard University, 1948), p. 82; and "Program of Nashville Meeting," *National Association Notes* 1 (September 1897), copy in Mary Terrell Papers, Howard University (hereafter MCT Papers, Howard).

9. Black publications proliferated in the late nineteenth century and gave attention to women's activities through columns that were often reprints from white periodicals. Those best known for women's interests included: *Our Women and Children, Ringwood's Journal*, and columns in the press: "Clara to Louise," "Hints to Girls," and "What a Lady Does Not Do," in the Washington *Bee*; "Woman's World," in Boston *Guardian*; "Doings of Women," in Chicago *Defender*; "Society Column," in Atlanta *Independent*; "Of Interest to Women," in Cleveland *Gazette*; and "Woman's Department" in both the *New York Age* and *New York Freeman*. Black women also provided advice through the early periodicals *Colored American* and *The Voice of the Negro*. Mary Terrell wrote a column, "Women's World," under the pen name of Euphemia Kirk. See Mary Terrell, *Colored Woman in a White World* (Washington: Ransdell, Inc., 1940), p. 222.

10. Lucy Laney, "Address Before the Women's Meeting," in W.E.B. Du Bois, ed., *Social and Physical Conditions of Negroes in Cities* 2 (Atlanta: Atlanta University Publications, 1897), p. 56.

11. Fannie Barrier Williams, "The Club Movement Among Colored Women in America," *Voice* 1 (March 1904): 101.

12. Georgia Swift King, "Mothers' Meetings," in Du Bois, ed., *Social . . . Negroes in Cities*, p. 61. To these black women, motherhood was a valued status. Terrell lost three babies only a few days after they were born during her first five years of marriage. Her diaries attest to the importance she placed on the maternal role. Ida Wells-Barnett felt motherhood was "one of the most glorious advantages of the development of their own womanhood." Alfreda Duster, ed., *Crusade for Justice* (Chicago: University of Chicago Press, 1970), p. 251. Similar attitudes about motherhood are expressed in the collections: Culp, *Twentieth Century Negro Literature* and the Atlanta University Publications, and in the autobiographies of the women.

13. Lucy Laney, "The Burden of the Educated Colored Woman," Paper read before the Hampton Negro Conference, July 1899, in Loewenberg and Bogin, eds., *Women in Nineteenth Century American Life*, p. 296.

14. *Ibid.*
15. Rosa Bowser, "What Role . . . Race?" in Culp, *Twentieth Century Negro Literature*, p. 180.
16. Mrs. M.E.C. Smith, "Is the Negro Morally Depraved As He Is Reputed To Be?" in Culp, *Twentieth Century Negro Literature*, p. 172.
17. Williams, "The Club Movement . . . America," in J.E. MacBrady, ed., *A New Negro for a New Century* (Chicago: American Publishing, 1900), p. 382.
18. Terrell, "Address to the NACW, September 15, 1897," copy in MCT Papers, LC.
19. Davis, *Lifting*, p. 44.
20. *Ibid.*
21. Terrell, "Address to the NACW, September 15, 1897," copy in MCT Papers, LC.
22. Mary White Ovington, *The Walls Came Tumbling Down* (New York: Harcourt, Brace and Company, 1947; reprint ed., New York: Arno Press, 1969), p. 106.
23. The leading Chicago clubwomen never received mention by name in Terrell or Wells-Barnett sources. According to the Chicago *Times Herald* and *Daily News*, August 14, 1899, the women included: Mrs. John A. Logan, Mrs. Shelby Cullom, Mrs. W.R. Harper, and Mrs. W.F. Tucker. Fannie Barrier Williams and Mrs. Charles Bentley were also leaders in the Chicago black female community. Clippings in MCT Papers, LC.
24. Duster, *Crusade for Justice*, pp. 258-60.
25. Chicago *Daily News*, August 14, 1899; Chicago *Chronicle*, August 17, 1899; in MCT Papers, LC; Duster, *Crusade for Justice*, p. 260; Terrell, *Colored Woman in White World*, p. 155; and Tulia Hamilton, "The National Association of Colored Women, 1896-1920," (Ph.D. dissertation, Emory University, 1978), p. 58.
26. Several sources relate the conflicts. In addition to the autobiographical accounts by Wells-Barnett and Terrell mentioned in note 25 above, consult the Chicago newspapers for those days.
27. "Refutations of the False Charges Made By the Woman's Era Club of Boston . . . Against the Officers and Delegates to the Last Convention of the National Association of Colored Women," Copy in MCT Papers, Howard.
28. John Daniels, *In Freedom's Birthplace: A Study of the Boston Negroes* (Boston: Houghton Mifflin, 1914), p. 210; Williams, "The Club Movement . . . America," pp. 402-405; *Press Comments from The Second Convention of the National Association of Colored Women*; "Our Club Women as Others Saw Them," n.p.: September 30, 1899; both in MCT Papers, Howard; Milwaukee *Sentinel*, n.d. clippings in MCT Papers, LC.
29. "Our Club Women as Others Saw Them," copy in MCT Papers, Howard.
30. Chicago *Times Herald*, August 17, 1899.
31. Quotation from the Chicago *Tribune* in "Refutations . . . NACW," p. 3.
32. Davis, *Lifting*, pp. 32-34, lists the following changes under "Officers of the National Association of Colored Women":

1897 of 14 offices: Massachusetts, Pennsylvania, and Washington = 2 each/New York, Kansas City, Maryland, Michigan, New Orleans, Tuskegee, Abbeville, S.C., and Minnesota = 1 each

1899 of 11 offices: 3 of the South

1901 of 11 offices: 5 of the South

1904 of 10 offices: 5 of the South

33. Detroit *Free Press*, July 14, 1906, clippings in MCT Papers, LC.

34. "Scrap in the Women's Federation," source unknown, clipping in MCT Papers, LC.

35. The elite's conscious tracing of white lineage is present in primary and secondary sources. Mary Terrell, *Colored Woman in a White World*, pp. 2-32 and 372-82 referred to her lineage from a Polynesian princess and white plantation owner; Duster, *Crusade for Justice*, pp. 1-24; W.E.B. Du Bois, *Dusk of Dawn* (New York: Harcourt, Brace, and World, 1940), p. 9; and Emmett Scott, "Mrs. Booker T. Washington's Part in Her Husband's Work," source unknown, in Tuskegee Institute Library, Tuskegee, Alabama. The advantages of light skin are delineated in August Meier, "Negro Class Structure and Ideology in the Age of Booker T. Washington," *Phylon* 23 (Fall 1962): 258-66; David Gerber, *Black Ohio and the Color Line, 1860-1915* (Urbana: University of Illinois Press, 1976); John Dittmer, *Black Georgia in the Progressive Era, 1900-1920* (Urbana: University of Illinois, 1977), pp. 50-62. Mary Berry and John Blassingame, *Long Memory* (New York: Oxford University Press, 1982), noted that lightness was not always a criterion for elite membership.

36. Ruth Bordin, *Women and Temperance: The Quest for Power and Liberty, 1873-1900* (Philadelphia: Temple University Press, 1981), p. 94.

37. Sources provide varied information about black female leadership in the WCTU. Ellen N. Lawson, "Sarah Woodson Early: Nineteenth Century Black Nationalist 'Sister,'" *UMOJA* 4 (Summer 1981): 22-23, said Early succeeded Harper as superintendent of the Colored Division from 1888-1892. Most other sources mention only Frances Harper as the leader until 1891. See: Clement Richardson, ed., *National Cyclopedia of the Colored Race* (Montgomery, Alabama: National Publishers, 1919), p. 563; E. Putnam Gordon, *Women Torch Bearers* (Evanston, Illinois: National W.C.T.U. Publishers, 1924); Edward T. James, ed., *Notable American Women* 3 vols. (Cambridge: Belknap Press, 1971), pp. 137-39; Mrs. N.F. Mossell, *The Work of the Afro-American Woman* (Nashville: Fisk University Press, 1894), pp. 14 and 177-78; Hallie Q. Brown, *Homespun Heroines* (Xenia: Aldine Publishing, 1926), pp. 128-32 and 176-77; and Harper's Annual Reports in the Minutes of the National W.C.T.U. For a background of black temperance activities see: Rosalyn V. Cleagle, "The Colored Temperance Movement, 1830-1860," (M.A. thesis, Howard University, 1969) and Hanes Walton, Jr. and James E. Taylor, "Blacks and the Southern Prohibition Movement," *Phylon* 32 (Summer 1971): 247-59.

38. Mossell, *The Work of the Afro-American Woman*, p. 178; Brown, *Homespun Heroines*, pp. 128-32.

39. Rosetta Douglass Sprague, "What Role Is the Educated Negro Woman to Play in the Uplifting of Her Race?" in Culp, *Twentieth Century Negro Literature*, p. 171; Brown, *Homespun Heroines*, pp. 165-68; College Writings File, MCT Papers, LC; Information about Mary Cordelia Booze in Montgomery Family Papers, Library of Congress (hereafter Montgomery Papers, LC); *The Woman's Journal*, October 18, 1890, January 30, 1892, November 1, 1902; "Mrs. Frances A. Joseph," *Colored American* 4 (December 1903): 218-21; *The Crisis* 11 (February 1916): 171.

40. In the South, the W.C.T.U. designated the segregated locals as "No. 2" instead of the common "colored" designation.

41. Brown, *Homespun Heroines*, p. 238.

42. Sprague, "What Role Is the Educated . . . Race?" p. 171; Brown, *Homespun Heroines*, pp. 176-77; Davis, *Lifting*, pp. 168-69; "Report of the Tuskegee Woman's Club, 1904-1905," in Gerda Lerner, ed., *Black Women in White America* (New York: Random House, 1972), p. 455; Richardson, *National Cyclopedia*, p. 215; Sylvia Dannett, ed., *Profiles of Negro Womanhood* (Chicago: Educational Heritage, 1964), p. 227.

43. Ida Joyce Jackson, "How to Cultivate a Taste for the Best Music," *National Notes* 7 (October 1904): 1.

44. Addie Hunton, "The National Association of Colored Women: Its Real Significance," *Colored American* 15 (July 1908): 417; *Woman's Journal*, September 5, 1908; Davis, *Lifting*, pp. 50-51; and Addie Hunton, "The National Association of Colored Women," *The Crisis* 2 (May 1911): 17-18.

45. M. Mossell Griffin, "Early History of Afro-American Women," *National Notes* 49 (March-April 1947), n.p. Copy in MCT Papers, LC.

46. Brown, *Homespun Heroines*, pp. 151-53; Dannett, *Profiles*, p. 309; Rosalyn Terborg-Penn, *Afro-American Woman*, pp. 21 and 27; *Woman's Journal*, October 18, 1890, January 30, 1892, March 3, 1894, October 7, 1899, and November 1, 1902; "Statement of Purpose," Colored Women's Progressive Franchise Association, Mary Ann Shadd Cary Papers, Howard University. Shadd Cary was a member of the National Woman Suffrage Association in 1881. See also, Dorothy Sterling, *We Are Your Sisters: Black Women in the Nineteenth Century* (New York: W.W. Norton, 1984), pp. 411-14.

47. For interest in woman suffrage see the papers and book reports in College Files of MCT Papers, LC; Duster, *Crusade*; Terrell, *Colored Woman in a White World*; Dannett, *Profiles*, pp. 217 and 235; *Woman's Journal*, May 5, 1893, March 7, 1896, May 13, 1899, and March 3, 1900; Hattie Cook, "The Franchise," speech delivered at the convention Northeastern Federation of Colored Women's Clubs at New Haven, Connecticut, August 1903, quoted in "Echoes From the Annual Convention of Northeastern Federation of Colored Women's Clubs," *Colored American* 4 (September 1903): 710.

48. Anti-suffrage leaders included Mabel Dodge, Mrs. Grover Cleveland, Mrs. Charles Seymour, Mrs. Andrew Carnegie, Mrs. Schuyler Van Rensselaer, Mrs. James Wadsworth, Ida Tarbell, Mrs. Francis M. Scott, Mrs. William A. Putnam, Mrs. William F. Northrup, and Mrs. Henry Seligman. For information about the anti-suffrage viewpoint see J. Stanley Lemons, *The*

Woman Citizen (Urbana: University of Illinois Press, 1973), pp. 36-37; Banner, *Women in Modern America*, pp. 88-90; John D. Buenker, "The Urban Political Machine and Woman Suffrage: A Study in Political Adaptability," *The Historian* 33 (February 1971): 276; Ida Tarbell, *The Business of Being a Woman* (New York: Macmillan, 1914) and Ann Watkins, "For the Twenty-Two Million: Why Most Women Do Not Want to Vote," *The Outlook* 101 (May 4, 1912): 26-30.

49. Terrell, *Colored Woman in a White World*, p. 144.

50. Brown, *Homespun Heroines*, p. 161.

51. Pettey, "What Role . . . Uplifting of Race?" in Culp, *Twentieth Century Negro Literature*, p. 184.

52. Washington, "Club Work Among Negro Women," in Gibson, *Progress of the Race*, p. 195.

53. Angelina Grimke, "Woman in the Home," Address, n.d. in Angelina Grimke Papers, Howard University.

54. For much of the information about Adella Hunt Logan, the writer has consulted her granddaughter, Adele Logan Alexander, on January 6, 1983; Adella Hunt Logan, "Woman Suffrage," *Colored American* 9 (June 1905): 45; *Woman's Journal*, July 4, 1903; "Report of the Tuskegee Women's Club, 1904-1905," in Gerda Lerner, ed., *Black Women in White America*, p. 456.

55. Charles Flint Kellogg, *NAACP: A History of the National Association for the Advancement of Colored People* (Baltimore: Johns Hopkins Press, 1967), p. 25.

56. Belle Kearney, "The South and Woman Suffrage," 1903, in Aileen S. Kraditor, ed., *Up From the Pedestal: Selected Writings in the History of American Feminism* (Chicago: Quadrangle, 1968), p. 265; Aileen S. Kraditor, *Ideas of the Women's Suffrage Movement, 1890-1920* (New York: Columbia University Press, 1965: reprint ed., New York: Doubleday, 1971), pp. 144-70; Terborg-Penn, *Afro-American Woman*, pp. 24-26; Robert L. Allen, *Reluctant Reformers: Racism and Social Reform Movements in the United States* (Washington: Howard University Press, 1974), pp. 121-65; and Banner, *Women in Modern America*, pp. 119-24.

57. Carrie Chapman Catt, "Testimony to the Senate," in Anne Firor Scott, ed., *One Half the People: The Fight for Woman Suffrage* (Philadelphia: Lippincott, 1975), pp. 102-105.

58. *Woman's Journal*, April 16, 1904.

59. Programe for the Seneca Falls Historical Society, May 23, 1908, and Mary Terrell's Diary, May 27, 1908 in MCT Papers, LC.

60. Terrell, *Colored Woman in a White World*, pp. 144-48; Duster, *Crusade*, pp. 345-47; Ida Wells Barnett, "How Enfranchisement Stops Lynching," *Original Rights Magazine* 28 (1910): 22.

61. Duster, *Crusade*, pp. 268-71; Emma Fields, "The Women's Club Movement," pp. 26 and 94-99; Terborg-Penn, *Afro-American Woman*, pp. 22-23.

62. Duster, *Crusade*, p. 270.

63. Fields, "The Women's Club Movement," pp. 24-25 and 96-100; Duster, *Crusade*, pp. 269-73.
64. Adella Hunt Logan, "Why the National Association of Colored Women Should Become Part of the National Council of Women," *National Association Notes* 2 (December 1899): 1. Copy in MCT Papers, LC.
65. *Ibid.*
66. *The Independent* 64 (July 14, 1904): 108. Copy in MCT Papers, LC.
67. Terrell, *Colored Woman in a White World*, p. 197.
68. Logan's article mentioned Sorosis, but did not mention the national club organization, the General Federation of Women's Clubs. This omission might have been intentional to avoid drawing attention to the racial participation in the individual clubs. See also the National Council of Women folder in MCT Papers, LC; Davis, *Lifting*, pp. 47-48; Terborg-Penn, *Afro-American Woman*, pp. 22-23.
69. The terms "league" and "association" seem to be used interchangeably when referring to the National League/Association for the Protection of Colored Women. Gilbert Osofsky used the term "League" in *Harlem: The Making of a Ghetto* (New York: Harper and Row, 1966), p. 58; Nancy Weiss also uses the term in *The National Urban League* (New York: Oxford University Press, 1974), p. 18. Frances Kellor in "Assisted Emigration from the South: The Women," *Charities* 15 (October 1905): 13, used the term "Association."
70. Victoria E. Matthews to Booker T. Washington, March 23, 1903, in Booker T. Washington Papers, Library of Congress. The Schomburg Collection, New York City Public Library System, has a copy of the *Annual Report*, White Rose Home, 1911. The condition of this copy is so poor that it can no longer be photocopied, but it can be used at the Schomburg.
71. Kellor, "Assisted Emigration . . .," p. 14.
72. Frances A. Kellor, "Opportunities for Southern Negro Women in Northern Cities," *Voice of the Negro* 2 (July 1905): 472-73; Frances A. Kellor, *Out of Work: A Study of Employment Agencies* (New York: n.p., 1904); Frances Kellor to W.E.B. Du Bois, February 10, 1905, in W.E.B. Du Bois Papers, University of Massachusetts, Amherst, Massachusetts (hereafter Du Bois Papers, UM); and W.E.B. Du Bois, ed., *Efforts for Social Betterment*, no. 14 (Atlanta: Atlanta University Publications, 1909): 102-103.
73. The interracial efforts of the two associations included few black women. In New York, Dr. Verina Morton Jones served as the chairman of the Committee on Education. In Philadelphia, Mrs. S.W. Layten served as agent for meeting migrants at the depots. See Kellor, "Assisted Emigration . . .," p. 14 and Weiss, *National Urban League*, p. 320, n. 15.
74. Due to the existence of protective associations in New York and Philadelphia under the direction of Frances Kellor, much inaccuracy exists about the date of the founding of the National League for the Protection of Colored Women. The following refer to the founding in 1905: Osofsky, *Harlem*, p. 58; Arvah E. Strickland, *History of the Chicago Urban League* (Urbana: University of Illinois Press, 1966), p. 10; L. Hollingsworth Wood, "The National Urban League Movement," *Journal of Negro History* 9 (April 1924):

117-26; and Jesse Thomas Moore, Jr., *A Search for Equality: The National Urban League, 1910-1961* (University Park: Pennsylvania State University Press, 1981), p. 40. According to the Kellor articles cited in notes 71 and 72 above, separate associations existed in the two main cities in 1905, but became national in 1906. Weiss, *National Urban League*, p. 18, refers to 1906 as the founding year of the National League for the Protection of Colored Women.

75. On October 16, 1911, the National Association for the Protection of Colored Women joined with two other organizations to form the National League on Urban Conditions Among Negroes.

76. "The Report of the National League for the Protection of Colored Women," in *Annual Report, 1910-1911*, p. 23, in National Urban League Papers, Library of Congress, Washington, D.C. (hereafter referred to as NUL Papers, LC): and E.M. Rhodes, "The Protection of Girls Who Travel: A National Movement," *Colored American Magazine* 13 (August 1907): 114-15.

77. Gladys G. Calkins, "The Negro in the Young Women's Christian Association: A Study of the Development of YWCA Interracial Policies and Practices in their Historical Setting" (M.A. thesis, George Washington University, 1960), p. 22.

78. Disagreement exists over which branch was first. Most sources written about the YWCA or existing National Board Archives list the Dayton organization as first. Eugene Kinckle Jones, "Social Work Among Negroes," *The Annals of the American Academy of Political and Social Science* 140 (November 1928): 288, lists the Philadelphia group as the first one in 1876. Discussion with officials of the YWCA in New York mentioned continual competition between these two branches over the primary position.

79. Grace Dodge had established services for white working-class girls in New York City, worked with the White Rose Home, and established the first non-sectarian Travelers' Aid Society in New York City prior to her assumption of the leadership position on the National Board of the YWCA in 1906. For information about Dodge and the National Board see Grace Dodge, "Working Girls' Societies," *The Chautauquan* 9 (October 1888): 223-25; Calkins, "Negro in the YWCA," pp. 23-24; Mary Sims, *The Natural History of a Social Institution—The Young Women's Christian Association* (New York: The Woman's Press, 1936), p. 173; Monroe Work, ed., *Negro Yearbook* (Tuskegee: Negro Yearbook Publishing Co., 1913), p. 95; and Addie Hunton, *Report*, YWCA National Board Archives, New York City (hereafter National Board Archives).

80. "Association in Colored Schools, 1909-1910, Student Associations, Table III," in National Board of the YWCA, *Annual Statistics for 1910* 4 (New York: National Board of the YWCA, 1910), Library of the National Board Archives.

81. Calkins, "Negro and the YWCA," p. 38.

82. Marion Cuthbert, "Negro Youth and the Educational Program of the YWCA," *Journal of Negro Education* 9 (July 1940): 363.

83. Calkins, "Negro and YWCA," p. 39; Jeanne C. Mongold, "Vespers and Vacant Lots: The Early Years of the St. Louis Phyllis Wheatley Branch YWCA," prepared for projected anthology *The Urban Black Woman: A Social*

History edited by Sharon Harley, 1979, Copy in Western Historical Collection, University of Missouri-St. Louis (hereafter WHC-UMSL).

84. "Traditional Position of the Young Women's Christian Association on Race," September 17, 1943, Records Files Collection YWCA, National Board Archives, New York City.

85. Jane Olcott Walters, compiler, *History of Colored Work, 1907-1920* (New York: National Board of the YWCA, December 1920), "Young Women's Christian Association Work Among Colored Women," n.a. (New York: National Board of the YWCA, 1921), both in Records Files in YWCA National Board Archives; Calkins, "Negro and YWCA," p. 33.

86. Elizabeth Ross, *Report*, December 3, 1908, YWCA National Board Archives.

87. Ross, *Report*, January 19, 1909, and October 27, 1909; March-April 1910 and June-September 1910; Mrs. W.A. Hunton, "Women's Clubs," *The Crisis* 2 (July 1911): 121.

88. Hunton, "Women's Clubs," p. 122.

89. "Third Address to the National Association of Colored Women, July 8, 1901," Copy in MCT Papers, LC.

90. "Our Club Women as Others Saw Them," no source: September 30, 1899, clipping in MCT Papers, LC.

91. Mary Terrell, "The Duty of the National Association of Colored Women to the Race, August 1899," Copy in MCT Papers, LC; Chicago *Times Herald*, August 15, 1899, clipping in MCT Papers, Howard.

92. *Ibid.*

93. Mary Terrell to Mrs. Stuyvesant Fish, n.d. in MCT Papers, LC.

94. Robert Zangrando, *The NAACP Crusade Against Lynching, 1909-1950* (Philadelphia: Temple University, 1980), p. 18.

95. Zangrando, *Ibid.*, pp. 11-13; Duster, *Crusade for Justice*, p. 254.

96. The (Galveston, Texas) *City Times*, May 2, 1908, clipping in MCT Papers, LC.

97. Duster, *Crusade for Justice*, pp. 262-63; "First Annual Meeting of the Michigan State Federation of Colored Women," p. 13, Copy in MCT Papers, LC; *Woman's Journal*, November 25, 1899; Mary Terrell, "Lynching from a Negro's Point of View," *North American Review* 178 (June 1904): 853-68; Mary Terrell, "Purity and the Negro," *The Light*, n.d., pp. 19-23; Nashville *Banner*, November 7, 1907, clippings and articles in MCT Papers, LC.

98. Addie Hunton presented resolutions against Jim Crow segregation. Her residence in Georgia made her aware of boycotts attempted in Atlanta, Augusta, and Rome, Georgia in 1900 and aware of Du Bois' protest against the discrimination of the Carnegie Library in Atlanta, 1902. See Addie Hunton, "The Detroit Convention of the N.A.C.W.," *Voice of the Negro* 3 (August 1906): 23; August Meier and Elliott Rudwick, "The Boycott Movement Against Jim Crow Streetcars in the South, 1900-1906," *Journal of American History* 55 (March 1969): 756-75; The Detroit *Free Press*, July 14, 1906, clipping in MCT Papers, LC.

99. Mrs. Booker T. Washington quoted in the Detroit *Free Press*, July 14, 1906.

100. Edna B. Johnson-Morris, "Queen Delta's Violets: A History of Delta Sigma Theta," Program of the Sixteenth National Conference, December 194[1], p. 2; "Our Oath," in Delta Sigma Theta File of MCT Papers, LC. Mary Terrell, "Dr. Sara Brown," *The Journal of the College Alumnae Club of Washington, D.C.* 18 (April 1950): 17-19. Lucy Slowe, one of the founders of Alpha Kappa Alpha, has several pieces of information about the sorority in her papers at Howard University, Washington, D.C.

CHAPTER THREE

1. Although the local aspects of social history have been neglected during this period, there are a few historians who have tried to delineate local, black, or female roles in the Progressive Era: David P. Thelan, *The New Citizenship: Origins of Progressivism in Wisconsin, 1885-1900* (Columbia, Missouri: University of Missouri Press, 1972); Robert L. Allen, *Reluctant Reformers: Racism and Social Reform Movements in the United States* (Washington: Howard University Press, 1974); David Southern, *Malignant Heritage: Yankee Progressives and the Negro Question, 1901-1914* (Chicago: Loyola University Press, 1968); Sharon Harley and Rosalyn Terborg-Penn, eds., *The Afro-American Woman* (Port Washington, New York: Kennikat Press, 1978); Dewey Grantham, Jr., "The Progressive Movement and the Negro," *South Atlantic Quarterly*, 54 (October 1955): 461-77; Gilbert Osofsky, "Progressivism and the Negro," *American Quarterly*, 16 (Summer 1964): 153-68; and Allen Davis, *Spearheads for Reform: The Social Settlements and the Progressive Movement, 1890-1914* (New York: Oxford University Press, 1973).

2. Josephine Goldmark, *Impatient Crusader: Florence Kelley's Life tory* (Urbana: University of Illinois Press, 1953), p. 25.

3. Arthur C. Holden, *The Settlement Idea: A Vision of Social Justice* (New York: Macmillan, 1922), p. 90.

4. Robert A. Woods, *The Neighborhood in Nation-Building* (Boston: Houghton Mifflin, 1923; reprint ed., New York: Arno Press, 1970), p. 99.

5. Frances Willard, *Glimpses of Fifty Years: The Autobiography of an American Woman* (Chicago: H.J. Smith and Co., 1889; reprint ed., New York: Source Book Press, 1970), p. 678.

6. For background information on organized charity and other forms of social welfare organizations see Kenneth Kusmer, "The Functions of Organized Charity in the Progressive Era: Chicago as a Case Study," *Journal of American History* 60 (December 1973): 657-77; James Leiby, *A History of Social Welfare and Social Work in the United States* (New York: Columbia University Press, 1978), chapters 8 and 9; Constance Smith and Anne Freedman, eds., *Voluntary Associations: Perspectives on the Literature* (Cambridge: Harvard University Press, 1972), pp. 124-71; Edyth Ross, ed., *Black Heritage in Social Welfare, 1860-1930* (Metuchen, New Jersey: Scarecrow Press, 1978); Robert A. Woods and Albert J. Kennedy, *The Settlement Horizon* (Philadelphia:

William Fell Printers, 1922; reprint ed., New York: Arno Press, 1970); and Holden, *The Settlement Idea*.

7. W.E.B. Du Bois, *Efforts for Social Betterment Among Negro Americans*, no. 14 (Atlanta: Atlanta University Publications, 1909): 42.

8. *Ibid.*, p. 77.

9. Du Bois, *Efforts for Social Betterment*, p. 68; Linda Perkins, "Black Women and Racial Uplift Prior to Emancipation," in *The Black Woman Cross Culturally*, Filomena C. Steady, ed. (Cambridge: Schenkman Publishing, 1981), p. 318; Leslie J. Pollard, "Black Beneficial Societies and the Home for the Aged and Infirm Colored Persons: A Research Note," *Phylon* 41 (Summer 1980): 231-32; John T. Emlen, "The Movement for the Betterment of the Negro in Philadelphia," *The Annals of the American Academy of Political and Social Sciences* 49 (September 1913): 89; *Charities* 15 (October 1905): 1-6; King E. Davis, *Fund Raising in the Black Community: History, Feasibility and Conflict* (Metuchen, New Jersey: Scarecrow Press, 1975), pp. 8-13; Gilbert Osofsky, *Harlem: The Making of a Ghetto* (New York: Harper and Row, 1966), pp. 54-57; and Mary White Ovington, *Half a Man: The Status of the Negro in New York* (New York: Longmans, Green and Company, 1911), pp. 114, 180.

10. Dorothy Sterling, *We Are Your Sisters: Black Women in the Nineteenth Century* (New York: W.W. Norton, 1984), p. 397.

11. Addie Hunton, "The National Association for Colored Women: Its Real Significance," *Colored American* 15 (July 1908): 423.

12. *Ibid.*

13. Darlene Clark Hine, *When the Truth Is Told: A History of Black Women's Culture and Community in Indiana, 1875-1950* (Indianapolis: The National Council of Negro Women, 1981), pp. 40-44; Display by the Indianapolis Section of the National Council of Negro Women, during the Black Women in the Midwest Project Conference, March 1983; Emma Lou Thornbrough, "The History of Black Women in Indiana," *Black History News and Notes* 12 (May 1983): 1, 4-8; Du Bois, *Efforts for Social Betterment*, p. 76.

14. Cleveland Home for Aged Colored People folder in the Lethia C. Fleming Papers, Western Reserve Historical Society, Cleveland, Ohio (hereafter WRHS).

15. The names of the women appear differently for the old and new elite women. The old elite used their husbands' names: Mrs. Harry Davis, Mrs. Charles Chesnutt. The new elite used their own names: Mrs. L.C. Fleming, Mrs. Lucy Early, Mrs. Sarah Green. This list also included Miss Jane Hunter, representative of the new elite. The men's auxiliary consisted of mostly husbands of the women's groups.

16. Cleveland Home for Aged Colored People folder in L.C. Fleming Papers, WRHS.

17. Cleveland Home for Aged Colored People, *Eighteenth Annual Report* (n.p.: 1914), pp. 3-4, and "Official Records [of] the Men's Auxiliary to the Home for Aged Colored People, 1909-1918," both in L.C. Fleming Papers, WRHS; Du Bois, *Efforts for Social Betterment*, p. 76; Kusmer, *A Ghetto Takes Shape*,

pp. 148-49; Eliza Bryant Home for the Aged, "Roll Book and Registers, 1898-1920," in the Eliza Bryant Home for the Aged Papers, WRHS.

18. Hallie Q. Brown, *Homespun Heroines* (Xenia: Aldine Publishing, 1926), p. 143; Sylvia Dannett, ed., *Profiles of Negro Womanhood* (Chicago: Educational Heritage, Inc., 1964), p. 309; Benjamin Brawley, *Women of Achievement* (Women's Baptist Home Mission Society, 1919), p. 11; and Du Bois, *Efforts for Social Betterment*, pp. 51, 75.

19. Addie Hunton called the New Bedford Home "the greatest accomplishment" among colored homes for the aged in "The National Association of Colored Women," *Colored American* 15 (July 1908): 423.

20. Mrs. N.F. Mossell, *The Work of the Afro-American Woman* (Nashville: Fisk University Press, 1894; reprint ed., New York: Books for Libraries Press, 1971), p. 31; Du Bois, *Efforts for Social Betterment*, pp. 67-68.

21. Dannett, *Profiles*, p. 285; Du Bois, *Efforts for Social Betterment*, pp. 65-66.

22. Constance Green, *The Secret City: A History of Race Relations in the Nation's Capital* (Princeton: Princeton University Press, 1967), p. 145; Du Bois, *Efforts for Social Betterment*, pp. 69-72.

23. W.E.B. Du Bois, ed., *The College-Bred Negro* no. 15 (Atlanta: Atlanta University Publications, 1910): 81; and Du Bois, *Efforts for Social Betterment*, pp. 70-73.

24. Addie Hunton, "The National Association of Colored Women," p. 423; Du Bois, *The College-Bred Negro*, pp. 80-81; *Efforts for Social Betterment*, pp. 59-62, 65-77; and "Joanna P. Moore," *The Crisis* 4 (August 1912): 170.

25. Hunton, "The National Association of Colored Women," p. 423.

26. Du Bois, *Efforts for Social Betterment*, pp. 55, 68, and 72-79; Tulia Kay Hamilton, "The National Association of Colored Women, 1896-1920," (Ph.D. dissertation, Emory University, 1978), p. 77; Elizabeth Davis, *Lifting as They Climb* (Washington: The National Association of Colored Women, 1933), pp. 132-37.

27. Examination of black newspapers representing various ideological perspectives found no conflict expressed about black homes and orphanages. Conflict did appear concerning black hospitals. The sources examined included Cleveland *Gazette*; Boston *Guardian*; Indianapolis *Freeman*; Washington *Bee*; Chicago *Defender*; New York *Age*; *Colored American*; Atlanta *Independent*; *The Crisis*; *The Voice of the Negro*.

28. For information about the hospitals and dispensaries consult Du Bois, ed., *Some Efforts . . . for Social Betterment* and *Efforts for Social Betterment*, pp. 87-88. This information is often incomplete, but usually it mentions names of founders and/or organizations responsible for maintaining the services. As with most information about black women during this period, the data is merely a beginning for further research at the local levels. The annual reports of the Lincoln Hospital and Home demonstrate how medical needs of the black community were increasingly accommodated by the black nursing graduates. The first six graduates in 1900 came from the New York area and became private duty nurses or married after graduation. Within a few years, black women came from as far away as Berkeley, California, for training and entered

public health fields, became superintendents of other black nurses, or worked as school nurses, visiting nurses, and settlement house nurses. See the Lincoln Hospital and Home, *Eightieth . . . and Eighty-First Annual Report* (n.p.: 1919 and 1920), pp. 44-52 and 62-71, both in the Schomburg Collection of the New York Public Library.

29. Mossell, *The Work of Afro-American Women*, p. 31; Dannett, *Profiles*, p. 295; "The Douglass Hospital of Philadelphia," *The Crisis* 3 (January 1912): 118-120; and Elliott Rudwick, "A Brief History of the Mercy-Douglass Hospital in Philadelphia," *Journal of Negro Education* 20 (Winter 1951): 50-66.

30. Du Bois, *Efforts for Social Betterment*, pp. 33-34, 58, 62, 92, 95; The Phyllis Wheatley Club, "Report," September 15, 1897, copy in MCT Papers, LC; *Colored American* 4 (January 25, 1902): 11; Hamilton, "The NACW," p. 76; Brawley, *Women of Achievement*, p. 11; and Du Bois, *College-Bred Negro*, pp. 80-81.

31. Dannett, *Profiles*, pp. 217, 277; Du Bois, *Efforts for Social Betterment*, p. 88; Fanny Jackson Coppin, *Reminiscences of School Life, and Hints on Teaching* (Philadelphia: AME Books, 1913), p. 155.

32. Du Bois, *Efforts for Social Betterment*, pp. 92, 88, 95, 57; and Dannett, *Profiles*, p. 241.

33. Margaret Murray Washington, "The Advancement of Colored Women," *Colored American* 9 (April 1905): 189.

34. Hine, *When the Truth . . .*, p. 38; Thornbrough, "The History of Black Women in Indiana," p. 7; Sterling, *We Are Your Sisters*, p. 441.

35. Mary Beard, *Woman's Work in Municipalities* (New York: D. Appleton and Co., 1915; reprint ed., New York: Arno Press, 1972), p. 56.

36. Mrs. E.C. Hobson and Mrs. C.E. Hopkins, *A Report Concerning the Colored Women of the South* (Baltimore: The Trustees of the John Slater Fund, 1896).

37. Beverly Guy-Sheftall, *Spelman: A Centennial Celebration, 1881-1981* (Atlanta: Spelman College, 1981), p. 38; and Sterling, *We Are Your Sisters*, p. 441.

38. Du Bois, *Efforts for Social Betterment*, p. 89.

39. Lincoln Hospital and Home, *Eightieth* and *Eighty-First Annual Reports*, pp. 44-52 and 62-71; lists of nurses' training schools tied to black hospitals are in Du Bois, *Efforts for Social Betterment*, pp. 87-95; Mary White Ovington to W.E.B. Du Bois, June 10, 1904, refers to Jessie Sleet working as a black visiting nurse for the Charity Organization Society, Du Bois Papers, University of Massachusetts, Amherst, Massachusetts (hereafter Du Bois Papers, UM); Beverly Guy-Sheftall, *Spelman*, p. 38, describes early nurses' training and the founding of MacVicar Hospital to serve as a practice school for Spelman nurses. For more information about the black female physicians see Dorothy Sterling, ed., *We Are Your Sisters*, pp. 440-45.

40. Mary Church Terrell, "What Role Is the Educated Negro Woman to Play in the Uplift of Her Race?" in D.W. Culp, ed., *Twentieth-Century Negro Literature* (Toronto: J.L. Nichols, 1902), p. 175.

41. Several centers displayed black-white cooperation. For further information about these centers see "The Gate City Free Kindergarten"; Helena Titus Emerson, "Children of the Circle: The Work of the New York Free

Kindergarten Association for Colored Children," *Charities* 15 (October 1905): 81-84; Rosa M. Bass, "Need of Kindergartens," in W.E.B. Du Bois, ed., *Social and Physical Conditions of Negroes in Cities,* no. 2 (Atlanta: Atlanta University Publications, 1897): 66-68; and Helen Cook, "The Work of the Woman's League: Washington, D.C.," in W.E.B. Du Bois, ed., *Some Efforts of American Negroes for their own Social Betterment,* no. 3 (Atlanta: Atlanta University Publications, 1898): 57-59.

42. "The Gate City Free Kindergarten," n.a., page 1. This five page typescript has a handwritten notation on the front page, "Written in 1917." It is from The Gate City Free Kindergarten File in the Neighborhood Union Papers, Woodruff Library, Atlanta University Center, Atlanta, Georgia. (Hereafter, Neighborhood Union, AUC.)

43. Du Bois, *Some Efforts . . . Betterment,* pp. 119-20; "The 'N' Street Day Nursery," *The Crisis* 3 (February 1912): 165-66; *The Fourth Annual Report of the Colored Woman's League, 1897* (Washington: F.D. Smith Printing, n.d.), p. 10, Copy in MCT Papers, LC; Helen Cook, "The Work of the Woman's League," pp. 57-59; and Sterling, *We Are Your Sisters,* p. 113.

44. Mary White Ovington, *The Walls Came Tumbling Down* (New York: Harcourt, Brace and Company, 1947; reprint ed., New York: Arno Press, 1969), p. 36; Emerson, "Children of the Circle," pp. 81-84; Bass, "Need of Kindergartens," pp. 66-68; Mary White Ovington to W. Du Bois, January 25, 1905 in W.E.B. Du Bois Papers, UM; and Mrs. Booker T. Washington, "The Gain in the Life of Negro Women," *Outlook* 74 (January 1967): 272.

45. Duster, *Crusade for Justice,* pp. 248-50; Allan H. Spear, *Black Chicago: The Making of a Negro Ghetto, 1890-1920* (Chicago: University of Chicago Press, 1967), p. 52.

46. Mrs. Selena Butler, "Need of Day Nurseries," in Du Bois, *Social and Physical . . . Cities,* p. 65.

47. The individuals included Mrs. David T. Howard, Mrs. J.W.E. Bowen, Mrs. George Burch, Mrs. A. Graves, Mrs. John Hope, and Mr. and Mrs. Alonzo F. Herndon.

48. E. (Ednah D.) Cheney to the editor of the Boston *Transcript,* n.d., Copy in the Archibald Grimke Papers, Howard University, Washington, D.C. (hereafter Archibald Grimke Papers, HU); Gerda Lerner, ed., "Club Activities," in *Black Women in White America,* p. 452; Du Bois, *Social and Physical . . . Cities,* pp. 32-34, 55-57, 63-68; "The Story of the Gate City Free Kindergarten," n.a./n.d.; Neighborhood Union, AUC; Louie D. Shivery, "The History of the Gate City Free Kindergarten Association," in Louie D. Shivery, "The History of Organized Social Work Among Atlanta Negroes, 1890-1935," (M.A. thesis, Atlanta University, 1936), pp. 258-64. Copy in Neighborhood Union Papers, AUC.

49. "The Story of the Gate City Free Kindergarten," p. 2; and Mary White Ovington, *Half a Man: The Status of the Negro in New York* (New York: Longmans, Green and Co., 1911), pp. 178-79.

50. "The Story of the Gate City Free Kindergarten," p. 4.

51. *Ibid.,* p. 5.

52. Terrell, "What Role Is the Educated Negro Woman to Play . . . Race?" p. 174.

53. Lois Banner, *Women in Modern America* (New York: Harcourt, Brace, Jovanovich, 1974), pp. 59-62; Mrs. Lena Jackson, "The Negro as a Laborer," in Culp, *Negro Literature*, pp. 304-308; W.E.B. Du Bois, *The Philadelphia Negro* (Philadelphia: University of Pennsylvania, 1899; reprint ed., New York: Schocken Books, 1967), pp. 230-33; Du Bois, *Efforts for Social Betterment*, pp. 119-20; Emlen, "The Movement . . . Philadelphia," *Annals*, p. 85; Caroline B. Chapin, "Settlement Work Among Colored People," *The Annals of the American Academy of Political and Social Science* 21 (January-June 1903): 336-37; and Addie Hunton, "The National Association of Colored Women," *Colored American* 15 (July 1908): 421.

54. Gussie Mims Logan, "The Carrie Steele Orphanage," *Voice* 1 (November 1904): 539; "History of the Carrie Steele Logan Home," n.a./n.d. in The Carrie Steele Orphanage File, Neighborhood Union Papers, AUC; Du Bois, *Efforts for Social Betterment*, pp. 52, 60-61.

55. Brawley, *Women of Achievement*, p. 11; Brown, *Homespun Heroines*, pp. 128-32; Davis, *Lifting*, pp. 293-94; and Du Bois, *Efforts for Social Betterment*, pp. 79-80.

56. The Leonard Street Orphanage File, Neighborhood Union Papers, AUC; Du Bois, *Efforts for Social Betterment*, pp. 59-66, 75-87; "Lincoln Colored Home," *National Notes* 32 (July 1930): 17, in L.S. Fleming Papers, WRHS; Stephen R. Fox, *The Guardian of Boston: William Monroe Trotter* (New York: Atheneum, 1970), p. 212; Davis, *Lifting*, pp. 132-37; Georgia Colored Industrial and Orphans Home, Macon, Georgia, folder 4 of the Long-Rucker-Aikens Papers, Atlanta Historical Society, Atlanta, Georgia (hereafter L-R-A Papers, AHS); Du Bois, *The College-Bred Negro*, pp. 80-81; Mary Terrell, "The Progress of the Colored Women," *Voice* 1 (July 1904): 293; Thomas C. Cox, *Blacks in Topeka, Kansas 1865-1915: A Social History* (Baton Rouge: Louisiana State University Press, 1982), p. 108; D.J. Jenkins of the Orphan's Aid Society to Archibald Grimke, January 2, 1915, in Archibald Grimke Papers, HU; Hunton, "The National Association of Colored Women," p. 421; and Chapin, "Settlement Work . . . People," pp. 336-37.

57. Mary Terrell, "The Progress of Colored Women," p. 293.

58. Fannie Barrier Williams, "The Negro and Public Opinion," *Voice* 1 (January 1904): 34.

59. Carlton Mabee, "Control by Blacks Over Schools in New York State, 1830-1930," *Phylon* 40 (March 1979): 37-40; Cox, *Blacks in Topeka*, pp. 111-113, 141; Duster, *Crusade for Justice*, pp. 274-78; and Clement Richardson, ed., *The National Cyclopedia of the Colored Race* (Montgomery, Alabama: National Publishers, 1969), p. 583.

60. Black women who founded schools include: Emma Wilson, Mayesville Educational and Industrial Institute, chartered by South Carolina, (1896); Lucy Laney, Haines Normal and Industrial Institute, Augusta, Georgia; Cornelia Bowen, Mt. Meigs Institute, Mt. Meigs, Alabama; Jennie Dean, Manassas Industrial School, Manassas, Virginia, (1894); Georgia Washington,

People's Village School, Mt. Meigs, Alabama, (1893); Nettie Wilmer, Gloucester (Virginia) Industrial School; Elizabeth E. Wright, Voorhees Normal and Industrial School, Denmark, South Carolina, (1897); Grace Morris Allen Jones founded school bearing her name in 1902 in Burlington, Iowa; Charlotte Hawkins Brown, Palmer Memorial Institute, Sedalia, North Carolina, (1902); Mary McLeod Bethune, Daytona Normal and Industrial Institute for Negro Girls, Daytona, Florida, (1904); Nannie Burroughs, National Training School for Women and Girls, Washington, D.C., (1909).

61. Cox, *Blacks in Topeka*, pp. 156-58; Terrell, "Progress of the Colored Woman," p. 293; and Du Bois, *Efforts for Social Betterment*, pp. 47, 56-57, 61.

62. Anna Cooper, *A Voice from the South: By a Black Woman of the South* (Xenia, Ohio: Aldine Printing House, 1892; reprint ed., New York: Negro Universities Press, 1969), p. 278.

63. Race history was becoming very popular among the elite during this period. Mary Terrell feared race suicide if the children were not taught their heritage. Jack Thorne of the Negro Society for Historical Research felt ignorance of racial history to be one of the race's greatest handicaps in upward mobility. Many black women wrote books or autobiographies to ensure some facets of race history were not overlooked. For information about the importance of race history consult Duster, *Crusade for Justice*, p. 5; Anna Cooper, *A Voice from the South*, p. 278; Brown, *Homespun Heroines*; Terrell, *Colored Woman in a White World*, p. 1; Jack Thorne, *A Plea for Social Justice for the Negro Woman* (Yonkers, New York: The Negro Society for Historical Research, 1912), copy in Cromwell Family Papers, Howard University; Mossell, *Work of the Afro-American Woman*; and Fannie Jackson Coppin, *Reminiscences of School Life* (Philadelphia: AME Books, 1913), p. 155.

64. Du Bois, *Efforts for Social Betterment*, pp. 55, 117-18; Lerner, *Black Women in White America*, pp. 132-43, 453.

65. Robert A. Woods, *The Neighborhood in Nation-Building*, p. 94.

66. Woods and Kennedy, *The Settlement Horizon*, p. 336.

67. Robert A. Woods and Albert J. Kennedy, eds., *The Handbook of Settlements* (Philadelphia: William F. Fell, 1911; reprint ed., New York: Arno Press, 1970), pp. v, 94.

68. Holden, *The Settlement Idea*, p. 169.

69. Ascertaining absolute numbers of settlements is difficult. Davis in *Spearheads for Reform* notes the existence of ten, but lists only the separate branches of the Henry Street Settlement, Philadelphia College Settlement, Robert Gould Shaw House, Wendell Philips Settlement, Cambridge Neighborhood House, and Frederick Douglass Center. Ruth Crocker, "Sympathy and Science: The Settlement Movement in Gary and Indianapolis, to 1930," (Ph.D. dissertation, Purdue University, 1982) delineates the activities of the Flanner House in Indianapolis; Jeffrey A. Hess, "Black Settlement House, East Greenwich, 1902-1914," *Rhode Island History* 29 (1970), pp. 113-27, describes another example. Depending on one's definition of settlement, one could include the Calhoun Colored School and Settlement (Alabama), Elizabeth Russell

Settlement (Tuskegee, Alabama), Locust Street Settlement (Hampton, Virginia), Washington Colored Social Settlement, Frederick Douglass Center (Chicago), Lincoln Social Settlement (New York), The White Rose Association (New York), and others noted by Davis above. For sources see Woods and Kennedy, *Handbook of Settlements*, pp. 5-6, 83, 118; Fannie Barrier Williams, "Social Bonds in the 'Black Belt' of Chicago," and Sarah C. Fernandis, "A Social Settlement in South Washington," both articles in *Charities* 15 (October 1905), pp. 40-44, 64-65.

70. For the social work involvement of leaders in the NAACP and the Urban League see Charles Flint Kellogg, *NAACP: A History of the National Association for the Advancement of Colored People* (Baltimore: Johns Hopkins University Press, 1967), pp. 12-19; Nancy Weiss, *The National Urban League, 1910-1940* (New York: Oxford University Press, 1974), pp. 48-70; and Davis, *Spearheads for Reform*, pp. 101-104.

71. Ovington, *The Walls Came Tumbling Down*, p. 41, and *Half a Man*, pp. 178-80; Woods and Kennedy, *Handbook of Settlements*, pp. 2-3; and Jacqueline Dowd Hall, "Revolt Against Chivalry: Jessie Daniel Ames and the Women's Campaign Against Lynching" (Ph.D. dissertation, Columbia University, 1974), pp. 91-93.

72. Pitt Dillingham, "The Black Belt Settlement Work," *The Outlook* 70 (October 12, 1902): 920.

73. Dillingham, "Black Belt Settlement," p. 921; Richardson, *National Cyclopedia*, pp. 28-29; Montgomery, *Bibliography of Settlements*, p. 17; and Mrs. Booker T. Washington, "Social Improvement for Plantation Women," *Voice* 1 (July 1904): 290.

74. Mary White Ovington, *Portraits in Color* (New York: Viking Press, 1927), p. 184.

75. *Ibid.*, pp. 181-92; Dannett, *Profiles*, p. 223; Edward T. James, Janet Wilson, and Paul Boyer, eds., *Notable American Women, 1607-1950* (Cambridge: Belnap Press, 1971), pp. 96-97; L.H. Hammond, *In the Vanguard of a Race* (New York: Council of Women Missions and Missionary Education Movement of the United States, 1922), pp. 78-93; and Irene McCoy Gaines, "Ten Living Negro Women Who Have Contributed Most to the Advancement of the Race," *Fisk News* 21 (May-June 1936): 10, copy in MCT Papers, LC.

76. Hammond, *In the Vanguard*, pp. 50-51; Dannett, *Profiles*, p. 239.

77. Mrs. E.C. Hobson and Mrs. C.E. Hopkins, *A Report Concerning the Colored Women of the South* (Baltimore: John F. Slater Fund, 1896), p. 10, praised the early efforts of Mrs. Washington to get the race to elevate itself. The authors saw the need for intelligent women to travel in rural districts to start mothers' meetings and schools that could offer sewing, cooking, first aid, cleanliness, and exposure to the value of clean air for the sick. Black schools and churches developed settlement work, as in the Locust Street Settlement (Hampton), Atlanta Baptist College, and Jacksonville (Florida) Baptist Church. Settlement work developed in Petersburg, Virginia, and Mt. Meigs, Alabama, through black schools. For reference to these types, see Du Bois, *Efforts for Social Betterment*, pp. 125-26; *The College-Bred Negro*, p. 80;

Washington, "Social Improvement for Plantation Women," p. 290; Max B. Thrasher, "Women and Their Work," New York *Evening Post*, August 22, 1900; Weiss, *National Urban League*, p. 19; and Montgomery, *Bibliography of Settlements*, p. 18.

78. Frances Kellor, "Assisted Emigration From the South: The Women," *Charities* 15 (October 1905): 12.

79. The first sectarian traveler's aid organization began in St. Louis, 1849. The first affiliated organization began in Chicago in 1888 as an adjunct of the YWCA. The first non-sectarian group started in Philadelphia in 1901. The official position of Traveler's Aid Society voiced nondiscrimination, but the times and the expanding numbers of migrating black women led to separate services for black women. Du Bois noted in *The Philadelphia Negro*, p. 357, the protective, rescue and reformatory work had not yet been applied to blacks in any degree. Mary L. Lewis, former president of the Board of Directors of the White Rose Home, said the White Rose Industrial Association performed the first travelers' aid in New York City. For further information see also David Katzman, *Seven Days a Week: Women and Domestics in Industrializing America* (New York: Oxford University Press, 1978) and the Travelers' Aid Collection, University of Illinois, Chicago Circle; Paul Kellogg Papers, Social Welfare History Archives, University of Minnesota, Minneapolis, Minnesota (hereafter SWHA).

80. The black women initially involved with the organization of the White Rose Mission in 1897 included Victoria E. Mathews, Mrs. J.S. Politte, Mrs. S.E. Wilkerson, Mrs. Pope, Mary L. Lewis, Mary Jane Bevier, Victoria Coles, Mrs. H.G. Miller, Mrs. Armand, Alice Moore (later married Paul Laurence Dunbar), and within a few years included a Miss Boyd, a Sunday School teacher at Mt. Olivet Church; Hattie Proctor, who met the travelers in Norfolk; and Mrs. Anna Rich, the sister of Victoria Mathews. See Mary L. Lewis, "The White Rose Industrial Association," *The Messenger* 7 (April 1925): 158.

81. Lassalle Best, *History of the White Rose Mission and Industrial Association* (New York: Federal Writers Project, n.d.); White Rose Home, *Annual Report*, 1911; both sources in the Schomburg Collection, New York.

82. Brown, *Homespun Heroines*, p. 212.

83. The problems facing young women coming to the city are discussed in Lewis, "The White Rose Industrial Association," p. 158; Lucy Friday, "Court Studies from Life," *Charities* 15 (October 1905): 212; Davis, *Lifting*, pp. 232-33; and Best, *History of the White Rose Mission*, pp. 17-20.

84. Green, *Secret City*, p. 144; Du Bois, *Efforts for Social Betterment*, p. 103; Hunton, "The National Association of Colored Women," p. 421.

85. Du Bois, *Efforts for Social Betterment*, p. 100.

86. *Ibid.*

87. Brawley, *Women of Achievement*, p. 11; Du Bois, *Efforts for Social Betterment*, p. 100; Gaines, "Ten Living Negro Women," p. 12; Fannie B. Williams, "Colored Women of Chicago," *Southern Workman* 43 (1914): 565-66; and Hine, *When the Truth Is Told*, pp. 40-44.

88. Du Bois, *Efforts for Social Betterment*, pp. 101-103, 55, 59, 66, 76; Du Bois, *The College-Bred Negro*, p. 80; Davis, *Lifting*, p. 116; and Hunton, "The National Association of Colored Women," p. 421.

89. Crocker, "Sympathy and Science," p. 187.

90. *Ibid.*, p. 221.

91. *Ibid.*, pp. 167-220; Woods and Kennedy, *Handbook of Settlements*, p. 83; Du Bois, *Efforts for Social Betterment*, pp. 124-25; Flanner Guild Industrial Neighborhood House, *Second Annual Report*, 1904; *Flanner Guild Report*, 1905; *Annual Report of the Flanner Guild*, 1910; all in the Flanner House Papers, Indiana State Library, Indianapolis; Indianapolis *News*, May 31, 1902; Thornbrough, "The History of Black Women in Indiana," pp. 1, 4-8; and Steve Vincent, "Hoosier History Revisited: Flanner House," *Black History News and Notes* 7 (February 1982): 4-5.

92. Maxine Seller, "The Education of the Immigrant Woman, 1900-1935," *Journal of Urban History* 4 (May 1978): 307-30.

93. Newark Social Settlement to W.E.B. Du Bois, April 7, 1905, Du Bois Papers, UM.

94. *Ibid.*; and information from Adelle Logan Alexander, granddaughter of Adella Hunt Logan.

95. Caroline Chapin, "Notes: Philanthropy, Charities and Social Problems," *Annals of American Academy of Political Science and Social Studies* 21 (January-June 1903): 336.

96. *Ibid.*, p. 337.

97. Other settlements included the Buffalo Colored Social Settlement, Greenwich House, Trinity Mission Settlement (Chicago) and those mentioned in note 69.

98. Anna Cooper, *The Social Settlement: What It Is and What It Does* (Washington: Murray Brothers, 1913), p. 10; copy in Anna Cooper Papers, Howard University.

99. Quotation of Commissioner H.B.F. Macfarland, November 6, 1905, in *Souvenir Booklet of the Social Settlement* (n.p.: ca. 1905), p. 1; copy in Cooper Papers, HU.

100. Du Bois, *Efforts for Social Betterment*, p. 122.

101. *Souvenir Booklet of the Social Settlement*; material in booklet almost directly corresponds with an article written by head resident Sarah Fernandis, "A Social Settlement in South Washington," *Charities* 15 (October 1905): 64-66; Mrs. Frank H. Montgomery, compiler, *Bibliography of Settlements* (Chicago: Blakely Press, 1905), p. 22, in the SWHA; Terrell, "Sara W. Brown," pp. 17-19; Du Bois, *Efforts for Social Betterment*, pp. 122-23; and the Colored Women's League folder in MCT Papers, LC.

102. Mary White Ovington to W.E.B. Du Bois, June 29, 1905, in Du Bois Papers, UM.

103. Du Bois, *Efforts for Social Betterment*, p. 122.

104. Ida Barnett to W.E.B. Du Bois, May 30, 1903, described Celia Parker Wooley as "a very good friend of the race" in Du Bois Papers, UM. Yet by 1905, Wells-Barnett voiced criticism of Wooley and Mrs. Plummer, another former friend of the race. See Duster, *Crusade*, pp. 278-88, for further delineation.

105. Richardson, *National Cyclopedia*, p. 143; Fannie Barrier Williams, "The Frederick Douglass Centre," *Voice* 1 (December 1904): 602-603; "A New Method of Dealing with Race," *Voice* 3 (June 1906): 302-303; "Social Bonds of the Black Belt of Chicago," pp. 43-44; Dannett, *Profiles*, p. 327; Montgomery, *Bibliography of Settlements*, p. 28; Allan Spear, "The Institutional Ghetto," in John H. Bracey, August Meier, and Elliott Rudwick, eds., *The Rise of the Ghetto* (Belmont, California: Wadsworth, 1971), pp. 171-72; and St. Clair Drake and Horace R. Cayton, *Black Metropolis: A Study of Negro Life in a Northern City* (New York: Harper and Row, 1945; reprint ed. New York: Harcourt, Brace and World, 1970), pp. 53-56.

106. *Ninth Annual Report of the Robert Gould Shaw House, Inc.*, 1916, and *Twelfth Annual Report of the Robert Gould Shaw House, Inc.*, 1919, copies in the Archibald Grimke Papers, HU; Isabel Eaton, "Robert Gould Shaw House Settlement," *The Crisis* 6 (July 1913): 142; and the Survey Associates Collection, SWHA.

107. Emlen, "The Movement for the Betterment of the Negro in Philadelphia," pp. 131-32.

108. Spear, "The Institutional Ghetto," n. 11, p. 174.

109. F. Ridgely Torrence, *The Story of John Hope* (New York: Macmillan, 1948), p. 138.

110. *Ibid.*

111. Mrs. John Hope, speech draft, ca. 1908-1909, Neighborhood Union Papers, AUC.

112. *Ibid.*

113. For information about Lugenia Hope, see Walter Chivers, "Neighborhood Union: An Effort of Community Organization," *Opportunity* 3 (June 1925): 178-79; Gerda Lerner, "Early Community Work of Black Club Women," *Journal of Negro History* 59 (April 1974): 158-66; Hall, "Revolt Against Chivalry," pp. 101-112; Chicago *Defender*, October 31, 1925; Interview by writer with Edward S. Hope, Lugenia Hope's son, August 17, 1982. See also Neighborhood Union, "Purposes," 1911; "The Neighborhood Union: An Experiment in Community Cooperation," n.d.; "Plan for the Neighborhood Union," n.d.; Mrs. Louie Shivery, "An Organization of Colored People for the Cultural Improvement of Their Community," fragmentary notes from her master's thesis; all in the Neighborhood Union Papers, AUC.

The personal side of Lugenia Hope's community and social interaction was clarified in an interview with her son, Edward S. Hope, on August 17, 1982. A recent book by Jacqueline Anne Rouse, *Lugenia Burns Hope: Black Southern Reformer* (Athens, Georgia: University of Georgia Press, 1989) provides the most information on Hope and her community to date.

CHAPTER FOUR

1. The NACW Biennial of July 11-15, 1910, followed the formation of the NAACP and the Committee on Urban Conditions Among Negroes in May 1910. For description about the formation of these organizations and the significant events, see Addie Hunton, "The National Association of Colored Women," *The Crisis* 2 (May 1911): 18; Alfreda Duster, ed., *Crusade for Justice: The Autobiography of Ida B. Wells* (Chicago: University of Chicago Press, 1970), pp. 328-30; Elizabeth Davis, *Lifting As They Climb* (Washington: The National Association of Colored Women, 1933), p. 51; and a brief study of clubwomen, Tullia Hamilton, "The National Association of Colored Women, 1896-1920" (Ph.D. dissertation, Emory University, 1978), p. 62.

2. "Proceedings," quoted in Davis, *Lifting*, p. 52.

3. William W. Griffin, "The Negro in Ohio, 1914-1939," (Ph.D. dissertation, Ohio State University, 1968), pp. 63-71; Mary White Ovington, *The Walls Came Tumbling Down* (New York: Harcourt, Brace, and Company, 1947; reprint ed., New York: Arno Press, 1969), pp. 110-111, 121; " 'N' Street Day Nursery," *The Crisis* 3 (February 1912): 165-66; Addie Hunton, "Women's Clubs Caring for the Children," *The Crisis* 2 (June 1911): 78; *Woman's Journal*, April 2, 1910; Chicago School of Civic and Philanthropy, "Employment of Colored Women in Chicago," *The Crisis* 1 (January 1911): 24-25; Mrs. John E. Milholland, "Talks About Women," *The Crisis* 1 (April 1911): 27; and Duster, *Crusade for Justice*, pp. 330-32.

4. Hunton, "Women's Clubs Caring," p. 78.

5. Material for this subject can be found mostly in black periodicals. The NAACP publication, *The Crisis*, is pertinent. See *The Crisis* 4 (May 1912): 38-39; Hunton, "Women's Clubs Caring," pp. 78-79; Hunton, "The National Association of Colored Women," pp. 17-18; Addie Hunton, "The Club Movement in California," *The Crisis* 4 (December 1912): 90-91.

6. Darlene Clark Hine, *When the Truth Is Told* (Indianapolis: National Council of Negro Women, 1981), pp. 43-44; "The Frederick Douglass Hospital of Philadelphia," *The Crisis* 3 (January 1912): 118-20; 1 (November 1910): 14; 2 (May 1911): 17; 1 (March 1911): 8; 2 (September 1911): 211-12; 8, 10, and 63; 9 (December 1914): 62. This last source in *The Crisis* listed the NACW membership as 700 clubs, 28 states, and 45,000 members. For further description of the clubs see Duster, *Crusade*, pp. 332-33; Fannie Barrier Williams, "Colored Women of Chicago," *Southern Workman* 43 (1914): 565; *Cleveland Gazette*, August 12, 1911; Constance Green, *The Secret City: A History of Race Relations in the National Capital* (Princeton: Princeton University Press, 1967), pp. 170-76; St. Clair Drake, *Churches and Voluntary Associations in Chicago* (Chicago: WPA research project, 1940), p. 127 which lists the women's clubs in Chicago, as of 1914:

Bethel AME Literary

Young Matrons Culture Club

Coleridge Taylor Club

Alpha Suffrage Club

Chicago Union Club

Ida B. Wells Women's Club

Frederick Douglass Club

Volunteer Workers Charity

Cornell Charity Club

Phyllis Wheatley Club

North Side Women's Club

7. Atlanta Lung Association, "Work of the Negro Race Department of the Educational Committee," 1915, p. 1, Atlanta Lung Association Papers, Atlanta Historical Society, Atlanta, Georgia (hereafter known as At. Lung Papers, AHS).

8. Jacqueline Hall, "Revolt Against Chivalry: Jessie Daniel Ames and the Woman's Campaign Against Lynching," (Ph.D. dissertation, Columbia University, 1974), pp. 91-92, footnote 3; Rosa Lowe to Amy Smith, June 18, 1920, in Neighborhood Union Papers, Atlanta University Center, Atlanta, Georgia (hereafter Neighborhood Union, AUC); Rosa Lowe, "City Tuberculosis Program for Negroes, 1914," "Work of the Negro Race Department, 1915," At. Lung Papers, AHS; Mrs. Louie D. Shivery, "Atlanta Health Campaign," and "Partial Report of the Work of the Neighborhood Union," n.d., both in Neighborhood Union, AUC.

9. Hamilton, "The National Association of Colored Women," pp. 76-77; Hine, *When the Truth Is Told*, pp. 38-39; *The Crisis* 11 (December 1915): 70; *National Notes* 21 (January 1917): 13, copy in Neighborhood Union, AUC; "Address to Committee of the House of Representatives of Georgia, 1915," in Neighborhood Union, AUC; H.H. Pace, *Report on the Work of the Negro Race Committee, 1915* (Atlanta: n.p., 1916); Rosa Lowe, untitled report issued through the Anti-Tuberculosis and Visiting Nurse Association, ca. 1916 or 1917, p. 4, both in At. Lung Papers, AHS.

10. *The Crisis* 1 (March 1911): 7-8, noted South = Virginia (2), Georgia (2), Florida (1), Tennessee (4), Texas (1), Alabama (1).

11. W.E.B. Du Bois, ed., *Efforts for Social Betterment*, no. 14 (Atlanta: Atlanta University Publications, 1909), pp. 127-29; *The Crisis* 1 (March 1911): 8; 2 (September 1911): 211; 1 (November 1910): 14; 2 (May 1911): 17; Williams, "Colored Women of Chicago," p. 565; Cleveland *Gazette*, August 12, 1911; and Duster, *Crusade*, pp. 332-33.

12. L.H. Hammond, *In the Vanguard of the Race* (New York: Council of Women in Home Missions and Missionary Education Movement, 1922), pp. 89-90.

13. Sadie Daniels, *Women Builders* (Washington: Associated Press, 1931), p. 68.

14. Davis, *Lifting*, pp. 53-55; Hammond, *In the Vanguard of the Race*, pp. 78-93; Mary White Ovington, *Portraits in Color* (New York: Viking Press, 1927), pp. 181-97; Sylvia Dannett, *Profiles of Negro Womanhood* (Chicago: Educational Heritage, 1964), p. 223; Edward T. James, Janet Wilson, and Paul Boyer, eds., *Notable American Women, 1607-1950* (Cambridge: Belnap Press, 1971), pp. 196-97; Daniels, *Women Builders*, pp. 53-78; Addie

Hunton, "A Social Center at Hampton," *The Crisis* 4 (July 1912): 145-46; 11 (November 1915): 13-14.

15. Hastings Hart quoted in Dannett, *Profiles*, p. 223. Similar information appeared in Ovington, *Portraits*, p. 186, and *When the Walls Came Tumbling Down*, p. 123.

16. See notes 8 and 11 above.

17. The National Training School for Women and Girls should not be confused with the reformatory the National Training School for Girls of the District of Columbia, which opened in 1893 to serve as a reformatory for black girls. The president of the United States appointed that Board of Trustees, all of whom were white, as were all of the employees. For sources dealing with Burroughs' school see Roscoe C. Bruce to Archibald Grimke, January 18, 1915, and Report of the Board of Trustees of the National Training School for Girls of the District of Columbia, 1913, both in the Archibald Grimke Papers, Howard University, Washington, D.C. (hereafter Arch. Grimke Papers, HU).

18. Nannie Burroughs Papers, Library of Congress, Washington, D.C. (hereafter Burroughs Papers, LC); Dannett, *Profiles*, p. 239; Hammond, *In the Vanguard of the Race*, pp. 47-62; Clement Richardson, ed., *The National Cyclopedia of the Colored Race* (Montgomery, Alabama: National Publishing, 1919), p. 411; Letterhead for the National Training School for Women and Girls, March 19, 1915, and "Ten Things the Negro Must Do For Himself," pamphlet, n.d., both in Archibald Grimke Papers, HU.

19. Davis, *Lifting*, pp. 55-57; Carlton Mabee, "Control by Blacks Over Schools in New York State, 1830-1930," *Phylon* 40 (March 1979): 37.

20. Women's Social Improvement Committee to the Board of Education, December 3, 1913, in Neighborhood Union, AUC.

21. *Ibid.*

22. William M. Slaton to Mrs. L.B. Hope, June 12, 1912; Survey of Clored (sic) Public Schools (1913-1914), p 1; Petition to the School Board, August 19, 1913; Rough Draft of School Petition, n.d.; *Annual Report of the Neighborhood Union*, 1913-1914, "Address to Committee of the House of Representatives of Georgia, 1915"; all in Neighborhood Union, AUC.

23. Unnamed black woman quoted in Mary Beard, *Woman's Work in Municipalities* (New York: D. Appleton and Company, 1915, reprint ed., New York: Arno Press, 1972), p. 211.

24. Hunton, "The National Association of Colored Women," p. 18; Hamilton, "The National Association of Colored Women," pp. 61-62; Davis, *Lifting*, pp. 53-55; Hunton, "A Social Center," pp. 145-46; *Woman's Journal* August 10, 1912, and August 24, 1912; Ovington, *The Walls Came Tumbling Down*, pp. 123-24; *The Crisis* 4 (June 1912): 113; Beard, *Women's Work in Municipalities*, pp. 210-17 and 182-95.

25. Program, February 27, 1913, printed by the New York *Age*, copy in the Mary Terrell Papers, Library of Congress (hereafter MCT Papers, LC); Ida B. Wells-Barnett, "Our Country's Lynching Record," *Survey* 24 (January 1913): 573-74.

26. *The Crisis* 5 (February 1913): 163; 7 (November 1913): 8; 6 (May 1913): 8, 10, 63; 9 (December 1914): 62; St. Clair Drake, *Churches and Voluntary Associations in Chicago*, p. 127; Zona Gale, "Mothers in Council," *The Crisis* 8 (October 1914): 285-88; M. Mossell Griffin, "Early History of Afro-American Women," *National Notes* 49 (March-April 1947), n.p., copy in MCT Papers, LC; Davis, *Lifting*, pp. 55-57.

27. Dannett, *Profiles*, pp. 188-89; Richardson, *National Cyclopedia of the Negro Race*, p. 263; Davis, *Lifting*, pp. 57-59; Osofsky, *Harlem*, p. 112; *New York Times*, September 2, 1917.

28. Hamilton, "The National Association of Colored Women," pp. 63-65; Davis, *Lifting*, pp. 57-59.

29. "The Frederick Douglass Home Again," Cleveland *Gazette*, n.d., clipping in the Archibald Grimke Papers, HU.

30. No name to Dr. Booker T. Washington, November 15, 1912, in Archibald Grimke Papers, HU.

31. Indianapolis *Freeman*, October 9, 1915, clipping in Archibald Grimke Papers, HU.

32. Robert H. Terrell to Mrs. Mary Talbert, November 1, 1916, in MCT Papers, LC.

33. Mary Talbert to Dear Co-Worker, December 9, 1916, copy in both the MCT Papers, LC, and Neighborhood Union Papers, AUC.

34. Mary Talbert, "The Frederick Douglass Home," *The Crisis* 13 (February 1917): 175.

35. Talbert, "The Frederick Douglass Home," p. 175.

36. Mortimer M. Harris to Mrs. Mary Talbert, July 27, 1916, copy in MCT Papers, LC; Mary Talbert, "Concerning the Frederick Douglass Home," *The Crisis* 14 (August 1917): 167-68. Copy of General Committee and Names Listed on Memorial Tablets (see Appendix) listed such committee members as Nannie Burroughs, Nettie Napier, Rev. Florence Randolph, Hallie Q. Brown, Maggie L. Walker, Elizabeth Carter, and Victoria Clay-Haley. Helen Douglass, the white second wife of Frederick Douglass, received some negative treatment from the black clubwomen. During an early national meeting of the clubwomen, Helen Douglass invited the delegates to tour the Douglass Home at Cedar Hill. After the tour, a Mrs. Jackson discourteously thanked Helen Douglass for having shown the group around the home of Annie Murray Douglass, the first wife of Frederick Douglass. Ida Wells-Barnett reported that Frederick Douglass told her that only Charlotte Grimke and herself had treated Helen Douglass with any kindness. Mary Terrell, however, recounted close personal relations with the couple. For these observations see Duster, *Crusade*, pp. 73-74; Terrell, *Colored Woman in a White World*; and Mary Terrell, "I Remember Frederick Douglass," *Ebony* 8 (October 1953): 76-78.

37. Historians differ as to when suffrage became a popular issue. Cynthia Neverdon-Morton, "The Black Women's Struggle for Equality in the South, 1895-1925," in Rosalyn Terborg-Penn and Sharon Harley, eds., *The Afro-American Woman* (Port Washington, New York: Kennikat Press, 1978), p. 53, noted the movement came of age after 1906. Eleanor Flexner, *Century of*

Struggle: The Woman's Rights Movement in the United States (Cambridge: Harvard University, 1959), pp. 262, 268, noted the growth after 1910 until 1914. Lois Banner, *Women in Modern America* (New York: Harcourt, Brace, Jovanovich, 1974), pp. 87-93, said the suffrage issue was not a major goal of reformers until 1915. Other sources agree that the suffrage movement gained momentum and popularity by mid-decade (around 1915); William L. O'Neill, *Everyone Was Brave* (Chicago: Quadrangle, 1969), pp. 15-55; Gerda Lerner, *The Woman in American History* (Menlo Park: Addison Wesley, 1971), pp. 98-158. Contemporary observations agree with the timing. Rheta Childe Dorr noted suffrage was dead before 1912. The General Federation of Women's Clubs finally endorsed the measure in 1914.

38. Martha Gruening to Resolution Committee Chairman, Louisville, Kentucky, c.a. 1911, in Du Bois Papers, UM.
39. Flexner, *Century of Struggle*, pp. 262-68; O'Neill, *Everyone Was Brave*, pp. 15-55; Terborg-Penn, *Afro-American Woman*, p. 53; *The Crisis* 1 (December 1910): 28; 1 (January 1911): 27; 10 (June 1915): 77; 4 (June 1912): 76; Kellogg, *NAACP*, p. 207; and NAWSA to Martha Gruening, November 14, 1911, in Du Bois Papers, UM.
40. Adella Hunt Logan, "Colored Women as Voters," *The Crisis* 4 (September 1912): 242.
41. Terrell, *Colored Woman in a White World*, pp. 144-48; Duster, *Crusade*, pp. 345-47; Ida Wells-Barnett, "How Enfranchisement Stops Lynching," *Original Rights Magazine* 28 (1910): 418; and Logan, "Colored Women as Voters," p. 243.
42. Duster, *Crusade*, p. 345.
43. *Alpha Suffrage Record*, March 18, 1914, p. 1. Copy in The Alpha Suffrage Club Papers, University of Illinois, Chicago Circle.
44. Duster, *Crusade*, pp. 344-50, 359-62; Chicago *Defender*, January 9 and 12, 1915; *The Woman's Journal*, September 4, 1915.
45. For accounts of the suffrage parade and the white leadership see Terrell, *Colored Woman in a White World*, pp. 210-11; W.E.B. Du Bois, "Hail Columbia," in Daniel Walden, ed., *W.E.B. Du Bois: The Crisis Writings* (Greenwich, Connecticut: Fawcett Publishing, 1972), pp. 342-44. For biographical information about Catt, Milholland, and Blatch, see James, *Notable American Women*.
46. Carrie W. Clifford, *The Crisis* 5 (April 1913): 296.
47. Clifford, *ibid.*, noted the representatives for Michigan and New York were Mary E. McCoy and a Mrs. Duffield. She listed the participants as Mary Terrell, Ida Wells-Barnett, Charlotte Steward, May H. Jackson, Bertha McNeel, Harriet Shadd, Caddie Park, Harriet G. Marshall, Georgia Simpson, Mrs. Daniel Murray, Dr. Amanda Gray, Dr. Eva Ross, Mrs. M.D. Butler, Carrie Clifford, Alice Dunbar Nelson, Asceola McCarthy Adams, Bertha Pitts Campbell, Mrs. Duffield, Mary McCoy, and the students from Howard University.
48. Clifford, *The Crisis* 5 (April 1913): 298.
49. Du Bois, "Hail Columbia," p. 343.

50. Bertha Campbell noted that black women received worse treatment from the hoodlums on the street than did the white suffrage marchers, whereas Clifford noted that they received no worse than the white women. For accounts of the treatment see Interview with Bertha Campbell by Amelia Fry, September 16, 1981; Amelia Fry, "Alice Paul and the South," Paper presented to the Southern Historical Association, November 12, 1981; Amelia Fry, "Alice Paul and the ERA," *Organization of American History Newsletter* 22 (February 1983): 13-16; Clifford, *The Crisis* 5 (April 1913): 296; Dannett, *Profiles*, p. 285; Kraditor, *Ideals of Woman's Suffrage*, pp. 167-68; *The Woman's Journal*, March 15, 1913; Terrell, *Colored Woman in a White World*, pp. 210-11; consultation with Adelle Logan Alexander, January 6, 1983; Cleveland *Courier*, March 1, 1950, in the Lethia Fleming Papers, WRHS; Duster, *Crusade*, pp. 229-30; and Flexner, *Century of Struggle*, pp. 263-66.

51. Rosalyn Terborg-Penn, "Black Male Perspectives on the Nineteenth-Century Woman," in Terborg-Penn, *Afro-American Woman*, pp. 29-42, and *The Crisis* 10 (August 1915): 178-92.

52. Cooper, *Voice from the South*, p. 75.

53. Logan, "Colored Women as Voters," p. 243.

54. Cooper, *Voice from the South*, p. 75; and Kelly Miller, "The Risk of Woman Suffrage," *The Crisis* 11 (November 1915): 37-38. For a critical response to Miller's argument see J.A. Rogers, "The Critic," *The Messenger* 7 (April 1925): 165-66.

55. Terrell, *Colored Woman in a White World*, p. 144.

56. In addition to the men cited in the text, black men who supported female suffrage included W.E.B. Du Bois, Alexander Crummell, A. Philip Randolph, James Weldon Johnson, Robert H. Terrell, William Monroe Trotter, T. Thomas Fortune, L.M. Hershaw, William S. Brathewaite, Ferdinand Barnett, Benjamin Brawley, William Pickens, Charles Chesnutt, John Hope, George Haynes, John Hurst, W.H. Crogman, John R. Lynch, Archibald and Francis Grimke, Oscar de Priest, W.H. Lewis, and C.W. Anderson. Their support has been acknowledged in Terborg-Penn, *Afro-American Woman*, p. 42; *The Crisis* 10 (August 1915): 178-92; Fox, *The Guardian of Boston*; Weiss, *The National Urban League*; or Kellogg, *NAACP*. Du Bois carried on as advisor to many black female leaders as his correspondence in his papers demonstrates. He noted in his autobiography (page 282): "My life . . . threw me widely with women of brains and great effort to work on the widest scale. I am endlessly grateful for these contacts."

57. Williams, "Colored Women of Chicago," p. 566.

58. *The Crisis* 6 (May 1913): 29.

59. *The Woman's Journal*, August 30, 1913, and April 14, 1914.

60. Female contributors to the issue included Nettie Asberry, Mrs. Clement Morgan, Mary Talbert, Alice Dunbar, Coralie Cook, Carrie Clifford, Dr. Mary Waring, Nannie Burroughs, Mary E. Jackson, Josephine St. Pierre Ruffin, Addie Hunton, Marie L. Baldwin, Anna Jones, Josephine Bruce, Elizabeth L. Davis, Mary Terrell, and Lillian A. Turner. Male contributors included Francis Grimke, Oscar de Priest, Benjamin Brawley, John Hurst, James Weldon

Johnson, Robert Terrell, W.H. Crogman, Charles W. Chesnutt, John Lynch, L. Hershaw, John Hope, Charles W. Anderson, W.H. Lewis, and William Braithewaite.

61. *The Woman's Journal*, January 9, 1916.
62. Other black women not previously mentioned but on record for having supported suffrage include Cora Horne, Naome Anderson, Victoria Clay Haley, Eva Buckner, Elizabeth Ensley, Nellie Griswold Francis, and Florence Randolph. Consult Delilah Beasley, *Negro Trailblazers of California* (Los Angeles: Times Mirror Publishing, 1919), p. 229; Dannett, *Profiles*, pp. 225, 299; *The Crisis* 20 (May 1920): 38; *The Woman's Journal*, September 26, 1914; Elizabeth Cady Stanton, Susan B. Anthony, and Matilda Gage, eds., *History of Woman Suffrage* (New York: Arno Press, 1969), pp. 310-11, 346-47, 358; Ida Husted Harper, ed., *History of Woman Suffrage, 1900-1910* (New York: Arno Press, 1969), p. 55, 59, 60; Susan B. Anthony and Ida Harper, eds., *History of Woman Suffrage, 1883-1900* (New York: Arno Press, 1969), pp. 395-96.
63. Addie Hunton, "Women's Clubs," *The Crisis* 2 (July 1911): 122.
64. Addie Hunton to W.E.B. Du Bois, fragment n.d. ca. 1911-12, in Du Bois Papers, UM.
65. Weiss, *The National Urban League*, p. 122.
66. Hunton, "Women's Clubs," p. 121.
67. Richardson, *National Cyclopedia*, p. 488; "Eva Bowles," *Woman's Press* n.v. (July 1932), n.p., clipping in Records File Collection, YWCA, National Board Archives, New York.
68. A.W. Hunton, *Report of the City Committee, September 24, 1913*, YWCA, National Board Archives, New York.
69. Hunton, *Report of the City Committee, January 6, 1913*, YWCA National Board Archives.
70. Jane Olcott Walters, *History of Colored Work, 1907-1920* (New York: National Board of the YWCA, December, 1920), pp. 17-24, YWCA, National Board Archives, New York; Jane Olcott, *The Work of Colored Women* (New York: National Board of YWCA—War Work Council, 1919), p. 7; "Women's Clubs," *The Crisis* 4 (May 1912): 38; and Du Bois, *Efforts for Social Betterment*, p. 126.
71. "History of the YWCA," copy in YWCA Metropolitan St. Louis Collection, University of Missouri-St. Louis Joint Collection (hereafter UMSL); Jeanne Mongold, "Vespers and Vacant Lots: The Early Years of the St. Louis Phyllis Wheatley Branch YWCA," 7, prepared for the 1979 projected anthology, *The Urban Black Woman: A Social History*, edited by Sharon Harley, copy of article in UMSL; Lillian Brandt, "The Negroes of St. Louis," American Statistical Association Publication 8 (March 1903), 263-64; Minutes of the Informal Dames, May 1901-January 1911, in St. Louis Association of Colored Women's Clubs Collection, UMSL.
72. The black elites opposed a black YMCA in 1911. Racial conditions worsened, black leadership changed, and black migration increased, so that by 1921, a black YMCA emerged. See Ruth Neely, ed., *Women of Ohio: A Record of*

Achievements in the History of the State, 3 vol. (n.p.: S.J. Clarke Publishing, n.d.), pp. 967-68; Dannett, *Profiles*, p. 271; Kenneth Kusmer, *A Ghetto Takes Shape: Black Cleveland, 1870-1930* (Urbana: University of Illinois Press, 1976), chapters 1-3; and Adrienne Lash Jones, "Jane Edna Hunter: A Case Study of Black Leadership, 1910-1950," (Ph.D. dissertation, Case-Western Reserve University, 1983).

73. Minutes of the Board of Directors, St. Louis YWCA, December 1, 1911, p. 149. YWCA of Metropolitan St. Louis Collection, UMSL.

74. Mongold, "Vespers and Vacant Lots," pp. 8-11; Julia Childs Curtis, "A Girls' Clubhouse," *The Crisis* 12 (October 1916): 294-96.

75. Jane Edna Hunter, *A Nickel and a Prayer* (Cleveland: Elli Kane Publishers, 1940), p. 88.

76. *Ibid.*, p. 90.

77. Conflicts between old and new elites are presented in Kusmer, *Ghetto Takes Shape*; Jones, "Jane Edna Hunter"; gleaning Harry Smith's Cleveland *Gazette* 1910-20; and Hunter, *A Nickel and a Prayer*, pp. 90-91.

78. Transcript of interview with Claretha Barrett, December 10, 1975, by Jeanne Mongold, in the Oral History Collection, UMSL.

79. Mrs. Frank L. Williams (Fannie B.) was another leader. Her information is in folder 8, The Auroran Club, St. Louis Association of Colored Women's Clubs, UMSL. Arsania Williams was the sole female on the organizing committee for Negro Day at the St. Louis Exposition according to Mongold, "Vespers and Vacant Lots," p. 10.

80. Jones, "Jane Edna Hunter," p. 29.

81. Hunter, *Nickel and a Prayer*, p. 97.

82. *Ibid.*

83. Jones, "Jane Edna Hunter," p. 29.

84. Black signers included Jane Hunter, R.K. Moon, Lethia Fleming, Charles Bundy, Cora Boyd, Miss A.B. Cohen, Miss R.E. Johnson, Ida M. Burton, Howard E. Murrell, Blanche Johnson, Lula Cox, Thomas Fleming, John P. Green, Minerva Taylor, John S. Hall, T.M. Farlice. The activities of these black leaders can also be ascertained through examination of the Cleveland NAACP, Cleveland Urban League, Lethia Fleming Papers, and A.M. Moon Papers, all in WRHS, Cleveland.

85. Mary McLeod Bethune, "A Century of Progress of Negro Women," An Address delivered before the Chicago Women's Federation, June 30, 1933, in Gerda Lerner, ed., *Black Women in White America*, p. 582.

86. Jones, "Jane Edna Hunter," p. 142, noted that the white Board of the Phillis Wheatley "almost duplicated that of the city's YWCA." Jones (153-54) also realized that Hunter's graduation from Ferguson-Williamson College equaled a high school education. Her nurses' training did not qualify her as a professional. Thus, the YWCA's requirement of a college degree for its secretaries and the additional training in some type of social work eliminated Hunter as the potential chief administrator of the Phillis Wheatley *if* taken over as a branch by the YWCA. See also, Hunter, *Nickel and a Prayer*, pp. 100-101; Minutes of the Phillis Wheatley Board of Trustees, Minutes of the

Joint Committee of the Phillis Wheatley Association and the YWCA, both in the Phillis Wheatley Association Papers, WRHS.

87. Curtis, "Girls' Clubhouse," p. 295.
88. Interview with Claretha Barrett.
89. Interview with Ellie Sutler, a co-worker of May Belcher, July 11, 1983, by Dorothy Salem.
90. *Christian Womanhood* 21 (March 21, 1912): 3, in YWCA Publications Collections, UMSL.
91. Mongold, "Vespers and Vacant Lots," pp. 16-17.
92. *Christian Womanhood* 18 (November 16, 1911): 5; newsclipping, n.d. said the group organized on December 4, 1911, and "took name of the Phyllis Wheatley on April 13, 1912"; Mongold, "Vespers and Vacant Lots," p. 8 and note 53 p. 16 attributed the name change time to an earlier period, January 1912. See also, Minutes of the Board of Directors, April 8, 1912 in YWCA of Metropolitan St. Louis Collection, UMSL; May Belcher, "Annual Report for 1912," *Christian Womanhood* 23 (February 13, 1913): 9 in YWCA Publications Collections, UMSL.
93. Du Bois, *Efforts for Social Betterment*, p. 99, said the YWCA never flourished among black women due to the social prejudices of white women. By 1909, however, the YWCA witnessed a growth of separate organizations. Carter Woodson, *The History of the Negro Church* (Washington: Associated Publishers, 1921) felt that the black churches discouraged participation in social welfare work, seeing such activity as a compromise with the devil. The YWCA and YMCA were not welcome among the black churches for many years. In addition to the women specifically mentioned, others included Frances Chase (Brooklyn), Adelle F. Ruffin (Norfolk), N.C.A. Vanderhoof (Gay Head, Mississippi), Bernice Morris (Philadelphia), Ida Cummins (sic) (Baltimore), Mrs. Jesse E. Moorland (Washington) and Alice Knight (Atlanta). See Hunton, *Report*, Records File Collection, YWCA, National Board Archives; *Young Women's Christian Association Work Among Colored Women* (New York: National Board of the YWCA, 1921), Records File Collection, YWCA; Mrs. W.A. Hunton, "Report," *Association Monthly* 12 (August 1912): 262, in YWCA Publications Collection, UMSL. Leila S. Frissell, *Report on the Third Conference*, and Mrs. W.A. Hunton, *Report on the Second Conference of Volunteer and Employed Workers, February 6-9, 1913 in Baltimore*, both in Secretary Reports, YWCA, National Board Library, New York.
94. Jane Olcott, *The Work of Colored Women*, p. 7.
95. Other women who made recommendations include: Katherine Hawes, Elizabeth MacFarland, Helen Davis, and Estelle Hawkins. See Olcott, *The Work of Colored Women*, p. 7.
96. Josephine Pinyon, *Report of the Louisville Conference, November 1915*, in Secretary Reports, YWCA, National Board Library, New York.
97. *Christian Womanhood* and *Association Monthly* included dialect jokes, use of black stereotypes, allusions to minstrels, and special identification of black branches as "Phyllis Wheatley" branches. See the *Christian Womanhood* 18 (December 14, 1911): 2, for specific example.

98. Josephine Pinyon quoted in Olcott, *The Work of Colored Women*, p. 11.
99. By 1915, the YWCA had 1 national colored secretary (Bowles), 16 local branches or centers, 9 local paid workers, and 101 other affiliated Negro schools (but no student staff), according to Eva Bowles, "Resume of Negro Work, 1915-1920," YWCA, National Board Archives, New York; Gladys G. Calkins, "The Negro in the Young Women's Christian Association: A Study of the Development of YWCA Interracial Policies and Practices in their Historical Setting" (M.A. thesis, George Washington University, 1960), pp. 45-46, 214; Jacqueline Hall, "Revolt Against Chivalry," pp. 106-107; Mongold, "Vespers and Vacant Lots," pp. 24-26; C.H. Tobias, "The Work of the YM and YWCAs with Negro Youth," *The Annals of the American Academy of Political and Social Science* 140 (November 1928): 283-86; and *The Crisis* 6 (May 1913): 63.
100. W.E.B. Du Bois, "A City Negro," speech delivered at the Brooklyn Lincoln Settlement, ca. 1910-1912, copy in Du Bois Papers, UM.

CHAPTER FIVE

1. Sources for the role in the Afro-American League/Council include Washington *Bee*, January 11, 1890; Chicago *Tribune*, August 18, 1899; Chicago *Times Herald*, August 20, 1899; Ida B. Wells-Barnett, "The National Afro-American Council," *Howard's American Magazine* 6 (May 1901): 415-18; Emma Lou Thornbrough, "The National Afro-American League, 1887-1908," *Journal of Southern History* 27 (November 1961): 494-512; Indianapolis *Freeman*, September 1, 1900; *Colored American* 4 (March 1903): 331-38; *Boston Guardian*, July 11, 1903; New York *Tribune*, October 11, 1906, and Program, National Afro-American Council, October 9-11, 1906, both in clippings of Mary Church Terrell Papers, Library of Congress (hereafter MCT Papers, LC).

   For sources dealing with the role of women in the Niagara Movement consult the Washington *Bee*, September 23, 1905; Mary Church Terrell, *Colored Woman in a White World* (Washington: Ransdell Press, 1940), p. 121; Mary Terrell to W.E.B. Du Bois, November 29, 1926; W.E.B. Du Bois to Anna Jones, January 23, 1906; Addie Hunton to W. Du Bois, April 8, 1907; Equal Suffrage League to W. Du Bois, August 25, 1907; all in W.E.B. Du Bois Papers, University of Massachusetts (hereafter Du Bois Papers, UM); Stephen R. Fox, *The Guardian of Boston: William Monroe Trotter* (New York: Atheneum, 1971), pp. 103-107, 122-25; *The Crisis* 2 (April 1912): 123; Mary White Ovington, *The Walls Came Tumbling Down* (New York: Harcourt, Brace and Company, 1947), p. 101; Nancy Weiss, *The National Urban League* (New York: Oxford University Press, 1974), p. 7; and Elliott Rudwick, "The Niagara Movement," *Journal of Negro History* 42 (July 1957): 183, 187-88.

   For the most helpful information about the role of black women in early racial advancement organizations, one most turn to contemporary sources. W.E.B. Du Bois in his books, *The Autobiography of W.E.B. Du Bois* (New

York: International Publishers, Inc., 1968) and *Darkwater: Voices from Within the Veil* (New York: Schocken Books, 1920), and his articles in *The Crisis* demonstrate his philosophical support of an active role for black women in the social reforms. Mary White Ovington in *Portraits in Color* (New York: Viking Press, 1927), *The Walls Came Tumbling Down*, and *Half a Man: The Status of the Negro in New York* (New York: Longmans, Green and Company, 1911) contain vignettes, insights, and organizational information not found in other biographical or organizational works. The autobiographies of black women provide other insights. Alfreda Duster, ed., *Crusade for Justice: The Autobiography of Ida B. Wells* (Chicago: University of Chicago Press, 1970) is useful for a critical perspective of white and black leadership from Wells-Barnett's point of view. She had great difficulty working in any organized group, so her viewpoints and frequently her dates have to be weighed with consideration to her other conflicts. Mary Terrell's autobiography, *Colored Woman in a White World*, is much more even in treatment, but it frequently smoothes over interorganizational conflicts.

Recent secondary sources that delineate the role of black women include Cynthia Neverdon-Morton, *Afro-American Women of the South and the Advancement of the Race, 1895-1925* (Knoxville: University of Tennessee Press, 1989) and Jacqueline Anne Rouse, *Lugenia Burns Hope: Black Southern Reformer* (Athens, Georgia: University of Georgia Press, 1989).

Most secondary sources about the Afro-American League/Council, the Niagara Movement, or the NAACP are of little help concerning the role of black women. Charles Flint Kellogg, *NAACP: The National Association for the Advancement of Colored People* (Baltimore: Johns Hopkins Press, 1967) seldom mentions the black female role, except in footnotes and, even then, female names are often misspelled, incomplete, or not identified as black women. Fox, *The Guardian of Boston*; Nancy Weiss, *The National Urban League*; and Robert L. Zangrando, *The NAACP Crusade Against Lynching, 1909-1950* (Philadelphia: Temple University Press, 1980) provide a few references to black women in the Boston reform community, the Urban League, and the antilynching movement.

2. "The Call," in Kellogg, *NAACP*, p. 298, and Mary White Ovington, "The National Association for the Advancement of Colored People," *Journal of Negro History* 9 (April 1924): 110.

3. Sources differ as to numbers of signers and women. Fox, *Guardian of Boston*, cited over fifty whites and seven blacks. "The Call" reprinted in Kellogg, *NAACP*, pp. 297-98, has sixty signers with seven noted black leaders, including Mary Terrell and Ida Wells-Barnett. Wilson Record, "Negro Intellectual Leadership in the National Association for the Advancement of Colored People: 1910-1940," *Phylon* 18 (Fall 1956): 380, said, "Only one Negro woman of note, Ida Wells-Barnett, was among the signers of the call." Apparently, Record did not know about the significance of Terrell or was not aware of her identity.

4. The white women who signed the call represented reform leadership in the suffrage, settlement house, child labor, labor, prison reform, pacifism, and

educational reform movements: Jane Addams, Harriet Stanton Blatch, Kate Claghorn, Mary E. Dreier, Florence Kelly, Mary E. McDowell, Leonora O'Reilly, Mary White Ovington, Jane Robbins, Anna Garland Spencer, Mrs. Henry Villard, Lillian Wald, Susan P. Wharton, Mary E. Wooley, Helen Stokes, Mrs. Rodman Wharton, and Helen Marot. For information about the individual women see Edward T. James, Janet Wilson, et. al., eds., *Notable American Women, 1607-1950* (Cambridge: Belnap Press, 1971) and further updated editions of the collection.

5. For Terrell's and Wells-Barnett's white contacts see Duster, *Crusade*, and Terrell, *Colored Woman in a White World*.

6. Clipping, source unknown, in MCT Papers, LC.

7. *Colored American* 4 (March 1903): 331-38; Thornbrough, "National Afro-American League," pp. 503-508; Fox, *Guardian of Boston*, pp. 46-60; Boston *Guardian*, July 11, 1903; Sylvia Dannett, *Profiles of Negro Womanhood* (Chicago: Educational Heritage Press, 1964), pp. 285, 309, 333; and Thomasine Corrothers, "Lucy Moten," *Journal of Negro History* 19 (1934): 102-106.

8. Gertrude Mossell of Philadelphia is listed as an organizer of the National Afro-American Council in Frank Lincoln Mather, ed., *Who's Who of the Colored Race* I (Chicago: Memento Edition Half-Century Anniversary of Negro Freedom in the United States, 1915; reprint ed., Detroit: Gale Research Company, 1976), p. 201. Since black women participated at the national level and served as delegates to various conventions, their participation on the local and state levels is assumed. Evidence of the local participation is lacking. The Washington *Bee*, January 11, 1890, discussed the need for leagues for civil and political protection, but no mention as to the formation of the actual structures. Since the coverage of the Afro-American League/Council is uneven, those conventions having the most amount of coverage about black female participation are given the broadest discussion in the paper. For more information see "Colored Men in Session," Chicago *Tribune*, August 18, 1899; Chicago *Times Herald*, August 20, 1899; both clippings in MCT Papers, LC; Duster, *Crusade*, pp. 255-63; Thornbrough, "National Afro-American League," pp. 494-512; Ida B. Wells-Barnett, "The National Afro-American Council," pp. 415-18; Fox, *Guardian of Boston*, pp. 46-48, 59; August Meier, *Negro Thought in America, 1880-1915* (Ann Arbor: University of Michigan, 1968), pp. 171-82. For information about Wells-Barnett, see Thomas C. Holt, "The Lonely Warrior: Ida B. Wells-Barnett and the Struggle for Black Leadership," in John Hope Franklin and August Meier, eds., *Black Leaders of the Twentieth Century* (Urbana: University of Illinois Press, 1982), p. 59, noted conflict Booker T. Washington contributed to her isolation. This author perceives the conflict with Washington to be symbolic of her personal style of interaction. She viewed no one—black or white—as righteous as she. Her perceptions were frequently accurate, but she did not take into account the sociopolitical context nor individual personalities. People found working with Wells-Barnett difficult. Yet, she was an excellent motivator for various causes. Her leadership approximates that of "an enthusiast" in social movements. She conflicted with

Washington supporters in women's clubs, politics, and racial advancement organizations ranging from the Afro-American League/Council to the NAACP. Washington's "style" and tactics, ideology in education and politics, and personality led to her open conflicts with the Washington camp. For further clarification see Ida B. Wells-Barnett, "Booker T. Washington and His Critics," *The World Today* 6 (April 1904): 518-21.

9. Press clippings, programs, and flyers, especially lecture tour booklets for the Interstate Lecture Bureau in the late 1890s, use these terms in MCT Papers, LC, and in Dannett, *Profiles*, p. 210.

10. Terrell, *Colored Woman*, pp. 189-93.

11. *Ibid.*, p. 191.

12. *Ibid.*, pp. 189-93; Mary Terrell, "The Colored Woman's Present Status and Aspiration," Address to the Congregational Association in New Jersey, 1899; "The Progress of Colored Women," "Uncle Sam and the Sons of Ham," Address to Ohio State Colored Educational and Industrial Exposition, August, 1906; and "Bright Side of a Dark Subject," Address to Columbia University, September 1906. Copies of speeches in MCT Papers, LC, and Mary Terrell Papers, Howard University (hereafter MCT Papers, HU). Mary Terrell's correspondence with W.E.B. Du Bois indicated friendly relations and discussed some of the same principles advocated by the "radical" camp. Du Bois also had been an early admirer of Washington and had supported the value of industrial education for training some blacks. See Mary Terrell to W.E.B. Du Bois, April 14, 1903, May 1, 1903, and October 6, 1904, in Du Bois Papers, UM.

13. Terrell, *Colored Woman*, p. 163.

14. Mary Terrell's speech before the National Purity Congress (Battle Creek, Michigan, in November 1907) repeated a message of an earlier speech, that black girls serving as domestics with Southern white homes were not safe. Mary Terrell, "A Plea for the White South," no source, 1906, in clippings file and Nashville *American*, November 3, 1907, in clippings file of MCT Papers, LC. Other speeches included an anti-lynching address to the Afro-American Council in October 1906 and to the Constitution League in February 1906. Her speech to St. Mark's A.M.E. Zion, October 1906 entitled "Educated Too Much?" attacked the basis of Washington's educational philosophy. For sources of these speeches, see the MCT Papers, LC and HU; Gladys B. Shepperd, *Mary Church Terrell: A Respectable Person* (Baltimore: Human Relations Press, 1959); and Terrell, *Colored Woman*.

15. "The Call" quoted in Kellogg, *NAACP*, p. 298.

16. Gloria T. Hull, "Researching Alice Dunbar-Nelson," in Gloria T. Hull, Patricia Bell Scott, and Barbara Smith, eds., *But Some of Us Are Brave* (Old Westbury, New York: The Feminist Press, 1982), p. 192.

17. Duster, *Crusade*, pp. 321-25; Nancy Weiss, "From Black Separatism to Interracial Cooperation: Origins of Organized Efforts for Racial Advancement, 1890-1920," in Barton Bernstein and Allen Matusow, eds., *Twentieth-Century America: Recent Interpretations* (New York: Harcourt, Brace, Jovanovich, 1972), p. 80; Ovington, *Walls Came Tumbling Down*, p. 111; B. Joyce Ross,

J.E. Spingarn and the Rise of the NAACP (New York: Atheneum, 1972); and Financial Statement, February 1-May 14, 1910, National Negro Committee in the Administrative Files of the NAACP Papers, Library of Congress show the travel expenses paid to Mrs. Wells-Barnett, Du Bois, and Mrs. Terrell. Wells-Barnett also described her accommodations arranged by the NAACP at Henry St. Settlement for this trip to New York in Duster, *Crusade*, pp. 327-28. For those black women having to travel distances to participate in the New York-based NAACP, travel expenses aided the financial burdens of such participation. Black women who participated from the New York-Brooklyn area included Dr. Verina Morton Jones, Maritcha Lyons, Mary Talbert, Bertha Johnson, Nina Wilson, Addie Hunton, and Frances Keyser.

18. The subcommittee of the National Negro Committee compiled a list of people who could work with others of differing opinions. This Committee of Forty was to organize the basic structure of next major meeting. Wells-Barnett's name was not included on the first list of names. Du Bois felt that Wells-Barnett did not trust white leadership and that Celia Parker Wooley could represent the Chicago reform perspective on the Committee of Forty. Wells-Barnett complained about her omission to Du Bois, and then to white leaders: John Milholland, Wooley, Charles Russell, and William E. Walling. Russell put her name back on the list, even though his action was not "legal" by deviating from subcommittee procedures. Wells-Barnett never forgave the NAACP the oversight. For discussion of this incident see Ovington, *Walls Came Tumbling Down*, p. 106; Duster, *Crusade*, pp. 321-28; Shirley Graham Du Bois, *His Day Is Marching One: A Memoir of W.E.B. Du Bois* (Philadelphia: J.B. Lippincott, 1971), p. 26; W.E.B. Du Bois, *Dusk of Dawn* (New York: Harcourt, Brace, 1940), p. 95; Fox, *Guardian of Boston*, pp. 126-29; Elliott Rudwick, "Booker T. Washington's Relations with the National Association for the Advancement of Colored People," *Journal of Negro Education* 29 (Fall 1960): 134-35; Elliott Rudwick, "The National Negro Committee Conference of 1909," *Phylon* 18 (Winter 1958): 414-16; Record, "Negro Intellectual Leadership in the NAACP," pp. 377-78.

19. Mary Terrell to Robert Terrell, June 14, 1909, in MCT Papers, LC.

20. Terrell, *Colored Woman*, pp. 160-61; Diary, 1908-1910, in MCT Papers, LC.

21. Duster, *Crusade*; and Holt, "The Lonely Warrior," pp. 39-61.

22. Hallie Q. Brown, *Homespun Heroines* (Xenia, Ohio: Aldine Press, 1926; reprint ed., Freeport, New York: Books for Libraries Press, 1971), p. 183.

23. Benjamin Brawley, *Negro Builders and Heroes* (Chapel Hill: University of North Carolina Press, 1937), pp. 278-79; Margaret Murray Washington, "Club Work Among Negro Women," in J.W. Gibson, ed., *Progress of the Race* (Naperville, Illinois: J.L. Nichols, 1920), pp. 186-89; Brown, *Homespun Heroines*, pp. 182-83; *The Crisis* 13 (April 1917): 281; and Kellogg, *NAACP*, pp. 298-301.

24. Fox, *Guardian of Boston*, p. 25.

25. John Daniels, *In Freedom's Birthplace: A Study of Boston Negroes* (Boston: Houghton Mifflin, 1914), p. 209.

26. Fox, *Guardian of Boston*, pp. 9-28, 105-105, 212; Elizabeth Davis, *Lifting As They Climb* (Washington: National Association of Colored Women, 1933), pp. 236-39; Dannett, *Profiles*, p. 309; Brown, *Homespun Heroines*, p. 151.

27. St. Clair Drake, *Churches and Voluntary Associations in the Chicago Negro Community* (Chicago: Works Progress Administration Report, 1940), pp. 21-22; "Some Chicagoans of Note," *The Crisis* 10 (September 1915): 237-42; Fannie B. Williams, "Colored Women of Chicago," *The Southern Workman* 43 (1914): 566; Charlotte Martin, *The Story of Brockport for 100 Years, 1829-1929* (Brockport, New York: Local History, Seymour Library, 1964), pp. 21, 36-37; Duster, *Crusade*; Dannett, *Profiles*, pp. 221, 269, 327; Richardson, *National Cyclopedia*, p. 143; Bert Loewenberg and Ruth Bogin, eds., *Black Women in Nineteenth-Century American Life: Their Words, Their Thoughts, Their Feelings* (University Park: Pennsylvania State University Press, 1976), pp. 263-64; Gertrude Mossell, *The Work of Afro-American Women* (Nashville: Fisk University Press, 1894; reprint ed., Freeport, New York: Books for Libraries Press, 1971), p. 112; Allan H. Spear, *Black Chicago: The Making of a Negro Ghetto, 1890-1920* (Chicago: University of Chicago Press, 1967), pp. 50-70. For discussion of the participation of the "radical" black woman, Chicagoan Lucy Parsons, in the labor reforms of the International Workers of the World, see Carolyn Ashbaugh, *Lucy Parsons: American Revolutionary* (Chicago: Charles Kerr, 1976). Drake (p. 125 cited above) claimed the Chicago middle class was not "caught on the horns of the Du Bois-Washington dilemma." The records of the national office of the NAACP continually reflect the need to motivate the Chicago branch, which the NAACP administration felt was in the hands of the conservatives. Duster also calls attention to the disagreements between the radical and conservative camps. For further discussion about the factionalism, see Kellogg, *NAACP*, pp. 124-25.

28. Terrell, Diary, January 7, 1908, in MCT Papers, LC.

29. Mary Terrell, "How, When, and Where Black Becomes White," Chicago *Sunday Tribune* (November 5, 1905), pp. 7-8; Mary Terrell, "Another Side of Washington's Race Question," (no source, ca. 1916); Mary Terrell, "Sara Brown," *The Journal of College Alumnae Club of Washington* 21 (April 1950): 17-19; all in clippings file of MCT Papers, LC. For further information about the Washington community see Constance Green, *The Secret City: A History of Race Relations in the Nation's Capital* (Princeton: Princeton University Press, 1967); Richardson, *National Cyclopedia*, p. 446; Dannett, *Profiles*, pp. 207-211, 245, 291, 311; Mary Terrell, "Colored Society in Washington," *Voice of the Negro* 1 (April 1904): 151-56; Mary Terrell, "Social Functions During Inauguration Week," *Voice of the Negro* 2 (April 1905): 237-40; and *The Crisis* 10 (September 1915): 243. From these sources, other black women in Washington included Mrs. J.R. Francis, Edith Wormley Minton, Lettie Langston Napier, Mrs. H.C. Tyson, and Mrs. A.M. Curtis.

30. The Empire State Federation and the New York State Federation were titles used interchangeably in the club movement.

31. Information on the New York clubwomen is found in Dannett, *Profiles*, p. 317; James, *Notable American Women*, II, pp. 576-77; Mrs. W. A. Hunton,

"Women's Clubs"; *The Crisis* 2 (September 1911):210-212 and 4 (May 1912): 38-39;and Members of Equal Suffrage League and National Association of Colored Women's Clubs to W.E.B. Du Bois, August 25, 1907, letter in Du Bois Papers, UM.

32. *The Crisis* 1 (November 1910): 122; Davis, *Lifting*, pp. 169-70; Dannett, *Profiles*, p. 231.

33. Program, National Negro Committee, Second Annual Conference, May 12-14, 1910, in MCT Papers, LC; Duster, *Crusade*, pp. 326-28; Minutes, Executive Committee, NAACP, November 29, 1910, pp. 1-2, in NAACP Papers, LC.

34. Announcement of Lecture-Recital at Berkeley Theatre, December 7, 1910, in MCT Papers, LC; Dannett, *Profiles*, p. 263.

35. Speech by W.E.B. Du Bois quoted in New York *Evening Mail*, December 7, 1910, clipping in MCT Papers, LC.

36. Mrs. John E. Milholland, "Talks About Women," *The Crisis* 1 (December 1910): 28.

37. Minutes, Executive Committee, January 3, March 7, April 11, and June 6, 1911, Board Minutes, NAACP Papers; Mary Talbert to M. Nerney, January 14, 1913, Mary Wilson to M. Nerney, March 10 and December 23, 1914, in NAACP Papers.

38. Program for Mass Meeting of NAACP, Young's Casino, January 12, 1913, in Archibald Grimke Papers, Howard University; Addie Hunton to M. Nerney, November 25, December 3 and 14, 1912, April 19 and May 25, 1913, in Special Correspondence, NAACP Papers.

39. In addition to note 38 above, see the periodic correspondence 1912-1913 between Hunton and Mrs. Butler Wilson in Special Correspondence Files, NAACP Papers.

40. Ovington, *Walls Came Tumbling Down*, p. 167.

41. Ronald Lawson and Stephen E. Barton, "Sex Roles in Social Movements: A Case Study of the Tenant Movement in New York City," *Signs* 6 (Winter 1980): 230-47, provides an analysis of women's roles in an urban social movement. A similar role existed for the black women in their grassroots organizational role in the early years of the NAACP.

42. Ovington, *Walls Came Tumbling Down*, p. 167.

43. Ovington, "The NAACP," p. 115.

44. *The Crisis* 8 (July 1914): 142; Kellogg, *NAACP*, p. 131; Kathryn Johnson to Roy Nash, August 19, 1916, Administrative Files, NAACP Papers.

45. Kathryn Johnson to May Nerney, January 6, 1914; Board Minutes, January 13 and February 2, 1915, NAACP Papers.

46. Kathryn Johnson to May Nerney, August 13, 1915, Administrative Files, NAACP Papers.

47. Wheatley YWCA, *Report*, to May Childs Nerney, September 11, 1915, in Administrative Records, NAACP Papers.

48. Kathryn Johnson to Roy Nash, July 11, 1916, Administrative Files; Board Minutes, May 10 and June 14, 1915, NAACP Papers.

49. Kathryn Johnson to May Nerney, September 17, 1915, Administrative Files, NAACP Papers.
50. *Ibid.*
51. Board Minutes, NAACP, October 11, 1915, and January 3, 1916, p. 22, both in Du Bois Papers, UM; Kathryn Johnson's dislike of accommodation to whites was clearly expressed in a letter to Du Bois ten years later, March 26, 1926, in Du Bois Papers.
52. May Childs Nerney to Mrs. Wilson, October 13, 1914, Administrative Files, NAACP Papers.
53. Mary Wilson to May Nerney, March 10 and October 29, 1914; Mary Ovington to Mary Wilson, December 23, 1914, in Administrative Files, NAACP Papers.
54. Branch Files, Brooklyn, New York, NAACP Files.
55. Branch applications for the following display female participation: Brooklyn Branch Files, Washington Branch Files, South Carolina (Columbia and Charleston) Branch Files, Houston Branch Files, all in NAACP Papers. The Secretary's Reports on Branch Organization are helpful in delineating female participation, especially M. Nerney to J.E. Spingarn, January 7, 1914, Administrative Files and Annual Conference, Reports of Branches.
56. Ovington, "The NAACP," p. 114.
57. Minutes, Executive Committee, May 10, 1911, in Board Minutes, NAACP Papers; Kellogg, *NAACP*, p. 120.
58. Mary Wilson to May Nerney, August 18, 1914; Board Minutes of NAACP for July 12, 1915, and January 3, 1916, NAACP Papers; Elizabeth C. Putnam to Archibald Grimke, April 16, 1915, in Archibald Grimke Papers, Howard University; and Kellogg, *NAACP*, p. 121.
59. Mary White Ovington to Joel Spingarn, July 20, 1913, in Washington, D.C., Branch Files, NAACP Papers.
60. May Childs Nerney to Joel Spingarn, July 31, 1913, in Washington, D.C., Branch Files, NAACP Papers.
61. Waldron accused his opposition of supporting Bruce and signing up new members who opposed Waldron. In a news clipping (no source of date in the Washington Branch Files) Waldron is quoted as urging black voters to "stand by their white friends in the South." Other descriptions of the conflict include: Memorandum, Joel Spingarn to May Childs Nerney, July 28, 1913, and other news clippings in Washington Branch Files, Board Minutes, May 6, July 1, and October 7, 1913, in NAACP Papers; Kellogg, *NAACP*, pp. 126-27.
62. Mary Terrell, "Sara Brown," pp. 17-19; Ovington, *Walls Came Tumbling Down*, pp. 124-25.
63. Kellogg, *NAACP*, pp. 126-27; Roscoe Conkling Bruce to Archibald Grimke, November 16, 1914, to discuss the possible consumer's league; copies of legislative bills intending to increase segregation in Washington, both bills and letter in Archibald Grimke Papers, Howard University.
64. Carrie Clifford, "National Association for the Advancement of Colored People," *The Crisis* 14 (October 1917): 306.
65. Carrie Clifford to W. Du Bois, November 15, 1916, in Du Bois Papers, UM.

66. Kellogg, *NAACP*, pp. 117-28; Duster, *Crusade*, pp. 325-28; John Milholland's proposal to merge the Constitution League with the National Negro Committee noted in Minutes, Special Meeting, National Negro Committee, April 7, 1910, NAACP Papers; Maritcha Lyons proposed a similar merger in Minutes, Board of Directors, NAACP, April 21, 1910, in NAACP Papers. The money raised by Gertrude Mossell is cited in *The Crisis* 13 (December 1916): 75.

67. Kellogg, *NAACP*, pp. 122-24; Brooklyn Branch Files, NAACP Papers; Davis, *Lifting*, pp. 205-206; Gail Lumet, "My Mother Lena Comes from a Line of Proud Women," *Ms.* 10 (August 1981): 46-47, 99; Du Bois, *Autobiography*, pp. 105-108; Brooklyn Branch Files, NAACP Papers; Gail Lumet, *The Incredible Hornes* (New York: Alfred A. Knopf, 1986).

68. *Annual Conference Report*, Baltimore, May 3-6, 1914, p. 1, Annual Conference Files, NAACP Papers.

69. Coralie F. Cook, "The Problems of the Colored Child," in *Annual Conference Report*, Baltimore, 1914, p. 9, Annual Conference Files, NAACP Papers.

70. Lucy Slowe Papers, Howard University: *Annual Conference Report*, Baltimore, 1914, Annual Conference Files, NAACP Papers.

71. Alice Dunbar, "The Colored Working Woman," in *Annual Conference Report*, Baltimore, 1914, p. 3, Annual Conference Files, NAACP Papers.

72. *Ibid.*, p. 7.

73. *The Crisis* 1 (November 1910): 14; Kellogg, *NAACP*, pp. 62-63; Ida B. Wells-Barnett to Joel Spingarn, April 21, 1911, Joel E. Spingarn Papers, Howard University (hereafter J. Spingarn Papers, HU).

74. Charles E. Bentley to J. Spingarn, April 29, 1912, and March 29, 1915, in J. Spingarn Papers, Howard; Minutes, Executive Committee, November 14, 1911, in Board Minutes, NAACP Papers; Kellogg, *NAACP*, pp. 117-28; Duster, *Crusade*, pp. 325-28; Davis, *Lifting*, pp. 179-83, 198, 263-66.

75. May Nerney to Joel Spingarn, "Notes on Branches," January 7, 1914, Administrative Files, NAACP Papers.

76. May Nerney to Joel Spingarn, January 22, 1914, Administrative Files, NAACP Papers.

77. *Ibid.*; *The Crisis* 6 (July 1913): 144.

78. Emma Lou Thornbrough, "The History of Black Women in Indiana," *Black History News and Notes* 14 (August 1983): 4-7; Darlene Clark Hine, *When the Truth Is Told: A History of Black Women's Culture and Community in Indiana, 1875-1950* (Indianapolis: National Council of Negro Women, 1981), pp. 46-56.

79. Dannett, *Profiles*, p. 243; Davis, *Lifting*, p. 200.

80. Davis, *Lifting*, pp. 173-76; R.W. Bagnall to Mary White Ovington, December 27, 1919, and November 3, 1920, Administrative Files, NAACP Papers; Lethia Fleming Papers, Western Reserve Historical Society, Cleveland, Ohio; Cleveland *Branch Bulletin* n.v. (October 1920): 8-9, copy in Cleveland Branch NAACP Papers, Western Reserve Historical Society; Kusmer, *A Ghetto Takes Shape*, pp. 259-63.

81. Delilah Beaseley, *Negro Trailblazers of California* (Los Angeles: Times Mirror Publishing, 1919), pp. 229-31; Davis, *Lifting*, pp. 230-31, 246-48.
82. Other sources of female participation in early branches can be ascertained from available photographs of original membership. The Du Bois Papers, Photographic Collection, University of Massachusetts, shows many examples of female presence in the organizing bodies. The NAACP Branch Files noted 81 women of 228 charter members of the Charleston, South Carolina, branch; 12 of 33 members of the Dallas branch; and 36 of 97 members of the Brooklyn branch.
83. Board Minutes, NAACP, January 4, 1912, and December 31, 1912, in Board Files, NAACP Papers, *The Crisis* 8 (October 1914): 220; Ovington, *Walls Came Tumbling Down*, pp. 110-11; Osofsky, *Harlem*, pp. 54, 67.
84. Minutes, Annual Meeting, January 3, 1916, in Board Files, NAACP Papers.
85. May Childs Nerney to Mrs. Butler Wilson, January 13, 1915, noted, "It is the first big opportunity we have to put the colored woman's position before such a representative suffrage body" in Administrative Files, NAACP Papers.
86. Minutes, July 12, 1915, and Minutes, Annual Meeting, January 3, 1916, in Board Files, NAACP Papers; Drake, *Churches and Voluntary Associations in Chicago*, p. 125; Dannett, *Profiles*, p. 255; Brown, *Homespun Heroines*, pp. 222-24.
87. Roy Nash to Kathryn Johnson, August 16, 1916, Administrative Files, NAACP Papers.
88. *Ibid.*
89. *Ibid.*
90. *Ibid.*
91. *Ibid.*
92. Roy Nash to Kathryn Johnson, January 17, 1916; Kathryn Johnson to Joel Spingarn, July 21, 1916; Kathryn Johnson to Roy Nash, August 15, 1916; Administrative Files, NAACP Papers, show that Johnson continued to direct letters to defend herself throughout August. Defensive in tone, her letters met the charges by Mary Wilson and continued to accuse other black women of undermining her. Mary Talbert and Addie Dickerson were specifically mentioned. The once-proud Johnson then stooped to sympathetic appeals, claiming she would have no money to survive if the NAACP went forward with her dismissal. For Johnson, the NAACP rejection seemed to symbolize the difficulties of interracial organization during that time. For sources dealing with the candidacy of black men and women, see Roy Nash to Kathryn Johnson, August 16, 1916, Administrative Files, NAACP Papers; Roy Nash to Joel Spingarn, October 27, 1916, J. Spingarn Papers; Kellogg, *NAACP*, n. 61, p. 132; and James Weldon Johnson, *Along This Way: An Autobiography of James Weldon Johnson* (New York: Viking, 1933), 314; Cleveland *Gazette*, July 22, 1916; Kellogg, *NAACP*, p. 218. These sources only verify the candidacy of Elizabeth Freeman, William Pickens, and John Hope. Other possible candidates could have included field workers such as Martha Gruening or Nettie Asberry.
93. Mary Terrell, *Colored Woman*, p. 195.

94. W.E.B. Du Bois, *The Amenia Conference: An Historic Negro Gathering* (Amenia, New York: Troutbeck Leaflet No. 8, September 1925), copy in MCT Papers, LC.
95. Categories used by Fox, *The Guardian of Boston*, pp. 31-41. Trotter's name appeared on the list, but according to Fox, Trotter did not attend. See Fox, pp. 202-31; Program, The Amenia Conference, August 24-26, 1916, copy in MCT Papers, LC.
96. Minutes, December 11, 1916, and January 8, 1917, Board Files, NAACP Papers.
97. The Minutes of the Meetings of the Board of Directors, December 11, 1916, and January 8, 1917, present a puzzling set of events. At the December meeting, the Report of the Committee on National Organizer was read by Mary White Ovington, the chairman of the committee. She reported the committee recommendation for the position of National Organizer as Mary E. Jackson, a black woman from Providence, Rhode Island. Jackson's contract was to begin January 1, 1917 for a period of one year's probation, three month's notice if terminated, and include a $2000 a year salary plus expenses when doing field work. Ovington recommended changing the title to "Field Secretary and Organizer" due to the type of work Jackson would have to carry out. Board members Paul Kennaday and William Sinclair moved that the committee report be approved. Discussion followed and that motion lost. Dr. Sinclair then moved for the matter to be laid on the table until the next board meeting. His motion also lost. Much of the interceding discussion is not officially recorded in the minutes, but suddenly a Mr. Studin moved and was seconded and voted that Mr. James Weldon Johnson be appointed as Field Secretary and Organizer and that a committee consisting of the Chairman (Spingarn) and one other be empowered to place Johnson under contract. Studin's motion carried with one dissenting vote (no names were mentioned, but those attending the meeting included Du Bois, Spingarn, Studin, Ovington, Sinclair, Kennaday, Dr. Holmes, Dr. Bishop, Mr. Crawford, Dr. Jones, Arthur Spingarn, Mr. Wilson, and Mr. Russell. From this list, I assume the dissenting vote was Ovington's. Joel Spingarn appointed Roy Nash to serve on the Committee to obtain Johnson. At the next meeting, January 8, 1917, James Weldon Johnson was present in the role as National Organizer and Field Secretary. Joel Spingarn appointed his brother, Arthur Spingarn, and Studin to a committee charged with working with James Weldon Johnson.

The Nominating Committee's recommendation of Mary Jackson is puzzling. Since Jackson lacked prominence in NAACP records and literature, her choice is difficult to understand, especially when coupled with the knowledge held by several members of the board that James Weldon Johnson had already accepted the position in his letter to Spingarn, November 5, 1916 (Joel Spingarn Papers, Howard University). The discussion of Johnson's appointment had been discussed since the Amenia Conference when Johnson impressed Spingarn with his abilities. See the following correspondence for further information about the Johnson appointment: Roy Nash to Joel Spingarn, October 27, 1916, Spingarn Papers, HU; Joel Spingarn to James

Weldon Johnson, October 28, 1916, in Oswald Garrison Villard Papers, Houghton Library, Harvard University; for Ovington's change in perception see Mary White Ovington to Joel Spingarn, September 26, 1917, in Spingarn Papers, HU. Johnson's appointment demonstrated weakness of female powers in the central administration of the NAACP. The fact that Sinclair and Kennaday moved for Ovington's recommendations shows that not all of the men on the board were in on the tactic to overrule the committee's recommendation. Jackson's nomination also showed the impact of female field work. Jackson was a close friend of Mary Wilson, wife of Butler Wilson. May Nerney sent Wilson's mail in care of Jackson during January 1915. As a national organizer for the NACW, Jackson had skills and contacts in the black female network. Within a few years, Jackson went on to leadership in the YWCA as the National Industrial Secretary of the YWCA Colored Work.

98. For information about Mary Talbert, Mary Wilson, Nettie Asberry, Mary Jackson, Agnes Adams, and Kathryn Johnson, see Mary Ovington, "The National Association for the Protection of Colored People," pp. 107-16; Fox, *Guardian of Boston*; Dannett, *Profiles*; Brown, *Homespun Heroines*; and special sections of *The Crisis* as "Women's Clubs" or "Men of the Month," e.g., Maria Baldwin is discussed in *The Crisis* 13 (April 1917): 281, "Votes for Women," 10 (August 1915): 178-92 mentions several women. For Mary Terrell's role, see Terrell, *Colored Woman*; Sammy Miller, "Woodrow Wilson and the Black Judge," *The Crisis* 74 (February 1977): 81-86; and "Robert H. Terrell: First Black D.C. Municipal Judge," *The Crisis* 73 (June/July 1976): 209-10.

99. *The Crisis* 13 (January 1917): 119; Dannett, *Profiles*, p. 317; Nannie Burroughs, "A Great Woman," no date, speech about Mary Talbert, copy in Nannie Burroughs Papers, Library of Congress; Mary Talbert to John Shillady, January 2, 1919 and May 15, 1920, Administrative Files, NAACP Papers; Mary White Ovington, Office Diaries, April 19, 1920, NAACP Papers; Addie Hunton to Du Bois, January 26, 1918, in Du Bois Papers, UM.

100. Johnson, *Along This Way*, p. 316.

101. *Ibid.*, pp. 314-15; Kellogg, *NAACP*, p. 135.

102. Mary Talbert to John Shillady, December 23, 1918, Administrative Files, NAACP Papers.

103. Mary Talbert, Report, in Talbert to Shillady, December 23, 1918; Mary Talbert to James Weldon Johnson, January 9, 1919 and February 25, 1919; Mary Talbet to John Shillady, May 16, 1919, Administrative Files, NAACP Papers.

104. Mary Talbert to James Weldon Johnson, February 12, 1919, Administrative Files, NAACP Papers.

105. Mary White Ovington, Office Diaries, April 7, 1919, Branch Files of Charleston, South Carolina, May 10 and December 17, 1917, all in NAACP Papers.

106. Ovington, Office Diaries, April 22, 1919, in NAACP Papers.

107. Mary Talbert to Addie Hunton, n.d., Administrative Files, NAACP Papers.

108. *Ibid.*

109. Addie Hunton to Walter White, September 15, 1920, Administrative Files, NAACP Papers.
110. W.E.B. Du Bois, Memorandum to the Chairman of the Board and the Committee on the Secretary, June 28, 1920, Administrative Files, NAACP Papers.
111. Catherine Lealtad was the first black woman to graduate (1915) from Macalester College in Minnesota, had the highest scholastic average of her class, and belonged to Alpha Kappa Alpha at the University of Minnesota, according to Earl Spangler, *The Negro in Minnesota* (Minneapolis: T.S. Denison, 1961), p. 77. She became a worker for the YWCA around 1918-19 noted in Catherine Lealtad, "The National Y.W.C.A. and the Negro," *The Crisis* 19 (April 1920): 317-18. Her position in the NAACP is noted in R.W. Bagnall to Katherine (sic) Lealtad, September 11, 1920, Administrative Files, NAACP Papers. For discussion of the change in black leadership see August Meier and Elliott Rudwick, "The Rise of the Black Secretariat in the NAACP, 1909-1935," in Meier and Rudwick, eds., *Along the Color Line* (Urbana: University of Illinois Press, 1976), pp. 94-127; B. Joyce Ross, *J.E. Spingarn and the Rise of the NAACP* (New York: Atheneum, 1972), pp. 103-15; Gary T. Marx and Michael Useem, "Majority Involvement in Minority Movements: Civil Rights, Abolition, Untouchability," *Journal of Social Issues* 27 (Spring 1971): 81-104. By 1919, 90 percent of the NAACP membership was black according to Kellogg, *NAACP*, p. 137; the old guard had passed from the scene, p. 291; and the circulation of *The Crisis* was at its height and influence great, p. 292.

CHAPTER SIX

1. Reynolds Farley, "The Urbanization of Negroes in the United States," *Journal of Social History* 1 (1967-1968): 255.
2. Nancy Weiss, *The National Urban League* (New York: Oxford University Press, 1974), pp. 13-14; Gilbert Osofsky, *Harlem: The Making of a Ghetto* (New York: Harper and Row, 1966), p. 67; and special issue devoted to the urban problems of blacks, *Charities* 15 (October 1905).
3. Frances A. Kellor, "Opportunities for Southern Negro Women in Northern Cities," *Voice of the Negro* 2 (July 1905): 473-73; Frances Kellor to W.E.B. Du Bois, February 10, 1905, in W.E.B. Du Bois Papers, University of Massachusetts, Amherst, Massachusetts (hereafter known as Du Bois Papers, UM); Weiss, *National Urban League*, pp. 3-20.
4. For a list and a description of the white and black membership of these organizations see Weiss, *National Urban League*, pp. 14-46, and notes 15 and 34 of chapter 2 and note 54 of chapter 3.
5. "The Report of the National League for the Protection of Colored Women," in *Annual Report, 1910-1911*, p. 23. National Urban League Papers, Library of Congress, Washington, D.C. (hereafter referred to as NUL Papers).

6. Minutes, Annual Meeting, October 8, 1913, NUL Papers.
7. *The Crisis* 13 (January 1917): 124-27.
8. Minutes of the Seventh Annual Meeting of the National League on Urban Conditions Among Negroes, December 4, 1918, p. 4, in NUL Papers. Unlike the biographical sources, the official records of the NAACP or the writings of the NAACP white leaders, the National Urban League or its leaders seldom mentioned the specific names of black women aiding their organization. Instead, they mentioned the particular activities or the organization, e.g., The White Rose Home, the Harlem Neighborhood Club, the Atlanta Neighborhood Union, or the Colored Social Settlement. Since black women provided the leadership and/or organization of the volunteer services of these organizations, the participation of black women in the League activities is evident. Until more research has been completed on the less well-known groups, e.g., the Amusement Club of New York City, the women will remain anonymous, as will the efforts of individuals who brought the delinquent black girls into their own homes, assumed the role of Big Sisters, and so on. For description of such activities see Committee for the Protection of Women, Minutes, January 6, February 3, April 7, October 21, and December 15, 1913; January 26 and April 13, 1914; *Annual Report, 1911-1912*, p. 26; and Minutes of the Seventh Annual Meeting of the National League on Urban Conditions Among Negroes, December 4, 1918, p. 4, all in NUL Papers (hereafter the individual organizational papers will be referred to as NLPCW for the National League for the Protection of Colored Women, CIICN for the Committee for Improving the Industrial Condition of Negroes in New York, and CUCAN for the Committee on Urban Conditions Among Negroes in New York).
9. Farley, "Urbanization of Negroes in U.S.," p. 255; W.E.B. Du Bois, *The Philadelphia Negro: A Social Study* (Philadelphia: University of Pennsylvania, 1899; reprint ed., New York: Schocken Books, 1967), pp. 50, 53; *Colored American* 4 (February 1902): 3; Constance Green, *The Secret City: A History of Race Relations in the National Capital* (Princeton: Princeton University Press, 1967), p. 151; Osofsky, *Harlem*, pp. 18, 128; Arvarh Strickland, *History of the Chicago Urban League* (Urbana: University of Illinois Press, 1966), pp. 22-23; Philip Hauser, "Demographic Factors in the Integration of the Negro," in John Bracey, August Meier, and Elliott Rudwick, eds., *The Rise of the Ghetto* (Belmont, California: Wadsworth, 1971), pp. 40, 41, 45; and Tables I, II, III, and IV in Appendix.
10. The title of Chapter 13 of E. Franklin Frazier, *The Negro Family in the United States* (Chicago: University of Chicago Press, 1939; revised and abridged, 1966), p. 210.
11. Osofsky, *Harlem*, p. 43; and Mary White Ovington, *Half a Man: Status of the Negro in New York* (New York: Longmans, Green and Co., 1911), pp. 18-26.
12. Kenneth Kusmer, *The Making of a Ghetto: Black Cleveland, 1890-1930* (Urbana: University of Illinois, 1978), pp. 55-57; and Alfreda Duster, ed.,

Crusade for Justice: The Autobiography of Ida B. Wells (Chicago: University of Chicago Press, 1970), pp. 371-74.

13. John Daniels, *In Freedom's Birthplace: A Study of Boston's Negroes* (Boston: Houghton Mifflin, 1914), p. 31.

14. Mary R. Beard, *Woman's Work in Municipalities* (New York: D. Appleton and Company, 1915; reprint ed., New York: Arno Press, 1972), p. 170; John Hope Franklin, *From Slavery to Freedom* (New York: Random House, 1969), pp. 436-37.

15. Quotation of Executive Secretary of the Chicago Urban League, A.L. Foster, in "Twenty Years of Inter-racial Goodwill Through Social Service," clipping n.d. in NUL Papers.

16. Strickland, *History of the Chicago Urban League*, pp. 36-39; Duster, *Crusade*, pp. 372-74.

17. Strickland, *ibid.*; Chicago League on Urban Conditions Among Negroes (hereafter CLUCAN), *Second Annual Report*, October 31, 1918, in Minutes of Annual Meeting, CUCAN, pp. 5, 7, 9, in NUL Papers.

18. CLUCAN, *Second Annual Report*, p. 11.

19. CLUCAN, *Second Annual Report*, pp. 8-9; Strickland, *History of the Chicago Urban League*, pp. 28-30, 36-37.

20. Strickland, *ibid.*, pp. 32-34.

21. CLUCAN, *Second Annual Report*; Weiss, *National Urban League*, p. 82; and Jesse Thomas Moore, Jr., *A Search for Equality: The National Urban League, 1910-1961* (University Park: Pennsylvania State University Press, 1981), pp. 57-58.

22. Wells-Barnett recounted her conflict with Mr. Meservey of the Travelers' Aid Society over organizational jurisdiction to meet black migrants at the train depots. Travelers' Aid objected to the Negro Fellowship League's representatives meeting the migrants and sent police officers to halt such activities. T. Arnold Hill of the Urban League gave his official blessing to the Travelers' Aid Society according to Wells-Barnett. For versions of her conflicts with the Urban League leadership see Duster, *Crusade*, pp. 372-74; Weiss, *National Urban League*, p. 112; and CLUCAN, *Second Annual Report*, p. 6.

23. National Urban League, *Annual Reports, 1912-1913*, pp. 15-18; *1913-1914/1914-1915*, pp. 18-22; *1915-1916*, pp. 11-13; *1916-1917*, pp. 19-22, *1920*, p. 20; and Weiss, *National Urban League*, p. 116.

24. Strickland, *History of the Chicago Urban League*, pp. 20-24; Charles Flint Kellogg, *NAACP: The National Association for the Advancement of Colored People* (Baltimore: Johns Hopkins Press, 1967), p. 128; and National Urban League, *Annual Report, 1912-1913*, pp. 20-22.

25. Weiss, *National Urban League*, pp. 90-92; National Urban League, *Annual Report, 1911-1912*, pp. 27-28; *1912-1913*, pp. 21-23; *1913-1914*, pp. 17-29; *1915-1916*, pp. 21-22, 39.

26. For information about Lugenia Hope and the Neighborhood Union see Walter Chivers, "Neighborhood Union: An Effort of Community Organization," *Opportunity* 3 (June 1925): 178-79; Gerda Lerner, "Early Community Work of Black Club Women," *Journal of Negro History* 59 (April

1974): 158-66; Jacqueline D. Hall, "Revolt Against Chivalry," (Ph.D. dissertation, Columbia University, 1974), pp. 101-12; Chicago *Defender*, October 31, 1925; F. Ridgely Torrence, *The Story of John Hope* (New York: Macmillan, 1948), p. 138; Interview by author with Edward S. Hope, August 17, 1982; Jane Addams to Mrs. John Hope, June 3, 1908, in Neighborhood Union Papers, Atlanta University Center, Atlanta, Georgia (hereafter Neighborhood Union Papers, AUC).

27. Neighborhood Union, Purposes, 1911, in Neighborhood Union Papers, AUC.

28. E.K. Jones to Mrs. Hope, May 26, 1914; Minutes, June 11, 1914; and folder for the Urban League, Atlanta Branch, 1910—; all in Neighborhood Union Papers, AUC.

29. Interview by author with Edward S. Hope, August 17, 1982.

30. For Hope's role in the club movement and YWCA, see chapters four and eight of this book.

31. Eugene Kinckle Jones to Mrs. Hope, May 26, 1914; May 15, 1916; May 12, 1917; Minutes of the Neighborhood Union, June 11, 1914; all in the Neighborhood Union Papers, AUC.

32. National Urban League, *Annual Report, 1920*, p. 5, NUL Papers.

33. National Urban League, *Annual Reports, 1914-1915*, p. 39; *1915-1916*, pp. 27-29; *1916-1917*, pp. 23-24; in NUL Papers.

34. Lucius S. Hicks, Secretary of the Boston Urban League, to Eugene Kinckle Jones, September 10, 1919; Report of the Executive Director, Boston Urban League, November 24, 1919; p. 4; Listing of the Local Executive Secretaries of the National Urban League, ca. 1920-1921, included Lucy Laney, Augusta, Georgia; Mrs. Stephen S. Duggan, Negro Welfare League of White Plains; Margaret J. Saunders, Plainfield Urban League; Mrs. S.W. Layton, Philadelphia Association for the Protection of Colored Women; Inez Summer, Westfield, New Jersey; and Catherine Barr, Los Angeles. All papers in NUL Papers. See also, Catherine Lealtad to Mrs. Hope, March 5, 1920, in Neighborhood Union Papers, AUC.

35. Minutes of the Executive Board, December 1, 1915, NUL Papers. For biographical information on Hope see note 26, on others see Sylvia Dannett, ed., *Profiles of Negro Womanhood* (Chicago: Educational Heritage, 1964), pp. 191-97; Edward James, et. al., eds., *Notable American Women* (Cambridge: Harvard University Press, 1979), pp. 530-31; Lily T. Hammond, *In the Vanguard of the Race* (New York: Council of Women for Home Missions and Missionary Education Movement of the United States and Canada, 1922), pp. 108-18; Sadie Daniels, *Woman Builders* (Washington: n.p., 1933), pp. 28-52.

36. National League on Urban Conditions Among Negroes, Minutes of the Third Annual Meeting, December 2, 1914; Minutes of Annual Meeting, February 4, 1920; December 16, 1919; October 19, 1920, all in NUL Papers; Weiss, *National Urban League*, pp. 60-62.

37. Weiss, *National Urban League*, pp. 78-79; National League on Urban Conditions Among Negroes, Minutes of Annual Meeting, October 8, 1913, in NUL Papers.

38. Weiss, *National Urban League*, pp. 74-76.
39. "Negro Advancement Society Doubles Membership," Press release of NAACP, December 20, 1919, in NAACP Papers, Library of Congress; Weiss, *National Urban League*, p. 112, noted 27 by 1918 and p. 175 noted 34 by 1930; Lucius Hicks to Mr. Jones, September 10, 1919, listed 32 in letterhead, NUL Papers; Chicago Urban League, *Second Annual Report, October 31, 1918*, listed 28, NUL Papers.
40. Associated Charities Auxiliary of Charlotte, North Carolina, March 18, 1917; Brooklyn Urban League File; Minutes of the National Urban League, February 4, 1920; National Urban League, *Annual Report, 1913-1914*, p. 18; *Annual Report, 1920*, p. 20. All in NUL Papers.
41. Weiss, *National Urban League*, p. 175.
42. Ruth S. Baldwin to Mr. L. Hollinsworth Wood, June 1, 1915, p. 2. NUL Papers.

CHAPTER SEVEN

1. Roger Rice, "Residential Segregation by Law, 1910-1917," *Journal of Southern History* 34 (May 1968): 179-99; and Clement E. Vose, *Caucasians Only: The Supreme Court, the NAACP, and the Restrictive Covenant Cases* (Berkeley: University of California Press, 1959).
2. John Hope Franklin, *From Slavery to Freedom: A History of Negro Americans* (New York: Random House, 1969), pp. 452-55; James Weldon Johnson, *Along This Way: An Autobiography of James Weldon Johnson* (New York: Viking Press, 1933, reprint ed. 1968), pp. 300-301, 306; Henry Blumenthal, "Woodrow Wilson and the Race Question," *Journal of Negro History* 48 (January 1963): 1-21; Kathleen Long Wolgemuth, "Woodrow Wilson and Federal Segregation," *Journal of Negro History* 44 (April 1959): 159-73; Jane L. Scheiber and Harry N. Scheiber, "The Wilson Administration and the Wartime Mobilization of Black Americans, 1917-1918," *Labor History* 10 (Summer 1969): 433-58; August Meier and Elliott Rudwick, "The Rise of Segregation in the Federal Bureaucracy, 1900-1930," *Phylon* 28 (Summer 1969): 178-84; Ida Wells-Barnett, "Our Country's Lynching Record," *Survey* 31 (January 1913): 573-74; and the years 1914-1915 in the Chicago *Defender* provide examples of increased legal and social discrimination.
3. Vose, *Caucasians Only*, pp. 210-21.
4. Alfreda Duster, ed., *Crusade for Justice: The Autobiography of Ida B. Wells* (Chicago: University of Chicago Press, 1970), pp. 375-80. Wells-Barnett's recollections often include erroneous dates. She attended the meeting of black leaders with President Wilson in the fall of 1913, but did not attend the notorious meeting in 1914. The recollections of Wells-Barnett reflect the bitterness that came with age and disappointment. For a more complete understanding of the incident, see the coverage in the black press and Christine A. Lunardini, "Standing Firm: William Monroe Trotter's Meeting

with Woodrow Wilson," *Journal of Negro History* 64 (Summer 1979): 244-64; Washington *Bee*, June 13 and 14, 1914; Chicago *Defender*, June 20 and 30, 1914; and Stephen R. Fox, *The Guardian of Boston: William Monroe Trotter* (New York: Atheneum, 1971), pp. 167-71.

5. Duster, *Crusade*, pp. 344-45; Delilah Beasley, *Negro Trailblazers of California* (Los Angeles: Times Mirror Publishing, 1919); Charles Flint Kellogg, *NAACP: The National Association for the Advancement of Colored People* (Baltimore: Johns Hopkins Press, 1967), pp. 127-29; Records of the Boston Branch of the NAACP, December 1915, in NAACP Papers, Manuscript Division, Library of Congress, Washington (hereafter referred to as NAACP Papers); and Elizabeth L. Davis, *Lifting As They Climb* (Washington: National Association of Colored Women, 1933), pp. 188-95.

6. Reynolds Farley, "The Urbanization of Negroes in the United States," *Journal of Social History* 1 (1967-1968): 253.

7. Gilbert Osofsky, *Harlem: The Making of a Ghetto* (New York: Harper and Row, 1961), p. 128; Philip Hauser, "Demographic Factors in the Integration of the Negro," in John Bracey, August Meier, and Elliott Rudwick, eds., *The Rise of the Ghetto* (Belmont, California: Wadsworth Publishing, 1971), p. 45; Kenneth Kusmer, *The Making of a Ghetto: Black Cleveland, 1870-1930* (Urbana: University of Illinois, 1978), pp. 10, 157; W.E.B. Du Bois, "The Migration of Negroes," *The Crisis* 14 (June 1917): 63-66; George Haynes, compiler, "Letters of Negro Migrants of 1916-1918," *Journal of Negro History* 4 (July 1919): 290-91, 300-301, 333, 337-38.

8. Boston Branch of the NAACP, Report, December 1915, NAACP Papers; and Kusmer, *Making of a Ghetto*, pp. 157-60.

9. *National Notes*, 32 (July 1930): 15-16, copy in Lethia Fleming Papers, Western Reserve Historical Society, Cleveland, Ohio (hereafter referred to as WRHS); Purpose and Objectives, 1908—, Phillis Wheatley Association Papers (Chicago), University of Illinois-Chicago Circle, Chicago, Illinois (hereafter referred to as Univ. Ill.-CC); Constance Green, *The Secret City: A History of Race Relations in the Nation's Capital* (Princeton: Princeton University, 1967): 184; Jeanne C. Mongold, "Vespers and Vacant Lots: Early Years of the St. Louis Phyllis Wheatley Branch, Y.W.C.A.," pp. 24-27, article intended for projected anthology, Sharon Harley, ed., *The Urban Black Woman: A Social History*, 1979, copy in Western Historical Collection, University of Missouri-St. Louis, St. Louis, Missouri (hereafter referred to as UMSL); "YWCA Among Colored Women and Girls," March, 1919, news release in Phyllis Wheatley Branch folder, YWCA of Metropolitan St. Louis Papers, UMSL; Phillis Wheatley Association Papers, WRHS; and Jane Hunter, *A Nickel and a Prayer* (Cleveland: Elli Kane Publisher, 1940), pp. 109-14.

10. Lugenia Hope to Mr. Z. Nespor, Field Secretary of the National War Department Commission, July 31, 1917, in Neighborhood Union Papers, Atlanta University Center (hereafter referred to as AUC); and Alice Dunbar Nelson, "Negro Women in War Work," in Edyth Ross, ed., *Black Heritage in Social Welfare* (Metuchen, New Jersey: Scarecrow Press, 1978), p. 387.

11. Allen Davis, "Welfare, Reform, and World War I," *American Quarterly* (Winter 1967): 516.
12. Stanley J. Lemons, *The Woman Citizen: Social Feminism in the 1920s* (Urbana: University of Illinois, 1973): 4-5, 15; Allen Davis, *Spearheads for Reform, 1890-1914* (New York: Oxford University Press, 1967); and A.B. Wolfe and Helen Olson, "Wartime Industrial Employment of Women," *Journal of Political Economy* 27 (October 1919): 640-69.
13. "Eva Bowles," clipping from the *Woman's Press*, July 1932, in Records File Collection, National Board Archives, YWCA, New York (hereafter referred to as YWCA National Board Archives); and Gladys G. Calkins, "The Negro in the Young Women's Christian Association: A Study of the Development of YWCA Interracial Policies and Practices in their Historical Setting," (M.A. thesis, George Washington University, 1960), p. 45.
14. Franklin, *From Slavery to Freedom*, p. 450.
15. Nelson, "Women in War Work," p. 386.
16. *Ibid.*, p. 392.
17. Chicago League on Urban Conditions, *Second Annual Report*, for the fiscal year ending on October 31, 1918, p. 6, in National Urban League Papers, Manuscript Division, Library of Congress (hereafter referred to as NUL Papers); and Nelson, "Women in War Work," pp. 392-94.
18. William J. Breen, "Black Women and the Great War: Mobilization and Reform in the South," *Journal of Southern History* 44 (August 1978): 422 n 4, 430; Lemons, *Woman Citizen*, pp. 16-17; Nelson, "Women in War Work," p. 392; and *The Crisis* 8 (May 1914): 8.
19. Breen, "Black Women and Great War," p. 431.
20. *The Crisis* 17 (January 1919): 137.
21. The seven organizations included the Jewish Welfare Board, the American Library Association, the National Catholic War Council, the National War Work Council of the YMCA, the Salvation Army, the War Camp Community Service, and the War Work Council of the YWCA. Source of list: letterhead of United War Work Campaign, Mary E.S. Colt to Lugenia Hope, November 22, 1918, in Neighborhood Union Papers, AUC. Of these organizations, only the War Camp Community Service and the YM/YWCA cooperative efforts allowed black women an active role and the Salvation Army offered "small but excellent field of service," according to Addie W. Hunton and Kathryn Johnson, *Two Colored Women with the American Expeditionary Forces* (Brooklyn: Brooklyn Eagle Press, 1921), p. 30 n 32.
22. Nelson, "Women in War Work," p. 386; Beasley, *Negro Trailblazers*, pp. 234-35; Davis, *Lifting*, pp. 196-200, 237, 219-24, 246-48; Hallie Q. Brown, *Homespun Heroines* (Xenia: Aldine Press, 1926; reprint ed., Freeport, New York: Books for Libraries Press, 1971), pp. 133-34, 160-68, 218-19; Wilhelmina S. Robinson, *Historical Biographies* (New York: Publishers Co., 1969), pp. 127-28; Clement Richardson, ed., *The National Cyclopedia of the Colored Race* (Montgomery: National Publications, 1919), p. 611; *The Crisis* 8 (May 1914): 8; and Gail Lumet, "My Mother Lena Comes from a Line of Proud Women," *Ms.* 10 (July 1981): 46-47, 99.

23. Davis, *Lifting*, pp. 196-97, 222-24, 264-65; Nelson, "Women in War Work," pp. 386-87; and Montgomery Family Papers, Manuscript Division, Library of Congress. Nelson's article refers to a Blanche Washington. Further information indicates her reference should be to Blanche Beatty of the Booker T. Washington Chapter.

24. Darlene Clark Hine, "The Call That Never Came: Black Women Nurses and WWI, An Historical Note," *Indiana Military History Journal* 15 (January 1983): 24; Nelson, "Women in War Work," pp. 387-88; and *The Crisis* 17 (December 1918): 84, and 17 (April 1919): 295.

25. Nelson, "Women in War Work," p. 387.

26. *Ibid.*

27. *Ibid.*, p. 386.

28. Susan Elizabeth Frazier (1864-1924) graduated from Hunter College. When she could not obtain a full-time position as a teacher in the New York City School System, she sued the system. After receiving a position, she dropped the suit. In the New York area, Frazier served as the president of the Woman's Loyal Union. Her activities with the military organizations led to her receipt of full military honors when she died. The memorial service, held in the 369th Regiment Armory with a flag-draped casket, was said to be "unique in the annals of Negro womanhood," according to Sylvia Dannett, ed., *Profiles of Negro Womanhood* (Chicago: Educational Heritage, 1964), p. 255. See also Nelson, "Women in War Work," p. 396; Brown, *Heroines*, pp. 222-24; and *The Crisis* 15 (July 1917): 140.

29. *The Crisis* 15 (July 1917): 140; Nelson, "Women in War Work," 396; and Brown, *Heroines*, pp. 222-24.

30. Hine, "The Call That Never Came," pp. 23-27; *The Crisis* 17 (March 1919): 243; Nelson, "Women in War Work," pp. 394-95; *Bulletin of the Circle for Negro War Relief, New York*, July 1, 1918, copy in the Neighborhood Union Papers; and *The Crisis* 17 (December 1918): 86, which noted sixty-one units in thirty states, 2,000 members, and fund-raising of over $50,000.

31. Nelson, "Women in War Work," pp. 388, 392, 394-96.

32. *Ibid.*, p. 397.

33. Dr. Louis T. Wright, president of the Colored American Society for Relief of French War Orphans to Lugenia Hope, July 6, 1917 and July 31, 1917, in Neighborhood Union Papers.

34. Figures differ in several sources. The YWCA National Board records and histories of the YWCA cited $400,000. See "The Colored Girl a National Asset," pamphlet, n.d. in the YWCA of Metropolitan St. Louis Papers, UMSL; and Eva Bowles, *Report, 1915-1920*, in YWCA National Board Archives. Nelson, "Women in War Work," p. 389 also cited that figure. A few sources quoted half that figure. See: *The Crisis* 15 (December 1917): 74; and "War Work Among Colored Girls and Women," June, 1918, copy in the Neighborhood Union Papers.

35. "War Work Among Colored Girls and Women," p. 1, copy in Neighborhood Union Papers.

36. Calkins, "The Negro and the YWCA," p. 49; and Nelson, "Women in War Work," p. 389.

37. Bowles, "Resume of Negro Work, 1915-1920," cited twelve national secretaries, forty-nine local centers or branches, and eighty-six paid workers (four student secretaries) by the end of 1919. A YWCA publication, *Young Women's Christian Association Work Among Colored Women* (New York: National Board of YWCA, 1920) noted fourteen national secretaries, sixty-four centers, and 100 paid workers by the end of 1920. See also Calkins, "The Negro and the YWCA," pp. 51-54; and Nelson, "Women in War Work," p. 389.

38. Jane Olcott, compiler, *The Work of Colored Women* (New York: National Board of the YWCA, 1919), p. 11.

39. Jacqueline D. Hall, "Revolt Against Chivalry: Jessie Daniel Ames and the Woman's Campaign Against Lynching," (Ph.D. dissertation, Columbia University, 1974), p. 100.

40. Calkins, "The Negro and the YWCA," pp. 48-56; and Jane Olcott, compiler, *The Work of Colored Women*, pp. 8-14, 40-50.

41. Bowles, *Report, 1915-1920*.

42. Joseph Odell, "The New Spirit of the New Army," *The Outlook* 121 (November 28, 1917): 3; and copies of the *War Work Bulletin* in YWCA National Board Archives.

43. "First Hostess House for Colored Troops," *War Work Bulletin* 31 (May 17, 1918): 1, copy in Neighborhood Union Papers; and Nelson, "Women in War Work," pp. 389-90.

44. Olcott, *Work of Colored Women*, p. 135.

45. Lugenia Hope, "Report, Camp Upton, Long Island," July 18, 1918, p. 2, copy in Neighborhood Union Papers.

46. *Ibid.*, p. 3.

47. Anna Cooper served at Camp Dix according to Anna Cooper to Genie, no date, in 1918-1919 file in Neighborhood Union Papers. State federations of the NACW raised funds for the hostess houses according to Olcott, *Work of Colored Women*, p. 28; and YWCA instruction booklets for hostess house workers, copies in Neighborhood Union Papers.

48. Olcott, *Work of Colored Women*, pp. 28, 30-32; and Hope, "Report, Camp Upton," pp. 2-3.

49. Olcott, *Work of Colored Women*, pp. 28-32; Eva Bowles to Lugenia Hope, March 27, 1918, in Neighborhood Union Papers.

50. Nelson, "Women in War Work," pp. 393-94; Florence Samuels, "A 'Clean-Up' Day for the Community," *The Crisis* 17 (March 1919): 226-28; *The Crisis* 17 (April 1919): 297 reported the War Camp Community Service assigned three women to Norfolk, Charleston, and Augusta; Davis, *Lifting*, pp. 199-200, 263-64; *The Crisis* 17 (December 1918): 84, mentioned the Women's Volunteer Service League, Newark, New Jersey; Anna Cooper, biographical introduction to her papers at Howard University; and Mary Church Terrell Papers, Manuscript Division, Library of Congress (hereafter referred to as MCT Papers, LC). For cooperative efforts with the Chicago Urban League,

see *Second Annual Report of the Chicago League on Urban Conditions Among Negroes*, fiscal year ending October 31, 1918, p. 6, in NUL Papers.

51. Breen, "Black Women and the Great War," p. 432; Davis, *Lifting*, pp. 59-62, 203-205, 237; Robinson, *Historical Negro Biographies*, pp. 127-28; Brown, *Heroines*, pp. 160-68, 219-19; Nelson, "Women in War Work," pp. 387-88; *The Crisis* 15 (February 1918): 243; and Colored Department of Atlanta Anti-Tuberculosis Association, *Report for Year 1918*, February 13, 1919, copy in the Atlanta Lung Association Papers, Atlanta Historical Society, Atlanta, Georgia (hereafter referred to as Lung Assoc. Papers, AHS).

52. Nelson, "Women in War Work," p. 397.

53. Emmett J. Scott to Mary Talbert, January 1919, quoted in Davis, *Lifting*, p. 62. For further information see *The Crisis* 17 (January 1919): 137, 15 (December 1918): 84; and Wolfe and Olson, "Wartime Industrial Employment of Women," pp. 639-69.

54. For information about the black working-class women see David M. Katzman, *Seven Days a Week: Women and Domestic Service in Industrializing America* (New York: Oxford University Press, 1978); Delores Hayden, *The Grand Domestic Revolution: A History of Feminist Designs for American Homes, Neighborhoods and Cities* (Cambridge: Massachusetts Institute of Technology, 1981); Gertrude MacDonald and Jessie Clark, *A New Day for the Colored Woman Worker* (New York: National Board of YWCA, 1919); Mary Church Terrell, *A Colored Woman in a White World* (Washington: Ransdell, 1940), pp. 248-58; and Olcott, *Work of Colored Women*, pp. 8, 79-80.

55. Rachel S. Gallagher of Cleveland's Free Labor Exchange, quoted in Mary E. Jackson, "The Colored Woman in Industry," *The Crisis* 17 (November 1918): 12. See also William W. Griffin, "The Negro in Ohio, 1914-1939" (Ph.D. dissertation, Ohio State University, 1968), pp. 26-28.

56. Mary E. Jackson, "Colored Girls in the Second Line of Defense," *The Association Monthly* 12 (October 1918): 363.

57. Jackson, "Colored Woman in Industry," pp. 12-17; Olcott, *Work of Colored Women*, pp. 69-79; J.W. Cromwell, "The War Work Council," *The Crisis* 17 (January 1919): 116-17; Nelson, "Women in War Work," p. 390; *The Crisis* (December 1919): 87.

58. Jackson, "Colored Woman in Industry," p. 16.

59. Jackson, "Colored Girls in Second Line," p. 363.

60. Hayden, *Grand Domestic Revolution* p. 170, indicates that in 1900 40 percent of the female servants were native-born white females.

61. Walter White, " 'Work or Fight' in the South," *New Republic*, March 1, 1919, pp. 144-46.

62. Katzman, *Seven Days*, chapters two and five; and Ruth Reed, "The Negro Women of Gainesville, Georgia," (M.A. thesis, University of Georgia, 1920), pp. 22-29.

63. Hunter, *Nickel and Prayer*; Mongold, "Vespers and Vacant Lots"; Phyllis Wheatley Association, *Annual Reports*, 1914-1920, in Phyllis Wheatley Association of Chicago Papers; Olcott, *Work of Colored Women*; and Cromwell, "The War Work Council," pp. 116-17.

64. Eva D. Bowles, *Report of Work Done for Colored Girls Under the War Work Council, South Central Field*, September 11, 1920, in YWCA National Board Archives; and "Broadening Opportunities for Colored Girls," *War Work Bulletin* 31 (May 3, 1918): 1, copy in Neighborhood Union Papers.
65. Bowles, *Report of Work Done*, 1920.
66. Camp Gicharbu in Harrod's Creek, Kentucky, is noted in brochures for YWCA activities, YWCA National Board Archives.
67. Olcott, *Work of Colored Women*, pp. 50-54, 62, 79, 92-94; "War Work Among Colored Girls and Women," June 1918, copy in Neighborhood Union Papers; and "Work Among Colored Women," n.d. in YWCA National Board Archives.
68. National Board of the YWCA, "The Colored Girl: A National Asset," n.d. in Metropolitan St. Louis YWCA Files, UMSL.
69. As of June 1918, only two of seven national staff women and one of twenty-two war workers was married. The hostess house supervisors had a higher percentage of married women: seven of twelve. By 1919, two of eleven national staff women and fifty-one of 187 war workers were married. Information from "War Work Among Colored Girls and Women," in Neighborhood Union Papers; and Olcott, *Work of Colored Women*, pp. 133-35.
70. Olcott, *Work of Colored Women*, p. 21; Adrienne Jones, "Jane Edna Hunter: A Case Study of Black Leadership, 1910-1950," (Ph.D. dissertation, Case-Western Reserve University, 1983); and Hunter, *Nickel and Prayer*.
71. Davis, *Lifting*, p. 247.
72. They requested a YMCA tent and other clubhouse facilities, recommended that the Public Safety Commission meet with the Street Railway Co. to ensure fair treatment of soldiers, advised all public parks and recreational facilities be equally accessible to all soldiers, and criticized the police harassment of the black soldiers. Source: "Educational Committee Report to the Atlanta Division of War Department Commission on Training Camp Activities," included in Colored Department of the Atlanta Anti-Tuberculosis Association, *Report for 1917*, 1918, in the Atlanta Lung Association Papers, AHS.
73. "Work Done by the Neighborhood Union," 1918, p. 2, copy in Neighborhood Union Papers.
74. Breen, "Black Women and Great War," pp. 432-36; Nelson, "Women and War Work," pp. 385-99; and Duster, *Crusade*, pp. 370-72.
75. Atlanta Anti-Tuberculosis Association, *Report of the Colored Department, 1918*, copy in Atlanta Lung Association Papers, AHS; Hunton and Johnson, *American Expeditionary*; and Files on Disabled Soldiers, MCT Papers, LC.
76. Breen, "Black Women and Great War," p. 436.
77. Breen, *ibid.*; Nelson, "Women in War Work," pp. 388-97; Mongold, "Vespers and Vacant Lots," pp. 25-27; "Plan of Work of the Atlanta Colored Women's War Council, 1918," in Neighborhood Union Papers; and Lemons, *Woman Citizen*, p. 17.
78. Breen, "Black Women and Great War," pp. 436-37; and Nelson, "Women in War Work," pp. 388-97.

79. Lincoln Hospital and Home, *Eightieth Annual Report for the Year Ending October 1, 1919* (New York: Irving Press, 1920), pp. 46-52, copy in Schomburg Collection, New York Public Library, New York (hereafter referred to as Schomburg Collection); and Beverly Guy-Sheftall and Jo Moore Stewart, *Spelman: A Centennial Celebration, 1881-1981* (Atlanta: Spelman College Press, 1981), p. 38.

80. Hammond, *In the Vanguard of the Race*, p. 93; and Minutes of the Inter-Racial Commission, November 17, 1920, in John J. Eagan File, Southern Education Foundation Papers, Atlanta University Center (hereafter Eagan File, SEF Papers, AUC).

81. Hammond, *In the Vanguard of the Race*, pp. 91-92.

82. *Report of the Colored Department for Year 1919*, p. 22, copy in Neighborhood Union Papers.

83. Breen, "Black Women and Great War," p. 438; the Neighborhood Union, Petition to Mayor Key and Park Commissin (sic), n.d., copy in Neighborhood Union Papers.

84. Advertisement for Second Annual Midway Carnival, 1919, copy in Neighborhood Union Papers.

85. Atlanta Colored Women War Council, *Report*, 1918, p. 2, copy in Neighborhood Union Papers; National Federation of Settlements, *Bulletins Conference* (Boston: Office of Secretary Robert Woods, 1919); and "War Work of Settlements," in *Ninth Conference of the National Federation of Settlements, Philadelphia*, May 29-31, 1919; both copies are in the National Federation of Settlement Papers, Social Welfare History Archives, University of Minnesota, Minneapolis (hereafter referred to as Settlements Papers, SWHA).

86. *Ibid.*

87. Atlanta Colored Women War Work Council, *Report, 1918*, p. 2, copy in Neighborhood Union Papers; Colored Department of Atlanta Anti-Tuberculosis Association, *Report for Year 1919*, pp. 21-22, in Atlanta Lung Association Papers, AHS.

88. "Social Progress," *The Crisis* 17 (January 1919): 141.

89. Nannie Burroughs quoted in "Jim Crow Invitation," January 31, 1918, no source, clipping in Nannie Burroughs Papers, Library of Congress.

90. "Atlanta Colored Women War Council, 1918," p. 2, copy in Neighborhood Union Papers and in Atlanta Lung Association Papers, AHS.

91. *Ibid.*

92. Atlanta Colored Women War Council, p. 1. For other views on racial labels: Niagara Movement used the term Negro American. Benjamin Brawley wanted the word Negro capitalized. The Afro-American Council used Afro-American and was the preferred term by Ida Wells-Barnett. But, the use of terms varied. Wells-Barnett still used black and colored in her writings, as did Anna Cooper in *Voice From the South*. Hallie Q. Brown used the word colored throughout *Homespun Heroines*, but referred to Madame Emma Hackley as "Pre-natally marked for everything black . . ." (p. 233). Mary Church Terrell preferred the word colored as used by the NAACP and National Association of Colored

Women. Terrell tried to get the word Negro banned due to its misuse as "nigra" or "nigger." Most of the Separate auxiliaries of reform organizations utilized the word colored as in the YWCA's Colored Work, the Colored Department of the Atlanta Anti-Tuberculosis Association; and Colored Auxiliary to the American Red Cross. Periodicals, too, varied as in the *Colored American* or *Voice of the Negro*.

93. Kellogg, *NAACP*, p. 265; and White, " 'Work or Fight' in the South," pp. 144-46.

94. Allen Grimshaw identified 1915-1919 as the period of greatest interracial disturbances during the period 1900-1949 in his research, "A Study in Social Violence" (Ph.D. dissertation, University of Pennsylvania, 1959), pp. 178-80. For other examples of racial violence see the Cleveland *Gazette*, November 17, 1917, August 10, 1918, and November 16, 1919.

95. Johnson, *Along This Way*, pp. 319-25; Kellogg, *NAACP*, pp. 260-62; Elliott M. Rudwick, *Race Riot at East St. Louis, July 2, 1917* (Carbondale, Illinois: Southern Illinois University Press, 1964); Edgar A. Schuler, "The Houston Race Riot of 1917," *Journal of Negro History* 29 (July 1944): 301-308; Arthur Waskow, *From Race Riot to Sit-In: 1919 and the 1960s* (Garden City: Doubleday, 1966); William Tuttle, Jr., *Race Riot: Chicago in the Red Summer of 1919* (New York: Atheneum, 1970); and Kenneth T. Jackson, *The Ku Klux Klan in the City: 1915-1930* (New York: Oxford University Press, 1967), pp. 235-49.

96. "New Negroes," *The Crisis* 17 (November 1918): 27.

97. NAACP, *Thirty Years of Lynching in the United States* (New York: NAACP, 1919); Kellogg, *NAACP*, pp. 216-32; and Cleveland *Gazette*, November 17, 1917, August 10, 1918, and November 17, 1919.

98. Atlanta Neighborhood Union, "To the President, the Cabinet, the Congress of the United States, the Governors and the Legislatures of the Several States of the United States of America," March 1, 1918, p. 2. Copy in Neighborhood Union Papers.

99. *Ibid*.

100. *Ibid*.

101. National Association of Colored Women, *Report from the Eleventh Biennial Convention*, ca. 1918, copy in clippings file of MCT Papers, LC; *The Crisis* 15 (February 1918): 243; and Tullia Hamilton, "The National Association of Colored Women," (Ph.D. dissertation, Emory University, 1978), pp. 65-66.

102. Mary Talbert to My Dear Co-Worker, November 18, 1921, copy in Neighborhood Union Papers.

103. Davis, *Lifting*, pp. 59-62; and NACW *Report from the Eleventh Biennial Convention*.

104. Board Minutes, NAACP, September 9, 1918, and October 14, 1918, in NAACP Papers.

105. Mary Terrell's War Camp Community Service file contains interviews and reports about women whom Terrell recommended for certain jobs. Terrell recommended Fannie B. Williams in her report, December 4, 1918, due to Williams' training and experience in social reform, MCT Papers, LC.

106. Mary Terrell, Report of the Colored Organization, War Camp Community Service, Pensacola, Florida, March 8, 1919, p. 1, copy in MCT Papers, LC.

107. Terrell, interview with Mr. Merritt, March 3, 1919, Pensacola, Florida, p. 3, copy in MCT Papers, LC.

108. Terrell, *Report of the Colored Organization*, War Camp Community Service, Gulfport, Mississippi, p. 5, copy in MCT Papers, LC.

109. Terrell, Interview with Miss Cutter, General Secretary of the YWCA, Macon, Georgia, p. 5, copy in MCT Papers, LC.

110. Terrell, *Colored Woman in a White World*, pp. 320-22; Terrell, interview with J.B. Edgar, February 10, 1919, p. 2, and Recommendations for Atlanta, Georgia, both in MCT Papers, LC; Atlanta Anti-Tuberculosis Association, *Report of the Colored Department for Year 1918*, p. 2, in Atlanta Lung Association, AHS.

111. Mary Terrell left for Zurich as one of twelve delegates to the International Congress of Women. See Terrell, *Colored Woman in a White World*, pp. 328-31.

112. Handwritten notation on top of Mary Terrell's Reports about the War Camp Community Service sent to the NAACP, March 12, 1919, copy in MCT Papers, LC.

113. Mary White Ovington, Office Diary, May 2, 1919, NAACP Papers. No indication about the outcome of the meeting could be found.

114. Duster, *Crusade*, pp. 377-82; "Denial of Passports," *The Crisis* 17 (March 1919): 237, noted Walker had been denied "because she was a woman."

115. Fox, *Guardian of Boston*, pp. 221-24; Clarence G. Conte, "Du Bois, the NAACP, and the Pan-African Congress of 1919," *Journal of Negro History* 56 (January 1971): 14-19; and Mary Terrell, "Impressions of My European Trip," *Howard University Record* 5 (December 1919): 100.

116. Hunton and Johnson, *American Expeditionary*, p. 135.

117. The husband of Helen Curtis was one of two black appointments made by the Wilson Administration. Judge Robert Terrell was the other black appointee reappointed as a municipal judge in Washington. A photograph of Helen Curtis appeared in *The Crisis* 11 (December 1915): 92. Information about the Curtis appointment can be found in Kathleen L. Wolgemuth, "Woodrow Wilson's Appointment Policy and the Negro," *Journal of Southern History* 24 (November 1958): 465-67; Clement Richardson, ed., *National Cyclopedia of the Colored Race* (Montgomery, Alabama: National Publications, 1919), p. 611.

118. Hunton and Johnson, *American Expeditionary*; W.E.B. Du Bois, "An Essay toward a History of the Black Man in the Great War," *The Crisis* 18 (June 1919): 87; "Some Colored Y Workers Overseas," *The Crisis* 19 (March 1919): 243.

119. Hunton and Johnson, *American Expeditionary*, pp. 136, 152-53. Those cited as canteen workers included Dr. N. Fairfax Brown, sister of Dr. Sara Brown; Mrs. Childs, Mrs. Williamson, Miss Thomas, Miss Evans, Mrs. Williams, Mrs. Craigwell, Miss Bruce, Miss Helen Hagan, Miss Barbon, Miss Rochon, Miss Edwards, Miss Phelps, Miss Suarez, Miss Turner, and Mrs. Mary Talbert. Some

of these names are identified as YMCA workers from a photo on pp. 26-27. Many of the names correspond with a list of War Workers of the YWCA cited in Olcott, *Work of Colored Women*, pp. 133-35.

120. Du Bois, *Dusk of Dawn*, pp. 260-61; Franklin, *From Slavery to Freedom*, pp. 468-69; Contee, "Du Bois, NAACP and Pan-African Congress," pp. 17, 21; Du Bois, "An Essay . . . Great War," pp. 63-87; Jane and Harry Scheiber, "The Wilson Administration and the Wartime Mobilization of Black Americans, 1917-1918," *Labor History* 10 (Summer 1969): 450-52; Joel E. Spingarn to W. Du Bois, October 9, 1918, in *The Crisis* 17 (December 1918): 60-61.

121. The black women had been active YWCA workers, but went to Europe under the direction of the YMCA. Hunton and Johnson refer to the YMCA group in their book, *American Expeditionary*. *The Crisis* 17 (March 1919): 243, identified the women as part of the "Y" workers. Mary Bethune, "A Century of Progress of Negro Women," in Lerner, ed., *Black Women in White America*, p. 582, also refers to the women as YMCA workers. See also, Terrell, *Colored Woman in White World*, pp. 327-31; Terrell, "Impressions of My European Trip," pp. 100-103; Mary B. Talbert to Emmet (sic) Scott, January 14, 1919, in NAACP Papers. For information about Pan-African Congress: Contee, "Du Bois and Pan-African Congress," p. 13, 24; "The Pan-African Congress," *The Crisis* 17 (April 1919): 271-74.

122. Terrell, "Impressions of My European Trip," p. 101.

123. Mary Talbert to Emmet (sic) Scott, January 14, 1919, and Mary Talbert to James Weldon Johnson, January 9, 1919, both in NAACP Papers.

124. Terrell, *Colored Woman in a White World*, pp. 332-41; and Hunton and Johnson, *American Expeditionary*.

125. Kellogg, *NAACP*, pp. 216-32, 235-46; Fox, *Guardian of Boston*, p. 214; Breen, "Black Women and Great War," p. 440; Scheiber, "Wilson Administration . . . Black Americans," pp. 436-51, 457; Johnson, *Along This Way*, pp. 341-42; Duster, *Crusade*, pp. 396-410; Du Bois, *Dusk of Dawn*, pp. 263-64; Weiss, *National Urban League*, pp. 141-42; "Negro and War," Cleveland *Gazette*, January 1919, clipping in Mary Branch Papers, Howard University.

126. Fox, *Guardian of Boston*, p. 232.

127. Atlanta Neighborhood Union, "To the President, the Cabinet, the Congress of the United States, the Governors and the Legislatures of the Several States of the United States of America," March 1, 1918, p. 1, in the Neighborhood Union Papers.

128. A Southern Colored Woman, "A Letter," *The Crisis* 19 (November 1919): 339.

CHAPTER EIGHT

1. Allan Spear, "Introduction," in Alain Locke, *The New Negro* (Chicago: Johnson Reprint Co., 1968), p. iii, noted that an "irrepressible optimism" was one of the most remarkable features of the New Negro.

2. The term New Negro came to describe black attitudes and behavior encompassing racial respect, militance against those accepting subordination, beauty and value in the non-white culture, and demands for better treatment of black Americans. In the Garvey movement, Harlem poetry, blues, and black business, the conglomeration of values emerged. For further discussion of the new militance and racial pride see Alain Locke, *The New Negro*; *The Crisis* 17 (November 1918): 26; and August Meier, *Negro Thought in America, 1880-1915* (Ann Arbor: University of Michigan Press, 1968), pp. 259-60. *The Crisis* attributed the growth of the New Negro to the critical position of the black press in the North and to the indeterminate policy of the state and federal governments toward lynching. Meier adds the influence of the development of a group economy, a professional class dependent on that group economy, and a black community with black social institutions.

3. Jacqueline D. Hall, "Revolt Against Chivalry: Jessie Daniel Ames and the Women's Campaign Against Lynching" (Ph.D. dissertation, Columbia University, 1974), p. 80. Hall attributed the new militance to the demographic changes of the Great Migration. The New Negro became an effective protest against the southern way of life. Meier, *Negro Thought*, p. 259, supports the idea that urbanization and northward migration together with the group economy influenced the militance.

4. Addie Hunton and Kathryn Johnson, *Two Colored Women with the American Expeditionary Forces* (Brooklyn: Brooklyn Eagle press, 1922), p. 157.

5. Eva Bowles to ———, January 5, 1920. Copy in Neighborhood Union Papers, Atlanta University Center (hereafter referred to as Neighborhood Union Papers, AUC).

6. Jeanne C. Mongold, "Vespers and Vacant Lots: The Early Years of the St. Louis Phyllis Wheatley Branch of the Y.W.C.A.," an article prepared for an anthology edited by Sharon Harley, *The Urban Black Woman: A Social History*, 1979, p. 27. Copy of article in Western Historical Manuscript Collection, University of Missouri-St. Louis Joint Collection (hereafter referred to as UMSL).

7. W.E.B. Du Bois, *Dusk of Dawn* (New York: Harcourt Brace, 1940), p. 185.

8. William Breen, "Black Women and the Great War: Mobilization and Reform in the South," *Journal of Southern History* 44 (August 1978): 440.

9. Mary White Ovington to John Shillady, July 16, 1918, Administrative Files, NAACP Papers, Library of Congress (hereafter NAACP Papers) noted, "The next person we take into our employ must be a woman . . . [due to their] enormous work."

10. Etrah Boutte, "Plan for Health Program of the Circle for Negro Relief," n.d. in Joel Spingarn Papers, Howard University (hereafter J. Spingarn Papers, HU); Darlene Clark Hine, "The Call That Never Came: Black Women Nurses

and World War I, An Historical Note," *Indiana Military History Journal* 15 (January 1983): 25-26, noted a continuation through the 1920s. The program included county health clubs, provided aid to community hospitals, established scholarships for training health care personnel, funded part of the cost for black visiting nurses in the South, and helped in the creation of new child care facilities.

11. Du Bois, *Dusk of Dawn*, pp. 265-66; James Weldon Johnson, *Along This Way* (New York: Viking Press, 1933), pp. 339-40; Charles Fling Kellogg, *NAACP* (Baltimore: Johns Hopkins Press, 1967), pp. 233-35.

12. Donald Lee Grant, "The Development of the Anti-Lynching Reform Movement in the United States: 1883-1932," (Ph.D. dissertation, University of Missouri, 1972), p. 288.

13. Charlotte Hawkins Brown, "What the Negro Woman Asks of the White Women of North Carolina," Speech, May 1920, copy in Charlotte Hawkins Brown Papers, Schlesinger Library, Radcliffe College; *The Crisis* 20 (June 1920): 100; Elizabeth L. Davis, *Lifting As They Climb* (Washington: National Association of Colored Women, 1933), pp. 218-19; and Grant, "Development of Anti-Lynching," pp. 270-71.

14. *The Crisis* 20 (June 1920): 100.

15. May Belcher to Mrs. John Hope, September 19, 1919, copy in Neighborhood Union Papers, AUC.

16. Mary B. Talbert to Dear Sister, September 20, 1922, in Neighborhood Union Papers, AUC.

17. Grant, "Development of Anti-Lynching," p. 288; Hunton and Johnson, *American Expeditionary*, pp. 135, 153; Mary Talbert to James Weldon Johnson, January 9, 1919, in Administrative Files, NAACP Papers; Clement Richardson, ed., *The National Cyclopedia of the Colored Race* (Montgomery: National Publications, 1919), p. 611; "First Hostess Houses for Colored Troops," *War Work Bulletin* 31 (May 17, 1918): 1, copy in Neighborhood Union Papers; Alice Dunbar Nelson, "Negro Women in War Work," in Edyth Ross, ed., *Black Heritage in Social Welfare* (Metuchen, New Jersey: Scarecrow Press, 1978), p. 392; *Bulletin of the Circle for Negro War Relief, New York*, n.d., copy in Neighborhood Union Papers; *The Crisis* 18 (June 1919): 92, and 19 (January 1920): 121; Jane Olcott, *The Work of Colored Women* (New York: National Board of the YWCA, 1919), p. 8.

18. Talbert frequently referred to her black "sisters." See Mary Talbert to Dear Sister, September 20, 1922 (which was also signed "Yours for a United Sisterhood") in Neighborhood Union Papers; Mary Talbert to Mrs. Booker T. Washington, November 7, 1922, mentioned "sisters" Hallie Q. Brown and Mary Bethune, copy in Mary Church Terrell Papers, Howard University (hereafter MCT Papers, HU).

19. Zona Gale and Florence Kelley, reformers who frequently worked with black women in the NACW, the NAACP, and the NAWSA, were just two of 200 white women of the NACW. See Grant, "Development of Anti-Lynching," p. 288.

20. For historical and contemporary accounts about the role of women in antilynching reform, see Hall, "Revolt Against Chivalry," pp. 139, 177-79; Mary White Ovington, *The Walls Came Tumbling Down* (New York: Harcourt, Brace and Co., 1947), p. 154; *Woman's Voice* 4 (January 1923): 1; and Kellogg, *NAACP*, pp. 216-21. William Pickens, the NAACP Field Secretary, called the women's work the "greatest effort of the Negro womanhood of this generation," in Minutes, Board of Directors, September 11, 1922, NAACP Papers.

21. Most of the black women had ties to the New York reform community and/or the NAACP. Cora Horne resided in Brooklyn. Addie Dickerson and Mary Terrell had ties to the New York reform community. As with the general peace movement which attracted genteel reformers, black female participation reflected elitism prior to World War I. The war transformed the American peace movement. Techniques and personnel of the woman suffrage movement became applied to the peace movement. In August 1914, Mrs. Henry Villard directed a dramatic public march down Fifth Avenue in New York City with 1,500 women dressed in mourning clothes. Involvement of minorities was never widespread due to the elitist nature of the participants. See Roland C. Marchland, *The American Peace Movement and Social Reform, 1898-1918* (Princeton: Princeton University Press, 1972), pp. 9, 7-13, 182; and Kellogg, *NAACP*, pp. 248-49.

22. After American entrance in World War I, most women reformers worked for domestic reform and the civilian war effort. Grace Abbott, Pauline Goldmark, Lillian Wald, and others worked with the Council of National Defense. Black women displayed similar patterns as with Mary Terrell working with the War Camp Community Service. See Marchand, *American Peace Movement*, pp. 257-62.

23. Mary Church Terrell, *A Colored Woman in a White World* (Washington: Ransdell Press, 1940), p. 171; Minutes of the Executive Board, Women's International League for Peace and Freedom, November 5, 1919, and December 4, 1919; Constitution, 1919, all in Women's International League for Peace and Freedom File, Mary Church Terrell Papers, Library of Congress (MCT Papers, LC). The WILPF became the Woman's Peace Party in 1915 according to Crystal Eastman to Paul Kellogg, November 10, 1915, in Paul Kellogg Papers 32/310, Social Welfare History Archives, University of Minnesota (hereafter SWHA). Mary Terrell noted the name change on April 11, 1921. As a member of the Executive Committee of the WILPF, Terrell noted the change in her file on that organization. No black women were listed in leadership positions of the American Union Against Militarism in letterhead dated July 26, 1917, in Paul Kellogg Papers, but many of the white women who worked with black women were listed: Zona Gale, Lillian Wald, Jane Addams.

24. Sylvia Dannett, *Profiles of Negro Womanhood* (Chicago: Educational Heritage Press, 1964), p. 255; and William Appleton Williams, "The Legend of Isolationism in the 1920s," *Science and Society* 18 (Winter 1954): 1-20.

25. Constitution, International Council of Women of Darker Races of the World, n.d., and Mrs. Booker T. Washington, "International Council of Women of the Darker Races of the World," November 10, 1924, copies of both in MCT Papers, HU; Addie Hunton to Margaret Murray Washington, September 16, 1922, in MCT Papers, HU; Margaret Murray Washington to Lugenia Hope, September 15, 1922, in Neighborhood Union Papers; "The National Association of Colored Women," *The Woman's Forum* n.v. (Fall 1922): 2-6, copy in MCT Papers, LC.

26. Mary McLeod Bethune, "Clarifying Our Vision with the Facts," *Journal of Negro History* 23 (January 1938): 12-15; The Circle for Peace and Foreign Relations letterhead of Executive Committee for the Fourth Pan-African Congress to Dr. Jesse Moreland, March 8, 1927 (not yet processed) Manuscript Division Howard University, listed the following names:
    Executive Committee: Addie Hunton, Lillian Alexander, Sadie Stockton, Minta B. Trotman, Dorothy R. Peterson, Nina G. Du Bois, Lottie Cooper, Minnie McAdoo Pickens, Annie M. Dingle.
    The Circle for Peace and Foreign Relations: A. Lucille Alleyne, Etnah R. Boutee, Tempie J. Burge, Casely Hayford, Florence J. Hunt, Ida Gibbs Hunt, Marie B. Johnson, Helen Fauset Lanning, Mattie B. McGhee, Adeline Proctor, Ruth Logan Roberts, Laura Jean Pollack, Ida L. Wallace, Jessie Fauset, Frances Gunner, Anna C. Hawley.

27. Ida Harper to Mary Terrell, March 18, 1918; Ida Harper to Elizabeth Carter, March 18, 1918, both in MCT Papers, LC; Aileen S. Kraditor, *Ideas of Woman's Suffrage Movement, 1890-1920* (New York: Columbia University, 1965; reprint ed., New York: Doubleday, 1971), pp. 170-71; Rosalyn Terborg-Penn and Sharon Harley, eds., *The Afro-American Woman* (Port Washington: Kennikat Press, 1978), pp. 25-26.

28. *New York Times*, February 17, 1919; Mary White Ovington to Vida Milholland, February 26 and April 8, 1919; Minutes, Executive Committee, March 10, 1919, in Board Minutes, both in NAACP Papers; Amelia Fry, "Alice Paul and the South," Paper delivered to the Southern Historical Association, November 12, 1981, emphasized the white-black cooperation for suffrage. Many of Paul's public statements were misinterpreted. According to Fry, "not a Southern-style prejudice or a white superiority complex" (p. 17) was evident, but instead a realization of a Southern white male oligarchy. Paul felt Negrophobia "irrelevant" and a tool of Southern politicians. For black views see: Mary Terrell, "Immediate Release," September 2, ———, copy in MCT Papers, LC; Addie Hunton to Mary White Ovington, March 25, 1921, Administrative Files, NAACP Papers; Nannie Burroughs, "The Negro Woman and Suffrage," *The West Virginia Woman's Voice* 18 (June 15, 1923): 1-2, copy in the Speeches and Writings Files, Nannie Burroughs Papers, Manuscript Division, Library of Congress.

29. George A. Mundy to Mary White Ovington, October 14, 1920, copy in Cleveland Branch NAACP Papers, Western Reserve Historical Society, Cleveland (hereafter referred to as WRHS).

30. *The Crisis* 19 (November 1919): 23, 18 (September 1919): 240, and 18 (August 1919): 190. For wartime suffrage work see *The Crisis* 10 (October 1915): 268, 17 (December 1918): 60-62, 15 (November 1917): 19-21, 178-92; Mabel E. Brown to W.E.B. Du Bois, July 27, 1917, in Du Bois Papers, University of Massachusetts, Amherst (hereafter referred to as Du Bois Papers, UM); Emma Lou Thornbrough, "The History of Black Women in Indiana," *Black History News and Notes* 13 (August 1983): 4-5.
31. Lugenia Hope to Mrs. Myrtle Cook, June 4, 1922, copy in Neighborhood Union Papers.
32. *National Notes* 27 (November 1925): 1, copy in MCT Papers, LC.
33. "The National Association of Colored Women," *The Woman's Forum* n.v. (Fall 1922): 3-6, copy in MCT Papers, LC. Anne Firor Scott, "After Suffrage: Southern Women in the Twenties," *The Journal of Southern History* 30 (August 1964): 309.
34. Mary Talbert's term on the board expired December 31, 1922. Verina Morton Jones was reelected to the board for a second term expiring December 31, 1923. See *The Crisis* 21 (December 1920): 73 and 78, 19 (January 1920): 124.
35. Nancy Weiss, *The National Urban League* (New York: Oxford University Press, 1974), pp. 158-60, noted the continued reliance on white money moderated the policies followed by the Urban League; and Lillian A. Turner, "The National Urban League," *The Crisis* 18 (May 1919): 25-26.
36. Weiss, *Urban League*, pp. 163-70, 75; "Announcement for the Atlanta School for Social Service," 1920, copy in Neighborhood Union Papers.
37. T.J. Woofter, Jr., "Inter-Racial Organizations in Northern Cities," Report of the Phelps Stokes Foundation, in Minutes of the Southeastern Federation of the Inter-Racial Commission, June 25, 1920, in J.J. Eagan Papers, Atlanta University Center (hereafter Eagan Papers, AUC).
38. Gladys G. Calkins, "The Negro in the Young Women's Christian Association: Study of the Development of YWCA Policies and Practices in their Historical Setting," (M.A. thesis, George Washington University, 1960), pp. 60-62.
39. Eva Bowles, *Report, September 26, 1919*, Records Files Collection, National Board Archives, YWCA, New York (hereafter called YWCA Board Archives).
40. Executive Director, *Report on the Boston Urban League*, November 24, 1919, copy in National Urban League Papers, Library of Congress (hereafter NUL Papers).
41. *The Crisis* 19 (April 1920): 317 listed Catherine Lealtad as one of four black secretaries. The other three were Juliette Derricotte, Adelle Ruffin, and May Belcher.
42. *Ibid.*
43. *Ibid.*, p. 318.
44. *Ibid.*
45. Adelle Ruffin received a great deal of criticism from her fellow southern black women during the 1920s. See note 52 for further clarification.
46. Catherine Lealtad to Mrs. John Hope, March 5, 1920, in Neighborhood Union Papers.

47. Beatrice D. Walker to Mrs. John Hope, n.d. (before April 6, 1920), in Neighborhood Union Papers.
48. *Ibid.*
49. Catherine Lealtad to Mrs. John Hope, March 5, 1920, in Neighborhood Union Papers.
50. *Ibid.*
51. *Ibid.*
52. Hunton's intentions to leave her position in the YWCA is mentioned in Mary White Ovington, Office Diaries, April 19, 1920, in NAACP Papers. Lealtad mentions aid from women outside the YWCA as Mary Talbert, who called Lealtad after hearing a rumor that Lealtad was about to be replaced with a white woman. Fellow YWCA worker Juliette Derricotte told Lealtad about the rumor at the Des Moines Conference. Lealtad complained about May Belcher's personal attacks, Ruffin's constant criticisms, and Bowles' lack of support in the YWCA organization. See *The Crisis* 19 (April 1920): 317-18 and Lealtad to Hope, March 5, 1920, in Neighborhood Union Papers.
53. Helen A. Davis, executive of the Field Work Department of the National Board, to Mrs. Hope, January 17, 1920; Eva Bowles to Mrs. Hope, January 25, 1920; and Lealtad to Hope, March 5, 1920; all in Neighborhood Union Papers.
54. "Conference to discuss the work of the YWCA among the colored women of the South," Minutes, April 6, 1920; Eva Bowles to Lugenia Hope, April 10, 1920, both in Neighborhood Union Papers.
55. Petition to the National Board of the Young Women's Christian Association, New York City, n.d., copy in Neighborhood Union Papers.
56. Lugenia Hope to ———, May 29, 1920, in Neighborhood Union Papers.
57. Calkins, "Negro in the YWCA," pp. 60-62.
58. "The Latest Farce from the YWCA," Cleveland *Advocate*, April 24, 1920, clipping in Neighborhood Union Papers.
59. "Too Much Paternalism in 'Ys'," Cleveland *Advocate*, May 1, 1920, clipping in Neighborhood Union Papers.
60. Nettie Napier to Lugenia Hope, May 4, 1920, in Neighborhood Union Papers.
61. Mrs. M.J. McCrorey to Lugenia Hope,. May 7, 1920, in Neighborhood Union Papers.
62. Lucy Laney to Lugenia Hope, May 4, 1920, in Neighborhood Union Papers.
63. Minutes, South Atlantic Field, YWCA, Richmond, July 3, 1920, in Neighborhood Union Papers. Hope wrote in the margins of this document, "Not true—Little Rock women were refused."
64. *Ibid.*
65. *Ibid.*
66. *Ibid.*
67. *Ibid.*
68. *Ibid.*; and Calkins, "Negro and the YWCA," pp. 62-65.
69. Atlanta City Federation to Mary McLeod Bethune, September 12, 1920, in Neighborhood Union Papers.

70. *The Crisis* 20 (June 1920): 100, 20 (September 1920): 244, 21 (December 1920): 57-58; *Report of the Twelfth Biennial Convention*, copy in MCT Papers, LC; "What the Colored Women Are Asking the YWCA," n.d., in Gerda Lerner, ed., *Black Women in White America* (New York: Random House, 1973), pp. 480-83; Petitions from the National Association of Colored Women to the YWCA, n.d., in Neighborhood Union Papers; Davis, *Lifting*, pp. 63-65; Hamilton, "The NACW," pp. 66-67.

71. *Report of the Twelfth Biennial Convention*, copy in MCT Papers, LC.

72. Charlotte Hawkins Brown, quoted in Hall, "Revolt Against Chivalry," p. 116.

73. "Agenda," n.d., in Neighborhood Union Papers; "The Colored Women's Statement to the Woman's Missionary Council," in Lerner, *Black Women in White America,* pp. 461-67; Grant, "Development of Anti-Lynching," pp. 249-50; Hall, "Revolt Against Chivalry," pp. 113-17. Charlotte Hawkins Brown was very proud of her white heritage and friendships with white women. Du Bois felt "Brown represents the White South," quoted in Du Bois to Robert B. Eleazer, March 12, 1926, in Commission for Interracial Cooperation Papers, Atlanta University Center. Brown's views are in Lerner, ed., *Black Women in White America*, pp. 375-76, 467-72. See also, Charlotte Hawkins Brown, Address, Memphis, Tennessee, October 8, 1920, copy in Commission for Interracial Cooperation Papers, AUC.

74. "Report of Woman's Conference, Memphis," in Minutes, Inter-Racial Commission, November 17, 1920, pp. 30-32, in John J. Eagan File, Southern Education Foundation Collection (hereafter SEF Colln.), Atlanta University Center.

75. Hall, "Revolt Against Chivalry," p. 125.

76. *Ibid.*, p. 15.

77. Grant, "Development of Anti-Lynching," p. 249.

78. "Report of Findings Committee, October 7, 1920," p. 31; Minutes, Inter-Racial Commission, June 1, 1920, p. 27, and November 17, 1920; both in John J. Eagan File (SEF Colln.). Hall, "Revolt Against Chivalry," p. 130, noted the first black female members of the Commission for Inter-Racial Cooperation were not chosen until 1922. But the Minutes, June 1, 1920, p. 27, noted a black woman from Louisiana, Edna Faure, as a member at that time.

79. "The Woman's Inter-Racial Memphis Conference, October 6-7, 1920," Neighborhood Union Papers.

80. Preamble and Seven Point Program, n.d., in Neighborhood Union Papers.

81. For the white woman's version of the seven points see, "Report of the Findings Committee, Woman's Conference, Memphis," in the Minutes of Inter-Racial Commission, November 17, 1920, pp. 32-35, in John J. Eagan Papers, SEF Colln.

82. Lugenia Hope to Mrs. Archibald Davis, March 1, 1921, in Neighborhood Union Papers.

83. *Ibid.*

84. Charlotte H. Brown to Mary Bethune, October 20, 1921, in Neighborhood Union Papers.

85. Only nineteen attended: Mrs. Robert R. Moten (sic), Tuskegee; Mrs. Mary McLeod Bethune, Daytona; Miss Nannie T. (sic) Burroughs, Washington; Mrs. Frank L. Williams, St. Louis; Georgia Nugent, Louisville; Charlotte Hawkins Brown, Sedalia; Mrs. John Hope, Atlanta; Emma S. Ransom, Oceanport, New Jersey; Helen Irvin Grossley, Alcorn, Mississippi; Elizabeth Ross Haynes, Washington; Mrs. R.W. Wilkinson, Orangeburg, South Carolina; Mrs. S. Joe Brown, Indianapolis; Mrs. Mary Jackson McCrorey, Charlotte; Lillian Brown, Indianapolis; Anna Hawley, Brooklyn; Mrs. A.W. Hunton, Brooklyn; Lucy Laney, Augusta; Grace Valentine, Bordentown, New Jersey; and Addie W. Dickerson, Philadelphia. Conference of Outstanding Colored Women, n.d. and "Executive Committee of National Board of YWCA Hostess to 19 Colored Women," new release, n.d., both in Records File Collection, YWCA National Board Archives; The earlier meeting of the International Conference on Woman Physicians, noted in *The Crisis* 19 (November 1919): 349, included black representatives: Dr. Iona Whipper, Dr. Sara Brown, and Dr. Rice. The YWCA hosted that event at the national headquarters.

86. Eva Bowles to Mrs. Hope, March 8, 1921; Mrs. Lapham to Charlotte Hawkins Brown, May 15, 1921; Brown to Mrs. Hope, June 16, 1921; and Ruth ——— to Mrs. Hope, November 1921, all in Neighborhood Union Papers; Hall, "Revolt Against Chivalry," p. 113.

87. Gertrude MacDougald and Jessie Clark, *A New Day for the Colored Woman Worker* (New York: National Board of the YWCA, 1919); Jane Olcott, *The Work of Colored Women* (New York: National Board of YWCA, 1919); and Jane Olcott-Walters, *History of Colored Work, 1907-1920* (New York: National Board of YWCA, 1920).

88. Eva Bowles, *Report, 1915-1920*, pp. 7-8, in Records File Collection, YWCA National Board Archives.

89. Eva Bowles, *Annual Report to the Department of Research and Methods*, 1920, p. 3, in Records File Collection, YWCA National Board Archives.

90. Eva Bowles, "Statement Addressed to Northern Cities Who Are Approaching Colored Work for the First Time," 1925, in Records File Collection, YWCA National Board Archives; Calkins, "Negro and the YWCA," p. 65.

91. Elizabeth Ross Haynes to Margaret Murray Washington, December 2, 1924, in MCT Papers, HU.

92. Eva Bowles, "Reports by the Secretary for Colored Work," in Lerner, *Black Women in White America*, pp. 484-85.

93. Anna Arnold Hedgeman, "Reminiscences of a YWCA Worker," in Lerner, *Black Women in White America*, pp. 484-85.

94. *Ibid.*, p. 491.

95. Eva Bowles noted strained relationships and white paternalism in the YWCA, see Lerner, *Black Women in White America*, pp. 485-86; Shirley Graham Du Bois, *His Day Is Marching On: A Memoir of W.E.B. Du Bois* (Philadelphia: J.B. Lippincott Co., 1971), pp. 33-36, recalled her own discrimination in the YWCA of Colorado Springs. Jane Olcott, author of several books and pamphlets for the YWCA, told Mary Ovington about the "largely superficial"

white women of the YWCA in Mary Ovington, Office Diaries, April 8, 1921, in NAACP Papers. White female reformer Jessie Daniel Ames called the YWCA "Rather wishy washy in their racial program," quoted in Hall, "Revolt Against Chivalry," p. 70. Jane Hunter's reply to the suggestion of making the Phillis Wheatley a black branch of the YWCA was, "we cannot," in Jane Hunter to Margaret Murray Washington, November 2, 1924, in MCT Papers, HU.

96. Davis, *Lifting*, pp. 93-94; *Report of the Twelfth Biennial Convention*, MCT Papers, LC.

97. Others included Lizzie Fouse (Kentucky), Elizabeth Carter and Minnie L. Bradley (Connecticut), as noted in letterhead of organization, Nannie Burroughs to Mrs. Washington, n.d. (before December 1922), in MCT Papers, HU. Both Burroughs and Bethune had demonstrated an early interest in organizing working women. Burroughs noted in "The Colored Woman and Her Relationship to Domestic Problems," 1902, quoted in Hamilton, "The National Association of Colored Women," p. 102: "If we hold in contempt women who are too honest, industrious, and independent, women whose sense of pride is too exalted to be debased by idleness, we will find our women becoming more and more slothful in this matter of supporting themselves. . . . This pulling aside of our silken skirts at the approach of the servant woman has materially affected the morals of the Negro woman." Bethune organized groups of women during the war years under the slogan, "A labor union with a purpose." Quoted in Hamilton, "NACW," p. 74. Mary Terrell's contacts with the Women's Trade Union League influenced her attempt to organize women who worked in hotels and restaurants. See the letter from Ethel Smith of the WTUL to Mary Terrell, December 10, 1919, in MCT Papers, LC. No record was found indicating the success or failure of the attempted organization.

98. See chapter two of this book for further discussion.

99. May Belcher gained access to Eli Lilly funding through her light appearance and demeanor as she had earlier gained access to the St. Louis white community. See Mongold, "Vespers and Vacant Lots," and interview by Dorothy Salem with Ellie Sutler, July 11, 1983. Adella Hunt Logan "passed" in her suffrage activities, according to her granddaughter, Adelle Logan Alexander, in a letter to Dorothy Salem, January 1983. Mary Terrell described her ability to pass in reform circles as noted in her autobiography and her Diaries, MCT Papers, LC.

100. Scott, "After Suffrage," p. 310.

101. Adrienne Jones, "Jane Edna Hunter: A Case Study in Black Leadership," (Ph.D. dissertation, Case Western Reserve University, 1983), frequently refers to Hunter's ability to put on the mask for her white benefactors.

102. Lugenia Hope used logic and principles to argue her case. Joined by other black women of the South, Hope advocated the use of tact and diplomacy. These women believed in the value of compromise. Hope's son, Edward S. Hope, described his mother as a fighter with great determination, yet never rash or insolent, more appraising than abrasive. Outwardly patient, she felt

dignity and respect were priceless possessions and a life of service was one of the highest planes to which a person could aspire. She was, said her son, energetic and "constructively restless." Interview with Edward S. Hope by Dorothy Salem, July 27, 1982, and examination of "My Mother," rough draft in possession of Edward S. Hope. Mary Terrell used some of the same arguments, but with less direct techniques. For further information see Cynthia Neverdon-Morton, *Afro-American Women of the South and the Advancement of the Race, 1895-1925* (Knoxville: University of Tennessee Press, 1989) and Jacqueline Anne Rouse, *Lugenia Burns Hope: Black Southern Reformer* (Athens, Georgia: University of Georgia Press, 1989).

103. Mr. A.D. Williams, Atlanta Branch, Report of the Annual Conference, Cleveland, June 21-29, 1919, p. 1. Copy in NAACP Papers.

104. Mr. A.C. McNeal, Chicago Branch, Report of the Annual Conference, Cleveland, June 21-29, 1919, p. 1. Copy in NAACP Papers.

105. Mary White Ovington, *Walls Came Tumbling Down*, p. 167.

106. "The Tenth Anniversary Conference," *The Crisis* 18 (June 1919): 88-89; "The Cleveland Conference," *The Crisis* 18 (August 1919): 189-91; "Brief Summary of Anti-Lynching Work," *The Crisis* 17 (February 1919): 182-83; "National Conference on Lynching," *The Crisis* 18 (May 1919): 23-25; Kellogg, *NAACP*, pp. 136-37; Mary Talbert to James Weldon Johnson, January 21, 1919, in NAACP Papers.

107. Mary Bethune, "A Century of Progress of Negro Women," Address before the Chicago Women's Federation, June 30, 1933, in Lerner, ed., *Black Women in a White World*, p. 580.

108. Cheryl T. Gilkes, "Successful Rebellious Professionals: The Black Woman's Professional Identity and Community Commitment," *Psychology of Women Quarterly* 8 (Spring 1982): 289-311.

Bibliography

MANUSCRIPT COLLECTIONS

Amherst, Massachusetts. University of Massachusetts.
W.E.B. Du Bois Papers
Atlanta, Georgia. Atlanta Historical Society.
Atlanta Kindergarten Alumnae Club
Atlanta Lung Association Papers
Long-Rucker-Aiken Papers
Mrs. D. Mitchell Cox Papers
Atlanta, Georgia. Atlanta University Center-Woodruff Library
Chautauqua Circle Papers
Commission on Interracial Cooperation Papers
Neighborhood Union Papers
Southern Education Foundation Papers
Cambridge, Massachusetts. Radcliffe College. Schlesinger Library.
Black Women's Oral History Collection
Charlotte Hawkins Brown Papers
Chicago, Illinois. University of Illinois Library at Chicago Circle.
Edith T. Ross Papers
Phyllis Wheatley Association Papers
Travelers' Aid Society Papers
Cleveland, Ohio. Western Reserve Historical Society.
Cleveland Branch, NAACP
Cleveland Urban League (Negro Welfare Association) Papers
Eliza Bryant Home for Aged Colored People Papers
Lethia C. Fleming Papers
Jane E. Hunter Papers
L. Pearl Mitchell Papers (Alpha Kappa Alpha File)
Phillis Wheatley Association Papers
YWCA, Cleveland Branch, Papers

Hampton, Virginia. Hampton University Archives
Faculty and Extension Collections
Indianapolis, Indiana. Indiana State Library.
Flanner House Papers
Madison, Wisconsin. Wisconsin State Historical Society.
Fannie Barrier Williams, "Present Status and Intellectual Progress . . ."
1898
Minneapolis, Minnesota. University of Minnesota. Social Welfare History Archives.
Paul Kellogg Papers
National Federation of Settlements
Survey Associates, Inc.
United South End Settlements
New York, New York. New York Public Library. Schomburg Collection.
Annual Reports, 1919 and 1920, Lincoln Hospital and Home
Annual Report, 1911, White Rose Home
New York, New York. YWCA, National Board Archives.
Records Files Collection
Reports of City Committee on Colored Work
St. Louis, Missouri. University of Missouri-St. Louis, Western Historical Joint Manuscript Collection.
St. Louis Association of Colored Women's Clubs Papers
St. Louis Louisiana Purchase Exposition Collection
YWCA, Metropolitan St. Louis, Papers
St. Paul, Minnesota. Macalester College.
Public Relations and Publications Department
Toledo, Ohio. Toledo-Lucas County Public Library.
Black American History Collection
Woman's Movement Papers
Washington, D.C. Howard University. Moorland-Spingarn Research Center.
Bethel Literary and Historical Association
Cromwell Family Papers
Anna Cooper Papers
Frederick Douglass Papers
Archibald H. Grimke Papers
Angelina Weld Grimke Papers
Lucy Diggs Slowe Papers
Joel E. Spingarn Papers
Mary Church Terrell Papers

Washington, D.C. Library of Congress. Manuscript Division.
Nannie Burroughs Papers
Frederick Douglass Papers
Montgomery Family Papers (Cordelia Booze)
National Association for the Advancement of Colored People Papers
National Urban League Papers
Mary Church Terrell Papers
Booker T. Washington Papers
Washington, D.C. National Association of Colored Women.
Reports and typewritten manuscripts

NEWSPAPERS AND PERIODICALS

Atlanta *Independent*
Boston *Guardian*
Chicago *Defender*
Cleveland *Gazette*
Indianapolis *Freeman*
New York *Age*
New York Times
Washington *Bee*
Colored American
The Crisis
The Voice (of the Negro)
Woman's Journal
Woman's Era

UNPUBLISHED MATERIALS

Calkins, Gladys G. "The Negro in the Young Women's Christian Association: A Study of the Development of YWCA Interracial Policies and Practices in their Historical Setting," M.A. thesis, George Washington University, 1960.

Cleagle, Rosalyn. "The Colored Temperance Movement, 1830-1860." M.A. thesis, Howard University, 1969.

Crocker, Ruth. "Sympathy and Science: The Settlement Movement in Gary and Indianapolis, to 1930." Ph.D. dissertation, Purdue University, 1982.

Fields, Emma L. "The Women's Club Movement in the United States." M.A. thesis, Howard University, 1948.

Fry, Amelia R. "Alice Paul and the Divine Discontent." Paper presented to the 13th Annual New Jersey History Symposium, December 5, 1981.

———. "Alice Paul and the South." Paper presented to the Southern Historian Association, November 12, 1981.

Giele, Janet Zollinger. "Social Change in the Feminine Role: A Comparison of Woman's Suffrage and Woman's Temperance, 1870-1920." Ph.D. dissertation, Radcliffe College, 1961.

Grant, Donald Lee. "The Development of the Anti-Lynching Reform Movement in the United States: 1883-1932." Ph.D. dissertation, University of Missouri, 1972.

Griffin, William W. "The Negro in Ohio, 1914-1939," Ph.D. dissertation, Ohio State University, 1968.

Hall, Jacqueline D. "Revolt Against Chivalry: Jessie Daniel Ames and the Woman's Campaign Against Lynching." Ph.D. dissertation, Columbia University, 1974.

Hall, Winona R. "Janie Porter Barrett, Her Life and Contribution to Social Welfare in Virginia." M.A. thesis, Howard University, 1954.

Hamilton, Tullia Brown. "The National Association of Colored Women, 1896-1920." Ph.D. dissertation, Emory University, 1978.

Jones, Adrienne L. "Jane Edna Hunter: A Case Study of Black Leadership, 1910-1950," Ph.D. dissertation, Case-Western Reserve University, 1983.

Mongold, Jeanne D. "Vespers and Vacant Lots: The Early Years of the St. Louis Phyllis Wheatley Branch Y.W.C.A." Prepared for projected anthology *The Urban Black Woman: A Social History.* Edited by Sharon Harley, 1979.

Reed, Ruth. "The Negro Women of Gainesville, Georgia." M.A. thesis, University of Georgia, 1920.

Shivery, Louie D. "The History of Organized Social Work Among Atlanta Negroes, 1890-1935." M.A. thesis, Atlanta University, 1936.

Stubbs, Carolyn A. "Angelina Weld Grimke: Washington Poet and Playwright." Ph.D. dissertation, George Washington University, 1978.

INTERVIEWS

Hope, Edward S. Cleveland, Ohio. Interview, July 27, 1982.

Sutler, Ellie. Cleveland, Ohio. Interview, July 11, 1983.

Turner, Carrie. Cleveland, Ohio. Interview, August 5, 1982.

BOOKS

Abbott, Edith. *The Tenements of Chicago, 1908-1935*. Chicago: University of Chicago Press, 1936; reprint edition, New York: Arno Press, 1970.

Allen, Robert L. *Reluctant Reformers: Racism and Social Reform Movements in the United States*. Washington: Howard University Press, 1974.

Anthony, Susan B. and Harper, Ida Husted, eds. *The History of Woman Suffrage*. 4 vols. Rochester, New York: 1902; reprint ed., New York: Arno Press, 1969.

Ashbaugh, Carolyn. *Lucy Parsons: American Revolutionary*. Chicago: Charles Kerr, 1976.

Badger, Reid. *The Great American Fair: The World's Columbian Exposition and American Culture*. Chicago: Nelson Hall, 1979.

Banner, Lois. *Women in Modern America: A Brief History*. New York: Harcourt, Brace, Jovanovich, 1974.

Bardolph, Richard. *The Negro Vanguard*. New York: Rinehart and Company, 1951.

Beard, Mary R. *Woman as Force in History: A Study in Traditions and Realities*. New York: Macmillan, 1946.

————. *Woman's Work in Municipalities*. New York: D. Appleton and Company, 1915; reprint ed., New York: Arno Press, 1972.

Beaseley, Delilah. *Negro Trailblazers in California*. Los Angeles: Times Mirror Publishing, 1919.

Best, Lassalle. *History of the White Rose Mission and Industrial Association*. New York: WPA, Federal Writers Project, n.d.

Billingsley, Andrew. *Black Families in White America*. Englewood Cliffs, New Jersey: Prentice-Hall, 1968.

Blassingame, John W. and Berry, Mary F. *Long Memory: The Black Experience in America*. New York: Oxford University Press, 1982.

Blocker, Jack S., Jr. *Alcohol, Reform, and Society: The Liquor Issue in Social Context*. Westport, Conn.: Greenwood Press, 1979.

Bordin, Ruth. *Woman and Temperance: The Quest for Power and Liberty, 1873-1900*. Philadelphia: Temple University, 1981.

Brawley, Benjamin. *A Social History of the Negro*. New York: Macmillan, 1921.

————. *Negro Builders and Heroes*. Chapel Hill: University of North Carolina Press, 1937.

————. *Women of Achievement*. Woman's Baptist Home Mission Society, 1919.

Brown, Hallie Q. *Homespun Heroines and Other Women of Distinction*. Xenia, Ohio: Aldine Press, 1926; reprint ed., Freeport, New York: Books for Libraries Press, 1971.

Butterfield, Stephen. *Black Autobiography in America*. Amherst: University of Massachusetts, 1974.

Chafe, William H. *Women and Equality: Changing Patterns in American Culture*. New York: Oxford University Press, 1977.

————. *The American Woman: Her Changing Social, Economic, and Political Roles, 1920-1970*. New York: Oxford University Press, 1972.

Cherrington, E.H., ed. *Standard Encyclopedia of the Alcohol Problem*. Westerville, Ohio: American Issue Publishing, 1926-30.

Cherry, Gwendolyn, and Thomas, Ruby. *Portraits in Color*. New York: Pageant Press, 1962.

Cooper, Anna. *A Voice from the South: By a Black Woman of the South*. Xenia, Ohio: Aldine Publishing, 1892; reprint ed., New York: Negro Universities Press, 1969.

Coppin, Fannie J. *Reminiscences of School Life, and Hints on Teaching*. Philadelphia: AME Book Concern, 1898.

Cox, Thomas C. *Blacks in Topeka, Kansas 1865-1915: A Social History*. Baton Rouge: Louisiana State University Press, 1982.

Croly, Jennie J. *The History of the Woman's Club Movement in America*. New York: Henry G. Allen and Co., 1898.

Cronon, Edmund B. *Black Moses: The Story of Marcus Garvey and the Universal Negro Improvement Association*. Madison, Wisconsin: University of Wisconsin, 1969.

Culp, D.W., ed. *Twentieth-Century Negro Literature*. Naperville, Illinois: J.L. Nichols and Co., 1902.

Daniels, John. *In Freedom's Birthplace: A Study of the Boston Negroes*. Boston: Houghton-Mifflin, 1914.

Daniels, Sadie. *Women Builders*. Washington, D.C.: Associated Press, 1931.

Dann, Martin E., ed. *The Black Press, 1827-1890: The Quest for National Identity*. New York: Putnam's Sons, 1971.

Dannett, Sylvia. *Profiles of Negro Womanhood*. Chicago: Educational Heritage, 1964.

Davis, Allen. *Spearheads for Reform, 1890-1914*. New York: Oxford University Press, 1967.

Davis, Ardelia. *Blacks in Ohio*. Cleveland: New Day Press, 1967.

Davis, Elizabeth L. *Lifting As They Climb*. Washington, D.C.: National Association of Colored Women, 1933.

Davis, King E. *Fund Raising in the Black Community: History, Feasibility and Conflict*. Metuchen, New Jersey: Scarecrow Press, 1975.

DeBenedetti, Charles. *The Peace Reform in American History*. Bloomington: Indiana University Press, 1980.

Degler, Carl N. *At Odds: Women and the Family in American from the Revolution to the Present*. New York: Oxford University Press, 1980.

Dittmer, John. *Black Georgia in the Progressive Era, 1900-1920*. Urbana: University of Illinois, 1977.

Drake, St. Clair. *Churches and Voluntary Associations in the Chicago Negro Community*. Chicago: Works Progress Administration, Federal Writers Project, 1940.

Drake, St. Clair, and Cayton, Horace R. *Black Metropolis: A Study of Negro Life in a Northern city*. New York: Harper and Row, 1945; reprint ed., New York: Harcourt, Brace and World, 1970.

Du Bois, Shirley Graham. *His Day Is Marching On: A Memoir of W.E.B. Du Bois*. Philadelphia: J.B. Lippincott, 1971.

Du Bois, W.E.B., ed., Atlanta University Publications. Atlanta: Atlanta University Press:

no. 2   *Social and Physical Conditions of Negroes in Cities*. 1897.

no. 3   *Some Efforts of American Negroes For Their Own Social Betterment*. 1898.

no. 4   *The Negro in Business*. 1899.

no. 6   *The Negro Common School*. 1901.

no. 7   *The Negro Artisan*. 1902.

no. 8   *The Negro Church*. 1903.

no. 14   *Efforts for Social Betterment*. 1909.

no. 15   *The College-Bred Negro*. 1910.

no. 16   *The Common School and the Negro American*. 1911.

no. 19   *Morals and Manners Among Negro Americans*. 1914.

———. *Dusk of Dawn*. New York: Harcourt, Brace, 1940.

———. *Darkwater: Voices From Within the Veil*. New York: Schocken Books, 1920.

———. *The Autobiography of W.E.B. Du Bois*. New York: International Publishing, 1968.

———. *The Philadelphia Negro: A Social Study*. Philadelphia: University of Pennsylvania, 1899, reprint ed., New York: Schocken Books, 1967.

———. *The Souls of Black Folks*. Chicago: A.C. McClung and Co., 1903.

Dunway, Abigail Scott. *Path Breaking: An Autobiographical History of the Equal Suffrage Movement*. New York: James, Kerns, and Abbott, 1914; reprint ed., New York: Schocken Books, 1971.

Duster, Alfreda M., ed., *Crusade for Justice: The Autobiography of Ida B. Wells*. Chicago: University of Chicago Press, 1970.

Factor, Robert L. *The Black Response to America: Man, Ideals, and Organizations from Frederick Douglass to the NAACP*. Reading, Massachusetts: Addison-Wesley, 1970.

Flexner, Eleanor. *Century of Struggle: The Woman's Rights Movement in the United States*. Cambridge: Harvard University Press, 1959.

Foner, Phillip. *Women and the American Labor Movement*. New York: Free Press, 1979.

Fox, Stephen R. *The Guardian of Boston: William Monroe Trotter*. New York: Atheneum, 1971.

Franklin, John Hope. *From Slavery to Freedom*. New York: Random House, 1969.

————, and Meier, August, eds., *Black Leaders in the Twentieth Century*. Urbana: University of Illinois, 1982.

Franklin, Vincent P., and Anderson, James D., eds., *New Perspectives on Black Educational History*. Boston: G.K. Hall and Company, 1978.

Frazier, E. Franklin. *The Negro Family in the United States*. Chicago: University of Chicago Press, 1939; revised ed., 1966.

Frederickson, George M. *The Black Image in the White Mind: The Debate on Afro-American Character and Destiny, 1817-1914*. New York: Harper and Row, 1971.

Gerber, David A. *Black Ohio and the Color Line, 1860-1915*. Urbana: University of Illinois Press, 1976.

Gibson, J.W., ed. *Progress of the Race*. Naperville, Illinois: J.L. Nichols, 1920.

Giddings, Paula. *When and Where I Enter*. New York: William Morrow, 1984.

Goldman, Eric F. *Rendezvous with Destiny: A History of Modern American Reform*. New York: Alfred A. Knopf, 1952; reprint ed., New York: Random House, 1977.

Goldmark, Josephine. *Impatient Crusader: Florence Kelley's Life Story*. Urbana: University of Illinois, 1953.

Gordon, Elizabeth P. *Women Torch Bearers: The Story of the Women's Christian Temperance Union*. Evanston: National Women's Temperance Union Publishers, 1924.

Gordon, Michael, ed. *The American Family in Social-Historical Perspective*. New York: St. Martin's Press, 1973.

Graham, Abbie. *Grace H. Dodge*. New York: Woman's Press, 1926.

Green, Constance. *The Secret City: A History of Race Relations in the Nation's Capitol*. Princeton: Princeton University Press, 1967.

Grimshaw, Allen, ed. *Racial Violence in the United States*. Chicago: Aldine, 1969.

Grichard, Parris, and Brooks, Lester. *Blacks in the City: A History of the National Urban League.* Boston: Little, Brown, 1971.

Guy-Sheftall, Beverly, and Stewart, Jo Moore. *Spelman: A Centennial Celebration, 1881-1981.* Atlanta: Spelman College, 1981.

Harlan, Louis. *Booker T. Washington: The Making of a Black Leader 1856-1901.* New York: Oxford University Press, 1972.

Haydn, Delores. *The Grand Domestic Revolution: A History of Feminist Designs for American Homes, Neighborhoods, and Cities.* Cambridge: MIT Press, 1981.

Haynes, George E. *Toward Interracial Cooperation.* New York: Federal Council of Churches, 1926.

Henry, Alice. *The Trade Union Woman.* New York: Burt Franklin, 1915.

Higham, John. *Strangers in the Land: Patterns of American Nativism 1860-1925.* New York: Atheneum, 1967.

Hine, Darlene C. *When the Truth Is Told: A History of Black Women's Culture and Community in Indiana, 1875-1950.* Indianapolis, Indiana: National Council of Negro Women, 1981.

Hobson, E.C. and Hopkins, C.E. *A Report Concerning the Colored Women of the South.* Baltimore: The Trustees of the John F. Slater Fund, 1896.

Holden, Arthur C. *The Settlement Idea: A Vision of Social Justice.* New York: Macmillan, 1922.

Holt, Rackam. *Mary McLeod Bethune: A Biography.* Garden City, New York: Doubleday and Co., 1964.

Hughes, William H. and Patterson, Frederick D. *Robert Russa Moton of Hampton and Tuskegee.* Chapel Hill: University of North Carolina Press, 1956.

Hull, Gloria T., Scott, Patricia B., and Smith, Barbara, eds. *But Some of Us Are Brave.* Old Westbury, New York: The Feminist Press, 1982.

Hunter, Jane. *A Nickel and a Prayer.* Cleveland: Elli Kane Publisher, 1940.

Hunton, Addie W., and Johnson, Kathryn M. *Two Colored Women with the American Expeditionary Forces.* Brooklyn: Brooklyn Eagle Press, n.d.

Jackson, Kenneth T. *The Ku Klux Klan in the City, 1915-1930.* New York: Oxford University Press, 1967.

James, Edward T., Wilson, Janet, and Boyer, Paul S., eds. *Notable American Women, 1607-1950: A Biographical Dictionary.* 3 vols. Cambridge: Belknap Press of Harvard University Press, 1971.

James, Felix. *The American Addition: History of a Black Community.* Washington, D.C.: University Press of America, 1979.

Jelinek, Estelle C., ed. *Women's Autobiography: Essays in Criticism.* Bloomington: Indiana University Press, 1980.

Johnson, James Weldon. *Along This Way: An Autobiography of James Weldon Johnson.* New York: Viking, 1933.

Katzman, Davis M. *Seven Days a Week: Women and Domestic in Industrializing America.* New York: Oxford University Press, 1978.

Kellogg, Charles Flint. *NAACP: The National Association for the Advancement of Colored People.* Baltimore: Johns Hopkins Press, 1967.

Kerber, Linda K., and Mathews, Jane DeHart, eds. *Women's America: Refocusing the Past.* New York: Oxford University Press, 1982.

Kraditor, Aileen S. *Ideas of Woman's Suffrage Movement, 1890-1920.* New York: Columbia University Press, 1965.

————, ed. *Up From the Pedestal: Selected Writings in the History of American Feminism.* Chicago: Quadrangle, 1968.

Kusmer, Kenneth. *The Making of a Ghetto: Black Cleveland, 1870-1930.* Urbana: University of Illinois, 1978.

Leiby, James. *A History of Social Welfare and Social Work in the United States.* New York: Columbia University Press, 1978.

Lemons, J. Stanley. *The Woman Citizen: Social Feminism in the 1920s.* Urbana: University of Illinois, 1973.

Lerner, Gerda, ed. *Black Women in White America.* New York: Random House, 1973.

————. *The Majority Finds Its Past.* New York: Oxford University Press, 1979.

————. *The Woman in American History.* Menlo Park: Addison Wesley, 1971.

Logan, Rayford. *The Betrayal of the Negro.* New York: Collier Books, 1954; reprint ed., New York: Macmillan, 1970.

Loewenberg, Bert, and Bogin, Ruth, eds. *Black Women in Nineteenth-Century American Life: Their Words, Their Thoughts, Their Feelings.* University Park: Pennsylvania State University Press, 1976.

Lumet, Gail. *The Incredible Hornes.* New York: Alfred A. Knopf, 1986.

MacBrady, J.E., ed. *A New Negro for a New Century.* Chicago: American Publishing House, 1900.

Majors, Monroe A. *Noted Negro Women: Their Triumphs and Activities.* Chicago: Donohue and Henneberry, 1893.

Marchand, C. Roland. *The American Peace Movement and Social Reform, 1898-1918.* Princeton: Princeton University Press, 1972.

Mather, Frank Lincoln, ed. *Who's Who of the Colored Race*, vol. I. Chicago: Memento Edition Half-Century Anniversary of Negro Freedom in United States, 1915; reprint ed., Detroit: Gale Research Company, 1976.

Meier, August. *Negro Thought in America, 1880-1915.* Ann Arbor: University of Michigan, 1968.

Meier, August, and Rudwick, Elliott. *Along the Color Line*. Urbana: University of Illinois Press, 1976.

Moore, Jesse Thomas, Jr. *A Search for Equality: The National Urban League 1910-1961*. University Park: Pennsylvania State University, 1981.

Mossell, Mrs. N.F. *The Work of Afro-American Women*. Nashville: Fisk University Library Negro Collection, 1894; reprint ed., Freeport, New York: Books for Libraries Press, 1971.

Moton, Robert Russa. *What the Negro Thinks*. New York: Doubleday, Doran, and Company, 1929; reprint ed., Garden City, New York: Garden City Publishing, 1942.

National Board of YWCA. *Annual Statistics for 1907 published in the June 1908 The Association Monthly*. New York: National Board of the YWCA of the United States of America, 1909.

————. *Yearbook Containing Directory and Statistical Report of the YWCA of the United States of America 1910-1911/1911-1912*. New York: Woman's Press, 1911/1912.

Neely, Ruth, ed. *Women of Ohio: A Record of Their Achievements in the History of the State, III*. Columbus: S.J. Clarke, n.d.

Neverdon-Morton, Chythia. *Afro-American Women of the South and the Advancement of the Race, 1895-1925*. Knoxville: University of Tennessee Press, 1989.

Noble, Jeanne L. *The Negro Woman's College Education*. New York: Teacher's College of Columbia University, 1956.

Norton, Mary Beth, ed. *Women of America: A History*. Boston: Houghton Mifflin, 1979.

Odegard, Peter H. *Pressure Politics: The Story of the Anti-Saloon League*. New York: Octagon Books, 1966.

Olcott, Jane, comp. *The Work of Colored Women*. New York National Board of the YWCA, 1919.

Olcott-Walters, Jane. *History of Colored Work 1907-1920*. New York: National Board of the YWCA, 1920.

O'Neill, William L. *Everyone Was Brave: The Rise and Fall of Feminism in America*. Chicago: Quadrangle, 1969.

Osofsky, Gilbert. *Harlem: The Making of a Ghetto. Negro New York: 1890-1920*. New York: Harper and Row, 1966.

Ovington, Mary White. *Half a Man: The Status of the Negro in New York*. New York: Longmans, Green and Company, 1911.

————. *Portraits in Color*. New York: Viking Press, 1927.

————. *The Walls Came Tumbling Down*. New York: Harcourt, Brace and Company; reprint ed., New York: Arno Press, 1969.

Paulson, Ross Evans. *Woman's Suffrage and Prohibition: A Comparative Study of Equality and Social Control.* Glenview, Illinois: Scott, Foresman and Co., 1973.

Pivar, David P. *Purity Crusade: Sexuality and Social Control, 1868-1900.* Westport: Greenwood Press, 1973.

Ransom, Roger L., and Sutch, Richard. *One Kind of Freedom: The Economic Consequences of Emancipation.* Cambridge, England, 1977.

Richardson, Clement, ed. *The National Cyclopedia of the Colored Race.* Montgomery: National Publishing, 1919.

Robinson, Wilhelmina, ed. *Historical Negro Biographies.* International Library of Negro Life and History. New York: Publishers Co., 1967-1969.

Ross, B. Joyce. *J.E. Spingarn and the Rise of the NAACP.* New York: Atheneum, 1972.

Ross, Edyth, ed. *Black Heritage in Social Welfare, 1860-1930.* Metuchen, New Jersey: Scarecrow Press, 1978.

Rouse, Jacqueline Anne. *Lugenia Burns Hope: Black Southern Reformer.* Athens, Georgia: University of Georgia Press, 1989.

Rudwick, Elliott. *Race Riot at East St. Louis, July 2, 1917.* Carbondale, Illinois: Southern Illinois University Press, 1964.

St. James, Warren D. *The National Association for the Advancement of Colored People: A Case Study in Pressure Groups.* New York: Exposition Press, 1958.

Scott, Anne F., ed. *The American Woman: Who Was She?* Englewood Cliffs: Prentice Hall, 1971.

———. *The Southern Lady: From Pedestal to Politics, 1830-1930.* Chicago: University of Chicago Press, 1970.

———. *One Half the People: The Fight for Woman Suffrage.* Philadelphia: J.B. Lippincott, 1975.

Scruggs, L.A. *Women of Distinction: Remarkable in Works and Invincible in Character.* Raleigh, North Carolina: L.A. Scruggs, 1893.

Sewell, May W., ed. *The World's Congress of Representative Women.* Chicago: Rand McNally, 1894.

Shepperd, Gladys. *Mary Church Terrell: Respectable Person.* Baltimore: Human Relations Press, 1969.

Sims, Mary S. *The Natural History of a Social Institution: The Young Women's Christian Association.* New York: The Woman's Press, 1936.

Sinclair, Andrew. *Prohibition: The Era of Excess.* Boston: Little Brown, 1962.

Smelser, Neil J. *The Theory of Collective Behavior.* New York: Free Press, 1963.

Smith, Constance, and Freedman, Anne. *Voluntary Associations: Perspectives on the Literature.* Cambridge: Harvard University Press, 1972.

Southern, Davis. *The Malignant Heritage: Yankee Progressives and the Negro Question, 1901-1914.* Chicago: Loyola University Press, 1966.

Spangler, Earl. *The Negro in Minnesota.* Minneapolis: T.S. Denison, 1961.

Spear, Allan H. *Black Chicago: The Making of a Negro Ghetto. 1890-1920.* Chicago: University of Chicago Press, 1967.

Spero, Sterling D., and Harris, Abram L. *The Black Worker: The Negro and the Labor Movement.* New York: Columbia University Press, 1931.

Staples, Robert. *The Black Woman in America.* Chicago: Nelson Hall, 1976.

Steady, Filomena C., ed. *The Black Woman Cross-Culturally.* Cambridge: Schenkman Publishing, 1981.

Sterling, Dorothy. *Black Foremothers: Three Lives.* Old Westbury, New York: Feminist Press, 1979.

————, ed. *We Are Your Sisters: Black Women in the Nineteenth Century.* New York: W.W. Norton, 1984.

Strickland, Arvarh E. *History of the Chicago Urban League.* Urbana: University of Illinois, 1966.

Tarbell, Ida M. *The Business of Being a Woman.* New York: Macmillan, 1914.

Terborg-Penn, Rosalyn, and Harley, Sharon, eds. *The Afro-American Woman.* Port Washington, New York: Kennikat Press, 1978.

Terrell, Mary Church. *A Colored Woman in a White World.* Washington: Ransdell, 1940.

Thelan, David. *The New Citizenship: Origins of Progressivism in Wisconsin, 1885-1900.* Columbia: University of Missouri Press, 1972.

Thompson, Daniel C. *The Negro Leadership Class.* Englewood Cliffs, New Jersey: Prentice Hall, 1963.

Thornbrough, Emma L. *Booker T. Washington.* Englewood Cliffs: Prentice Hall, 1969.

Torrence, F. Ridgely. *The Story of John Hope.* New York: Macmillan, 1948.

Tuttle, William M. *The Race Riot: Chicago in the Red Summer of 1919.* New York: Atheneum, 1970.

Walsh, Mary Roth. *"Doctors Wanted: No Women Need Apply": Sexual Barriers in the Medical Profession, 1835-1975.* New Haven: Yale University Press, 1977.

Waskow, Arthur. *From Race Riot to Sit-in, 1919 and the 1960s.* Garden City, New York: Doubleday, 1966.

Weiss, Nancy. *National Urban League, 1910-1940.* New York: Oxford University Press, 1974.

Wellington, Joseph. *The Power of Womanhood: A Speech*. New York: The Standard Book Co., 1912.

White, Walter F. *A Man Called White: An Autobiography of Walter White*. New York: Viking, 1948.

Wiebe, Robert H. *The Search for Order, 1877-1920*. New York: Hill and Wang, 1967.

Willard, Frances E. *Glimpses of Fifty Years: The Autobiography of an American Woman*. Chicago: B.J. Smith and Company, 1889; reprint ed., New York: Sources Books Press, 1970.

———. *Woman and Temperance or, The Work and Workers of the Woman's Christian Temperance Union*. Hartford: Park Publishing, 1883; reprint ed., New York: Arno Press, 1972.

Witherspoon, Margaret J. *Remembering the St. Louis World's Fair*. St. Louis: Folkestone Press, 1973.

Woods, Robert A. *The Neighborhood in Nation-Building*. Boston: Houghton Mifflin, 1923; reprint ed., New York: Arno Press, 1970.

———. *The Settlement Horizon*. Philadelphia: William Fell, 1911; reprint ed., New York: Arno Press, 1970.

———, and Kennedy, Albert J., eds. *Handbook of Settlements*. Philadelphia: William Fell Co., 1911; reprint ed., New York: Arno Press, 1970.

Woodson, Carter G. *History of the Negro Church*. Washington: Associated Publishers, 1921.

Woodward, C. Vann. *The Strange Career of Jim Crow*. Revised edition. New York: Oxford University Press, 1966.

Work, Monroe. *Negro Yearbook*, Tuskegee: Tuskegee Institute Press, 1913.

Zangrando, Robert L. *The NAACP Crusade Against Lynching, 1909-1950*. Philadelphia: Temple University Press, 1980.

ARTICLES

Athey, Louis L. "Florence Kelley and the Quest for Negro Equality," *Journal of Negro History* 61 (October 1971): 249-61.

Baker, Ray Stannard. "The Tragedy of the Mulatto," *American Magazine* n.v. (April 1908): 583-98.

Barnett, Ida B. Wells. "Booker T. Washington and His Critics," *The World Today* 6 (April 1904): 518-21.

———. "The National Afro-American Council," *Howard's American Magazine* n.v. (May 1901): 415-18.

————. "Our Country's Lynching Record," *Survey* 31 (February 1913): 573-74.

Bennett, Lerone, Jr. "No Crystal Stair: The Black Woman in History," *Ebony* 22 (August 1977): 164-65.

Bethune, Mary McLeod. "How the Bethune-Cookman College Campus Started," in *Women's America*, pp. 260-62. Edited by Linda Kerber and Jane De Hart Mathews. New York: Oxford University Press, 1982.

Bigglestone, W.E. "Oberlin College and the Negro Student," *Journal of Negro History* 56 (July 1971): 198-219.

Bliss, William D. Porter. "The Church and Social Reform Workers," *Outlook* 82 (January 20, 1906): 122-25.

Blumenthal, Henry. "Woodrow Wilson and the Race Question," *Journal of Negro History* 48 (January 1963): 1-21.

Boylan, Anne M. "Women in Groups: Analysis of Women's Benevolent Organizations in New York and Boston, 1797-1840," *Journal of American History* 71 (December 1984): 497-523.

Brancher, Nahum D. "Cleveland: A Representative American City," *Voice* 2 (August 1905): 532-36.

Breen, William J. "Black Women and the Great War: Mobilization and Reform in the South," *Journal of Southern History* 44 (August 1978): 421-40.

Buenker, John D. "The Urban Political Machine and Woman Suffrage: A Study in Political Adaptability," *The Historian* 30 (February 1971): 264-79.

Burnham, John C. "The Progressive Era Revolution of American Attitudes Towards Sex," *Journal of American History* 59 (March 1973): 885-908.

Chapin, Caroline B. "Philanthropy, Charities and Social Problems: Settlement Work Among Colored People," *The Annals of the American Academy of Political and Social Science* 21 (January-June 1903): 336-37.

Chicago School of Clubs and Philanthropy. "Employment of Colored Women in Chicago," *The Crisis* 1 (January 1911): 24-25.

Chivers, Walter R. "Neighborhood Union: An Effort of Community Organization," *Opportunity* 3 (June 1925): 178-79.

Clifford, Carrie. "National Association for the Advancement of Colored People: Our Children," *The Crisis* 14 (October 1917): 306-307.

Contee, Clarence G. "Du Bois, the NAACP, and the Pan-African Congress of 1919," *Journal of Negro History* 56 (Spring 1971): 13-28.

Conway, Jill. "Women Reformers and American Culture, 1870-1930," *Journal of Social History* 5 (Winter 1971-72): 162-77.

Cook, Blanche W. "Female Support Networks and Political Activism." In *A Heritage of Her Own*, pp. 412-44. Edited by Nancy Cott and Elizabeth Pleck. New York: Simon and Schuster, 1979.

Crowe, Charles. "Racial Violence and Social Reform: Origins of the Atlanta Riot of 1906," *Journal of Negro History* 53 (July 1968): 234-56.

Curtis, Julia Childs. "A Girl's Clubhouse," *The Crisis* 6 (October 1913): 294-96.

Cuthbert, Marion. "Negro Youth and the Educational Program of the YWCA," *Journal of Negro Education* 9 (July 1940): 363-71.

Davis, Allen. "Welfare, Reform and World War I," *American Quarterly* 19 (Winter 1967): 516-29.

————. "WTUL: Origins and Organization," *Labor History* 5 (Spring 1964): 3-17.

De Graaf, Lawrence. "Race, Sex and Region: Black Women in the American West, 1850-1920," *Pacific Historical Review* 49 (May 1980): 285-313.

————. "The City of Black Angels: Emergence of the Los Angeles Ghetto, 1890-1920," *Pacific Historical Review* 39 (August 1970): 310-17.

Dillingham, Pitt. "The Settlement Idea in the Cotton Belt," *Outlook* 70 (April 12, 1902): 920-22.

Dodge, Grace. "Working Girls' Societies," *The Chautauquan* 9 (October 1888): 223-25.

Du Bois, W.E.B. "An Essay Toward a History of the Black Man in the Great War," *The Crisis* 18 (June 1919): 63-88.

————. "Strivings of the Negro People," *Atlantic Monthly* (August 1897): 194.

Eaton, Isabel. "The Robert Gould Shaw House," *The Crisis* 6 (July 1913): 141-43.

Emerson, Helena Titus. "Children of the Circle: The Work of the New York Free Kindergarten Association for Colored Children," *Charities* 15 (October 1905): 81-83.

Emlen, John T. "The Movement for the Betterment of the Negro in Philadelphia," *The Annals of the American Academy of Political and Social Science* 49 (September 1913): 81-92.

Enck, Henry S. "Black Self-Help in the Progressive Era: The 'Northern Campaigns' of Smaller Southern Black Industrial Schools, 1900-1915," *Journal of Negro History* 61 (January 1976): 73-87.

Farley, Reynolds. "The Urbanization of Negroes in the United States," *Journal of Social History* 1 (Winter 1967-68): 241-53.

Fernandis, Sarah Collins. "A Social Settlement in South Washington," *Charities* 15 (October 1905): 64-66.

Freedman, Estelle B. "The New Woman: Changing Views of Women in the 1920s," *Journal of American History* 61 (September 1974): 372-93.

Friday, Lucy F. "Court Studies from Life," *Charities* 15 (October 1905): 79-80.

Gale, Zona. "Mothers in Council," *The Crisis* 8 (October 1914): 285-88.

Gilkes, Cheryl T. "Successful Rebellious Professionals: The Black Woman's Professional Identity and Community Commitment," *Psychology of Women Quarterly* 6 (Spring 1982): 289-311.

Giddings, Paula. "The Black Woman," *The Crisis* 87 (December 1980): 540-45.

Ginger, Ray. "The Women at Hull House." In *Women's America*, pp. 263-74. Edited by Linda Kerber and Jane De Hart Mathews. New York: Oxford University Press, 1982.

Gordon, David E. "Manual Training for Negro Children," *Charities* 15 (October 1905): 84.

Grant, Jacqueline. "Black Women and the Church." In *But Some of Us Are Brave*, pp. 141-52. Edited by Gloria T. Hull, Patricia B. Scott, and Barbara Smith. New York: The Feminist Press, 1982.

Grantham, Dewey. "The Progressive Movement and the Negro," *South Atlantic Quarterly* 54 (October 1955): 461-77.

Griffin, M. Mossell. "Early History of Afro-American Women," *National Notes* 49 (March-April, 1947): 2-4.

Griffin, William. "The Mercy Hospital Controversy Among Cleveland's Afro-American Civic Leaders, 1927," *Journal of Negro History* 61 (October 1976): 327-50.

Griggs, A.C. "Lucy Craft Laney," *Journal of Negro History* 19 (January 1934): 97-102.

Grimke, Francis J., et. al. "Votes for Women," *The Crisis* 10 (August 1915): 178-92.

Gruening, Martha. "Two Suffrage Movements," *The Crisis* 4 (September 1912): 245-47.

Gusfield, Joseph. "Social Structure and Moral Reform: A Study of the Woman's Christian Temperance," *American Journal of Sociology* 61 (November 1955): 221-32.

Harper, Frances Ellen. "Duty to Dependent Races." In *Transactions of the National Council of Women in the United States*, pp. 86-91. Philadephia: National Council of Women, 1891.

———. "National Women's Christian Temperance Union," *A.M.E. Church Review* 5 (1889): 242-45.

Hauser, Philip. "Demographic Factors in the Integration of the Negro." In *The Rise of the Ghetto*, pp. 40-43. Edited by John Bracey, Jr., August Meier, and Elliott Rudwick. Belmont, California: Wadsworth, 1971.

Hay, May Garett, et. al. "Votes for All," *The Crisis* 15 (November 1917): 19-21.

Haynes, George E., compiler. "Letters of Negro Migrants of 1916-1918," *Journal of Negro History* 4 (July 1919): 290-91, 300-301, 333, 337-38.

———. "Additional Letters of Negro Migrants of 1916-1918," *Journal of Negro History* 4 (October 1919): 413, 432, 439.

Henle, Ellen, and Merrell, Marlene. "Antebellum Black Coeds at Oberlin College," *Oberlin Annual* 60 (Winter 1980): 8-11.

Hine, Darlene Clark. "The Call That Never Came: Black Women Nurses and World War I, An Historical Note," *Indiana Military History Journal* 15 (January 1983): 23-27.

Holt, Thomas C. "The Lonely Warrior: Ida B. Wells-Barnett and the Struggle for Black Leadership." In *Black Leaders of the Twentieth Century*, pp. 39-61. Edited by John Hope Franklin and August Meier. Urbana: University of Illinois, 1982.

Hunton, Addie W. "Negro Womanhood Defended," *Voice* 1 (July 1904): 280-82.

———. "The Club Movement in California," *The Crisis* 5 (December 1912): 90-91.

———. "The Detroit Convention of the National Association of Colored Women," *Voice* 3 (August 1906): 280-82.

———. "The National Association of Colored Women: Its Real Significance," *Colored American* 15 (July 1908): 417-21.

———. "The National Association of Colored Women," *The Crisis* 2 (May 1911): 17-18.

———. "Women's Clubs," *The Crisis* 2 (May 1911): 17-18.

———. "Women's Clubs Caring for the Children," *The Crisis* 2 (June 1911): 78-79.

Isetts, Charles. "A Social Profile of the Women's Temperance Crusade: Hillsboro, Ohio." In *Alcohol, Reform and Society: The Liquor Issue in Social Context*, pp. 104-107. Edited by Jack S. Blocker, Jr. Westport, Connecticut: Greenwood Press, 1979.

Jackson, Mary E. "Colored Girls in the Second Line of Defense," *The Association Monthly* 16 (October 1918): 363-65.

———. "The Colored Woman in Industry," *The Crisis* (November 1918): 12-17.

Jenkins, William D. "Housewifery and Motherhood: The Question of Role Change in the Progressive Era." In *Woman's Being, Woman's Place*, pp. 142-53. Edited by Mary Kelley. Boston: G.K. Hall, 1979.

Jensen, Richard. "Family, Career and Reform in the Progressive Era." In *The American Family*, pp. 267-78. Edited by Michael Gordon. New York: St. Martin's Press, 1973.

Johnson, Georgia Douglass. "Frederick Douglass and Paul Laurence Dunbar at the World's Fair," *National Notes* 49 (January-February 1947): 10, 29.

Johnson, Kenneth. "Kate Gordon and the Woman Suffrage Movement in the South," *Journal of Southern History* 38 (August 1972): 365-92.

Jonas, Rosalie. "Brother Baptis' on Woman Suffrage," *The Crisis* 4 (September 1912): 247.

Jones, Anna H. "The American Colored Woman," *Voice* 1 (July 1904): 282.

Jones, Eugene Kinckle. "Social Work Among Negroes," *The Annals of the American Academy of Political and Social Sciences* 140 (November 1928): 287.

Kellor, Frances A. "Assisted Emigration from the South," *Charities* 15 (October 1905): 11-14.

———. "Opportunities for Southern Negro Women in Northern Cities," *Voice* 2 (July 1905): 472-73.

Kenneally, James. "Women and Trade Unions, 1870-1920," *Labor History* 14 (Winter 1973): 42-55.

Kessler, Sidney H. "The Organization of Negroes in the Knights of Labor," *Journal of Negro History* 37 (July 1952): 248-75.

Kousser, Morgan J. "Progressivism—For Middle Class Whites Only: North Carolina Education, 1880-1910," *Journal of Southern History* 46 (May 1980): 169-94.

Kusmer, Kenneth L. "The Functions of Organized Charity in the Progressive Era: Chicago as a Case Study," *Journal of American History* 60 (December 1973): 657-77.

Lamplugh, George R. "The Image of the Negro in Popular Magazine Fiction, 1875-1900," *Journal of Negro History* 57 (April 1972): 177-89.

Lawson, Ellen. "Sarah Woodson Early: Nineteenth Century Black Nationalist 'Sister,' " *UMOJA* 2 (Summer 1981): 12-14.

Lawson, Ronald, and Barton, Stephen E. "Sex Roles in Social Movements: A Case Study of the Tenant Movement in New York City," *Signs* 6 (Winter 1980): 230-47.

Lealtad, Catherine D. "The National YWCA and the Negro," *The Crisis* 14 (October 1917): 317-18.

Lerner, Gerda. "Early Community Work of Black Club Women," *Journal of Negro History* 59 (April 1974): 158-66.

————. "New Approaches to the Study of Women in American History," *Journal of Social History* 3 (Fall 1969): 53-62.

————. "Women's Rights and American Feminism," *American Scholar* 40 (Spring 1971): 235-48.

Lewis, Diane K. "A Response to Inequality: Black Women, Racism, and Sexism," *Signs* 3 (Winter 1977): 339-61.

————. "The Black Family: Socialization and Sex Roles," *Phylon* 36 (Fall 1975): 221-37.

Lewis, Mary L. "The White Rose Industrial Association: The Friend of the Strange Girl in New York," *The Messenger* 7 (April 1925): 158-65.

Logan, Adella Hunt. "Colored Women as Voters," *The Crisis* 4 (September 1912): 242-43.

Lumet, Gail. "My Mother Lena Comes from a Line of Proud Women," *Ms.* 10 (August 1981): 46-47, 99.

Lunardini, Christine A. "Standing Firm: William Monroe Trotter's Meeting with Woodrow Wilson," *Journal of Negro History* 64 (Summer 1979): 244-64.

Mabee, Carlton. "Control by Blacks Over Schools in New York State, 1830-1930," *Phylon* 40 (March 1979): 29-37.

McCoy-Gaines, Irene. "Ten Living Negro Women Who Have Contributed Most to Advancement of the Race," *Fisk News* 40 (May-June 1936): 10-13.

Marx, Gary T., and Useem, Michael. "Majority Involvement in Minority Movements: Civil Rights, Abolition, and Untouchability," *Journal of Social Issues* 27 (Spring 1971): 81-104.

Mays, Benjamin. "The Most Extraordinary Black Women I Have Ever Known," *Ebony* 22 (August 1977): 139-40.

Meier, August. "Booker T. Washington and the Negro Press," *Journal of Negro History* 39 (January 1953): 67-90.

————. "Negro Class Structure and Ideology in the Age of Booker T. Washington," *Phylon* 23 (Fall 1962): 258-66.

————. "Some Observations on the Negro Middle Class," *The Crisis* 53 (October 1957): 460-69.

————, and Lewis, David. "A History of the Negro Upper Class in Atlanta, Georgia, 1890-1958," *Journal of Negro Education* 28 (Spring 1959): 128-39.

————, and Rudwick, Elliott. "The Origins of Nonviolent Direct Action in Afro-American Protest." In *Along the Color Line*, pp. 307-404. Edited by August Meier and Elliott Rudwick. Urbana: University of Illinois, 1976.

————, and Rudwick, Elliott. "The Rise of the Black Secretariat in the NAACP, 1909-1935." In *Along the Color Line*, pp. 94-127.

Milholland, Inez. "Talks About Women," *The Crisis* 1 (December 1910): 28.

Miller, M. Sammy. "Mary Church Terrell's Letters from Europe to Her Father," *Negro History Bulletin* 39 (October 1976): 615-18.

———. "Robert H. Terrell: First Black D.C. Municipal Judge," *The Crisis* 80 (June-July 1976): 209-10.

———. "Woodrow Wilson and the Black Judge," *The Crisis* 84 (February 1977): 81-86.

Moton, R.R. "Organized Negro Effort for Racial Progress," *The Annals of the American Academy of Political and Social Sciences* 140 (November 1928): 257-63.

Nelson, Alice Dunbar. "Negro Women in War Work." In *Black Heritage in Social Welfare*, pp. 388-99. Edited by Edyth Ross. Metuchen, New Jersey: Scarecrow Press, 1978.

Neverdon-Morton, Cynthia. "Black Woman's Struggle for Equality in the South, 1895-1925." In *The Afro-American Woman*, pp. 43-53. Edited by Rosalyn Terborg-Penn and Sharon Harley. Port Washington, New York: Kennikat Press, 1978.

Osofsky, Gilbert. "Progressivism and the Negro, New York, 1900-1915," *American Quarterly* 16 (Summer 1964): 153-68.

Ovington, Mary White. "Fresh Air Work Among Colored Children in New York," *Charities and the Commons* 17 (October 1906): 115-17.

———. "The National Association for the Advancement of Colored People," *Journal of Negro History* 9 (April 1924): 107-16.

Perkins, Linda. "Black Women and Racial 'Uplift' Prior to Emancipation." In *The Black Woman Cross-Culturally*, pp. 317-34. Edited by Filomena Steady. Cambridge: Schenkman, 1981.

Pleck, Elizabeth H. "The Two-Parent Household: Black Family Structure in Late Nineteenth Century Boston," *Journal of Social History* 6 (Fall 1972): 3-31.

Pollard, Leslie J. "Black Beneficial Societies and the Home for Aged and Infirm Colored Persons: A Research Note," *Phylon* 41 (Summer 1980): 230-34.

Porter, Dorothy. "The Organized Educational Activities of Negro Literary Societies, 1828-1846," *Journal of Negro Education* 5 (October 1936): 555-74.

Record, Wilson. "Negro Intellectual Leadership in the National Association for the Advancement of Colored People, 1910-1940," *Phylon* 18 (Winter 1956): 375-89.

Rice, Roger L. "Residential Segregation by Law, 1910-1917," *Journal of Southern History* 34 (May 1968): 179-99.

Ross, B. Joyce. "Mary McLeod Bethune and the National Youth Administration: A Case Study of Power Relationships in the Black Caginet of Franklin D. Roosevelt," *Journal of Negro History* 60 (January 1975): 1-28.

Rudwick, Elliott. "Booker T. Washington's Relations with the National Association for the Advancement of Colored People," *Journal of Negro Education* 29 (Summer 1960): 134-44.

———. "Brief History of Mercy-Douglass Hospital in Philadelphia," *Journal of Negro Education* 20 (Winter 1951): 50-66.

———. "The National Negro Committee Conference of 1909," *Phylon* 18 (December 1958): 413-19.

———. "The Niagara Movement," *Journal of Negro History* 42 (July 1957): 177-200.

———, and Meier, August. "Black Man in the 'White City': Negroes and the Columbian Exposition, 1893," *Phylon* 26 (Winter 1965): 354-61.

Scheiber, Jane L., and Harry N. "The Wilson Administration and the Wartime Mobilization of Black Americans, 1917-1918," *Labor History* 10 (Summer 1969): 433-58.

Schuler, Edgar A. "The Houston Race Riot of 1917," *Journal of Negro History* 29 (July 1944): 301-308.

Scott, Anne F. "After Suffrage: Southern Women in the Twenties," *Journal of Southern History* 30 (August 1964): 298-314.

Sprague, Rosetta Douglass. "Anna Murray Douglass—My Mother As I Recall Her," *Journal of Negro History* 8 (January 1923): 93-101.

Talbert, Mary B. "Concerning the Frederick Douglass Memorial," *The Crisis* 14 (August 1917): 167-78.

———. "The Frederick Douglass Home," *The Crisis* 13 (February 1917): 174-76.

Terborg-Penn, Rosalyn. "Discrimination Against Afro-American Women in the Women's Movement." In *The Afro-American Woman*, pp. 17-27. Edited by Rosalyn Terborg-Penn and Sharon Harley. Port Washington, New York: Kennikat Press, 1978.

———. "Black Male Perspectives on the Nineteenth-Century Woman." In *The Afro-American Woman*, pp. 28-42. Edited by Rosalyn Terborg-Penn and Sharon Harley. Port Washington, New York: Kennikat Press, 1978.

Terrell, Mary Church. "Club Work of Colored Women," *Southern Workman* 30 (August 1901): 435-36.

———. "History of the Club Woman's Movement," *Aframerican Woman's Journal* 1 (Summer-Fall 1940): 33-38.

———. "History of the High School for Negroes in Washington," *Journal of Negro History* 2 (July 1917): 252-66.

———. "History of the National Association of Colored Women," *The Sooner Woman* 1 (September 1950): 3-4.

———. "How, When and Where Black Becomes White," (Chicago) *Sunday Tribune*, November 5, 1905, p. 7.

———. "I Remember Frederick Douglass," *Ebony* 8 (October 1953): 73-76, 78-80.

———. "Impressions of My European Trip," *Howard University Record* 5 (December 1919): 100-103.

———. "Justice of Woman Suffrage," *The Crisis* 4 (September 1912): 243-45.

———. "Lynching from a Negro's Point of View," *North American Review* 23 (June 1904): 853-68.

———. "Progress of Colored Women," *Voice* 1 (June 1906): 293.

———. "Sara W. Brown," *The Journal of the College Alumnae Club of Washington* 30 (Memorial Edition, April 1950): 17-19.

———. "Susan B. Anthony: A Tribute," *Voice*, 410-16.

———. "Society Among the Colored People of Washington," *Voice* 1 (April 1904): 150-56.

Thelen, David P. "Social Tensions and the Origins of Progressivism," *Journal of American History* 56 (Fall 1969): 323-41.

Thornbrough, Emma Lou. "The History of Black Women in Indiana," *Black History News and Notes*, Part one: 12 (May 1983): 1, 4-8; Part two: 13 (August 1983): 4-7.

———, ed. *This Far By Faith: Black Hoosier Heritage.* Indianapolis: Indiana Historical Society, 1982.

———. "The National Afro-American League, 1887-1908," *Journal of Southern History* 27 (November 1961): 494-512.

Tucker, David M. "Miss Ida. B. Wells and Memphis Lynching," *Phylon* 32 (Summer 1971): 112-22.

Tuttle, William M., Jr. "Labor Conflict and Racial Violence: The Black Worker in Chicago, 1894-1919," *Labor History* 10 (Summer 1969): 408-32.

Villard, Fanny Garrison. "A Woman's Suffrage Symposium," *The Crisis* 4 (September 1912): 240-42.

Vincent, Steve. "Hoosier History Revisited: Flanner House," *Black History News and Notes* 7 (February 1982): 4-5.

Walton, Hanes, Jr., and Taylor, James E. "Blacks and the Southern Prohibition Movement," *Phylon* 32 (Summer 1971): 247-58.

Washington, Mrs. Booker T. "Club Work Among Negro Women." In *Progress of a Race*, pp. 177-209. Edited by John W. Gibson. Naperville, Illinois: J.L. Nichols and Co., 1920.

——. "Social Improvement for Plantation Women," *Voice* 1 (July 1904): 290.

——. "The Advancement of Colored Women," *Colored American* 8 (April 1905): 271-74.

——. "The Gain in the Life of Negro Women," *Outlook* 76 (January 1904): 271-74.

Weiss, Nancy. "Black Separatism and Interracial Cooperation: Origins of Organized Efforts for Racial Advancement, 1890-1920." In *Twentieth Century America: Recent Interpretations*, pp. 52-87. Edited by Barton Bernstein and Allen J. Matusow. New York: Harcourt, Brace, Jovanovich, 1972.

White, Walter. " 'Work or Fight' in the South," *The New Republic* (March 1, 1919): 144-46.

Williams, Fannie Barrier. "A Northern Negro's Autobiography," *The Independent* (July 14, 1904): 166-68.

——. "A New Method of Dealing with Race," *Voice* 3 (June 1906): 302-303.

——. "Colored Women of Chicago," *Southern Workman* 43 (June 1914): 564-66.

——. "Extension of the Conference Spirit," *Voice* 1 (July 1904): 302-303.

——. "Industrial Education—Will It Solve the Negro Problem?" *Colored American* 7 (July 1904): 493-96.

——. "Social Bonds of the 'Black Belt' of Chicago," *Charities* 15 (October 1905): 40-44.

——. "The Club Movement Among Colored Women in America," *Voice* 1 (March 1904): 94-100; and in *A Negro for a New Century*, pp. 379-97. Edited by Booker T. Washington. Chicago: American Press, 1900.

——. "The Colored Girl," *Voice* 2 (June 1905): 400-403.

——. "The Colored Woman and Her Part in Race Regeneration." In *A Negro for a New Century*, pp. 398-405. Edited by Booker T. Washington. Chicago: American Publishing, 1900.

——. "The Frederick Douglass Center," *Voice* 1 (December 1904): 602-603.

——. "The Smaller Economies," *Voice* (May 1904): 184-85.

——. "Woman's Part in Man's Business," *Voice* 1 (November 1904): 543-47.

Williams, Lee. "Newcomers to the City: A Study of Black Population Growth in Toledo, Ohio, 1910-1930," *Ohio History* 89 (January 1980): 5-24.

Williams, William Appleman. "The Legend of Isolationism in the 1920s," *Science and Society* 18 (Winter 1954): 1-20.

Williamson, Emily E. "Settlement Work Among Colored People," *The Annals of the American Academy of Political and Social Science* 21 (January-June 1903): 336-37.

Wolgemuth, Kathleen Long. "Woodrow Wilson's Appointment Policy and the Negro," *Journal of Southern History* 24 (November 1958): 457-71.

Wolfe, H.B., and Olson, Helen. "Wartime Industrial Employment of Women," *Journal of Political Economy* 27 (October 1919): 640-69.

Wood, L. Hollingsworth. "The Urban League Movement," *Journal of Negro History* 9 (April 1924): 117-24.

Wood, Mary I. "Civic Activities of Women's Clubs," *The Annals of American Academy of Political and Social Science* 56 (November 1914): 78-87.

Yates, Josephine Silone. "The Equipment of the Teacher," *Voice* 1 (June 1904): 248-52.

———. "Thought Power in Education," *Voice* 1 (June 1904): 243.

GOVERNMENT PUBLICATIONS

United States Department of Commerce, Bureau of the Census. *Women in Gainful Occupations, 1870-1920.* Census Monograph No. 9; Washington, D.C.: Government Printing Office, 1929.

United States Department of Labor, Women's Bureau. *Women's Occupations Through Seven Decades,* by Janet Hooks. Bulletin No. 218, Washington, D.C.: Government Printing Office, 1947.

Index

Black Women in
United States History:
A Guide to the Series

PUBLISHER'S NOTE

The sixteen volumes in this set contain 248 articles, in addition to five monographs. This *Guide to the Series* is designed to help the reader find *every* substantive discussion of a topic of interest in the articles. Included in the subject index are general topics such as education and family life, as well as individuals to whom articles are devoted. Geographical locations are included when they are an important part of the article. Professions are also included. Thus, one can look up Fannie Lou Hamer (three articles), Kansas (two articles), or nursing (four articles). The more than 200 authors represented in the index to authors are a who's who of contemporary scholarship.

For topics in the five monographs and for specific discussions in the articles, please see the comprehensive indexes for every title. The more than 10,000 entries in these indexes make this series a virtual encyclopedia of black women's history.

Contents of the Series

3

Volumes 1-4, continued

Volumes 1-4, continued

59. Oden, Gloria C. *The Journal of Charlotte L. Forten: The Salem-Philadelphia Years (1854-1862) Reexamined.*
60. Parkhurst, Jessie W. *The Role of the Black Mammy in the Plantation Household.*
61. Perkins, Linda M. *Heed Life's Demands: The Educational Philosophy of Fanny Jackson Coppin.*
62. Perkins, Linda M. *The Black Female American Missionary Association Teacher in the South, 1861-1870.*
63. Perkins, Linda M. *The Impact of the 'Cult of True Womanhood' on the Education of Black Women.*
64. Perkins, Linda M. *Black Women and Racial 'Uplift' Prior to Emancipation.*
65. Pleck, Elizabeth H. *The Two-Parent Household: Black Family Structure in Late Nineteenth Century Boston.*
66. Porter, Dorothy B. *Sarah Parker Remond, Abolitionist and Physician.*
67. Quarles, Benjamin. *Harriet Tubman's Unlikely Leadership.*
68. Riley, Glenda. *American Daughters: Black Women in the West.*
69. Reiff, Janice L., Michael R. Dahlin, and Daniel Scott Smith. *Rural Push and Urban Pull: Work and Family Experiences of Older Black Women in Southern Cities, 1880-1900.*
70. Schafer, Judith K. *'Open and Notorious Concubinage': The Emancipation of Slave Mistresses by Will and the Supreme Court in Antebellum Louisiana.*
71. Sealander, Judith. *Antebellum Black Press Images of Women.*
72. Seraile, William. *Susan McKinney Steward: New York State's First African-American Woman Physician.*
73. Shammas, Carole. *Black Women's Work and the Evolution of Plantation Society in Virginia.*
74. Silverman, Jason H. *Mary Ann Shadd and the Search for Equality.*
75. Sloan, Patricia E. *Early Black Nursing Schools and Responses of Black Nurses to their Educational Programs.*
76. Soderlund, Jean R. *Black Women in Colonial Pennsylvania.*
77. Sterling, Dorothy. *To Build A Free Society: Nineteenth-Century Black Women.*
78. Sumler-Lewis, Janice. *The Forten-Purvis Women of Philadelphia and the American Anti-Slavery Crusade.*
79. Tate, Claudia. *Pauline Hopkins: Our Literary Foremother.*
80. Terborg-Penn, Rosalyn. *Black Women Freedom Fighters in Early 19th Century Maryland.*
81. Thompson, Priscilla. *Harriet Tubman, Thomas Garrett, and the Underground Railroad.*
82. Tucker, David M. *Miss Ida B. Wells and Memphis Lynching.*
83. Vacha, John E. *The Case of Sara Lucy Bagby: A Late Gesture.*
84. Wade-Gayles, Gloria. *Black Women Journalists in the South, 1880-1905: An Approach to the Study of Black Women's History.*
85. White, Deborah G. *The Lives of Slave Women.*

Vols. 5-8. BLACK WOMEN IN AMERICAN HISTORY: THE TWENTIETH CENTURY, Edited with a Preface by Darlene Clark Hine

1. *Votes for Women: A Symposium by Leading Thinkers of Colored America.*
2. Anderson, Karen T. *Last Hired, First Fired: Black Women Workers During World War II.*
3. Anderson, Kathie R. *Era Bell Thompson: A North Dakota Daughter.*
4. Blackwelder, Julia Kirk. *Quiet Suffering: Atlanta Women in the 1930s.*

Volumes 5-8, continued

5. Blackwelder, Julia Kirk. *Women in the Work Force: Atlanta, New Orleans, and San Antonio, 1930 to 1940.*
6. Brady, Marilyn Dell. *Kansas Federation of Colored Women's Clubs, 1900-1930.*
7. Brady, Marilyn Dell. *Organizing Afro-American Girls' Clubs in Kansas in the 1920's.*
8. Breen, William J. *Black Women and the Great War: Mobilization and Reform in the South.*
9. Brooks, Evelyn. *Religion, Politics, and Gender: The Leadership of Nannie Helen Burroughs.*
10. Brown, Elsa Barkley. *Womanist Consciousness: Maggie Lena Walker and the Independent Order of Saint Luke.*
11. Bryan, Violet H. *Frances Joseph-Gaudet: Black Philanthropist.*
12. Cantarow, Ellen and Susan Gushee O'Malley. *Ella Baker: Organizing for Civil Rights.*
13. Carby, Hazel V. *It Jus Be's Dat Way Sometime: The Sexual Politics of Women's Blues.*
14. Chateauvert, Melinda. *The Third Step: Anna Julia Cooper and Black Education in the District of Columbia, 1910-1960.*
15. Clark-Lewis, Elizabeth. *'This Work Had a End:' African-American Domestic Workers in Washington, D.C., 1910-1940.*
16. Coleman, Willi. *Black Women and Segregated Public Transportation: Ninety Years of Resistance.*
17. Ergood, Bruce. *The Female Protection and the Sun Light: Two Contemporary Negro Mutual Aid Societies.*
18. Farley, Ena L. *Caring and Sharing Since World War I: The League of Women for Community Service—A Black Volunteer Organization in Boston.*
19. Feinman, Clarice. *An Afro-American Experience: The Women in New York City's Jail.*
20. Ferguson, Earline Rae. *The Women's Improvement Club of Indianapolis: Black Women Pioneers in Tuberculosis Work, 1903-1938.*
21. Ford, Beverly O. *Case Studies of Black Female Heads of Households in the Welfare System: Socialization and Survival.*
22. Gilkes, Cheryl Townsend. *'Together and in Harness': Women's Traditions in the Sanctified Church.*
23. Gilkes, Cheryl Townsend. *Going Up for the Oppressed: The Career Mobility of Black Women Community Workers.*
24. Gilkes, Cheryl Townsend. *Successful Rebellious Professionals: The Black Woman's Professional Identity and Community Commitment.*
25. Gunn, Arthur C. *The Struggle of Virginia Proctor Powell Florence.*
26. Guzman, Jessie P. *The Social Contributions of the Negro Woman Since 1940.*
27. Harley, Sharon. *Beyond the Classroom: Organizational Lives of Black Female Educators in the District of Columbia, 1890-1930.*
28. Harley, Sharon. *Black Women in a Southern City: Washington, D.C., 1890-1920.*
29. Haynes, Elizabeth Ross. *Negroes in Domestic Service in the United States.*
30. Helmbold, Lois Rita. *Beyond the Family Economy: Black and White Working-Class Women during the Great Depression.*
31. Hine, Darlene Clark. *The Ethel Johns Report: Black Women in the Nursing Profession, 1925.*
32. Hine, Darlene Clark. *From Hospital to College: Black Nurse Leaders and the Rise of Collegiate Nursing Schools.*
33. Hine, Darlene Clark. *Mabel K. Staupers and the Integration of Black Nurses into the Armed Forces.*
34. Hine, Darlene Clark. *The Call That Never Came: Black Women Nurses and World War I, An Historical Note.*

Volumes 5-8, continued

35. Hine, Darlene Clark. *'They Shall Mount Up with Wings as Eagles': Historical Images of Black Nurses, 1890-1950.*
36. Hull, Gloria T. *Alice Dunbar-Nelson: Delaware Writer and Woman of Affairs.*
37. Hunter, Tera. *The Correct Thing: Charlotte Hawkins Brown and the Palmer Institute.*
38. Jacobs, Sylvia M. *'Say Africa When You Pray': The Activities of Early Black Baptist Women Missionaries Among Liberian Women and Children.*
39. Jacobs, Sylvia M. *Afro-American Women Missionaries Confront the African Way of Life.*
40. Jacobs, Sylvia M. *Their 'Special Mission': Afro-American Women as Missionaries to the Congo, 1894-1937.*
41. Janiewski, Dolores. *Seeking 'a New Day and a New Way': Black Women and Unions in the Southern Tobacco Industry.*
42. Janiewski, Dolores. *Sisters Under Their Skins: Southern Working Women, 1880-1950.*
43. Jones, Beverly W. *Race, Sex and Class:Black Female Tobacco Workers in Durham, North Carolina, 1920-1940, and the Development of Female Consciousness.*
44. Kendrick, Ruby M. *'They Also Serve': The National Association of Colored Women, Inc., 1895-1954.*
45. Lee, Don L. *The Achievement of Gwendolyn Brooks.*
46. Leffall, Dolores C. and Janet L. Sims. *Mary McLeod Bethune—The Educator; Also Including a Selected Annotated Bibliography.*
47. Lerner, Gerda. *Early Community Work of Black Club Women.*
48. Matthews, Mark D. *'Our Women and What They Think,' Amy Jacques Garvey and the Negro World.*
49. McDowell, Deborah E. *The Neglected Dimension of Jessie Redmon Fauset.*
50. McDowell, Margaret B. *The Black Woman As Artist and Critic: Four Versions.*
51. Nerverdon-Morton, Cynthia. *Self-Help Programs as Educative Activities of Black Women in the South, 1895-1925: Focus on Four Key Areas.*
52. Newman, Debra L. *Black Women Workers in the Twentieth Century.*
53. O'Dell, J. H. *Life in Mississippi: An Interview With Fannie Lou Hamer.*
54. Parks, Rosa. *Interview.*
55. Peebles-Wilkins, Wilma. *Black Women and American Social Welfare: The Life of Fredericka Douglass Sprague Perry.*
56. Pleck, Elizabeth H. *A Mother's Wages: Income Earning Among Married Italian and Black Women, 1896-1911.*
57. Porter, Dorothy B. *Maria Louise Baldwin, 1856-1922.*
58. Ross, B. Joyce. *Mary McLeod Bethune and the National Youth Adminstration: A Case Study of Power Relationships in the Black Cabinet of Franklin D. Roosevelt.*
59. Saunders, Deloris M. *Changes in the Status of Women During The Quarter Century (1955-1980).*
60. Seraile, William. *Henrietta Vinton Davis and the Garvey Movement.*
61. Smith, Elaine M. *Mary McLeod Bethune and the National Youth Administration.*
62. Smith, Sandra N. and Earle H. West. *Charlotte Hawkins Brown.*
63. Stetson, Erlene. *Black Feminism in Indiana, 1893-1933.*
64. Still, Judith Anne. *Carrie Still Shepperson: The Hollows of Her Footsteps.*
65. Terborg-Penn, Rosalyn. *Discontented Black Feminists: Prelude and Postscript to the Passage of the Nineteenth Amendment.*
66. Trigg, Eula S. *Washington, D.C. Chapter—Links, Incorporated: Friendship and Service.*
67. Tucker, Susan. *A Complex Bond: Southern Black Domestic Workers and Their White Employers.*

Volumes 5-8, continued

68. Woods, Sylvia. *You Have to Fight for Freedom.*
69. Woodson, Carter G. *The Negro Washerwoman: A Vanishing Figure.*
70. Yancy, Dorothy C. *Dorothy Bolden, Organizer of Domestic Workers: She Was Born Poor But She Would Not Bow Down.*

Vols. 9-10. BLACK WOMEN'S HISTORY: THEORY AND PRACTICE, Edited with a Preface by Darlene Clark Hine

1. Aldridge, Delores. *Black Women in the Economic Marketplace: A Battle Unfinished.*
2. Allen, Walter R. *Family Roles, Occupational Statuses, and Achievement Orientations Among Black Women in the United States.*
3. Allen, Walter R. *The Social and Economic Statuses of Black Women in the United States.*
4. Armitage, Susan, Theresa Banfield, and Sarah Jacobus. *Black Women and Their Communities in Colorado.*
5. Biola, Heather. *The Black Washerwoman in Southern Tradition.*
6. Bracey, John H., Jr. *Afro-American Women: A Brief Guide to Writings from Historical and Feminist Perspectives.*
7. Brown, Minnie Miller. *Black Women in American Agriculture.*
8. Collier-Thomas, Bettye. *The Impact of Black Women in Education: An Historical Overview.*
9. Dickson, Lynda F. *Toward a Broader Angle of Vision in Uncovering Women's History: Black Women's Clubs Revisited.*
10. Dill, Bonnie Thornton. *Race, Class, and Gender: Prospects for an All-Inclusive Sisterhood.*
11. Dill, Bonnie Thornton. *The Dialectics of Black Womanhood.*
12. Fox-Genovese, Elizabeth. *To Write My Self: The Autobiographies of Afro-American Women.*
13. Higginbotham, Evelyn Brooks. *Beyond the Sound of Silence: Afro-American Women in History.*
14. Hine, Darlene Clark. *An Angle of Vision: Black Women and the United States Constitution, 1787-1987.*
15. Hine, Darlene Clark. *To Be Gifted, Female, and Black.*
16. Hine, Darlene Clark. *Opportunity and Fulfillment: Sex, Race, and Class in Health Care Education.*
17. Hine, Darlene Clark. *Lifting the Veil, Shattering the Silence: Black Women's History in Slavery and Freedom.*
18. Jackson, Jacquelyne Johnson. *A Partial Bibliography on or Related to Black Women.*
19. Katz, Maude White. *The Negro Woman and the Law.*
20. Katz, Maude White. *She Who Would Be Free—Resistance.*
21. King, Deborah K. *Multiple Jeopardy, Multiple Consciousness: The Context of a Black Feminist Ideology.*
22. Ladner, Joyce A. *Racism and Tradition: Black Womanhood in Historical Perspective.*
23. Lewis, Diane K. *A Response to Inequality: Black Women, Racism, and Sexism.*
24. Marable, Manning. *Groundings with my Sisters: Patriarchy and the Exploitation of Black Women.*
25. Palmer, Phyllis Marynick. *White Women/Black Women: The Dualism of Female Identity and Experience in the United States.*
26. Patterson, Tiffany R. *Toward a Black Feminist Analysis: Recent Works by Black Women Scholars.*

Volumes 9-10, continued

27. Reagon, Bernice Johnson. *My Black Mothers and Sisters, or On Beginning A Cultural Autobiography.*
28. Reagon, Bernice Johnson. *African Diaspora Women: The Making of Cultural Workers.*
29. Rector, Theresa A. *Black Nuns as Educators.*
30. Render, Sylvia Lyons. *Afro-American Women: The Outstanding and the Obscure.*
31. Scales-Trent, Judy. *Black Women and the Constitution: Finding Our Place, Asserting Our Rights.*
32. Shockley, Ann Allen. *The Negro Woman in Retrospect: Blueprint for the Future.*
33. Smith, Eleanor. *Historical Relationships between Black and White Women.*
34. Snorgrass, J. William. *Pioneer Black Women Journalists from 1850s to the 1950s.*
35. Strong, Augusta. *Negro Women in Freedom's Battles.*
36. Terborg-Penn, Rosalyn. *Historical Treatment of Afro-Americans in the Woman's Movement, 1900-1920: A Bibliographical Essay.*
37. Terborg-Penn, Rosalyn. *Teaching the History of Black Women: A Bibliographical Essay.*
38. Thornbrough, Emma Lou. *The History of Black Women in Indiana.*
39. Walker, Juliet E. K. *The Afro-American Woman: Who Was She?*
40. Yellin, Jean Fagan. *Afro-American Women 1800-1910: A Selected Bibliography.*

Vol. 11. Daughters of Sorrow: Attitudes Toward Black Women, 1880-1920, by Beverly Guy-Sheftall

Vol. 12. Jane Edna Hunter: A Case Study of Black Leadership, 1910-1950, by Adrienne Lash Jones; Preface by Darlene Clark Hine

Vol. 13. Quest for Equality: The Life and Writings of Mary Eliza Church Terrell, 1863-1954, by Beverly Washington Jones
including Mary Church Terrell's selected essays:

1. *Announcement* [of NACW].
2. *First Presidential Address to the National Association of Colored Women.*
3. *The Duty of the National Association of Colored Women to the Race.*
4. *What Role is the Educated Negro Woman to Play in the Uplifting of Her Race?*
5. *Graduates and Former Students of Washington Colored High School.*
6. *Lynching from a Negro's Point of View.*
7. *The Progress of Colored Women.*
8. *The International Congress of Women.*
9. *Samuel Coleridge-Taylor.*
10. *Service Which Should be Rendered the South.*
11. *The Mission of Meddlers.*
12. *Paul Laurence Dunbar.*
13. *Susan B. Anthony, the Abolitionist.*
14. *A Plea for the White South by A Coloured Woman.*
15. *Peonage in the United States: The Convict Lease System and Chain Gangs.*
16. *The Disbanding of the Colored Soldiers.*
17. *What It Means to Be Colored in the Capital of the United States.*
18. *A Sketch of Mingo Saunders.*
19. *An Interview with W.T. Stead on the Race Problem.*
20. *The Justice of Woman Suffrage.*
21. *Phyllis Wheatley—An African Genius.*
22. *The History of the Club Women's Movement.*
23. *Needed: Women Lawyers.*
24. *Dr. Sara W. Brown.*
25. *I Remember Frederick Douglass.*

Vol. 14. **To Better Our World: Black Women in Organized Reform, 1890-1920**, by Dorothy Salem

Vol. 15. **Ida B. Wells-Barnett: An Exploratory Study of an American Black Woman, 1893-1930**, by Mildred Thompson

including Ida B. Wells-Barnett's Selected Essays

1. *Afro-Americans and Africa.*
2. *Lynch Law in All Its Phases.*
3. *The Reason Why the Colored American is not in the World's Columbian Exposition.* Chapter IV. *Lynch Law,* by Ida B. Wells Chapter VI. *The Reason Why,* by F.L. Barnett

4. *Two Christmas Days: A Holiday Story.*
5. *Lynch Law in America.*
6. *The Negro's Case in Equity.*
7. *Lynching and the Excuse for It.*
8. *Booker T. Washington and His Critics.*
9. *Lynching, Our National Crime.*
10. *How Enfranchisement Stops Lynchings.*
11. *Our Country's Lynching Record.*

Vol. 16. **Women in the Civil Rights Movement: Trailblazers and Torchbearers, 1941-1965**

Edited by Vicki Crawford, Jacqueline A. Rouse, Barbara Woods; Associate Editors: Broadus Butler, Marymal Dryden, and Melissa Walker

1. Black, Allida. *A Reluctant but Persistent Warrior: Eleanor Roosevelt and the Early Civil Rights Movement*
2. Brock, Annette K. *Gloria Richardson and the Cambridge Movement*
3. Burks, Mary Fair. *Trailblazers: Women in the Montgomery Bus Boycott.*
4. Cochrane, Sharlene Voogd. *'And the Pressure Never Let Up': Black Women, White Women, and the Boston YWCA, 1918-1948.*
5. Crawford, Vicki. *Beyond the Human Self: Grassroots Activists in the Mississippi Civil Rights Movement.*
6. Grant, Jacquelyn. *Civil Rights Women: A Source for Doing Womanist Theology.*
7. Knotts, Alice G. *Methodist Women Integrate Schools and Housing, 1952-1959.*
8. Langston, Donna. *The Women of Highlander.*
9. Locke, Mamie E. *Is This America: Fannie Lou Hamer and the Mississippi Freedom Democratic Party.*
10. McFadden, Grace Jordan. *Septima Clark.*
11. Mueller, Carol. *Ella Baker and the Origins of 'Participatory Democracy.'*
12. Myrick-Harris, Clarissa. *Behind the Scenes: Doris Derby, Denise Nicholas, and the Free Southern Theater.*
13. Oldendorf, Sandra. *The South Carolina Sea Island Citizenship Schools.*
14. Payne, Charles. *Men Led, But Women Organized: Movement Participation of Women in the Mississippi Delta.*
15. Reagon, Bernice Johnson. *Women as Culture Carriers in the Civil Rights Movement: Fannie Lou Hamer.*
16. Standley, Anne. *The Role of Black Women in the Civil Rights Movement.*
17. Woods, Barbara. Modjeska Simkins and the South Carolina Conference of the NAACP.

Author Index

Boldface indicates volume numbers and roman
indicates article numbers within volumes.

Subject Index

Boldface indicates volume numbers and roman
indicates article numbers within volumes.